The Foreign Policy Discourse
in the United Kingdom and the United States
in the "New World Order"

The Foreign Policy Discourse in the United Kingdom and the United States in the "New World Order"

Edited by

Lori Maguire

The Foreign Policy Discourse in the United Kingdom and the United States
in the "New World Order", Edited by Lori Maguire

This book first published 2009

Cambridge Scholars Publishing

12 Back Chapman Street, Newcastle upon Tyne, NE6 2XX, UK

British Library Cataloguing in Publication Data
A catalogue record for this book is available from the British Library

ISBN (10): 1-4438-0131-3, ISBN (13): 978-1-4438-0131-7

TABLE OF CONTENTS

CHAPTER ONE

INTRODUCTION

LORI MAGUIRE

This book aims to examine some of the major foreign policy debates in the United Kingdom and the United States in the period from 1992 to 2008.[1] The dates have been chosen because of their particular significance. 1992 makes a logical starting point for several reasons. First, in January 1991, the original Gulf War began with the air bombing of Iraq. Within a short time Kuwait would be liberated but the problem of Saddam Hussein and Iraq would not disappear and would continue to poison international relations throughout the following years. Two months later, in March, then President George H.W. Bush told Congress:

> Until now, the world we've known has been a world divided—a world of barbed wire and concrete block, conflict and cold war.
> Now, we can see a new world coming into view. A world in which there is the very real prospect of a new world order. In the words of Winston Churchill, a "world order" in which "the principles of justice and fair play ... protect the weak against the strong ..." A world where the United Nations, freed from cold war stalemate, is poised to fulfil the historic vision of its founders. A world in which freedom and respect for human rights find a home among all nations.[2]

He went on to state that: "the Gulf war put this new world to its first test, and, my fellow Americans, we passed that test." He argued that Americans had been true to their principles by fighting for Kuwait and insisted that "the hard work of freedom still calls us forward". He seemed to be announcing a far more interventionist policy in the future and even used the term "mission" so that the speech was broadly messianic. Certainly the term "new world order" did not go unnoticed and was frequently repeated. But what exactly, many commentators wondered, was this "new world order"?

When George Bush gave his speech, the Berlin wall had already fallen and the end of communism was obviously near. In December 1991 the Soviet Union collapsed and the Cold War came to its official end. The United States was now the world's only superpower, although a superpower afflicted with weaknesses, especially, at this time, economic ones. The "new world order" seemed to mean an American hegemony. But where did other nations fit in? In particular, what was the role for a middle-level power and long-time ally like the U.K.? 1992, then, is an extremely significant date as the first full post-cold war year as well as seeing the start of a new phase in the continuing conflict with Iraq. 1992, exceptionally, also saw elections in both the United States and the United Kingdom. Although the results differed–the Conservatives hung onto power in Britain while the Democrats, under Bill Clinton, returned in the United States, the date does provide a convenient launch point to consider certain major foreign policy developments of the 1990s and the 2000s.

2008 also provides a logical concluding point. Tony Blair had resigned the previous year leaving a weakened Labour Party behind him. The new Prime Minister, Gordon Brown, made a number of mistakes and became progressively more and more unpopular in his first year in office. Even more important, 2008 saw the election of Democrat Barack Obama to the White House which promised great change. By 2008 there was the feeling of the end of an era in both nations. Furthermore, by this point the "new world order" did not seem so new or so strongly American. The period saw the terrorist attacks against the U.S. of 11 September 2001, military problems for the superpower in Afghanistan and Iraq and, by the summer of 2008, near economic collapse. In all of these developments, Britain shared to a lesser or a greater extent.

During these years, the United States and the United Kingdom shared a great deal and diverged in a number of significant ways. Too often the policy of a nation–whether domestic or foreign–is considered in isolation from that of other countries. While there have been a number of studies of the foreign policy of each country, there has been no major attempts at comparative analysis. A number of books do exist on Anglo-American relations but our goal does not limit itself to the question of dealings between the two nations but considers a wide-range of issues in order to present an overall comparison of major foreign policy debates in each country. Clearly, they differ in terms of relative power on the world scene and in their geographic positions–both of which have had a profound impact on their foreign policy. At the same time, both obviously have had a lot in common: economic *rapprochement* with their closest neighbours, a global war on terrorism, and interventions in ex-Yugoslavia, Afghanistan and Iraq, for example. It is hoped that this book will shed an important light both on each nation and on the so-called "special relationship" between the two. In particular, it will try to analyse the extent of American exceptionalism. Does being "the world's only superpower" make American foreign policy completely unique? Or can we see similar developments in a middle-range power like the United Kingdom?

This book is also not specifically concerned with policy or how policy is made but with the debate around policy and the rhetoric used to present different points of view. We aim to show the discussion of these questions on different levels: among policymakers, legislatures, theorists, the press and the public. We will examine this theme from the point of view of rhetoric and content, considering, for example, the choice of language and its relationship to the subject of a speech and to the history of speech-making in the English-speaking world.

Discourse

The word "discourse" has become a highly contentious term. Merriam Webster gives its main meanings as "a verbal interchange of ideas, especially conversation... a formal and orderly and usually extended expression of thought as a subject; connected speech or writing, a linguistic unit (as a conversation or a story) larger than a sentence... a mode of organizing knowledge, ideas or experience that is rooted in language and its concrete contents (as history or institutions).[3] Related to this last definition, the word has taken on a whole number of subsidiary meanings in recent years and discourse analysis has become a major field of study in a number of disciplines. The list of people who have made important contributions to its study is long but, unfortunately, we do not have the space here to give more than just a brief overview of the subject.

In particular, discourse has been used to criticise empiricism. Empiricists believe that the human mind learns from experience and organizes its impressions into knowledge of the world. This knowledge, then, is expressed through language. The French philosopher, Michel Foucault, however, argued that if we are the sum of our experiences and if those experiences are the source of our knowledge, then those who control our early experiences have a great deal of power over how we think.[4] Knowledge becomes something relative which can change over time. Furthermore, knowledge is based on discourses that existed before a person's own experiences. The discourse we hear shapes our identity. According to Foucault:

Education may well be, as of right, the instrument whereby every individual, in a society like our own, can gain access to any kind of discourse. But we well know that in its distribution, in what it permits and in what it prevents, it follows the well-trodden battle-lines of social conflict. Every educational system is a political means of maintaining or of modifying the appropriation of discourse, with the knowledge and the powers it carries with it.[5]

Those who control discourse, then, possess immense power. Foucault argued that every institution has a dominant discourse that identifies what is normal and excludes those who do not fit in. As he put it:

In every society the production of discourse is at once controlled, selected, organised and redistributed according to a certain number of procedures, whose role is to avert its powers and its dangers, to cope with chance events, to evade its ponderous, awesome materiality.[6]

There are a series of unspoken rules in each area that defines what discourse is acceptable and those who break them are condemned to madness and silence. But these rules are not static. Foucault sees truth, morality and even meaning itself as changing. They are not universal ideas but created through discourse. Change, therefore, is linked to possessing the means of communication, and, therefore, being able to alter the dominant discourse.

Social and political power, thus, are gained through discourse. The French Marxist, Louis Althusser stressed the importance of ideology and its link with discourse.[7] For Althusser, the political analysis of Rousseau and Marx lays out a structuralism whose key foundation is that of socially determined speech. Other scholars have studied the history of "resistances" to the dominant discourse. For, while one discourse is normally dominant, there are competing discourses. Different groups have their own discourse that expresses their thoughts, beliefs and history. Since politics is about power, political discourse has come under particular scrutiny. Much has been written about the relationship between language, ideology and power. The most obvious propagators of discourse in this arena are the political parties. They fight wars of words to express their own ideology and myths. They compete for control of the media and try to manipulate it as much as possible.

Indeed, some scholars have seen media as being far more important than content. Marshall McLuhan, notably, wrote that "the media is the message".[8] He saw media as extensions of our human senses, as well as massaging our senses. McLuhan also examined how people have seen the world at various times and how these views have been changed by media.

A number of other scholars have scrutinized the relationship between media and politics and how politicians use various media to gain votes.

Not surprisingly, the subject has attracted a great deal of attention in linguistics, and discourse analysis has become a major field there. The American, Noam Chomsky, is probably the most famous figure to have explored this area and he has produced thousands of articles speeches and books. He has argued that the mass media, far from presenting an unbiased vision of the news, tends to focus only on the point of view of the rich and powerful. In his book *Necessary Illusions: Thought Control in Democratic Societies*, he presents the mass media as little more than vehicles for propaganda. For him, media and politics are inseparable. A number of other scholars have followed in his direction. Recently, the British academic Norman Fairclough has worked to link linguistic analysis with social research. In the introduction to his book, *Analysing Discourse*, he explains his goal:

> This book aims to provide a useable framework for analysing spoken or written language for people in social sciences and humanities with little or no background in language study, presented in a way which suggests how language analysis may enhance research into a number of issues which concern social scientists.[9]

For this reason, he has devoted a great deal of effort to political discourse, notably in relation to New Labour.

This book, while taking into account these and other ideas, does not try to place itself within any specific theory. There are certainly many important reasons to look at discourse. For one thing, discourse and policy do not always agree and politicians frequently say things and not act upon them or do not act in the way expected. Politicians certainly adopt rhetoric to voters' expectations since one of their primary goals is to win elections. A classic case is that of the veteran cold warrior Richard Nixon who, to the surprise of many, initiated the policy of détente. So all discourse is subject to *realpolitik*. It is also well known that all discourse on foreign policy is also heavily subject to domestic policy, which clearly preoccupies voters. This can be seen most clearly in relation to trade and economic matters. During our period, NAFTA is a classic case as many workers feared that it would hurt their jobs and wages. Britain's failure to adopt the euro is another case. Lack of support for the euro in public opinion and in the press led both the Labour party and, eventually, the Liberal Democrats, to distance themselves from previously favourable statements. International economic issues, then, depend to a certain extent on political considerations within the country.

But discourse also takes place within a specific political context and political culture. Furthermore, international relations frequently raise questions relating to a nation's own identity. Studying discourse then can help us understand how a people view themselves and their history. And, of course, current foreign policy discourse does not stand in isolation but is part of a long rhetorical tradition. Placing recent speeches within the framework of past pronouncements shows changes (or not) in the nation and its image of itself.

Anglo-American Values

The United States was founded by English colonisers who brought their language and their culture with them. Although the two nations diverged afterwards, they still possessed, and possess, a great deal in common–and that includes discourse and rhetoric. This came to the fore in World War II when the "special relationship" was born, but it had many precursors. In the twentieth century, one of the most influential was Woodrow Wilson. Wilson came to see World War I in terms we associate more commonly with World War II. He told the Senate:

> This is a people's war and the people's thinking constitutes its atmosphere and morale, not the predilections of the drawing room or the political considerations of the caucus. If we be indeed democrats and wish to lead the world to democracy, we can ask other peoples to accept in proof of our sincerity and our ability to lead them whither they wish to be led nothing less persuasive and convincing than our actions. Our professions will not suffice. Verification must be forthcoming when verification is asked for.[10]

The immediate subject here is a constitutional amendment for women's suffrage, but, obviously, much more is implied. In calling this a "people's war" Wilson is rejecting traditional great power diplomacy: all parts of the population are concerned in the struggle and their desires must be taken into account. And Wilson is confident that he knows what the people of the world want–American democracy which will allow them to pursue happiness (another quintessentially American notion)–and that it is the duty of the United States to lead the world in that direction. To so this, they must become a model of democracy and for this, none of their citizens must be excluded from full rights. In a discourse of 1915, Wilson expressed his belief that the United States had a mission in the world, which he saw as one of "peace and good will among men"–the proclamation of the angels at Christ's birth.[11] America's mission is divinely inspired. Furthermore, America is uniquely able to do this because it is a nation of immigrants. In the same allocution he said: "America has been made up of the nations of the world and is the friend of the nations of the world." A nation whose citizens come from all over the world, Wilson believes, is able to speak to the world with a power and understanding that more homogenous nations cannot equal. Wilson has had a profound effect on American rhetoric. He is one of the leading exponents of ideas of American exceptionalism, that the United States is fundamentally different from other nations.

World War II formally united American and British traditions of rhetoric and, from the Atlantic Charter onwards, the two nations presented their war aims in consciously similar terms. Both Roosevelt and Churchill emphasised the superiority of their values and stressed that the combat had a missionary dimension. In his famous speech of the 18th of June 1940, after France's demand for an armistice, Churchill said:

> What General Weygand called the Battle of France is over. I expect that the battle of Britain is about to begin. Upon this battle depends the survival of Christian civilisation. Upon it depends our own British life, and the long continuity of our institutions and our Empire. The whole fury and might of the enemy must very soon be turned on us. Hitler knows that he will have to break us in this island or lose the war. If we can stand up to him, all Europe may be free and the life of the world may move forward into broad, sunlit uplands. But if we fail, then the whole world, including the United States, including all that we have known and cared for, will sink into the abyss of a new Dark Ages made more sinister, and perhaps more protracted, by the lights of perverted science. Let us therefore brace ourselves to our duties and so bear ourselves that, if the British Empire and its Commonwealth last for a thousand years, men will still say, "This was their finest hour."[12]

According to Churchill, the survival of Western values and civilisation (whose pinnacle he seems to have found in Great Britain) depends on that nation's continued resistance to Germany–whatever its citizens may suffer. The Battle of Britain is a cosmic battle in which Good and Evil fight for control of the world and only Britain's self-sacrifice–her remaining true to the nation's values–can secure victory for the side of Right. Not only will Britain herself be saved by this action but she will ultimately bring a higher level of civilisation to the world and allow it to progress.

Churchill has frequently been called a "Whig" historian. This term comes from Herbert Butterfield, who in his 1931 book, *The Whig Interpretation of History*, used it to describe a view of British history as one of progress towards constitutional monarchy and the rule of law.

Political leaders of the past were generally portrayed either as heroes who had advanced these causes or villains who had tried to stop their inevitable victory. In particular, "Whig" historians presented the British system of government as the zenith of human political achievement.

In his eighth State of the Union address on the "four freedoms" given nearly a year before the United States entered the war–Roosevelt committed the American people to aiding the opponents of Nazi Germany in all ways short of war. Although he began by speaking of the needs of his fellow citizens, by the end of the speech he had, like Churchill, adopted a messianic tone, extending his project to the entire world:

> In the future days, which we seek to make secure, we look forward to a world founded upon four essential human freedoms.
> The first is freedom of speech and expression–everywhere in the world.
> The second is freedom of every person to worship God in his own way–everywhere in the world.
> The third is freedom from want–which, translated into world terms, means economic understandings which will secure to every nation a healthy peacetime life for its inhabitants–everywhere in the world.
> The fourth is freedom from fear–which, translated into world terms, means a worldwide reduction of armaments to such a point and in such a thorough fashion that no nation will be in a position to commit an act of physical aggression against any neighbour–anywhere in the world.[13]

Obviously this speech is not nationalistic in the sense that Churchill's is. Roosevelt wants to establish the "four freedoms" in the world but he does not portray them as particularly American and Roosevelt rarely uses the language of American exceptionalism. Still, they are American war aims (although the U.S. is not yet at war) and putting them into effect depends on Allied success.

Since the first and probably the quintessential speech of the Cold War was given by Churchill–that of the "iron curtain", it is not surprising to see a continuation of the themes of World War II in the new conflict. The Cold War was generally portrayed, in official circles at least, as a battle between Good and Evil. In his speech of 1947, outlining what became known as the Truman Doctrine, Harry Truman contrasted the Western democracies and communism:

> At the present moment in world history nearly every nation must choose between alternative ways of life. The choice is too often not a free one. One way of life is based upon the will of the majority, and is distinguished by free institutions, representative government, free elections, guarantees of individual liberty, freedom of speech and religion, and freedom from

political oppression. The second way of life is based upon the will of a minority forcibly imposed upon the majority. It relies upon terror and oppression, a controlled press and radio, fixed elections, and the suppression of personal freedoms.[14]

John Kennedy, in his inaugural address in 1961, insisted that "here on earth God's work must truly be our own" which he defined as "defending freedom in its hour of maximum danger".[15] Reagan used some of the most morally charged language, famously saying:

> I urge you to beware the temptation of pride - the temptation of blithely declaring yourselves above it all and label both sides equally at fault, to ignore the facts of history and the aggressive impulses of an evil empire, to simply call the arms race a giant misunderstanding and thereby remove yourself from the struggle between right and wrong and good and evil.[16]

Reagan here describes the Cold War in stark Manichean terms–some of the starkest of the entire conflict, especially since the 1950s.

While the subject figured less prominently in British discourse, one can still see important similarities. In a speech to the House of Commons on the formation of NATO, Ernest Bevin, Labour Foreign Minister, insisted that "no nation innocent of aggressive intentions need have the slightest fear or apprehension about it"–thus not too subtly implying that the USSR had exactly these intentions. He also spoke of Western civilisation as "founded on principles of democracy, individual liberty and the rule of law between nations."[17] Later Harold Macmillan spoke of the Cold War as "a struggle for the minds of men" with Western civilisation representing "freedom and order and justice".[18] Margaret Thatcher used harsh terms to talk of the conflict. She mocked the Soviets for having to buy wheat from the United States and refused criticisms of Western life:

> Is it not time we spoke up for our way of life? After all, no western nation has to build a wall round itself to keep its people in.[19]

The end of the Cold War gave rise to a certain triumphalism, especially in the United States, where many argued that Western values had finally defeated all opposition. The end of history in the Hegelian sense was actually announced in 1989 in an article by Francis Fukuyama and then in a book he wrote in 1992. He argued that:

> What we may be witnessing is not just the end of the Cold War, or the passing of a particular period of post-war history, but the end of history as such: that is, the end point of mankind's ideological evolution and the

universalization of Western liberal democracy as the final form of human government.[20]

Of course, the events of 11 September 2001 shattered this complacency. Some people now saw a new ideological conflict and as America and the United Kingdom had fought fascism and communism earlier–each time seeing their values triumph and spread to new parts of the world–now they had to defeat the threat of radical Islam.

These ideas were much stronger in the United States than in Britain and are particularly associated with a group known as neo-conservatives. The term neoconservative originally referred to a group of politicians and political thinkers who tended towards the Left on domestic issues but were strongly anti-communist. Over time it has come to refer to those who hold an aggressively moralist foreign policy and who favour unilateral action by the United States. They sympathize with Woodrow Wilson's idealistic desire to spread American values in the world–especially those related to democracy–but do not accept Wilson's espousal of international organizations. Many of them have long argued that the United States should imitate Israel and use pre-emptive strikes against potential enemies. A number of commentators, most notably a former director of the CIA, have even talked of World War IV (World War III having been the Cold War) being fought since the 9/11 attacks.[21] There is no equivalent movement in Britain but there are rhetorical similarities between the neo-conservatives and many of Tony Blair's statements, as we shall see in chapter 11.

Having said all this, a sense of national destiny is by no means peculiar to the English-speaking world, or even the West, and, indeed, has taken far more ominous paths as the case of Nazi Germany shows. Nor does it have to be associated with one particular country for communism is a messianic philosophy. It may be that all peoples like to think they are special in some way and have an exceptional role to play in the world.

The "Special Relationship"

At the centre of this book is Anglo-American relations and the changes they underwent during the period. A number of books have been written on this subject and so we will only give a brief overview here.[22] It was, apparently, Churchill who coined the term, most famously in his "iron curtain" speech of 1946, which was given in Missouri with President Truman in attendance. Essentially, Churchill states here that a "special relationship" existed during World War II but he is afraid that it might not continue afterwards. Much of the speech is an attempt to alert the Americans to the seriousness of the international situation. He actually sees it as a special relationship between all English-speaking countries:

> Neither the sure prevention of war; nor the continuous rise of world organisation will be gained without what I have called the fraternal association of the English-speaking peoples. This means a special relationship between the British Commonwealth and Empire and the United States... Fraternal association requires not only the growing friendship and mutual understanding between our two vast but kindred systems of society, but the continuance of the intimate relationship between our military advisers.[23]

As the speech goes on, he specifies how he wants the military link to continue. He wants the two nations to use similar weapons and instruction books, to arrange exchanges of officers and cadets and to continue joint use of air force and naval bases. He even suggests the establishment of common citizenship. Perhaps most importantly, he calls for the "common study of potential dangers", obviously hoping to increase British influence over American policy. Clearly, Churchill fears Soviet aggression in Europe and wants America to continue its presence there as a counterbalance.[24]

Of course, Churchill did not limit British foreign policy to Anglo-American relations. He saw British influence as being exercised in three circles: the Atlantic partnership, the Commonwealth and Empire, and Europe.[25] In the period since 1945, the importance of the Commonwealth declined considerably while that of Europe grew substantially. The relationship with the United States, however, in spite of ups and downs, tended to remain steady. Meanwhile, throughout this period, the United States normally was the leading economic and military power of the world. The disproportion in power has led many to see Britain as having exaggerated the importance of their influence and of the "special relationship" and, indeed, as having been often subservient to the larger power. John Dumbrell insists that the "special relationship" has to be considered from the point of view of policy, culture and sentiment.[26] With regard to policy, it has been almost exclusively a British preoccupation. Dumbrell also writes of the debate between those who take a purely *realpolitik* view of Anglo-American relations[27] and those who emphasize shared culture, values and traditions. Part of the purpose of this book is to analyse the similarities and differences between British and American discourse since the end of the Cold War and this obviously deals with the question of shared culture and values.

Anglo-American Relations since the End of the Cold War

The first Gulf War demonstrated that, although the Cold War was ending, Anglo-American relations remained close. Certainly Margaret Thatcher portrayed them as such. After lamenting, in her memoirs, the close relationship between Germany and George Bush's America, Thatcher insisted that the Gulf War had made the Bush administration understand who their true friends were:

> Anglo-American relations suddenly lost their chill; indeed by the end [of 1990] they had hardly been warmer. The protectionism of that "integrated" Europe, dominated by Germany, which the Americans had cheerfully accepted, even encouraged, suddenly started to arouse American fears and threaten to cost American jobs. But this change of heart was confirmed by the aggression of Saddam Hussein against Kuwait which shattered any illusion that tyranny had been everywhere defeated. The UN might pass its resolutions; but there would soon be a full-scale war to fight. Suddenly a Britain with armed forces which had the skills, and a government which had the resolve, to fight alongside America, seemed to be the real European "partner in leadership".[28]

From the Iraqi invasion of Kuwait in August 1990 to her resignation in November of that year, Thatcher repeatedly pressed on the Americans her enthusiasm for a military solution to the conflict. However, an examination of American sources tends to show that Thatcher exaggerated her own role in stiffening Washington's resolve and the importance of the British contribution in U.S. eyes. Bush's Secretary of State, James Baker, for example, roughly equated the British and French contribution in his memoirs.[29] The diplomatic correspondent, John Dickie argued that the Gulf War was the last blossom of the special relationship.[30] Indeed, it became rather fashionable in the 1990s to talk of its end.

The period of the Clinton presidency, at least at first, seemed to support this. Although Clinton had been a Rhodes Scholar at Oxford, as had other members of his administration, his personal relationship with John Major, the then British premier, got off to a rocky start. This was primarily Major's fault as he had cooperated with the Bush re-election campaign in 1992. But Major also found irritating Clinton's interventions in Northern Ireland.[31] Furthermore, Clinton had very early on stated his desire to concentrate on domestic and trade policy, with the famous slogan "it's the economy, stupid.[32] He also made Russia the centrepiece of his foreign policy.[33]

The arrival of Blair at 10 Downing Street saw a renewed warmth in Anglo-American relations. Blair and New Labour openly admired Clinton and the new Democrats; indeed, they had modelled many of their programmes and strategies on the Americans. Added to this Blair, unlike Major, welcomed Clinton's involvement in the Northern Ireland peace process. And finally, Blair and Clinton genuinely liked each other and enjoyed being in each other's company–a fact which is shown by their continued friendship even after both have left office.

They did, however, have some differences, in particular over Kosovo. In 1999 Blair addressed the Chicago Economic Club. At this time the air campaign in Kosovo was going on and was less successful than NATO leaders had hoped. Blair worried about what would happen if Milosevic could not be stopped solely by air power and wished to have American agreement to prepare for a land war. Clinton, however, refused to give Blair any such assurances. The Prime Minister arrived in Washington just before a major NATO summit on 21 April and met with Clinton the same day. The next day he gave this speech which had obviously been designed well in advance to put pressure on the American President.

Among the many subjects he discussed was the international situation and, in particular, the war then taking place in Kosovo. In this discussion, Blair asserted that:

> This is a just war, based not on any territorial ambitions but on values. We cannot let the evil of ethnic cleansing stand. We must not rest until it is reversed. We have learned twice before in this century that appeasement does not work. If we let an evil dictator range unchallenged, we will have to spill infinitely more blood and treasure to stop him later.[34]

Blair emphasizes here the moral dimension of the question and his text is full of emotionally charged words. In particular, "evil" appears twice in this short extract alone. Opposed to the "evil" of Milosevic stands the morality of the nations who fight against him: their cause is righteous. They seek nothing for themselves and their actions reflect their "values" Having established this Manichean division, Blair goes on to allude to the failure of earlier attempts at "appeasement"–another highly charged word that automatically brings to mind the 1930s and Neville Chamberlain's attempts to placate Hitler in order to avoid war. This analogy is increased by the use of the term "evil dictator". Although never specifically stated, Blair has summoned up the earlier conflict between Chamberlain and Churchill over how to deal with Hitler–and thus, the tragedy of the Second World War–to support his own position.

The crux of the speech came towards the end where Blair argued that:

No longer is our existence as states under threat. Now our actions are guided by a more subtle blend of mutual self-interest and moral purpose in defending the values we cherish. In the end values and interest merge. If we can establish and spread the values of liberty, the rule of law, human rights and an open society then that is in our national interests too. The spread of our values makes us safer. As John Kennedy put it: "Freedom is indivisible and when one man is enslaved who is free?"

The word "values" appears four times in this short extract. Blair believes–and this clearly reflects Blair's conviction and not just that of his speechwriter–that foreign policy must be based on morality. More than this, the use of the word "spread", which appears two times, shows that Blair feels that these values, British and American political ideals, must be disseminated throughout the world. There is thus a messianic element to Blair's philosophy. Note also his argument that "self-interest" and "moral purpose" coincide in this case, for this reasoning will recur in the Iraq conflict. It is interesting to observe that along with Milosevic, Blair singles out Saddam Hussein in this speech, describing both dictators as "dangerous and ruthless men". Given the similarities between what Blair said over Kosovo and much neo-conservative rhetoric, it is not very surprising that the Labour Prime Minister got along almost as well with the Republican George W. Bush. But this will be discussed in more detail in the last two chapters.

Political Parties and the Left/Right Axis

The Cold War saw an important division between Left and Right but one which should not be exaggerated. In the United States, both Democrats and Republicans were hostile to the Soviet Union and a general consensus existed on stopping the spread of communism. Although some of the strongest anti-communist rhetoric was associated with the Republican party, ideology rarely won out over *realpolitik*. Nixon, that ardent cold warrior, went to China and Reagan, who talked of an "evil empire", met with Gorbachev. In Britain, the post-war Labour government pushed for the establishment of NATO and the Marshall Plan. There did, however, exist a group of extreme leftwing sympathisers within the Labour party and, in particular in the 1980s, a polarised discourse did exist.

In the post-Cold War world we can notice a frequently polarised discourse in the American political scene. From 1994, foreign policy issues were repeatedly used by a Republican dominated Congress to attack a Democratic president. The origins of this lay within the United States and are outside the scope of this book for they can only be examined in detail in relation to domestic policy discourse. Interestingly enough, this renewed polarisation often reflected debates of the Cold War. The fight against globalisation and NAFTA, with all its anti-capitalist overtones, became a preoccupation of many leftwing groups and influenced Democratic party policy. Criticisms of Russia and China were used by the Right to attack the Clinton government.

In general, British politics do not show the same degree of polarisation. Little difference existed on issues like the euro, relations with former Cold War enemies or even military interventionism. Of course, participation in the War in Iraq was highly controversial but the fact that a Labour government spearheaded it, seemed to divide opponents–at least at first. On the whole, Labour appears to have succeeded in taking the centre ground and building a consensus while the Conservatives still seem to be seeking to rebuild their party.

The Organisation of the Book

This book is divided into three sections and the first concerns relations with international groupings We begin with Martine Azuelos' chapter on NAFTA where she shows us the importance of trade issues since the end of the Cold War. These questions have gained both in prominence and controversy and, have consequently, become more and more partisan. Professor Azuelos shows how NAFTA had been negotiated by the first President Bush's administration, as part of the "new world order". Bush hoped it would help the U.S. develop a closer relationship with its southern neighbours and believed its impact, on the U.S. at least, would be more political than economic. The treaty had been signed but not ratified by the end of Bush's term and so its future was left to the new Democratic government. Given the importance of trade issues to the Clinton administration, it is not surprising to see that they worked for its approval. However, the debate about NAFTA only grew after its ratification and became embroiled in the escalating partisanship of the American political scene. Clinton had underestimated the hostility to it among certain important groups within the Democratic party. Workers and unions feared that freer trade with underdeveloped countries would hurt their jobs and wages. Clinton's alliance with Republicans to pass NAFTA undermined its support in the Democratic camp. As a result, in the 2008 primaries, very few Democratic candidates had anything good to say about it. This article shows clearly how foreign policy questions, especially those involving trade (and thus jobs) can be strongly affected by domestic considerations. Furthermore, it involves debates, not only about economics but also about immigration and, ultimately, national identity.

The next two chapters consider Britain's relationship with the European Union. The first, by Pauline Schnapper, examines the discourse among the leaders at a time that saw the vote on the Maastricht Treaty, the "mad cow" crisis, a massive expansion in EU membership and the debate on the European constitution, among other things. Europe obviously raises questions about national identity since it is by nature supranational. Added to this, the British have, historically, seen themselves as fundamentally different from their European neighbours. Prof. Schnapper shows that no political leaders have been able to articulate a positive vision of Europe in relation to British identity and that the question has, therefore, attracted little popular support or interest. While, in the period since 1992, Labour has been consistently less hostile to Europe than the Conservatives, neither has shown much enthusiasm for it and both have resorted to the use of military and defensive vocabulary. Even the Liberal Democrats have dampened their own interest for it, primarily because of a lack of popular support.

The third chapter, by Carine Berberi, analyses specifically the debate over British membership in the European single currency. Neither major party came out in favour of joining the economic union, although they have flirted with it, but they base their opposition on different grounds. Labour's main objections have been economic; the Conservatives' political and constitutional. Labour has certainly had a more positive attitude but lack of support in public opinion and in the press has hampered it. Indeed, Labour has become less pro-European more because of public opinion and divisions within its own party than over somewhat debateable economic reservations. In the end, while the discourse in the parties has been somewhat dissimilar, their policy has not been very different.

Finally, Fatma Ramdani looks at American discourse at the United Nations. She examines the exportation of the political divide in the United States over questions related to gender–notably abortion and family policy, feminism and women's rights. Of course, this has occurred because controversy over these questions exists in other nations. In the 1970s, development was a major issue at the U.N. and the American Republican administrations insisted that women were key players. In international conferences of the time, the U.S. linked control of population growth to development–a position fiercely attacked by many developing nations. In the 1990s, the U.S. was still exercising a leadership role and working for women's rights but this time under a Democratic administration. Their active work at the U.N., however, stimulated those within the U.S. who had more traditional views on gender related issues to organize themselves on an international level and seek allies among developing nations. Some of them decided to use the U.N. as a forum to counterattack a secular feminist agenda–and this in spite of much hostility to the U.N. and international institutions among many in their ranks.

The second section of the book concerns relations with former Cold War players. We begin by looking at the discourse within the U.K. relating to Hong Kong. This undoubtedly belongs to the long history of British imperial discourse and, as such, is linked to concepts of national identity. Certainly, two often repeated words in the debate were "mission" and "legacy"–both harking back to nineteenth century imperial rhetoric. In the second half of the twentieth century, before becoming independent, colonies were supposed to receive training in British values, notably with regard to democracy and human rights. Hong Kong, the U.K.'s last major colony, did not become independent but was returned to China–a significant difference, especially since China's record on human rights was notoriously poor. The population of Hong Kong was afraid of their future, especially after Tiananmen. Much of British discourse, then focussed on how to ensure, as much as possible, the survival of British values there and on trying to reassure the population. To leave with honour, in other words. Little difference existed between the parties either on this need or on the way to do this, although the last governor's attempts to put this policy into effect hurt relations with Beijing. But most politicians seem to have felt this was an acceptable price to pay, although, once Hong Kong was returned, Blair's government immediately moved to improve relations.

In the next article Juliette Bourdin examines U.S./China relations which show, as with the British, a conflict between *realpolitik* and moral values. In Washington, the subject became increasingly linked to the growing partisanship of American politics. Under Clinton, China became an issue in the tug-of-war between a Republican Congress and a Democratic president as the Republicans attacked Clinton's policy. Here we see clearly how trade can be linked to the spread of American values and, indeed, how capitalism can be considered to be one of the most important of these values. *Realpolitik* and support for the spread of capitalism dictated closer economic relations with China and many argued that the best way to westernise China was to engage it in Western institutions. Others wanted to limit relations with China because of its poor human rights record. Finally, we can see the continued existence of Cold War rhetoric in this debate.

We can see a similar situation in the following chapter which deals with British and American discourse on Russia. In his first term, Clinton made assistance for Russia a major element of his administration's foreign policy. He argued that it would help bring Russia into the Western camp and remove it as a security threat. There was much bipartisan support for this policy, even in Congress. But like China, after the 1994 election, Russian policy became yet another part of the partisan debate between the Republican-dominated Congress and the Democratic President. In Britain there was more consensus between the parties but this did not prevent relations from worsening. Transforming Russia into a democracy proved more difficult than hoped and Yeltsin did not live up to expectations. Putin, although showing promise after the 11 September 2001 attacks, became more hostile and threatening to both the U.S. and Britain (especially the latter)–especially after the invasion of Iraq. In both Western nations we can see a return to the rhetoric of the Cold War (some might argue it had never really disappeared). Certainly, much of the rhetoric relating to Russia, whether in Britain or the U.S., presents it as a nation that must be taught how to behave properly and can seem patronising– especially to the Russians.

The last chapter in this section, by Ann Lane, concerns British discourse on ex-Yugoslavia, notably with regard to Western interventions in Bosnia-Herzegovina and Kosovo. Since each situation was multifaceted and morally unclear, British political debate about a response was equally complex. The intense coverage events there generated in the international media and its closeness to the Cold War further complicated the matter. Deliberations over British involvement in ex-Yugoslavia showed that the Left/Right axis of foreign policy debate during the Cold War had shattered and split in an indefinable way that did not always follow party lines. Paradoxically, British confidence in its military ability was weaker under the Conservative government of John Major than under the Labour government of Tony Blair. Blair's conviction politics could build a consensus for intervention (not only in ex-Yugoslavia). In fact, Dr. Lane suggests at the end that Blair may have helped forge a new consensus over intervention that would develop more strongly after the 11 September attacks.

The third section considers the Middle East, terrorism and the Iraq War which became the most urgent question of foreign policy for both nations. We begin with Lars Berger's chapter considering different approaches to America's Middle East policy. As he points out, the U.S. has generally managed to reconcile two seemingly irreconcilable aims–to have its cake and eat it too–by maintaining close relations with both Israel and the oil-producing Arab countries. Certainly, many countries in the Middle East found the neo-conservative discourse patronising: the U.S., Israel and Europe will teach the Arab world how to behave. This undoubtedly increased the difficulties the Bush administration had in those areas. The repeated problems encountered in Iraq and Afghanistan discredited to some extent the neo-conservative discourse and, towards the end of his second term, Bush's policy moved closer to *realpolitik*.

In the next chapter, Jon Roper examines the rhetoric of Blair and Bush in more detail and looks at their relationship to rhetorical traditions in both Britain and the United States. He shows how Blair, although from the Labour Party, resembles, in many ways, the great nineteenth century Liberal statesman, William Gladstone. Much has already been written about the Wilsonian (as in Woodrow Wilson) origins of neo-conservative thought in America. Prof. Roper shows the links between the two men's ideas. Blair is by no means Bush's poodle but believes sincerely in his moral vision and shares a similar outlook to the American President. Both believe in the superiority of their nations' values and the need to spread them throughout the world. However, Blair places more emphasis on ideas of international community while Bush stresses American internationalism.

Finally, our last chapter, by James Bergeron, focuses on the importance of choosing an all-encompassing name for the post-9/11 conflicts. The Bush administration certainly would not agree with Shakespeare's assessment that "a rose by any other name would smell as sweet". Several terms were tried before the War on Terror became the generally accepted appellation. Dr. Bergeron also compares Blair's and Bush's rhetoric after the 11 September attacks. In spite of remarkable similarities there were important differences. Bush emphasized that they were an attack on the United States and used vocabulary related to war. Blair, on the other hand, talked of an attack on democracy and placed greater emphasis on policy more than war.

It would be impossible in a book of this size to give a comprehensive view of British and American foreign policy discourse and we have not tried to do so. Major areas are missing: Africa hardly appears; Asia, outside China, is neglected as is much of Latin America. Our goal was not to give a comprehensive view but to examine those areas that figured most strongly in foreign policy debate within the two nations during the period.

Notes

[1] I would like to thank Susan Ball, Lilli Parrott, Allan Potofsky and Henri Zuber for their help.

[2] George H.W. Bush, "Address before a Joint Session of Congress on the Cessation of the Persian Gulf Conflict", March 6, 1991, in *Public Papers of the Presidents: George Bush, 1991, vol. 1* (Washington, D.C.: 1993) 220-221.

[3] Merriam Webster Dictionary Online, www. Merriam-webster.com/dictionary/discourse (accessed October 16, 2008).

[4] See *The Essential Works of Michel Foucault, 1954-1984, vol. 3, Power*, ed. Paul Rabinow (London: Penguin, 2002)

[5] Michel Foucault, "The Discourse on Language" in *The Archaeology of Knowledge and The Discourse on Language*, trans. A.M. Sheridan Smith (New York: Pantheon Books, 1972) 227

[6] *Ibid.*, 216

[7] See, for example, Louis Althusser, *Essays on Ideology* (London: Verso, 1984)

[8] See, for example, Marshall McLuhan, *The Media is the Massage: An Inventory of Effects* (Harmondsworth: Penguin, 1967)

[9] Norman Fairclough, *Discourse Analysis : Textual Analysis for Social Research* (London : Routledge, 2003) 1.

[10] Woodrow Wilson, "Address to the Senate" September 30, 1918, in *The Papers of Woodrow Wilson, Vol. 51*, ed. Arthur Link (Princeton: Princeton University Press, 1985) 158.

[11] Woodrow Wilson, November 4, 1915, in *The Papers of Woodrow Wilson, Vol. 35*, ed. Arthur Link (Princeton: Princeton University Press, 1981) 353.

[12] Winston Churchill, *Blood, Toil, Tears and Sweat: Winston Churchill's Famous Speeches*, ed. David Cannadine (London: Cassell, 1989) 177-8

[13] *Ibid.*, 200-1

[14] Harry Truman, "Speech to Congress", March 12, 1947, in *Public Papers of the Presidents: Harry Truman: 1947* (Washington: USGPO, 1966) 178-9.

[15] John Kennedy, "Inaugural Address", January 21, 1961, in *Public Papers of the Presidents: John Kennedy, 1961* (Washington: D.C., USGPO) 3

[16] Ronald Reagan, "Remarks at the Annual Convention of the National Association of Evangelicals, Orlando, Florida", March 8, 1983, in *Speaking My Mind: Selected Speeches* (New York: Simon & Schuster, 1989) 179.

[17] Ernest Bevin, *House of Commons Debates*, 18/3/1949, 5th Series, vol. 462, cols. 2533-6

[18] Harold Macmillan, speech in Cape Town, 3 February 1960 in *Pointing the Way* (London: Macmillan, 1972) 476

[19] Margaret Thatcher, Speech at the Conservative Party Conference at Brighton, October 10, 1975 in *Let Our Children Grow Tall: Selected Speeches, 1975-77* (London: Centre for Policy Studies, 1977) 31.

[20] Francis Fukuyama, "The End of History?", *The National Interest* (1989)

[21] See James Woolsey, "World War IV", lecture at the Center for the Study of Popular Culture, 16 Nov. 2002; Eliot Cohen, "World War IV: Let's Call This Conflict What It Is", *The Wall Street Journal*, November 20, 2001

[22] See, for example, John Dumbrell, *A Special Relationship* (Basingstoke: Palgrave, 2nd edition, 2006); D.M. Andrews, ed. *The Atlantic Alliance under Stress: U.S.-European Relations after Iraq* (Cambridge: Cambridge University Press, 2005); John Baylis, *Anglo-American Relations since 1939: The Enduring Alliance* (Manchester: Manchester University Press, 1997); Alex Danchev, *On Specialness: Essays in Anglo-American Relations* (Basingstoke: Macmillan, 1998); John Dickie, *"Special No More": Anglo-American Relations: Rhetoric and Reality* (London: Weidenfeld & Nicolson, 1994); Alan Dobson, *Anglo-American Relations in the Twentieth Century* (London: Routledge, 1995); J. Hollowell, ed., *Twentieth Century Anglo-American Relations* (Basingstoke: Palgrave, 2001); Beatrice Heuser, *Transatlantic Relations: Sharing Ideals and Costs* (London: Pinter/RIIA, 1996) and any others which there is not the space to list.

[23] Churchill, op.cit.

[24] While Churchill may have had a romantic idea of England, its dependence on and need for the U.S. was one of the major themes of his war speeches. Even his speech after Dunkirk terminates with, after the famous "We shall fight..." sequence, the recognition that, the only way Britain can be saved is through the assistance of the United States.

[25] Winston Churchill, Speech to the Conservative Party Conference, October 9, 1948, in *Never Give In! The Best of Winston Churchill's Speeches*, edited by Winston Churchill (London: Pimlico, 2004) 448.

[26] Dumbrell, 6.

[27] Alex Danchev calls them the "functionalists" in "On Specialness", *International Affairs*, 72:4 (1996): 737-51

[28] Margaret Thatcher, *The Downing Street Years*, (London: Harper Collins, 1993) 769

[29] James Baker, *The Politics of Diplomacy* (New York: Putnam, 1995) 381.

[30] See Dickie, *op. cit.*

[31] For more on this see Dumbrell.

[32] For more on this see I.M. Destler "Foreign Economic Policy Making under Bill Clinton" in James Scott, ed. *After the End: Making US Foreign Policy in the Post-Cold War World* (London: Duke University, 1998) and John Dumbrell, *American Foreign Policy: Carter to Clinton* (Basingstoke: Macmillan, 1997)

[33] See chapter 8.

[34] Tony Blair, Speech to the Chicago Economic Club, April 22, 1999, at www.pbs.org/newshour/bb/international/jan-june99/blair_doctrine4-23.html

PART I:

RELATIONS WITH INTERNATIONAL GROUPINGS

CHAPTER TWO

NAFTA AND BEYOND: FREE TRADE IN U.S.
POLICY DEBATES FROM 1992 TO 2007

MARTINE AZUELOS

While foreign trade had not been a major bone of contention in the
United States between the 1930s and the late 1980s, the negotiation of the
North American Free Trade Agreement with Mexico and Canada in the
early 1990s marked the beginning of a new era. Indeed, NAFTA sparked
off an acrimonious debate which has durably affected the perception of
and discourse on foreign trade in the U.S. As public opinion became
increasingly concerned with the impact of trade liberalisation on the
everyday lives of U.S. citizens, the free trade issue gained greater visibility
and moved to the foreground of the political agenda. Trade politics
became more partisan, and the bipartisan consensus which had prevailed
since the Roosevelt Administration evaporated, thus often leading to
political deadlock.

In an attempt to account for these developments, this paper first draws
attention to methodological issues: in particular, it posits that discourse
matters in trade policy making. The second part studies the making of
NAFTA: after analysing the institutional framework which determines the
way trade policy is made in the U.S., it focuses on debates and discourse
in the 1990-1993 period, i.e. during the negotiation and prior to ratification
of the agreement. Finally it examines the legacy of NAFTA, i.e. the way in
which the discourse on trade liberalisation, which grew out of the debate
on NAFTA, has informed political debate and political action since that
period.

1. Why discourse matters in trade policy making

The literature on trade policy making in the U.S. has traditionally
emphasized the role of actors and institutions. Elected officials are seen as

suppliers of trade policies, and voters as demanders of these policies. Within this scenario, the interests of producers and workers are crucial in determining the demands of voters. This is why the role of interest groups is so important, particularly as the U.S. institutional framework makes it possible for groups representing relatively small interests to have a large influence on Congress. Thus, as Destler has observed, the political imbalance between concentrated interests seeking protection and dispersed interests benefiting from trade expansion has often ensured victory of the former.[1] Treating voters as rational agents also explains why it makes sense, given the complexity of trade economics and trade policy, for these voters not to try and waste too much time understanding these complex issues. This can account for the knowledge gap between elites and the general public which, as has often been observed, has been wider on the issue of international trade than on any other policy issue since the 1930s.[2] It can also explain why the most visible impact of trade liberalisation, such as the damage it may do to uncompetitive sectors of the economy, will attract public attention, while its more diffuse benefits, such as lower import prices for consumers, will often go unnoticed.

The approach here focuses on the institutional dimension of discourse and borrows from discursive institutionalism, which sees discourse as "an interactive process", both framed by the institutional context in which it is developed and which serves "to enhance political institutional capacity to impose or negotiate reform".[3] For discursive institutionalists discourse is not just about ideas, it is a social construct, in line with critical discourse analysis. Where critical theorists like Foucault or Fairclough see discourse as an instrument for creating and sustaining relations of power, however, discursive institutionalists are interested in discourse as an agent of political reform and change. Discourse can be "coordinative", when built among policy actors and can serve to generate ideas, and be "communicative", when addressed to the public and meant to inform about those ideas. Reform will occur when discourse can persuade "key policy actors and/or the public to shift their preferences."[4]

In view of the intensity of the debate NAFTA has generated in the U.S. and the enduring impact this has had on the shaping of U.S. trade policy, this discursive approach seems particularly appealing. This paper uses this analytical framework to supplement the political economy and political science approaches. Discourse is seen as an interactive process defining the terms of the trade policy debate, the way in which this debate is framed, and also largely determining the outcome of the debate, i.e. whether a change in policy can take place or not. This approach can hopefully shed fresh light on the policy debates which NAFTA has generated and on the political action or political deadlock which have resulted from the interaction between political actors, public opinion and interest groups.

2. The making of NAFTA

The institutional framework: how trade policy
is made in the United States

Article 1, section 8, of the Constitution of the United States grants Congress sole "power to regulate ... commerce with foreign nations" and to "lay and collect (tariff) duties". Thus the executive branch of government is given no authority whatsoever over the making of trade policy. Indeed, until the 1930s, the President hardly played any role in this area. But in 1934, Congress passed the Reciprocal Trade Agreements Act. This Act first delegated authority to the President to cut tariffs by up to 50 % in the course of a negotiation with foreign partners to grant the United States similar ("reciprocal") concessions. The fundamental reason underlying this transfer of authority had to do with pressures which special interests traditionally exert on Congress: "Because the President was less accountable to local interests than Members of Congress were, the President could negotiate reciprocal reductions in tariffs (within the limits allowed) without the political liability faced by Members".[5] This authority, which was subsequently renewed repeatedly, was instrumental in enabling the President to negotiate tariff cuts in the six rounds of multilateral negotiations which were held under the auspices of the General Agreement on Tariffs and Trade (GATT) between the end of World War II and the late 1960s. Thus the average U.S. tariff rate on all goods (dutiable and duty free) fell from over 19 % in 1933 to 6.5 % in 1970.

In the early 1970s, it thus became clear that, for trade liberalisation to proceed any further, the scope of multilateral negotiations would have to include non-tariff barriers. As the Tokyo Round was about to be launched, President Nixon asked Congress for a new type of negotiating authority. However, the prevailing economic conditions, including the first oil shock and rising unemployment, and the political climate of Watergate, meant that Congress was unwilling to sign Nixon a blank cheque. The Trade Act of 1974 thus enacted a compromise between the White House and both houses of Congress in establishing what has, since then, become known as "Fast Track Authority". This provides for a mechanism under which Congress gives the President temporary authority to negotiate non-tariff trade agreements while limiting his margin of manoeuvre and keeping his representatives under close congressional scrutiny throughout the negotiation. Congress specifies negotiating objectives and requires the President to a) consult with appropriate congressional committees before and during the negotiation and b) notify Congress at least 90 days before entering into an agreement. Once the agreement is signed, the President has to submit implementing legislation which Congress has 60 days to accept or reject with no possibility of amending it.

Fast-Track authority was first granted for a five-year period, but was subsequently extended until 1994. It was instrumental in enabling the United States to negotiate and implement the major multilateral trade agreements reached during the Tokyo and Uruguay Rounds of the GATT negotiations, as well as the bilateral free trade agreement with Canada[6], and the North American Free Trade Agreement[7]. Since 1974, no agreement has been disapproved under Fast-Track procedures, which gives considerable credit to administrations benefiting from this authority. Conversely, the international credibility of a President to whom Congress has not granted Fast Track Authority is undermined, since partners of the United States may reasonably doubt whether the agreement they are negotiating with its representatives will eventually be ratified by Congress—and therefore implemented. This was precisely what happened between 1994 and 2002, a period during which the President was without Fast Track Authority. This situation was largely a side-effect of the mounting opposition to free trade which was fuelled by the conditions under which NAFTA was negotiated and ratified.

Negotiating and winning approval for NAFTA

One year after the inception of the U.S.-Canada Free Trade Agreement, Mexican President Carlos de Salinas de Gortari approached U.S. President George Bush with a view to reaching an agreement of the same kind with its Northern neighbour. Indeed, he saw trade liberalisation as a means of bolstering the free-market reforms which his country had started implementing after the very severe crisis which it had experienced in the early 1980s. For its part, the U.S. administration was fully aware that creating a North American free trade area made sense at a time when the Uruguay Round talks were stalled and when Europe was making rapid progress towards the building of a single market. It was also aware that given the huge asymmetry between the U.S. economy and that of Mexico, the economic impact of such an agreement on the U.S. would be modest[8]. Thus the goal it pursued on entering the negotiation was mostly political. As Destler observes, "The initial impetus for NAFTA was political, not economic".[9] Weintraub concurs: "NAFTA ... used trade and investment as the route to long term political embrace".[10] As the collapse of the Soviet Union ushered in a "New World Order", strengthening the alliance with one's Southern "distant neighbours" was seen as a strategic priority, and this may have led the White House to underrate the political impact that the projected agreement would have domestically.[11]

Throughout the two and a half years from June 1990, when bilateral talks with Mexico were initiated, to December 1992 when the agreement was signed, the Bush Administration repeatedly emphasized the mutual economic benefits that the partners would reap from the proposed NAFTA. In particular, it argued that trade liberalisation would promote growth and create jobs across North America:

> By building, together, the largest free-trading nation in the world, Mexico, the United States, and Canada are working together to ensure that the future will bring increased prosperity, trade, and new jobs for the citizens of each of our countries.[12]

NAFTA was also presented as a means of addressing other concerns, such as illegal drug trafficking, environmental protection, and immigration. It was also presented as a stepping stone towards broader hemispheric integration:

> The United States is a neighbor and friend of Canada and Mexico. NAFTA provides a unique opportunity to draw North America even closer by building a solid foundation for stronger cooperation, integration, and growth. A trade agreement will give economic and political impetus to US efforts to address other North American problems, such as the environment, the flow of drugs, and immigration. NAFTA will help forge a US-Mexican partnership that could lead to closer cooperation on other foreign policy issues.
> A North American trade agreement also is important as the cornerstone of a comprehensive Western Hemisphere policy. It will send a strong, encouraging signal throughout Latin America to a new generation of leaders pledged to democracy, human rights, and market economies. Its successful conclusion will provide further impetus to President Bush's long-range vision of a hemisphere-wide system of free trade.[13]

The Bush administration's rhetoric thus focused attention on the fact that NAFTA's success would pave the way to wider U.S. influence in Latin America.[14]

The project met with little initial opposition from Congress, where bipartisan consensus on support for free trade still prevailed. The

Administration could count on overwhelming Republican backing. The business community, a traditional supporter of the Republican party, was also clearly in favour of increased integration of the North American economies, which it saw as a potential source of improved competitiveness for U.S.-based firms. A majority of Congressional Democrats were also unwilling to abandon the legacy of Roosevelt's Secretary of State, Cordell Hull, who had linked free trade to prosperity and security, and leading figures such as Ways and Means Committee Chairman Dan Rostenkowski (D-IL) in the House and Finance Committee Chairman Lloyd Bentsen (D-TX) in the Senate supported NAFTA. So did a majority of American citizens. Indeed, an opinion survey conducted by the Chicago Council on Foreign Relations in October and November 1990 showed that a majority (73%) of Americans agreed that "the United States should have a free-trade agreement with Mexico, as (they had) with Canada".[15]

Yet jarring notes were soon heard. First, the proposed agreement was met with great suspicion by labour unions, who expressed fear that it would lead to job losses and wage cuts for U.S. workers. Environmentalists also claimed that accelerated industrialisation on the Mexican side of the U.S.-Mexican border would increase pollution and deplete water resources in the south west of the United States.[16] Thus, as economic conditions deteriorated during the recession of 1990-91, causing unemployment to rise until mid-1992, the NAFTA project could easily feed public anxiety. Mounting grass-roots protests orchestrated by the AFL-CIO and organisations like Public Citizen or the Sierra Club put pressure on an increasing number of Democratic Congressmen to oppose NAFTA. Thus, while the Omnibus Trade and Competitiveness Act of 1988 was passed by overwhelming majorities in both the House (376-45) and the Senate (85-11), in May 1991 the resolution extending Fast Track Authority for 2 years was passed by a much narrower margin (231-192 in the House, 59-36 in the Senate). The fact that a majority of Democrats in the House voted against it (170-91) was evidence that opposition to NAFTA had strengthened in Democratic ranks.[17]

The debate on NAFTA grew more acrimonious in 1992, which was an election year. George H. W. Bush, the incumbent Republican President, was challenged by a rival Republican candidate, Patrick Buchanan. Although Buchanan did not succeed in winning the presidential nomination, he managed to gather some 3 million votes in state primary elections and seriously challenge Bush, whose popularity was waning, on the NAFTA project. The presidential campaign was also marked by the emergence of an independent candidate, Ross Perot, who was also very critical of NAFTA. Perot managed to capture 19.5% of the vote in the November 1992 election, and pursued his battle against NAFTA throughout 1993. His widely circulated book drew the public's attention to the "giant sucking sound" that could be heard as the elimination of trade barriers encouraged firms to relocate facilities in Mexico, thus causing millions of manufacturing jobs to be lost in the United States.[18] The AFL-CIO expressed serious reservations about the proposed agreement, which it saw as "social dumping".[19] Under such circumstances, the Democratic presidential candidate could not avoid declaring where he stood on NAFTA. After winning the Democratic presidential ticket in the summer of 1992, Bill Clinton and Al Gore defined an economic strategy focusing on export promotion on the promise that it would lead to job creation: "Because every $1 billion of increased American exports will create 20,000 to 30,000 new jobs, we will move aggressively to open foreign markets to quality American goods and services".[20] They were also committed to supporting free trade with Mexico "so long as it provides adequate protection for workers, farmers, and the environment on both sides of the border".[21] In October, when the Bush administration had finalised NAFTA, Clinton endorsed it while calling for negotiation of side agreements on the environment and labour standards to avoid antagonizing core democratic constituencies.

Negotiation of these supplementary side agreements began shortly after Clinton was inaugurated in January 1993. With unemployment at 7.0 % of the labour force for the best part of the first half of that year, concern over job losses mounted and was established as the central NAFTA issue.[22] An opinion poll published in *Time* on June 7 asked "Do you agree with Clinton's view that the free trade agreement will create jobs, or with Perot's view that it will cost US jobs?" Only 25 % of respondents shared Clinton's view, while 63% agreed with Perot. At the time, it therefore seemed highly unlikely that Clinton might turn the public debate around and win Congressional approval on NAFTA. Yet he did, and the final vote cast by the House of Representatives was won by a fairly wide margin (234-200, with 102 Democrats and 132 Republicans supporting the implementing bill). This success was partly due to Clinton's bargaining skills. It also owed much to the administration's, but also the business community's, communicative skills. In the face of rising public opinion doubts about the potential benefits of free trade with Mexico, communications campaigns were mounted in September and October 1993.[23] Building on this, Al Gore's forceful arguments in his debate with Ross Perot on the national talk show "Larry King Live" seem to have had a determining impact on public opinion just 8 days before the

House of Representatives cast its crucial vote.[24] William Safire's analysis of the contrast between the discourse of the two politicians in the essay he published in the *New York Times* on November 11, 1993, sheds light on the way in which Gore managed to impress public opinion favourably:

> In a classic rendition of "Mr. Nice Guy Goes for the Jugular," Vice President Al Gore poked, prodded and needled Ross Perot into revealing himself as a bossy old billionaire bully who blows his cool when confronted in a fair fight. The debate on CNN ... wasn't even close. Gallup scored audience reaction as almost 2-to-1 for Gore. Was this event an elucidation of the issue of free trade versus protectionism? Of course not; the scrap taking place in the arena of NAFTA has little to do with foreign economic policy. It is the old grudge fight between the politics of hope against the politics of fear (as the free traders put it) or the cultural elite against the pee-pul (as the protectionists put it). That's why the Clinton decision to have his Vice President take on Perot was a media masterstroke. ... The President saw how to dramatize a dull issue -- by anointing one volatile villain as spokesman for NAFTA's opposition. ... The White House strategy was to provoke Perot into blowing his cool, into getting visibly mean and verbally abusive when cornered. Gore's tool in peeling off the veneer of folksiness was an accusation of hypocrisy: since Perot personally profited from his land around a free-trade zone near Mexico, why did the billionaire oppose everybody else getting the same free-trade break? That threw him on the defensive. In truth, Perot is not in the NAFTA opposition for the money he can make; he's only in it for the power he can grab. But the charge of financial hypocrisy rattles him because it undermines his appeal to populist resentment. When Perot launched his customary attack on lobbyists, Gore landed the counterpunch related to that conflict of interest: "I served in the Congress," said Gore, "and I don't know of any single individual who lobbied the Congress more than you did . . . to get tax breaks for your companies."[25]

The television audience's empathy with Gore ricocheted on Congressional politicians, especially in the House of Representatives who, as the *New York Times* observed were "the real target of the debate." The vote cast on November 17 showed that a majority of them thought that the ground was safe enough to tread.

A report published by the U.S. Department of Commerce in October 1993 emphasized the "opportunities for U.S. industries" which NAFTA would provide, but also its benefits for workers and the environment. It also stressed that NAFTA's approval would "demonstrate America's strong commitment to global leadership."[26] Indeed, in the new global environment that the end of the Cold War had created, the Clinton administration saw U.S. global leadership on trade as the centrepiece of

national security. On signing the bill into law, Clinton underlined this
trade, security and prosperity linkage:

> For this new era, our national security we now know will be determined as
> much by our ability to pull down foreign trade barriers as by our ability to
> breach distant ramparts. Once again, we are leading. And in so doing, we
> are rediscovering a fundamental truth about ourselves. When we lead, we
> build security; we build prosperity for our own people.[27]

Seen in this broader perspective, NAFTA strengthened U.S. national
security and global leadership. Geopolitical concerns therefore played as
fundamental a role in shaping the Clinton administration's stance on
NAFTA as it had under the Bush administration. They certainly informed
its rhetoric.

> The Cold War is over. The grim certitude of the contest with communism
> has been replaced by the exuberant uncertainty of international economic
> competition. And the great question of this day is how to ensure security
> for our people at a time when change is the only constant.
> Make no mistake, the global economy with all of its promise and peril is
> now the central fact for hardworking Americans. It has enriched the lives
> of millions of Americans; but for many those same winds of change have
> worn away at the basis of their security.[28]

Clinton's victory nevertheless left deep rifts in his own party. Instead
of rallying a majority of Congressional democrats behind the banner of
free trade, as Cordell Hull had done in the 1930s, his alliance with House
Republicans and the close resemblance between his discourse and that of
the Bush administration undermined support for free trade in the
Democratic camp. As *Business Week* noted, "the bitter debate inflamed
class and ethnic hostilities, pitted labor against management, and set New
Democrats against their liberal brethrens".[29] It was therefore not difficult
to predict that the wounds would not heal easily. With the benefit of
hindsight, the view that the Clinton administration won a victory and that
the anti-NAFTA coalition failed in November 1993 needs to be qualified.
Under the circumstances, victory or defeat may, indeed, have hinged on
discourse more than on anything else. The fact that labour unions and
environmentalists had met on the same ground with populists like
Republican right-winger Patrick Buchanan and protectionists like Ross
Perot could hardly go unnoticed. For each of the groups forming the anti-
NAFTA coalition the NAFTA debate had been a learning process. In the
space of two and a half years they had become fully aware of the
resonance that the jobs and environment issues could have in public

opinion and they were now determined to capitalize on the popularity of these issues to gain more public attention and support for their cause in the future. In the process, a common body of discourse was constructed and this discourse continued to gain ground in the months and years following the passage of NAFTA. As a result, the idea of trade liberalisation became increasingly associated with negative overtones. Thus, despite NAFTA's overall benefits and Clinton's apparent success, the history of its negotiation and ratification paved the way for future battles which he was not going to be in a position to win. As Bhagwati insightfully comments,

> While the President is credited by the pro-free-trade media and by unsophisticated economists with his success on NAFTA ... it was in fact a Pyrrhic victory... In particular, the NAFTA debate had crystallized ... the fears of workers and the labor unions that freer trade with all but rich countries could imperil their real wages... One serious legacy of NAFTA was the plague it visited on future trade liberalisation, by accentuating and politicizing these fears ... and aligning the unions and their Congressional supporters against the further freeing of trade and against the passage of fast track.[30]

3. The NAFTA legacy, rising opposition to free trade since 1994

Taking stock of NAFTA

The agreement which came into effect on January 1st, 1994 provided for eliminating all tariffs and most other trade barriers between the U.S., Canada and Mexico. Some of the tariffs were to be dropped immediately, but most were to be phased out gradually over 15 years. Thus, most of the last remaining obstacles to tripartite trade were eliminated on January 1st, 2008. NAFTA also established a dispute settlement procedure, a Commission for Environmental Cooperation and a Commission for Labour Cooperation which have worked reasonably well. Insofar as it has expanded trade and investment across North America, NAFTA has clearly proved a success, as successive administrations have consistently argued[31] and most economists shown since 1994[32]. Overall trade in goods among the United States, Canada and Mexico grew from $297 billion in 1993 to $883 billion in 2006, an increase of 198%. U.S. merchandise exports to Canada and Mexico grew more rapidly, at 157%, than U.S. exports to the rest of the world, at 108%. U.S. service exports to Canada and Mexico grew 125% over the same period, reaching $61.7 billion in 2006. U.S. foreign direct investment in Canada and Mexico increased even more rapidly, by 289%, reaching $331.2 billion in 2006. As a result, production has become more integrated across North America, which has improved the competitiveness of the three economies.

Critics have nevertheless consistently questioned these positive outcomes and stressed that NAFTA has resulted in job losses and reduced wages in the U.S. while causing havoc in Mexican agriculture, therefore displacing Mexican farmers and increasing illegal immigration to the U.S. The Economic Policy Institute, together with the AFL-CIO and Public Citizen, has been prominent in voicing these criticisms, as the following statement illustrates:

> NAFTA's basic economic assumptions clearly were wrong. Its promoters told American workers not to worry about losing jobs to low-wage Mexican labor because free trade by itself would create a booming Mexican economy and a huge middle-class market for U.S. goods. They confidently predicted that our trade surplus with Mexico would grow, generating net new good jobs in the United States and at the same time reducing illegal immigration from Mexico. But neither the Mexican boom nor the vast middle-class market materialized. The gap between wages in the two countries actually widened. And the trade surplus turned to a chronic deficit, moving hundreds of thousands of American jobs south of the border. At the same time, imports of highly subsidized U.S. and Canadian grain and other agricultural products undercut Mexico's rural economy and drove over 2 million family farmers off the land. With no jobs in the cities, they swelled the migrant stream north. After NAFTA, annual illegal immigration from Mexico doubled.[33]

In view of these criticisms, the Bush and Clinton administrations' discourse was probably flawed. As Weintraub observes, this discourse was based on "unadulterated mercantilism".[34] Indeed with "no automatic relationship between increased export value and job creation", there was a major risk of selling NAFTA on the promise that it would create jobs: any job losses resulting from plant closures, which were bound to happen as the United States adjusted to globalisation, could then easily be used in making the case against NAFTA, while the overall macroeconomic benefits of trade liberalisation would be discounted just as easily.[35] The Bush and Clinton administrations' discursive strategy led NAFTA's opponents to develop a "mirror discourse" focusing on job losses. Thus quantitative data and stories of plant closures and offshoring became the building blocks on which the anti-NAFTA coalition cemented its opposition to free trade. The gradual erosion of public support for NAFTA may be interpreted as evidence that its communicative discourse was effective. In the end, NAFTA's opponents managed to frame the trade liberalisation debate.

As the authors of *Globaphobia* explain, "open borders create losers as well as winners"—in other words globalisation does not lift all boats. Its welfare effects are fairly evenly spread among consumers, while its disruptive effects are born by highly visible minorities. Thus, they argue, while "the losses suffered by displaced workers in the auto, apparel, and shoemaking industries are vividly portrayed on the nightly news", "few Americans recognize that cars, clothes, or shoes are cheaper, better made, or more varied as a result of their country's openness to the rest of the world".[36] That indeed seemed to be the prevailing attitude when those lines were written, even if recent polls have revealed interesting shifts in public opinion. It seems that Americans have grown more sophisticated about free trade than they were in the 1980s or early 1990s. Today majorities of Americans acknowledge the benefits of open borders. A report published by the Chicago Council on Foreign Relations in 2004 revealed that 64% of Americans believed that globalization was mostly good for the United States, and that 57% viewed international trade as good for the U.S. economy. Even more said that international trade was good for consumers like themselves (73%) and for their own standard of living (65%). However this report also revealed the complex public reaction to NAFTA ten years after its inception, showing that 42% of Americans saw it as good, and 43% saw it as bad for the U.S. economy. In another report, published by World Public Opinion.org in 2005, 47% felt that NAFTA had been good for the United States, while 39% felt that it had been bad. In an Ipsos Reid poll conducted in 2005, 47% saw the United States as a loser and 43% as a winner in NAFTA. Interpreting these results is not easy, but the CCFR reports shed some light on what may motivate the American public's mixed feelings: a majority of Americans felt that NAFTA was good for consumers like them (55%) and good for their standard of living (51%), but a majority (56%) also felt that NAFTA was bad for creating jobs in the U.S. and for the job security of American workers (60%). Thus, while supporting NAFTA, majorities expressed reservations about its impact on specific groups within U.S. society and questioned its fairness between the three countries. The overall impression conveyed by these surveys is that Americans now fully realize that, as consumers, they have substantially benefited from the internationalisation of the U.S. economy. But they are also aware that this internationalisation threatens them as workers.

One reason for this ambivalence may have to do with the inadequacy of U.S. policy designed to assist workers who lose their jobs as a result of trade liberalisation. Federal government funding of the Trade Adjustment Assistance (TAA) programme[37] is far too modest. The unemployment benefits, retraining assistance and health insurance it provides[38] thus fall short of providing adequate remedies to worker dislocation.

The failure of Trade Adjustment Assistance to provide efficient insurance against trade dislocation thus goes a long way to explain why anti-NAFTA sentiment could flourish and nourish wider, anti-free trade sentiment among U.S. workers. Yet the U.S. economy created 25 million jobs from 1993 to 2006, which dwarfs the job losses caused by NAFTA.[39] In fact, as Kletzer has shown, there is a set of industries facing sustained import competition where the rate of job loss has been high, but outside these industries, the number of job losses associated with imports is much weaker.[40] This means that increasing imports play a small role in aggregate job losses, but a larger role in import competing industries. Why is it, then, that globalisation should be seen as threatening much larger categories of workers? Scheve and Slaughter argue that one key feature of the way globalisation is *perceived* to affect the U.S. economy is through its broader effects on labour markets—stagnating or falling incomes, rising inequalities, diminished job security.[41] Thus TAA may incorrectly presume that the key issue in the current state of public opinion on globalisation lies in "transitions across jobs for workers in trade-exposed industries." Whether the linkage between these developments and globalisation can firmly be established is a matter of dispute among economists, but the fact remains that the wider public believes that such a linkage exists: "Because the pressures of globalization are spread economy-wide ... there is concern about income and job security among workers employed in all sectors".[42] This perception seems to have played a key role in causing *globaphobia*.[43] Addressing this concern should therefore have been a prerequisite to any further trade liberalisation. Inability to do so could only fuel opposition to free trade.

Rising opposition to free trade: from free trade to fair trade

In the closing paragraphs of the speech he delivered on signing the NAFTA implementing into law, Bill Clinton called for further trade liberalisation. He mentioned the impending conclusion of the GATT Uruguay talks and insisted that the Administration and Congress "seek to reconstruct the broadbased political coalition for expanded trade".[44] His following sentences echoed both Cordell Hull and J.F. Kennedy:[45]

> For decades, working men and women and their representatives supported policies that brought us *prosperity and security*. This was because we

recognized that expanded trade benefited us all, but that we have an
obligation to protect those workers who do *bear the brunt* of competition
by giving them a chance to be retrained and to go on to a new and different
and, ultimately, more secure and more rewarding way of work. In recent
years, this social contract has been sundered; it cannot continue.[46]

In an attempt to rebuild the broad-based consensus on trade, which had
prevailed in the United States from the mid-1930s to the early 1990s,
Clinton offered a promise that was going to deadlock future trade
negotiations with third world countries:

We will seek new institutional arrangements that leaves *the world* cleaner
than before. We will press for workers *in all countries* to secure rights that
we now take for granted, to organize and earn a decent living.[47]

Protecting the environment and labour rights thus became a
"negotiating priority" for the Clinton administration. These "fair trade"
goals, as they were soon labelled, were added to the "free trade" goals of
the U.S. foreign trade agenda. "Fair trade", a phrase which had originally
be used by Ronald Reagan in the 1980s to counter dumping or other
"unfair trade practices" by emerging competitors like Japan, was now
given a much wider meaning. The implicit sports metaphor—derived from
"fair play"—conjured up the picture of a "level playing field" which all
nations participating in trade liberalisation should enter. For this "field" to
be "level", all these nations had to abide by the same rules, but the scope
of these rules was no longer limited to the trade practices that had
originally been listed in the GATT in the immediate post-war era. It was to
encompass the two major societal issues which had surfaced during the
negotiation of NAFTA, i.e. workers' rights and the environment. As I.M.
Destler observes, "An important feature of American trade politics over
the decade beginning in 1995 was the rise of issues involving the
relationship between trade and other prominent policy concerns".[48] While
from the foundation of the American republic to the 1980s, U.S. trade
politics had been "dominated by economic interests in general and
producer interests in particular", in the 1990s, the advent of globalisation
changed the status of trade in the political agenda. It weakened the
resistance of special interest groups to free trade but also fuelled broader
social concerns, so much so that "trade became too important to be left to
the trade specialists".[49] As trade negotiations increasingly bore on "non-
tariff barriers" to trade, issues like subsidies, product standards,
intellectual property, human rights, labour rights and environmental
protection were included in the sphere covered by U.S. trade policy.

Six years later, at Seattle, as Clinton hosted the WTO Ministerial conference that was to launch the "Millenium Round", U.S. officials' insistence on the inclusion of these "fair trade" goals on the negotiating agenda found an echo in the slogans shouted by the thousands of demonstrators in the streets surrounding the convention centre. The rampage they caused in downtown Seattle was evidence of their determination and drew the world's attention to the strength their movement had gathered. It was also evidence of the stalemate trade liberalisation was facing. The deadlock at Seattle reflected the fact that the United States' willingness to impose its own views and rules in this broader sphere met with fierce opposition from a number of its trading partners. Emerging nations, such as India or Brazil, were not prepared to accept what they considered as neo-imperialist practices[50]. Thus, as Jeffrey Schott observes, "the WTO meeting fell victim not to protests outside the streets, but rather to serious substantive disagreements inside the convention centre among both developed and developing countries."[51] The collapse of the talks meant that the launching of a new WTO round of negotiations had to be postponed. It was only two years later, in November 2001, that the new Doha Round was launched. This required President G.W. Bush, who had succeeded Bill Clinton in January 2001, to ask Congress to renew Fast Track Authority (now renamed "Trade Promotion Authority"). In the lengthy process which ensued, leading to the passing of the Trade Act of 2002, the AFL-CIO and environmentalists campaigned for inclusion of provisions preventing the President from signing trade agreements that would not include labour and environmental protection clauses. The Bush administration and a majority of Republican Congressmen were unwilling to accept this provision as they realized that it would probably paralyse future negotiations with many partners in the third world. Thus, they were not included in the Trade Act. But this also paved the way for major domestic difficulties, fuelling opposition of the "Fair Trade" coalition which now focused its discourse on these two issues and led a majority of Democrats to oppose trade agreements that would not include those clauses. Once Democrats were again a majority in Congress (after January 2007) this jeopardized progress on trade policy.

The outsourcing controversy

The resonance of Ross Perot's metaphor of the "giant sucking sound" marked the beginning of the outsourcing controversy in the United States. Of course, outsourcing existed before NAFTA and before Perot made it an electoral issue, but until the early 1990s it seemed as if the general public had not fully realized that it did. The state of public opinion on this issue is better known today than it was twenty or thirty years ago as in-depth surveys of public attitudes to foreign trade and globalisation have only been conducted on a regular basis since the 1990s.[52] Reports published by the Chicago Council on Foreign Relations in the 1970s and 1980s, when the U.S. economy was widely perceived as losing competitiveness, revealed rising public concern about *foreign competition* and its impact on U.S. jobs—a view that the press also largely echoed.[53] Americans were then anxious about rising *foreign* imports flooding the U.S. market and saw *foreign* companies like Toyota, Sony, or Honda challenging former American champions whose competitiveness was being eroded. Clearly, to the average American, the challenge then came from abroad. It pitted foreigners ("them") against Americans ("us"). Of course trade liberalisation, declining U.S. competitiveness and rising foreign competition meant that more and more U.S. workers, especially in "smokestack" industries, were being "displaced". They did lose their jobs, but these jobs were seen as being lost to *foreign* competition, and not as being "shipped overseas" as a result of strategies implemented by U.S. companies and U.S. free trade policies.

This perception was increasingly inaccurate, however. But it was the NAFTA debate which drew the public's attention to the fact that "offshoring" or "outsourcing" were becoming common practices for firms. As trade barriers were lowered or eliminated, technological advances in transportation and communications drove firms to cut costs by breaking up their production processes and participating in global supply chains "in which the many tasks required to manufacture complex industrial goods (or … provide knowledge intensive services) are performed in several, disparate locations", systematically taking advantage of the competitive advantage of each of these locations.[54] Robert Reich had made these facts of globalisation familiar to a wide reading public as early as 1992. He argued that the process could not be stopped and that to successfully adjust to the forces of the global economy, the United States was required to put more emphasis on education. A better-educated workforce would be able to take on the highly-skilled, well-paid jobs that the U.S. economy could create, thus ensuring greater national prosperity in the future.[55] Strong job creation from 1994 to 2000, combined with confidence that the "New Economy", fuelled by high technologies and globalisation, had restored prosperity, meant that few heard the call. When unemployment started to rise again sharply from 2001 to 2003 as the bursting of the internet bubble plunged the economy into recession, the picture changed swiftly.

Offshoring and outsourcing become a major source of concern—and a major electoral issue—in the 2004 presidential campaign. The number of press articles published on the subject in 2003 and 2004 gave resonance to concerns voiced by the AFL-CIO and populists.[56] This could have been merely a repetition of what had happened a decade before, when NAFTA was being negotiated. There was, however, a major difference. Offshoring undermined support for free trade among wider ranks of politicians, and the economic profession itself began to think again. Research was thus increasingly devoted to an issue which was threatening to tear the fabric of U.S. society apart.[57]

Presidential candidates widely expressed their views on the subject. One particular occasion on which they did was the October 13, 2004 presidential debate in which they were questioned on economic and social issues. Two questions bore on the issue of offshoring.[58] The answers given by the two candidates shed light on their attitudes to free trade and globalisation. First, while implicitly sharing the view that globalization is good for the United States, they did not say so, and this silence spoke for itself. Expressing positive views on free trade was probably considered too risky by both of them, which confirms what was said previously on the success of the anti-free trade coalition in framing the debate on trade policy. Second, the two candidates expressed different views on measures which the Federal government could implement to tackle the issue of offshoring. G.W. Bush spoke first:

> And so the person you talked to, I say, here's some help, here's some trade adjustment assistance money for you to go a community college in your neighborhood, a community college which is providing the skills necessary to fill the jobs of the 21st century. And that's what I would say to that person.[59]

As one *Business Week* commentator noted, "Although Bush is derided by foes for his mangled syntax, he's smart enough to have figured one thing out: Words are weapons … The key to Bushspeak is 'simplicity and relevance'."[60] This statement is a good illustration of the way in which Bush uses discourse, bearing in mind the huge gap between the general public and elites on trade policy matters. Bush's speech mannerisms are used here to convey his message to his main target—ordinary Americans. What strikes most in this short statement is that it is supposed to reproduce an informal conversation with an ordinary displaced American worker: the words and syntax used by Bush are so simple that this worker would have no difficulty understanding what he is talking about. Thus Bush manages to convey his proximity with and understanding of the American people, as well as his optimism for the future ("the jobs of the 21st century"). Yet elites also get the reference to TAA benefits and retraining allowance—which is the object of broad bipartisan consensus. Republicans get what they want to hear on individual responsibility—as each individual's willingness to retrain ("for you to go to a community college") is presented as a key determinant of his ability to find a replacement job, in line with traditional Republican emphasis on self-reliance and on free market economists' insistence on TAA as the only remedy for labour market displacement resulting from trade liberalisation. A very subtly crafted statement indeed if one bears in mind that all that matters here is effectiveness of communication.

Kerry's answer differed radically in both manner and content:

> Outsourcing is going to happen. I've acknowledged that in union halls across the country. I've had shop stewards stand up and say, "Will you promise me you're going to stop all this outsourcing?" And I've looked them in the eye and I've said, "No, I can't do that." What I can promise you is that I will make the playing field as fair as possible, that I will, for instance, make certain that with respect to the tax system that you as a worker in America are not subsidizing the loss of your job. Today, if you're an American business, you actually get a benefit for going overseas. You get to defer your taxes.[61]

While obviously candid and far more articulate than the President, his Democratic challenger was probably less effective a communicator. The length and fairly technical content of his message made it more difficult for ordinary Americans to understand. In fact his target was narrow—the union members he referred to accounting for less that 12% of the labour force. Taking up themes that were promoted by the AFL-CIO ("fair" trade, the need to reform existing tax legislation granting unfair advantages to businesses investing abroad), his statement failed to reach beyond this constituency. In particular, it conveyed a sense of doom boding ill of America's future ("outsourcing is bound to happen") and highlighted the limitations of government action ("I can't do that", "as fair as possible") which were unlikely to infuse widespread confidence in his own ability to address the economic anxieties of a majority of Americans.

These answers provide the background which has shaped the trade debate since 2004. A majority of Congressional Democrats have relentlessly brandished the demand for "fair trade" or a "level playing field" as a prerequisite to their approval of any further trade liberalisation. The Bush administration and a majority of Congressional Republicans have pushed for trade liberalization and have argued that a more generous

TAA is the best instrument for addressing the problems of the losers of globalization. Failure to reach a bipartisan compromise on these issues has resulted in a stalemate which the debate over Fast-Track has revealed.

The stalemate over fast track

In the aftermath of the NAFTA "victory", the Clinton administration sought to repair its frayed relations with key Democratic constituencies, particularly labour unions and environmentalists. This led them to emphasize trade-related labour and environmental issues as priority negotiating objectives, which antagonized business interests. As a result, it was impossible to include a provision renewing Fast-Track authority, which expired in 1994, under the Trade Act of 1994.[62] Republican victory in the November 1994 congressional elections meant that in the years that followed the rift between Congress and the Clinton administration widened. The peso crisis and the resulting swing of the U.S. trade balance with Mexico from surplus to deficit strengthened the anti-NAFTA coalition in 1996, and made Clinton's position even more difficult in a re-election year. It was thus only in 1997 that he sought renewal of Fast-Track authority. In October of that year, however, after months of negotiations with Congress, it became clear that it would be impossible to reach a compromise reconciling the diverging goals of majorities in both parties, so Clinton chose to withdraw the bill rather than face the humiliation of a negative vote. In 1998, it was the Congressional Republicans who proposed to reauthorize Fast-Track, but this proposal was defeated by a House vote in September. Thus from April 1994 to August 2002, when Clinton's successor managed to get Congress to grant him "Trade Promotion Authority", the President was not given the essential instrument to credibly negotiate trade agreements. The relabeling of Fast-Track is another illustration of the Bush administration's crafty use of discourse. As a former Clinton aide commented, "When creating a new term the goal is to choose 'inclusive language' that reaches out beyond your political base. "You're looking for words that people can readily understand without putting you in one ideological camp."[63] This was of particular importance over as contentious an issue as trade liberalization. It suggests that the fair trade coalition had managed to associate Fast-Track with such negative overtones that the administration no longer found it fit to use the phrase. The renaming of Fast-Track was part of a discursive counter strategy meant to associate "trade" with positive overtones ("promotion"). The absence of an adjective before "trade" revealed that by avoiding to choose between "free" and "fair" trade, the administration meant to reach across party lines. This, however, was unrealistic given the extent to which party polarization now dominated Congressional trade politics.

Party polarization on trade issues increased sharply in the 1990s and 2000s, as votes on major trade agreements reveal. The one-vote majority, by which the renewal of fast track authority was won in 2002, made it another Pyrrhic victory for the Presidency. It required huge concessions to special interests (farmers, steel producers[64]) which cast doubt on the administration's commitment to free trade and on its ability to win approval of future trade agreements. These conflicting objectives tied the hands of the U.S. in a way which led to deadlock both in the Doha round and in the negotiation over the Free Trade Areas of the Americas (FTAA).

Votes in Major Trade Legislation, 1974-2006

Title of legislation	Vote in H.R.	Vote in Senate
Trade Act of 1974	272-140	72-4
Trade Agreements Act of 1979	395-7	90-4
Omnibus Trade and Competitiveness Act of 1988	376-45	85-11
United States–Canada Free Trade Agreement Implementation Act of 1988	366-40	83-9
North American Free Trade Implementation Act (1993)	234-200	61-38
Uruguay Round Agreements Act (1994)	288-146	76-24
Trade Act of 2002	215-212	64-34
United States-Chile Free trade Agreement Implementation Act (2003)	270-156	65-32
United-States-Singapore Free Trade Agreement Implementation Act (2003)	272-155	66-32
United-States-Australia Free Trade Agreement Implementation Act (2004)	314-109	80-16
United States-Morocco Free Trade Agreement Implementation Act (2004)	323-99	Unanimous consent, no recorded vote
Dominican Republic-Central America-United States Free Trade Agreement Implementation Act (2005)	217-215	55-45
United States–Bahrain Free trade	327-95	Unanimous

Agreement Implementation Act (2006)		consent, no recorded vote
United States–Oman Free Trade	221-205	62-32
Agreement Implementation Act (2006)		

Source : Smith 2007.

The doomed FTAA

The creation of a free trade area of the Americas had first been promoted by Ronald Reagan in the 1980 presidential campaign, but in the "lost decade" of the 1980s the debt crisis and repeated U.S. military interventions in Latin America were hardly conducive to progress on trade liberalisation issues. Just a few weeks after the U.S. agreed to negotiate NAFTA, President George H.W. Bush announced the "Enterprise for the Americas Initiative" (EAI) which was designed to promote democracy and market-oriented reforms across Latin America by expanding regional trade and investment and reducing these countries' debt burden. It was only after NAFTA and the Uruguay Round agreements had been ratified, however, that the Clinton administration gave the EAI new momentum. The Summit of the Americas convened in Miami in December 1994 launched negotiations with a view to progressively eliminating trade and investment barriers among 34 countries from Alaska to Tierra del Fuego (only Cuba was not invited to participate). The negotiation, which was targeted for completion no later than January 2005, made reasonable progress in the first few years. But enthusiasm gradually dampened in the United States as well as among its major partners in Latin America and talks finally collapsed at the November 2005 Summit of the Americas in Mar del Plata (Argentina).

The collapse of the FTAA project has given rise to various interpretations. While in Latin America and Europe it has been widely seen as a defeat for the Bush administration and a setback for U.S. economic "imperialism", U.S. observers have focused on the erosion of U.S. interest in the project. From the start it was clear that strong political, social and economic heterogeneity across Latin America would make it difficult to agree on one common agenda, but from the U.S. viewpoint it seemed worthwhile to attempt to do so. In sharp contrast with its swift response to Mexico's peso crisis in 1994-1995, however, the United States did not rush to rescue Argentina from the severe depression in which it was plunged in 1999 and, in the aftermath of September 11, security concerns and the war on terror pushed all other foreign policy goals to the background. This was evidence that trade policy was no longer a priority of government action, all the more so when it concerned partners with which trade and investments flows were growing modestly—which was the case of Latin America.[65] In Latin America, the rise to power of left-leaning governments in 11 countries between 1998 and 2007 weakened support for cooperation with the United States while reinforcing the drive toward bilateral ad sub-regional agreements, as well as toward partnerships with the European Union or Asia. Thus while Andean Community or Mercosur members were seeking to deepen their relations, U.S. Trade Representative Robert Zoellick made it clear that the U.S. would seek "competitive liberalisation", a concept first coined by C. Fred Bergsten[66]:

> We will promote free trade globally, regionally and bilaterally, while rebuilding support at home. By moving forward on multiple fronts, the United States can exert its leverage for openness, create a new competition in liberalization, target the needs of developing countries, and create a fresh political dynamic by putting free trade on to the offensive.[67]

The United States thus opened bilateral negotiations with Chile, Peru, Panama, Colombia, as well as with four Central American countries (Ecuador, Guatemala, Nicaragua and Honduras) and the Dominican Republic. And the "salami tactics" were successful in enabling the U.S. to reach agreements with these 9 Latin American partners. The trade agreement with Chile was swiftly negotiated and ratified by Congress in 2002. Another, with Peru, was signed in 2006 and ratified in 2007.

Yet approval of the sub-regional agreement with Central America and the Dominican Republic, known as CAFTA-DR, was hard-won (it passed by a 2-vote margin in the House of Representatives) and the agreements with Panama and Colombia were still expecting Congressional approval at the beginning of 2008, despite the bipartisan "compromise" on trade reached in May 2007. As Destler observes, "House Democrats lack the option of legislating a trade expansion policy based on partisan majorities".[68] The fact that in the 2008 primaries campaign Democratic candidates Hillary Clinton and Barack Obama both vowed to renegotiate NAFTA was evidence of the resonance of the free trade issue with key Democratic constituencies. Yet the Bush administration, the Democratic leadership in Congress and business interests still viewed the geopolitical and economic concerns which had prevailed when NAFTA was negotiated as overriding goals of trade policy.[69] These discordant discourses illustrated the polarization of trade politics and the specific challenge it posed for Democrats. Clearly, the NAFTA legacy was here to stay.

Bibliography

Azuelos, Martine, Maria Eugenia Cosio de Zavala, and Jean-Michel Lacroix, eds. *Intégration dans les Amériques. Dix ans d'ALENA.* Paris: Presses Sorbonne Nouvelle, 2004.

Azuelos, Martine. "Mondialisation et politique sociale aux États-Unis: le cas de la *Trade Adjustment Assistance*", in *Marginalité et politiques sociales: réflexions autour de l'exemple américain*, ed. Taoufik Djebali and Benoît Raoulx. Caen: Presses de l'Université de Caen, 2008.

Baldwin, Robert E. and Christopher S. Magee. *Congressional Trade Votes: from NAFTA Approval to Fast-Track Defeat.* Washington, D.C. : Institute for International Economics, 2000.

Bhagwati, Jagdish. *Free Trade: Why AFL-CIO, The Sierra Club and Congressman Gephart Should Like It.* Memphis, Tenn.: P. K. Seidman Foundation, 1999.

—. *The Wind of the Hundred Days. How Washington Mismanaged Globalization.* Cambridge, Mass.: MIT Press, 1999.

—. *Free Trade Today*, Princeton: Princeton University Press, 2002.

Binder, Alan. "Offshoring: The Next Industrial Revolution?" *Foreign Affairs*, (March-April, 2007).

Burtless, Gary, Robert Z. Lawrence, Robert E. Litan, and Robert J. Shapiro. *Globaphobia. Confronting Fears about Open Trade.* Washington, D.C.: Brookings Institution, 1998.

Chicago Council on Foreign Relations. *American Public Opinion and U.S. Foreign Policy 1991.* Chicago: Chicago Press Corporation, 1991.

—. *WorldView 2004.* Chicago: Chicago Press Corporation, 2004.

Clinton, Bill and Al Gore. *Putting People First. How We Can All Change America.* New York: Times Books, 1992.

Clinton, Bill. "Remarks by the President in NAFTA Bill Signing Ceremony, Mellon Auditorium, Washington, DC." The White House. Office of the Press Secretary, 1993. http://www.clintonfoundation.org/legacy/120893-speech-by-president-in-nafta-bill-signing-ceremony.htm (Accessed February 15, 2008).

Coughlin, Cletus C. "The Controversy Over Free Trade. The Gap Between Economists and the General Public". *The Federal Reserve Bank of Saint Louis Review* (January-February, 2002) 1-21.

Destler, I.M. "The United States and a Free Trade Area of the Americas: A Political-Economic Analysis". In *Integrating the Americas. FTAA and Beyond,* ed. Antoni Estevadeordal, Dani Rodrik, Alan M. Taylor, and Andrés Velasco, 397-416. Cambridge, Mass.: Harvard University Press, 2004.

—. *American Trade Politics.* Washington, D.C.: Institute for International Economics, 4th ed., 2005.

Dobbs, Lou. *Exporting America: Why Corporate Greed Is Shipping American Jobs Overseas.* New York: Warner Books, 2004.

Faux, Jeff and William Spriggs. *US Jobs and the Mexico Trade Proposal,* Washington, D.C.: Economic Policy Institute, 1991.

Faux, Jeff. "The Effect of George Bush's NAFTA on American Workers: Ladder Up or Ladder Down?" Briefing Paper, Washington, D.C.: Economic Policy Institute, 1992.

—. *The Failed Case for NAFTA. The Ten Common Claims for the North American Trade Agreement and Why they Don't Make Sense.* Briefing Paper, Washington, D.C.: Economic Policy Institute, 1993.

—. *Broken promises. NAFTA Cost U.S. Jobs and Reduced Wages.* Washington, DC: Economic Policy Institute. (October, 2006). http://www.epi.org/content.cfm/webfeatures_snapshots_20061004. (Accessed March 3, 2008).

—. *Overhauling NAFTA.* Washington, D.C.: Economic Policy Institute. February 29, 2008. http://www.epi.org/content.cfm/webfeatures_viewpoints_overhauling_ nafta (Accessed March 3, 2008).

Feenstra, Robert C. "Globalization and Its Impact on Labor", Global Economy Lecture. Vienna Institute for International Economic Studies, February, 2007. http://www.wiiw.ac.at/e/global_economy_lecture<.html (Accessed April 2007).

Feenstra, Robert C. and Gordon H. Hanson. "Globalization, Outsourcing, and Wage Inequality", *American Economic Review*, 86:2 (May, 1996): 240-245.

Friedman, Sheldon. "NAFTA as Social Dumping". *Challenge*, (September-October, 1992) 27-32.

Grossman, Gene M. and Esteban Rossi-Hansberg. "The Rise of Offshoring: It's Not Wine and Cloth Anymore." Federal Reserve Bank of Kansas City, Symposium on "The New Economic Geography. Effects and Policy Implications." July, 2006. http://www.kc.frb.org/PUBLICAT/SYMPOS/2006/PDF/Grossman-Rossi.Hansberg.paper.0728.pdf (Accessed April 2007).

Hufbauer, Gary Clyde. *NAFTA. An Assessment,* Washington, D.C.: Institute for International Economics, 1993.

—. *Western Hemisphere Economic Integration.* Washington, D.C.: Institute for International Economics, 1994.

Hufbauer, Gary Clyde and Jeffrey J. Schott. *North American Free Trade. Issues and Recommendations*, Washington, D.C.: Institute for International Economics, 1992.

Hufbauer, Gary Clyde and Jeffrey J. Schott. *NAFTA Revisited. Achievements and Challenges.* Washington, D.C.: Institute for International Economics2004.

Koechlin, Timothy and Mehreene Larudee. "The High Cost of NAFTA". *Challenge*, (October-November, 1992), 19-32.

Kletzer, Lori G. *Job Loss from Imports: Measuring the Costs.* Washington, D.C.: Institute for International Economics, 2001.

__. "Imports, Exports, and American Jobs: Understanding the Links and What they Mean for U.S. Workers," Center for National Policy, *Trade Policy: Forging a New Consensus.* A Series of Discussion Papers. July, 2003.

Krugman, Paul R. "Is Free Trade Passé?" *Journal of Economic Perspectives*, 1:2 (Fall, 1987): 131-144.

__. "The Uncomfortable Truth About NAFTA: It's Foreign Policy, Stupid". *Foreign Affairs,* (November-December, 1993) 13-19.

Lustig, Nora, Barry Bosworth, and Robert Z. Lawrence. *North American Free Trade. Assessing the Impact.* Washington, D.C.: Brookings Institution, 1992.

Nader, Ralph, Jerry Brown, Margaret Atwood, and William Greider. *The Case Against Free Trade: GATT, NAFTA and the Globalization of Corporate Power.* Berkeley: North Atlantic Books, 1993.

Perot, Ross and Pat Choate. *Save your Jobs, Save Your Country: Why NAFTA Must Be Stopped,* New York: Hyperion, 1993.

Program on International Policy Attitudes (PIPA). "Americans on Globalization. A Study of US Public Attitudes". March, 2000. http://www.pipa.org (Accessed April 2007).

Public Citizen. "NAFTA's Broken Promises. The Border Betrayed", Public Citizen's Global Trade Watch, January, 1996.

—. 2001. "Americans Oppose Fast Track and Unfettered Free Trade". http://www.citizen.org/pctrade/FastTrack/tradepolling.htm

Reich, Robert B. *The Work of Nations. Preparing Ourselves for 21st Century Capitalism.* New York : Albert A. Knopf, 1991.

Riding, Alan. *Distant Neighbors. A Portrait of the Mexicans.* New York: Albert A. Knopf, 1984.

Rosen, Howard. "Strengthening the Commitment to American Workers, Firms, Farmers and Fishermen and Communities Adversely Affected by International Trade and Investment." Testimony Before the House Ways and Means Committee. June 14, 2007.

http://waysandmeans.house.gov/media/pdf/110/Rosen%20TESTIMON Y.pdf (Accessed February 15, 2008).

Scheve, Kenneth F. and Matthew J. Slaughter. *Globalization and the Perceptions of American Workers*. Washington, D.C.: Institute for International Economics, 2001.

Scheve, Kenneth F. and Slaughter, Matthew J. "A New Deal for Globalization". *Foreign Affairs*, (July-August, 2007).

Schmidt, Vivien A. "U.S. and European Market Economies and Welfare Systems: The Differences in State Strategies, Political Institutional Capacity, and Discourse." *Critique internationale*, 27 (April, 2005).

Schott, Jeffrey J. *The WTO after Seattle*. Washington, D.C.: Institute for International Economics, 2000.

Scott, Robert E. *NAFTA's Pain Deepens. Job Destruction Accelerates in 1999 with Losses Everywhere*. Briefing Paper, Washington, D.C.: Economic Policy Institute, 1999.

—. *The Facts about Trade and Job Creation*. Issue Brief. Washington, D.C.: Economic Policy Institute, 2000.

—. *Distorting the Record. NAFTA's Promoters Play Fast and Lose with Facts*. Issue Brief. Washington, D.C.: Economic Policy Institute, 2001.

—. *NAFTA at Seven. Its Impact on Workers in All Three Nations*. Washington, D.C.: Economic Policy Institute, 2001.

—. *Fast Track to Lost Jobs. Trade Deficits and Manufacturing Decline Are the Legacies of NAFTA and the WTO*. EPI Briefing Paper no 117. Washington, D.C.: Economic Policy Institute. October, 2001.

Sek, Leonore. *Fast-Track Authority for Trade Agreements (Trade Promotion Authority): Background and Developments in the 107th Congress*. Congressional Research Service. Issue Brief for Congress. May 14, 2001.

Skonieczny, Amy. "Constructing NAFTA: Myth, Representation and the Discursive Construction of U.S. Foreign Policy". *International Studies Quarterly*, 45:3 (September, 2001): 433-454.

Smith, Carolyn C. *Trade Promotion Authority and Fast-Track Negotiating Authority for Trade Agreements: Major Votes*. Congressional Research Service Report for Congress, 2007.

United States Chamber of Commerce. *A Guide to the North American Trade Agreement : What it Means for U.S. Business*. Washington, D.C.: U.S. Chamber of Commerce, 1992.

United States Department of Commerce. *North American Free Trade Agreement. Opportunities for US Industries. NAFTA Industry Sector Reports*. Washington, D.C.: U.S. Government Printing Office, 1993.

United States Department of State. "Commitment to Reach North American Trade Agreement–Address by President George Bush", *Dispatch*, vol. 3, no 29, July 20, 1992.
http://dosfan.lib.uic.edu/ERC/briefing/dispatch/1992/html/Dispatchv3n o29.html (Accessed February 15, 2008).

United States International Trade Commission. "The Likely Impact on the United States of a Free Trade Agreement with Mexico". Report to the Committee on Ways and Means of the United States House of Representatives and the Committee on Finance of the Senate on Investigation No 332-297 under Section 332 of the Tariff Act of 1930. U.S. International Trade Commission Publication 2553. Washington, D.C. February, 1991.

—. *Impact of the North American Free Trade Agreement on the US Economy and Industries. A Three Year Review,* Washington, D.C.: U.S. Government Printing Office, 1997.

United States Trade Representative. *NAFTA Reports.*
http://www.ustr.gov/Trade_Agreements/Regional/NAFTA/NAFTA_R eports/Section_Index.html (Accessed February 15, 2008).

Weintraub, Sidney. *NAFTA. What Comes Next?* Washington, D.C.: Center for Strategic and International Studies, 1994.

—. *NAFTA at Three. A Progress Report.* Washington, D.C.: Center for Strategic and International Studies, 1997.

Weintraub, Sidney, ed. *NAFTA's Impact on North America. The First Decade.* Washington, D.C.: Center for Strategic and International Studies, 2004.

Weintraub, Sidney. *Commentaries on International Political Economy.* Washington, D.C.: Center for Strategic and International Studies, 2004.

Notes

[1] I.M. Destler, *American Trade Politics*, (Washington, D.C.: Institute for International Economics, 4th ed., 2005).

[2] This gap has been noted by authors such as Paul Krugman, "Is Free Trade Passé?" *Journal of Economic Perspectives*, 1:2 (Fall, 1987): 131-144 or Cletus Coughlin, "The Controversy Over Free Trade. The Gap Between Economists and the General Public". *The Federal Reserve Bank of Saint Louis Review*, January-February, 2002, 1-21. Evidence of it is given in the CCFR Report on American Public Opinion and U.S. Foreign Policy for 1983, 24.

[3] Vivien Schmidt, "U.S. and European Market Economies and Welfare Systems: The Differences in State Strategies, Political Institutional Capacity, and Discourse", *Critique internationale*, 27 (April, 2005).

[4] *Ibid.*, 2005, 8

[5] Leonore Sek, "Fast-Track Authority for Trade Agreements (Trade Promotion Authority): Background and Developments in the 107th Congress". Congressional Research Service. Issue Brief for Congress. May 14, 2001.

[6] The U.S.-Canada Free Trade Agreement was signed in 1988 and implemented as of January 1st, 1989.

[7] NAFTA was signed in 1992, ratified by the U.S. Congress in 1993, and implemented as of January 1st, 1994.

[8] In 1989 U.S. GDP reached $5 201 billion, while Mexico's GDP reached a bare $201 billion, or 3.9 % of that of the U.S. Economists then widely agreed that NAFTA would mostly affect intra-industry trade across North America, thus causing shifts in the location of production. The impact on U.S. jobs and wages would be minimal and mostly affect unskilled U.S. workers.

[9] I.M. Destler, "The United States and a Free Trade Area of the Americas: A Political-Economic Analysis". In *Integrating the Americas. FTAA and Beyond*, ed. Antoni Estevadeordeal, Dani Rodrik, Alan M. Taylor, and Andrés Velasco, 397-416. (Cambridge, Mass.: Harvard University Press, 2004) 408

[10] Sidney Weintraub, ed., *NAFTA's Impact on North America. The First Decade*, (Washington, D.C.: Center for Strategic and International Studies, 2004) 137.

[11] Alan Riding, *Distant Neighbors. A Portrait of the Mexicans* (New York: Albert A. Knopf, 1984).

[12] United States Department of State. "Commitment to Reach North American Trade Agreement–Address by President George Bush", *Dispatch*, vol. 3, no 29, July 20, 1992. http://dosfan.lib.uic.edu/ERC/briefing/dispatch/1992/html/Dispatchv3no29.html (Accessed February 15, 2008).

[13] *Ibid.*

[14] See below, section on the doomed FTAA project.

[15] Chicago Council on Foreign Relations, *American Public Opinion and U.S. Foreign Policy 1991*. Chicago: Chicago Press Corporation, 1991) 27.

[16] Jeff Faux and William Spriggs. *US Jobs and the Mexico Trade Proposal*, (Washington, D.C.: Economic Policy Institute, 1991).

[17] Destler, *American Trade Politics*, 198

[18] Ross Perot and Pat Choate. *Save Your Jobs, Save Your Country: Why NAFTA Must Be Stopped* (New York: Hyperion, 1993).

[19] See Sheldon Friedman, "NAFTA as Social Dumping". *Challenge*, (September-October, 1992) 27-32; Timothy Koechlin and Mehreene Larudee. "The High Cost of NAFTA". *Challenge*, (October-November, 1992) 19-32.

[20] Bill Clinton and Al Gore, *Putting People First. How We Can All Change America* (New York: Times Books, 1992) 13.

[21] *Ibid.*, 156.

[22] Jeff Faux, *The Failed Case for NAFTA. The Ten Common Claims for the North American Trade Agreement and Why they Don't Make Sense.* Briefing Paper, (Washington, D.C.: Economic Policy Institute, 1993); Ralph Nader, Jerry Brown, Margaret Atwood, and William Greider, *The Case Against Free Trade: GATT, NAFTA and the Globalization of Corporate Power*, (Berkeley: North Atlantic Books, 1993). Robert Kuttner, "Seeing through NAFTA's New Clothes". *Business Week*, September 20, 1993: 9.

[23] Amy Skonieczny, "Constructing NAFTA: Myth, Representation and the Discursive Construction of U.S. Foreign Policy", *International Studies Quarterly*, 45:3 (September, 2001): 433-454.

[24] This was acknowledged by Clinton in the speech he delivered on signing the NAFTA bill into law. See Bill Clinton, 1993. *Remarks by the President in NAFTA Bill Signing Ceremony, Mellon Auditorium, Washington, DC*. The White House. Office of the Press Secretary.
http://www.clintonfoundation.org/legacy/120893-speech-by-president-in-nafta-bill-signing-ceremony.htm
(Accessed February 15, 2008).

[25] William Safire, "Gore Flattens Perot", *New York Times,* November 11, 1993, 27, col.5.

[26] US Department of Commerce, *North American Free Trade Agreement. Opportunities for US Industries. NAFTA Industry Sector Reports*, (Washington, D.C.: U.S. Government Printing Office, 1993) 6-7

[27] Clinton, 2

[28] *Ibid.*

[29] Susan B. Garland, et al., "Sweet Victory. The NAFTA War is Won. Now Clinton Must Mend Fences". *Business Week*, November 8, 1993: 26

[30] Jagdish Bhagwati, *Free Trade: Why AFL-CIO, The Sierra Club and Congressman Gephart Should Like It*, (Memphis, Tenn.: P. K. Seidman Foundation, 1999) 6.

[31] The yearly editions of the *Economic Report of the President*, as well as reports posted on the Office of the United States Trade Representative website provide illustrations of the consistency with which the Clinton and Bush Administrations have stressed the benefits of NAFTA since its inception.

[32] See bibliography for publications by Hufbauer and Schott, Lustig, or Weintraub.

[33] Jeff Faux, "Overhauling NAFTA". Washington, D.C.: Economic Policy Institute. February 29, 2008.
http://www.epi.org/content.cfm/webfeatures_viewpoints_overhauling_nafta
(Accessed March 3, 2008).

[34] Weintraub, *NAFTA at Three. A Progress Report*. (Washington, D.C.: Center for Strategic and International Studies, 1997) 5.

[35] *Ibid.*

[36] Gary Burtless, Robert Z. Lawrence, Robert E. Litan, and Robert J. Shapiro, *Globaphobia. Confronting Fears about Open Trade*. (Washington, D.C.: Brookings Institution, 1998) 9-10.

[37] Trade Adjustment Assistance was first instituted by the Trade Act of 1962, as the Kennedy Administration wished to stave off potential opposition from organised labour. Kennedy made it plain that "Those injured by (that) trade competition should not be required to bear the full brunt of the impact. Rather, the burden of economic adjustment should be borne in part by the federal government ... (T)here is an obligation to render assistance to those who suffer as a result of national trade policy". (Howard Rosen, 2002. "Reforming Trade Adjustment Assistance: Keeping a 40-Year Promise". (Washington, DC: Institute for International Economics, 2002) 1. Specific provisions were included in NAFTA establishing NAFTA-TAA, which was abolished by the Trade Act of 2002 which unified and expanded TAA coverage. See Martine Azuelos, "Mondialisation et politique sociale aux États-Unis: le cas de la *Trade Adjustment Assistance*", *in Marginalité et politiques sociales: réflexions autour de l'exemple américain*, ed. Taoufik Djebali and Benoît Raoulx. (Caen: Presses de l'Université de Caen, 2008).

[38] Health care coverage was added when TAA was reformed in 2002.

[39] Quantifying those job losses has been the object of much controversy. The most pessimistic count is that of the Economic Policy Institute, which estimates that 1 million jobs have been lost in the U.S. because of NAFTA since 1994 (Faux, *Broken Promises. NAFTA Cost U.S. Jobs and Reduced Wages*, (Washington, DC: Economic Policy Institute, October, 2006). http://www.epi.org/content.cfm/webfeatures_snapshots_20061004.   (Accessed March 3, 2008).

[40] Lori Kletzer, "Imports, Exports, and American Jobs: Understanding the Links and What they Mean for U.S. Workers," Center for National Policy, *Trade Policy: Forging a New Consensus*. A Series of Discussion Papers. (July, 2003)

[41] Kenneth F. Scheve, and Matthew J. Slaughter, "A New Deal for Globalization". *Foreign Affairs*, (July-August, 2007)

[42] *Ibid.*

[43] Globaphobia is borrowed from Burtless et.al. The authors coined the word to refer to the widespread anxiety that globalization has caused in the U.S.

[44] Clinton, 3

[45] See note 37.

[46] *Ibid*, italics mine.

[47] *Ibid*, italics mine.

[48] Destler, *American Trade Politics*, 253

[49] *Ibid*, 254.

[50] See, for example, the statements of India or Brazil Ministers at the Seattle conference. These can be accessed on the WTO website.

[51] Jeffrey J. Schott, *The WTO after Seattle*. (Washington, D.C.: Institute for International Economics, 2000) 5.

[52] Scheve and Slaughter, *Globalization and the Perceptions of American Workers*, (Washington, D.C.: Institute for International Economics, 2001. For the 1970s and 1980s, see the reports published by the Chicago Council on Foreign Relations. For the 1990s and 2000s, see also publications by PIPA, the Program on International

Policy Attitudes established in 1993 at the University of Maryland, or by World Public Opinion.org.

[53] Martine Azuelos, "Les Etats-unis et la mondialisation : de l'ébranlement de la puissance nationale à l'émergence d'un nouveau défi américain," in *Mondialisation et domination économique. La dynamique anglo-saxonne*, eds Marie-Claude Esposito and Martine Azuelos. (Paris: Economica, 1997).

[54] Gene M. Grossman and Esteban Rossi-Hansberg, "The Rise of Offshoring: It's Not Wine and Cloth Anymore", Federal Reserve Bank of Kansas City, Symposium on "The New Economic Geography. Effects and Policy Implications." July, 2006, 2. http://www.kc.frb.org/PUBLICAT/SYMPOS/2006/PDF/Grossman-Rossi.Hansberg.paper.0728.pdf (Accessed April 2007).

[55] Robert B. Reich, Robert B. 1991. *The Work of Nations. Preparing Ourselves for 21st Century Capitalism*. (New York : Albert A. Knopf, 1991).

[56] Lou Dobbs, *Exporting America: Why Corporate Greed Is Shipping American Jobs Overseas*, (New York: Warner Books, 2004).

[57] Robert Feenstra and Gordon H. Hanson. "Globalization, Outsourcing, and Wage Inequality", *American Economic Review*, 86:2 (May, 1996): 240-245; Alan Binder, "Offshoring: The Next Industrial Revolution?" *Foreign Affairs*, (March-April, 2007); Scheve and Slaughter, "A New Deal for Globalization"

[58] The incumbent President, George W. Bush, was first asked: "what do you say to someone who's lost his job to someone overseas who gets paid a fraction of what he earned?" His challenger, Democratic Senator John Kerry, was asked: "Is it fair to blame the administration entirely for this loss of jobs?"

[59] *Ibid.*

[60] Richard S. Dunham, "When Is a Tax Cut Not a Tax Cut? When it's a "refund." George W.'s winning way with words," *Business Week*, March 19, 2001.

[61] *Ibid.*

[62] Destler, *American Trade Politics*, chapter 8

[63] Dunham, *op. cit.*

[64] The Farm Bill passed in the Spring of 2002 substantially increased subsidies for farmers. The temporary surcharge imposed on steel imports in March 2002 followed a safeguard action introduced by the U.S. International Trade Commission in 2001.

[65] Destler, "The United States and a Free Trade Area of the Americas: A Political-Economic Analysis". The Western Hemisphere accounted for 43% of U.S. exports and 34% of U.S. imports in 2006, but Canada and Mexico make up the bulk of these. Excluding Mexico, Latin America accounts for only 8% of U.S. trade. U.S. trade with the Asia-Pacific region has, conversely, grown very rapidly over the past decade, and now accounts for over one third of the total.

[66] C. Fred Bergsten, *Competitive Liberalization and Global Free Trade: A Vision for the 21st Century*, Working Paper 96-12. (Washington: Institute for International Economics, 1996).

[67] Robert B. Zoellick, "Unleashing the Trade Winds: A Building-block Approach". *The Economist*, December 7, 2002, 27-29.

[68] Destler, "American Trade Politics in 2007: Building Bipartisan Compromise". Peterson Institute Policy Brief No. PB07-5 (May, 2007). http://www.iie.com/publications/interstitial.cfm?ResearchID=741 (Accessed March 3, 2008)
[69] See U.S. Trade Representative Susan Schwab's comments to the U.S. Chamber of Commerce, Washington, D.C., January 17, 2008 : "None of us–not the Administration, not the Congressional leadership–wants to look back in a few years and ask "Who lost Latin America?"

CHAPTER THREE

THE BRITISH PARTY LEADERS'
DISCOURSE ON EUROPE

PAULINE SCHNAPPER

"The dilemma of a British Prime Minister over Europe is acute to the point of the ridiculous. Basically you have a choice: co-operate in Europe and you betray Britain; be unreasonable in Europe, be praised back home, and be utterly without influence in Europe"[1]

Political discourse in general never takes place in an intellectual vacuum. Since the politicians' first aim is to attract and keep the loyalty of voters, they adapt their rhetoric in a way which they believe to be compatible with voters' expectations and representations. In other words, discourse takes place in a specific political context and political culture, where some historical references, images, norms, symbols and values are widely shared.[2] This is true in general, but particularly of discourse about Europe in Britain, where the issue of the involvement in the European project has always been problematic and divisive. It raised deep questions about the nature of British identity after the end of the Second World War, as Britain was losing its empire and experiencing a relative economic decline of historic proportions, questions that most of the elite was not really ready to address, at least until the 1960s. Europe was only the third of Churchill's "three circles" for British post-1945 foreign policy, coming after the Empire/Commonwealth and the transatlantic community. Attachment to parliamentary sovereignty and trade with the Commonwealth, added to the feeling of being still a major power, led British leaders, both Conservative and Labour, to turn down participation in the first efforts at European integration in the 1950s. The anti-Common Market consensus of the late 1940s and 1950s broke down in the following decade, when Macmillan first decided to apply for membership of the then European Community. The debates that followed pitted proponents and opponents of membership, and when this was concluded by the 1975 referendum, were conducted around the level of British commitment in the EEC as well as the general direction of European integration, in particular its federal nature.

Any discourse about Europe, in whatever member-state, has two audiences. One is external, being addressed to partner governments and, to a lesser extent, public opinion in other European countries. The other is the domestic audience, which in the British case has proved to be crucial because of the general lack of enthusiasm towards Europe among the public. Whereas it was diplomatically encouraged, except in the case of Margaret Thatcher, to be consensual and accommodating in tone with one's European partners, discourse meant for the domestic audience has tended to be much more negative. Indeed, throughout this period, political discourse about Europe was conducted in somewhat simplistic terms of "us" versus "them", as if the continent continued to be the "other" that Linda Colley identified.[3] The rejection of "federalism", in particular, was common to almost all political actors. Joining the Community was a last resort option when the economic difficulties had become unbearable, not a positive choice. The political project behind the EC/EU was either downplayed (by supporters of British membership) or rejected as alien to the British constitutional tradition (by the critics). But in a way the terms of the debate remained similar, based on a pragmatic assessment of costs and benefits and/or discussion of the extent to which national sovereignty would be undermined. The so-called defence of British interests was constantly referred to, though rarely defined beyond general terms. No positive vision of Europe in relation to British identity was ever really articulated.[4] In this sense, there has been a single narrative about Europe in Britain, from which few leaders have differed, apart from a few exceptions like Edward Heath or the Liberal Democrats.

If we turn to the specific period under review here, 1992 to 2007, we can try and assess whether this general pattern of the British debate about Europe remained true, looking at the way party political leaders talked about the EU. This period covers two governments not just led by two different political parties, but also with, in theory at least, different visions of British participation in the European project and, perhaps even more important, two very different domestic political situations. The Major government had, following the April 1992 general election, a very small majority in the House of Commons and had to manage a thoroughly divided and increasingly Eurosceptic party, leading his premiership to be totally dominated by the European question. In contrast, Tony Blair came to power with an overwhelming majority in 1997 and with a party behind him which was more united on Europe than it had ever been since the

1960s. Yet, because the domestic context in which they were operating was not really different, as illustrated by opinion polls and the influence of the Eurosceptic press, their European rhetoric was in the end not as contrasted as would have be expected. Even the Liberal Democrats, who were the only party not accepting the terms of the debate, have softened their rhetoric towards a more mainstream, therefore critical, discourse about the EU.

John Major: at the "heart of Europe"?

When John Major was elected as leader of the Conservative party in November 1990, his party was in complete disarray over Europe, which had proved highly damaging for its electoral prospects. The last years of the Thatcher governments had been dominated by conflicts about Europe, particularly on projects for an economic and monetary union (EMU) as well as political union, which the Prime Minister rejected vehemently. Her 1988 Bruges speech had sharply divided the party, her opposition to British participation in the European Exchange Rate Mechanism and, more generally, her attitude to Europe, led to the resignation of increasingly senior members of her Cabinet, and ultimately, was one element which led to her own downfall. In this context, John Major was elected as a compromise candidate between her extreme views and those of the other, more Europhile, candidates, Michael Heseltine and Douglas Hurd. But he was only a second best for the Eurosceptics in the party, who were becoming more and more influential.[5] He therefore had to balance, in his rhetoric as well as in his policies, the demands emanating from the still powerful pro-European voices in his party and the Eurosceptics inspired by Thatcher. This balance was maintained until the ratification of the Maastricht treaty, but then collapsed under Eurosceptic pressure.

The first signal sent by Major was interpreted as a realignment from Thatcher's extreme position towards the EU: in a speech in Bonn (interestingly, to a European rather than domestic audience), he talked of putting Britain back where it belonged, "at the heart of Europe". In his mind, this was more a change of tactics than of policy: like his predecessor, he opposed political union, the Social Chapter envisaged in the intergovernmental conference and had strong reservations about EMU. But he believed Thatcher's confrontational opposition to be counter-productive and wanted to build alliances within the EC.[6] The ambiguity of the sentence was such, nevertheless, that the Eurosceptics interpreted it as a shift away from Thatcher's policy. Still, the balance was maintained until the spring of 1992. The negotiations on the European Union treaty led to an agreement in Maastricht which enabled Major to claim that he had successfully defended British interests by obtaining an opt-out on EMU and the Social Chapter, secured the pillar structure which ensured the common foreign and security policy (CFSP) would remain intergovernmental and the removal of any reference to a "federal" objective for the EU. It was a military and defensive vocabulary which was used after the European Council in Maastricht, with much talk of battles fought and won against "federalists", particularly Jacques Delors, François Mitterrand and Helmut Kohl, who were becoming hate figures for the Eurosceptic tabloid press:

> The Community can fulfil its role properly only if it responds to the needs of its European citizens. It must respect national identity and national traditions. It must not, in the name of some wider European ambition, override the democratic wishes of the people of any one of its member states.
> That is why the treaties now agreed at Maastricht were so hard-fought. Real British national interests were at stake in those discussions. The Government's job was to safeguard and to advance those interests. It was not to sign up, without critical examination, to anything that was presented to us with a European label.[7]

This presentation of the treaty was successful at first, since the Conservative majority in Parliament praised the Prime Minister after the Maastricht summit, with few criticisms emanating from the Eurosceptic benches. Similarly, the party manifesto for the April 1992 general elections heralded the results obtained by Major in Maastricht:

> The Maastricht Treaty was a success both for Britain and for the rest of Europe. British proposals helped to shape the key provisions of the Treaty including those strengthening the enforcement of Community law defence, subsidiarity and law and order. But Britain refused to accept the damaging Social Chapter proposed by other Europeans, and it was excluded from the Maastricht treaty.

But, while insisting on Britain's full commitment to some aspects of EC policy, the party leader continued to stress "resistance" towards further moves, which could satisfy both wings of this party:

> We will continue to resist changes to the Treaty of Rome that would damage British business.
> We will resist Commission initiatives which run counter to the principle that issues should be dealt with on a national basis wherever possible. ...

> We will insist on more effective control over Community spending and
> will resist pressure to extend Community competence to new areas.[8]

The Conservative party won that election, but with a majority reduced to
21 and a new intake of MPs who were generally more sceptical towards
Europe. This might not have been too much of a problem for the leader
without the events of the following spring and summer, which destroyed
his careful rhetorical balance. The unexpected "no" vote in the Danish
referendum on the ratification of the Maastricht treaty on 2 June whetted
Eurosceptic appetites, especially as polls indicated a possible negative vote
in France too. Above all, the dramatic ejection of the pound from the ERM
on "Black" Wednesday in September proved fatal to Major's ambitions of
appealing to both pro and anti-Europeans. The ratification of the treaty
was delayed, and became a long tortuous process, where emboldened
Eurosceptics, often supported by the opposition, tried every parliamentary
tactic to defeat the treaty.[9] Throughout that drama, Major tried to convince
the Eurosceptics that they were wrong about the treaty. At the annual party
conference he explained: "If I believed what some people said about the
treaty I would vote against it. But I don't. So I'm going to put the real
treaty–the one I negotiated–back to the House of Commons".[10] On 29
October, he addressed a backbench committee, assuring them that he
examined carefully all European proposals and that therefore he was "the
greatest eurosceptic in the Cabinet".[11] This failed to appease the rebels, as
well as all his other statements in Parliament. The bulk of his argument
was summed up during the debate of 4 November on the resumption of
consideration of the Bill:

> There are important decisions to be made, now and in the immediate
> future, about the way in which the Community develops. We can develop
> as a centralist institution, as some might want, or we can develop as a free-
> market, free-trade, wider European Community more responsive to its
> citizens. I am unreservedly in favour of the latter form of the Community,
> and I believe that that is the overwhelming view of this country. But there
> is only one way in which we can bring that Community about, and I
> believe that it is this–by Britain playing a full part in the Community, by
> arguing its case, by forming alliances, by exercising its influence and
> authority, by persuading, by pushing, by fighting for its interests and,
> sometimes, by digging our toes in and saying no as we did over the social
> chapter and the single currency.[12]

He stuck to the argument that, indeed, there were many things wrong
in the EC, but that Britain could only amend them by ratifying the treaty,

throughout the lengthy debates, as appears on the final debate about the Social Chapter, on 22 July 1993:

> Too often over the years, the dominant political attitude has been to object to the ways others have wanted to develop the EC, rather than to set out our plans, our prospects and our hopes and then fight for them to deliver the type of community that is right for this country. Many hon. Members are right in their opposition to the way in which the EC operates. Some of the ways that it operates need to be changed—I strongly support that. I want to see the EC reformed, as do my hon. Friends and many Opposition Members, but if we are to reform the EC, Britain must have influence in the EC. We will not have influence if we do not ratify the treaty that we have agreed after consultations in the House.[13]

This balancing act had no effect on the Eurosceptics, who won a number of tactical victories, like the vote on the composition of the Committee of the Regions on 8 March 1993 and another one, supported by Labour, on the Social Chapter in July. The treaty was eventually ratified in August, following a confidence vote, but this late victory did nothing to restore the Prime Minister's authority over his own party. The continuing pressure from the Eurosceptics in the months and years that followed led to a gradual change in Major's rhetoric about Europe. He obviously denied this shift was due to internal party politics, claiming that his own views on Europe had changed after "Black" Wednesday and that party considerations came only second, but it beggars belief.[14]

A first hint of this evolution appeared in an article Major published in *The Economist* in September 1993. The audience here was both domestic and European, and his tone was more critical of the EU than it had been before:

> It is for nations to build Europe, not for Europe to attempt to supersede nations. I want to see the Community become a wide union, embracing the whole of democratic Europe, in a single market and with common security arrangements firmly linked to NATO. ... A Community which ceases to nibble at national freedoms, and so commands the enthusiasm of its member nations.[15]

A year later, in a speech he gave in Leyden, he again criticized plans for an "inner core" of member-states being then aired by German Christian Democrats and suggested the EU adopt a "variable geometry" approach, each member-state being free to opt in or out of different policies—a suggestion he knew would be unacceptable to his European partners but could appeal to British Conservatives.

In policy terms, this rhetoric was translated into vetoes and crises in the EU. First, in March 1994, Major opposed a reweighing of qualified majority voting for the next round of enlargement in 1995. The dispute was resolved in the so-called Ioannina compromise. Then he vetoed the candidacy of the Belgian Prime Minister, Jean-Luc Dehaene, as new president of the European Commission, on the ground that he was a Belgian federalist and that France and Germany could not impose their candidate on the rest of the EU. He agreed on the appointment of Jacques Santer, who was equally federalist but a less powerful candidate, as events showed later. The biggest crisis took place after March 1996 over "mad cow" disease, when the European Commission imposed a ban on the export of British beef. Faced with a domestic outcry, Major announced a policy of non cooperation with the European institutions, leading the British representatives in Brussels to veto all decisions which had to be taken unanimously for several months. This was an unprecedented gesture, which resulted in a major crisis with the other member-states. Finally, his approach to the 1996 intergovernmental conference was one of appearing to dig in his heels and not agreeing on any further extension of EU competence.

During all this period, the domestic debate on Europe was still dominated by the question of whether to join EMU, in spite of the Maastricht opt-out. The Conservative Eurosceptics demanded that the government rule out membership indefinitely, something that, to his credit, Major refused to do–the demand made little sense anyway from a purely constitutional point of view, since a Parliament cannot bind its successors:

> The House knows, from the Maastricht negotiations and the opt-out that I negotiated there, that I am wary of a single currency for those economic reasons--wary of its economic impact and of the serious political and constitutional implications. However, if some of our partners do go ahead, there will be implications for this country in any event, albeit different ones... It is for that reason that I believe that it is in our own national and economic interests to keep open the option of going into a single currency and equally to keep open the option of deciding that it will not be in our national interest to go in.[16]

But the relentless pressure from his backbenchers led the Prime Minister to a crucial compromise in early 1996, when he agreed that should his government decide in the next Parliament to adopt the single currency, the decision would be put to a referendum. This was to have long-term consequences, since New Labour soon felt compelled to adopt the same position.

John Major's way of talking about Europe therefore shifted from a cautious but broadly positive discourse to a much more critical and defensive one at the end of his premiership, which was mostly due to his domestic troubles. But he always stopped short of conceding what the die-hard Eurosceptics demanded, which was to rule out adopting the European single currency in the future. Interestingly, despite the obvious differences in their attitude and management of their own party, Tony Blair's premiership was marked by an eerily similar evolution.

Smith and Blair: breaking the mould?

The Labour party followed an opposite direction to the Conservative party in the 1990s, becoming increasingly pro-European as the Conservative party was becoming more sceptical. The process started under Neil Kinnock and was reinforced by John Smith, who was leader between 1992 and 1994 and had always been pro-European.[17] In the 1992 election, Europe was hardly mentioned in the Labour manifesto, for fear of reawakening past divisions, but the few signals given were positive, in particular in their support for the Social Chapter and the principle of British participation in EMU. Smith criticized the opt-outs and accused the government of leaving Britain isolated in Europe. This gave him justification to vote against the government during the ratification of the Maastricht treaty in spite of his professed support for the treaty:

> As we have repeatedly made clear,... our commitment is to closer economic and political co-operation in Europe. But we have a different agenda for the Community from the Conservatives. We want a Community for people, not just a market for business. That is why we will continue our efforts to overturn the foolish opt-out from the social chapter, which is regarded as essential by all the other 11 member states.[18]
> I could not understand how the Prime Minister could argue that we had to be involved in decision making in the Community while also arguing the justification for an opt-out. Once again, decisions will be arrived at and policies forged in Britain's absence.[19]

When first elected as leader in 1994, Tony Blair followed his predecessor's steps. In particular, he made it clear he supported the adoption of the single currency in principle, though he was very careful in his choosing of words, and more generally made few mentions of Europe as Leader of the Opposition. The need to attract middle class voters and to have support from a largely Eurosceptic press was more important, hence the extraordinary article that Blair published in *The Sun* in April 1997, where he wrote about "(his) love of the pound".[20] The 1997 manifesto was very cautious:

> Any decision about Britain joining the single currency must be determined by a hard-headed assessment of Britain's economic interests.... However, to exclude British membership of EMU forever would be to destroy any influence we have over a process which will affect us whether we are in or out....
>
> In any event, there are three pre-conditions which would have to be satisfied before Britain could join during the next Parliament: first, the Cabinet would have to agree; then Parliament; and finally the people would have to say "Yes" in a referendum.

But in more general terms, Blair criticized the marginalisation of Britain on the European scene under John Major's government and went further, regretting the missed opportunities of the past: "Britain's relations with Europe have too often been ambivalent or indifferent, Indeed, I believe Britain's hesitation over Europe was one of my country's greatest miscalculations of the post-War years".[21] He pledged, in terms which were not completely different from those of Major in 1991, to put Britain at the centre of the European debate and influence the EU through a "constructive engagement". This was an approach which broke with the recent past. His own attitude towards the EU was very relaxed:

> I come to this with my own perspective. I am not marked by personal experience of the scars of war. Or by painful memories of British post-war readjustment to a new world. Britain has been a member state for the entire period of my adult life. To me and most of my generation, Europe is simply the political, economic and commercial world in which I have naturally lived.[22]
>
> I believe in a Europe of enlightened self-interest. Without chauvinism. It is the nation-state's rational response to the modern world. If globalisation of the world economy is a reality; if peace and security can only be guaranteed collectively; if the world is moving to larger blocs of trade and cooperation and look at ASEAN or Latin America: if all this is so, then the EU is a practical necessity. I happen to share the European idealism. I am by instinct internationalist. But even if I weren't, I should be internationalist through realism.[23]

Another key word in Blair's first discourse was "leadership", which the new Prime Minister wanted to exercise in Europe in order to steer it in a direction suitable to British interests.[24] He insisted on the need for "change" and "reform" in Europe, along the lines of the "third way" he was implementing his own country.[25] He added economic reform and, crucially, a strengthening of the European voice on the international scene, through the common foreign and security policy, which was a clear break from Major's days.

But if the general approach differed starkly from those of his opponents, the actual policy aims stated did much less so: completion of the single market, reform of the common agricultural policy, enlargement, strengthening of the intergovernmental dimension–beyond the spectacular, but largely symbolic, signing of the Social Chapter, change was limited. The rhetoric of opposition to "a federal superstate" continued, clearly aimed at a domestic audience rather than grounded in any reality.[26]

On EMU, official policy was announced, not by Blair but by Gordon Brown, the Chancellor of the Exchequer, in November 1997: no opposition in principle, but the right economic conditions were necessary and five tests would have to be met before the UK could adopt the euro. This was put in more positive terms by Blair in January 1998:

> Britain has set out its own position clearly. We believe a single currency can make sense in a Single European market. There is no insuperable constitutional barrier to our joining. The test is whether the economic benefits of EMU are demonstrably clear and unambiguous. Barring unforeseen circumstances, we want Britain to be in a position to take a decision on whether to be part of a successful single currency early in the next parliament, should the economic conditions be met. All this is settled. It is a practical and constructive approach well in line with mainstream British opinion.[27]

For him then, at this point at least, the decision would be a political one, and he never developed the economic argument beyond general sentences like the one above. In 1999, he sponsored the creation of a non-partisan organisation, Britain in Europe, which was supposed to present the pro-European case and stand up to the Eurosceptic arguments which were much more heard in the public debate. But from the start, Blair prevented it from making a specific case for joining the euro and made it stick to a general agenda about the benefits of the EU. As a result, it had little impact on public opinion. By the end of 2000, and indeed of 2001, there was no indication of a change in the assessment of the obstacles to joining the euro:

> I have said the political case for Britain being part of the single currency is strong. I don't say political or constitutional issues aren't important. They are. But to my mind, they aren't an insuperable barrier. What does have to be overcome is the economic issue. It is an economic union. Joining

prematurely simply on political grounds, without the economic conditions
being right, would be a mistake.[28]
As for the Euro, the conclusion of this argument is not that we go in
regardless of the economic conditions. It is that if the economic tests are
met, political or constitutional barriers should not prevent us joining. And
of course the final decision rests with the people in a referendum.[29]

Yet, in the meantime, New Labour had won a decisive second victory
in the 2001 general election. The argument that the electorate should not
be frightened by the prospect of adopting the euro in the run-up to a
general election, which was widely heard at the time, was no longer valid.
But the Conservative party, supported by a majority of the national press,
was campaigning relentlessly to "Keep the Pound". Furthermore, the
respective economic situation of Britain and the eurozone countries made
it difficult to argue forcefully in favour of the euro–the main indicators,
especially growth and employment, showed Britain was doing better than
the eurozone countries. By 2001, the issue had effectively been hijacked
by the Chancellor, who was very wary of the European Central Bank, and
it was becoming difficult for the Prime Minister to take his country into
the euro. Indeed, Blair's speeches after 2001 made little or no reference to
the issue. The events of 9/11, the war in Iraq and the European constitution
obliterated most references to the euro, to which Blair paid only lip
service.[30] This was confirmed by the result of the 2002-2003 assessment of
the five tests defined by Brown in 1997, conducted by the Treasury, which
concluded that the five tests for British adoption of the euro had not been
met. By then, Blair had given up all hope of changing policy on the euro.
During Blair's second term as Prime Minister, between 2001 and 2005,
much of the debate about the EU in Britain was rather about Europe's
place in the world, particularly in the context of the war against terrorism,
then about plans for a European constitution to replace existing treaties.
Blair's rhetoric then emphasized the need for "reform" in the EU, and
when need be, the strengthening of EU institutions to ensure the successful
"alliance of European and national government", as opposed, once again,
to a federation.[31] In contrast to his predecessors, Blair supported the idea
of a constitution but with a mandate that fitted the British vision of
Europe:

We do need a proper Constitution for Europe, one which makes it clear
that the driving ideology is indeed a union of nations not a superstate
subsuming national sovereignty and national identity. This should be spelt
out in simple language.[32]

Still, he favoured the establishment of a fixed term presidency of the Council of Ministers and was not opposed to an increase in qualified majority voting to improve governance in an enlarged EU, nor to the communitisation of Justice and Home Affairs, provided Britain kept its opt-in in this field. This positive attitude contrasted with his previous reluctance to contemplate the drafting of a constitution, apparent in his Warsaw speech.[33] But Blair refused to have the Charter of Fundamental Rights incorporated into the constitution, refused the creation of a European Foreign Minister (or rather, the use of the name) as well as any coordination of economic policies. He also put forward what he called British "red lines", which were non negotiable, like the adoption of qualified majority voting on taxation, social security or criminal law. As the Convention made progress, the British attitude became more defensive, against the backdrop both of the mounting crisis over Iraq and attacks from the Conservatives and the Eurosceptic press at home.[34] One of the issues on which these attacks focussed was the question of a referendum on the future constitution, which the Conservative party demanded. The Prime Minister first refused to grant it, arguing that there was no more need for a referendum on this treaty than there had been for the Single Act or Maastricht, both signed and ratified by Conservative governments, and that a referendum would only be justified if there was a major change in the relationship between the member-states and the EU.[35] But he yielded under domestic pressure, and announced in the Commons on 20 April 2004 that there would be a referendum on the future constitution after it was debated and ratified in Westminster. The justification for this U-turn was not, of course, that he yielded to any pressure, but that he would welcome a debate on the real issue behind Conservative opposition to the constitution, which was their wish to withdraw from the EU:

> It is time to resolve once and for all whether this country, Britain, wants to be at the centre and heart of European decision making or not; time to decide whether our destiny lies as a leading partner and ally of Europe or on its margins. Let the Eurosceptics, whose true agenda we will expose, make their case. Let those of us who believe in Britain in Europe—not because of Europe alone, but because we believe in Britain and our national interest lying in Europe—make our case, too.[36]

The dispute with France and Germany over Iraq in 2003 led to a stiffening of Blair's attitude towards the EU, which was reflected in his rhetoric. Indeed, he took comfort from the 2004 enlargement to central

Europe, which was going to redress the EU balance towards the British
view:

> For these 10 (countries), by and large, share the same outlook, an outlook
> both familiar and welcome to Britain: in favour of economic reform,
> wedded, after their history of oppression and struggle, to a Europe of
> nation states; and for the same reason, unequivocally committed to the
> transatlantic alliance.[37]

Blair was actually almost silent on Europe in 2004 and 2005, except
for his acclaimed speech to the European Parliament after the "no" votes
in France and the Netherlands in the referendums on the constitutional
treaty. He focussed instead on global issues related to world trade
negotiations, aid to Africa and the fight against terrorism. Globalization
was the main challenge for industrialised countries. This was also the topic
of the three major foreign policy speeches he gave in 2006. That same
year, following the long dispute with France over the EU budget and the
British rebate, he did give a speech on Europe in Oxford in which, though
repeating the mantra that Britain's future lay in Europe, was very critical
of the way the EU and some member-states functioned:

> Too often in recent times, Europe has been used not to answer a question
> but to avoid answering it. ...
> Do not misunderstand me. I believe that the single currency will ultimately
> be to Europe's benefit and Britain, of course, retains the option of joining
> it. My point is very simple. The economics had to be got right and the
> politics follow. Instead, a political decision was taken by France and
> Germany (whilst Britain concentrated on a largely presentational opt-out);
> a timetable imposed and the economics made to fit. In time, this will sort
> itself out. But it will take time.
> The best example lies in the debate over Europe's Constitution. We spent 2
> or 3 years in an intense institutional debate. Giscard, with characteristic
> brilliance, negotiated a solution. There was only one drawback. Apart from
> better rules of internal governance, no-one in Europe knew what it was
> meant to solve. As the problems of the citizen grew ever more pressing,
> instead of bold policy reform and decisive change, we locked ourselves in
> a room at the top of the tower and debated things no ordinary citizen could
> understand. And yet I remind you the Constitution was launched under the
> title of "Bringing Europe closer to its citizens".
> Worse, there became a growing mood amongst European people, that
> Europe, unable to solve its actual problems, took to solving imaginary
> ones: by regulation no-one wanted, implemented in ways everyone hated.[38]

In this speech, the familiar war-like words came back: "resisting", "battling off". Although attacking the Conservatives for their "baleful lurch into an almost wholly negative view of Europe", he praised what he called a "practical scepticism", a "genuine intellectual and political concern about Europe as practised; not about Europe as an ideal or a vision". Though remaining broadly positive about Europe, this rhetoric was very different from the early speeches where he was claiming to want to reconnect the British public with the European project. Indeed, he admitted that because of the British media's attitude, he had "long since given up trying to conduct a serious debate about Europe in certain quarters".

By then, it was therefore clear that Blair no longer hoped to reconcile the British public with Europe. The domestic crisis over the Iraq war had undermined his leadership on foreign policy questions, and any attempt, in particular, to "sell" the euro was abandoned.[39] Although at first breaking with the traditional mould of British leaders' discourse about Europe, Blair had, by the end of his premiership, largely come back to it, even if his general attitude remained rhetorically more positive.

Conservative leaders since 1997: ever more Eurosceptic

The Conservative party in opposition tried four different leaders in their ten years out of government under New Labour, differing only slightly in their degree of Euroscepticism and rejection of the government's "new" approach to the European Union. In spite of the damage the divisions about Europe had created within the party, William Hague, leader between 1997 and 2001, chose to focus much of his and his party's opposition to the government on the question of the single currency. This was apparently an issue on which opinion polls showed the Conservatives to be more in tune with the wider public than New Labour.[40] He managed to marginalise what was left of the traditional pro-Europeans within the party and reinforced the Eurosceptic voices in the shadow Cabinet. Once again, the economic and political arguments against the euro were presented in stark contrast and military vocabulary: "The battle for the pound is a battle for the economic prosperity of the British people and a battle for the independence of the British nation."[41] This was clearly a step further towards an anti-European course compared with Major, who had always refused to rule out joining the single currency in the long-term future. Hague's general European policy was summed up in the slogan "In Europe, not run by Europe", though the precise implications of this were never really spelled out. Patriotism was called for, abandoning

the pound being presented as the corollary of losing national
independence:

> This Labour Government is taking us down the road to a European
> superstate. ...
> Now we must champion the cause of a flexible, free trading, low tax,
> lightly regulated Europe. A Europe that goes with the grain of the new
> global economy, in which nations combine in different combinations for
> different purposes to different extents. We will be the champions of that
> flexible Europe. And we will be the champions of Britain's right to govern
> itself.[42]

The 2001 general election defeat was followed by Hague's resignation
and the election as leader of Iain Duncan Smith, who had been one of the
Maastricht rebels. The Conservative shift towards anti-Europeanism could
not have been more clearly illustrated. His leadership was a short one
(2001-2003) but followed the steps of his predecessor on Europe:
opposition to the euro, and then opposition to the European constitution.
On the euro, his main arguments were economic: the performance of the
British economy was much better than the eurozone's, British
competitiveness would be undermined by joining the single currency. He
saw the constitution as "centralizing", and asked instead for a repatriation
of some of EU policies to the national level.[43] The only difference between
him, as well as Michael Howard after him, and Hague was that the next
two leaders spoke much less about Europe–they had realized that, however
broadly Eurosceptic the electorate might be, the British public were mostly
uninterested by the EU. Also, as the prospect of a quick adoption of the
euro subsided, the issue lost its salience. As for the constitution, the
Conservatives only took up the issue in late 2003, as the negotiations drew
to their end.[44] So there was, once again, very little difference between
Duncan Smith and Howard's discourse, which took place in the context of
a resurgent UKIP (United Kingdom Independence Party), particularly in
the 2004 European election. The UKIP advocated complete withdrawal
from the EU, and most of their members and electors came from
Conservative ranks. So opposition to the European constitution *per se* was
restated by Michael Howard (leader from 2003 to 2005), as well as the
more general aim to "renegotiate" Britain's relations to the EU:

> The British people don't want to be part of a European super state. But
> other European governments are determined to press ahead with ever
> closer integration. Britain has tried to stop them. ... Some of our European
> partners want to integrate further. I'll say to them–"fine. Britain will no

longer try and stop you. But we must have something in return. We want to
bring powers back from Brussels to Britain".

It is not enough to say No to the European Constitution–though a
Conservative Government will. It is not enough to say No to the Euro–
though a Conservative Government will. It's time we went further. We
want out of the social chapter, which is a threat to British jobs. We want
out of the common fisheries policy, which is destroying communities. And
we want more British aid to be distributed from London and less from
Brussels. It's time to bring powers back to Britain.[45]

The Conservative policy was to support a "two-speed" Europe,
whereby British governments would be free to opt in or opt out of *all* EU
policies.[46] This remained unchanged under David Cameron, who became
leader in December 2005, following the third consecutive Conservative
defeat in the general election. Indeed, one of the most striking facts about
Cameron's leadership has been that his modernizing agenda has not
encompassed European policy, which remains broadly similar to his
predecessors, testifying to the depth of Euroscepticism in the party. For the
first year or so of his leadership, Cameron said little about Europe, except
for suggesting that the Conservative party leave the EPP (European
People's Party) group in the European Parliament–an idea already aired by
Duncan Smith but dismissed by Howard. Only in 2007 did he deliver a
speech on Europe, in which familiar themes were repeated:

There are two ways that a British politician can speak in Europe. One way
is to posture for the TV cameras back home and boast of your
determination to stand up for the national interest. And then, later–
inevitably–to agree to whatever proposal is on the table. Let me give an
example–our negotiations over the EU Constitution. At the beginning of
the process, Tony Blair and Gordon Brown called for the EU to listen to
the people of Europe, and to reform. They spoke of the "red lines" which
the government would not, under any circumstances, cross. But in the
event, they gave their total assent to the text. ... I'm against a European
Constitution and I'm in favour of a referendum if one is ever proposed. My
approach to European negotiations will be different. I believe that the best
way to pursue your national interest, is not to posture–but to persuade. I
will be polite, but solid and consistent. I will work to create a flexible
Europe by building alliances with those who share our interests and our
ideas.[47]

But some other parts of this speech were reminiscent of Blair's discourse
at that time: the challenges of globalisation, climate change and global
poverty made it necessary to have an outward, not inward-looking Europe,
able to reform its economy along the lines of the Lisbon agenda, to reform

its agriculture policy and pursue enlargement–without further integration. Cameron therefore managed to blend what had become established Conservative rhetoric on Europe with New Labour's slightly disillusioned post-2003 discourse.

The Liberal Democrats: still apart?

The Liberal party, then the Liberal Democrats, are the only mainstream party to have developed a distinctively pro-European discourse in the last fifty years, which was outside the linguistic mould to which the two main parties stuck. In particular, they favoured federalism, both at the national and European levels, and supported every institutional move towards further integration, including EMU. Yet two developments were notable in the Liberal Democrat discourse between 1992 and 2007: a toning down of their pro-European rhetoric and the blurring of their distinctive approach, which is now hard to differentiate from New Labour's.

During the Maastricht debates, Ashdown made his party's position clear: they opposed the two opt-outs negotiated by the government and were in favour both of the Social Charter and the single currency. But, unlike Labour, he supported the ratification of the treaty and voted with the government, on the grounds that it was a first step, that a future pro-European government could opt in, and that voting against the treaty would prevent any progress in Europe.[48] He supported the idea of a referendum on the euro, as later on the European constitution, in order to have a proper debate on the UK's place in Europe.

The evolution started in the 1990s, when Paddy Ashdown was still leader of the party. As talks with New Labour about a possible coalition went under way before the 1997 general election, Ashdown abandoned the reference to federalism in Europe. The 1997 manifesto said instead: "Our vision is of a European Union that is decentralised, democratic and diverse. A strong and united Europe, but one that respects cultural traditions and national and regional identities." On the single currency, the approach was hardly more positive than New Labour's although the party leader had clearly expressed his support for it in the Maastricht treaty and had criticized the Labour party's "opportunism" during the ratification debates:

> Being part of a successful single currency will bring low inflation and low interest rates. Staying out will result in less investment and a loss of influence. However, three conditions must be met before Britain can join. First, the single currency must be firmly founded on the Maastricht criteria.

Second, Britain must meet those criteria. Third, the British people must have agreed to it in a referendum.[49]

Paddy Ashdown was among the founders of Britain in Europe, which was launched in 1999. But he and his successor, Charles Kennedy, followed Blair's line in never really developing a case for the euro within the organisation, and never really put a meaningful pressure on the government in the years that followed. Indeed from 2003, the party's stance on Iraq, which was to oppose the government's decision to go to war, quickly superseded the debate on the euro and enabled the party to distance itself from the government and establish itself as the only party in tune with public opinion on the war.

On the constitution, Charles Kennedy broadly supported the government's position, especially on the "red lines". His only difference, and line of attack on the Prime Minister at that point, was to join the Conservatives in demanding a referendum.[50] It therefore became more and more difficult to draw a line between both parties on this issue, or to hear a distinctive Liberal voice on the EU. This can be explained, as with other parties, by the fear of antagonizing the electorate, which in the Liberal Democrat case is less pro-European than the leadership. In many marginal constituencies, particularly in the south of England, the Liberal Democrats try to attract or keep voters who used to support the Conservatives, and are therefore likely to be less enthusiastic about Europe. This probably explains the toning down of the pro-European rhetoric, even if on the whole, the Lib Dems' discourse remains the most positive of the three main parties.

The conclusion that can easily been drawn from this analysis is that there has indeed been only one discourse about Europe in the contemporary British political debate, with only short variations within it between relative Europhiles and Eurosceptics. Major may have represented a middle-of-the-road figure in this respect, Blair a more pro-European voice, later Conservative leaders a more negative one, but the vocabulary and the arguments used belong to the same category. It is a narrative which insists on British national interests, although they are rarely defined, on the refusal of federalism and a European superstate, although no member state wants it, and is defined in mostly negative terms, i.e. what Britain does not want from the Union. No political leader in the recent past has been immune to this rhetoric, whether through belief or electoral tactic. Even the apparently positive objectives set for the future of the EU, like enlargement, flexibility or free trade, have defensive undertones: it is enlargement as opposed to the kind of integration favoured by other member states, "outward-looking" means that agricultural subsidies should be scrapped and/or policy repatriated at the national level, etc. It is the discourse which is deemed acceptable to the British public, and a framework from which it is difficult to extract oneself. Indeed, in spite of Tony Blair's professed aim to look critically at this discourse in his early speeches, no effort has been made to change the nature of the debate about Europe in the last ten years. Political leaders share responsibility for this situation with the media, above all the popular press, which has developed a violent anti-European campaign since the early 1990s, which has never been properly dispelled by politicians. The consequence of this settled discourse is that it is very difficult, if at all possible, to present a positive case for Europe in the UK.

Bibliography

Alexandre-Collier, Agnès, Bernard d'Hellencourt and Pauline Schnapper, eds. *Le Royaume-Uni et l'Union Européenne depuis 1997.* Dijon: Editions Universitaires Dijonnaises, 2007.

Almond, Gabriel and Sydney Verba. *Civic Culture.* Boston: Little, Brown & Company, 1963.

Baker, David, Andrew Gamble and Steve Ludlam. "Whips or Scorpions? The Maastricht Vote and the Conservative Party". *Parliamentary Affairs*, 46:2 (1993): 151-166.

Blair, Tony. "Britain's role in Europe", speech to the European Research Institute, Birmingham, November 23, 2001.

—. "Change: A Modern Britain in a Modern Europe", speech in The Hague, January 20, 1998.

—. "A Clear Course for Europe", speech, November 28, 2002.

—. "Committed to Europe, Reforming Europe" speech in Ghent, February 23, 2000.

—. "Speech at the Foreign Office Conference", January 7, 2003.

—. "Speech in Warsaw", May 30, 2003.

—. "Speech on the Future of Europe", Oxford, February 2, 2006.

—. "Speech to the French National Assembly", March 24, 1998.

—. "Speech to the Lord Mayor's Banquet", November 10, 2003.

—. "Speech to the Polish Stock Exchange", October 6, 2000.

Cameron, David. "The EU–A New Agenda for the 21st Century", speech at the Movement for European Reform, March 6, 2007.

Colley, Linda. *Britons: Forging the Nation 1707-1837.* New Haven: Yale University Press, 1992.

Cowley, Philip. "Chaos or Cohesion? Major and the Conservative Parliamentary Party". In *The Major Premiership 1990-1997: Politics and Policies under John Major*, edited by Peter Dorey, 1-26. Basingstoke: Palgrave, 1999.

Duncan-Smith, Iain. "Speech to the British-Swiss Chamber of Commerce", May 19, 2003.

Hague, William. "Speech to the Second Congress for Democracy", July 9, 1999.

Hague, William. "Speech to the Conservative Party Conference, October 5, 2000

Hix, Simon. "Britain, the EU and the Euro". In *Developments in British Politics 6*, 47-68. Basingstoke: Palgrave, 2000.

Holden, Russell. *The Making of New Labour's European Policy*. Basingstoke: Palgrave, 2002.

Howard, Michael. "Speech to the Conservative Party Conference", October 5, 2004.

Larsen, Henryk. "British Discourses on Europe: Sovereignty of Parliament, Instrumentality and the Non-Mythical Europe". In *Reflective Approaches to European Governance*, edited by Knud Erik Jorgensen, 109-127. Basingstoke: Macmillan, 1997.

—. *Foreign Policy and Discourse Analysis: France, Britain and Europe*. London: Routledge, 1997.

Lynch, Philip. *The Politics of Nationhood: Sovereignty, Britishness and Conservative Politics*. Basingstoke: Palgrave, 1999.

Major, John. *The Autobiography*. London: Harper Collins, 1999.

—. "Raise your eyes, there is a land beyond", *The Economist*, September 25, 1993.

Menon, Anand. "Britain and the Convention on the Future of Europe". *International Affairs* 79:5 (2003): 963-978.

Riddell, Peter. "Europe". In *The Blair Effect 2001-2005*, edited by Anthony Seldon and Dennis Kavanagh. Cambridge: Cambridge University Press, 2005.

—. *The Unfulfilled Prime Minister: Tony Blair's Quest for a Legacy*. London: Politico's, 2005.

Risse, Thomas. "The Euro between National and European Identity", *Journal of European Public Policy*, 10: 4 (2003): 487-505.

Roth, Andrew, "Michael Howard: the First Jewish Prime Minister?" *Political Quarterly*, 75:4 (2004): 362-366.

Young, Hugo. *This Blessed Plot: Britain and Europe from Churchill to Blair*. London: Macmillan, 1998.

Notes

[1] Tony Blair, "Speech on the Future of Europe", Oxford, 2 February 2006. The author wishes to thank Anand Menon, Stephen Wall, Aude de Mézerac, Agnès Alexandre-Collier and Eric Guilyardi for comments on earlier drafts.

[2] Gabriel Almond and Sydney Verba, *Civic Culture*, (Boston: Little, Brown & Company, 1963).

[3] See Linda Colley, *Britons: Forging the Nation 1707-1837*, (New Haven: Yale University Press, 1992); HugoYoung, *This Blessed Plot: Britain and Europe from Churchill to Blair*, (London: Macmillan, 1998); Henryk Larsen, *Foreign Policy and Discourse Analysis: France, Britain and Europe*, (London: Routledge,1997); and Larsen, "British Discourses on Europe: Sovereignty of Parliament, Instrumentality and the Non-Mythical Europe". In *Reflective Approaches to European Governance*, edited by Knud Erik Jorgensen, 109-127. Basingstoke: Macmillan, 1997.

[4] Thomas Risse, "The Euro between National and European Identity", *Journal of European Public Policy*, 10: 4 (2003): 487-505.

[5] Philip Cowley, "Chaos or Cohesion? Major and the Conservative Parliamentary Party", in *The Major Premiership 1990-1997: Politics and Policies under John Major*, edited by Peter Dorey, (Basingstoke: Palgrave, 1999) 1-26.

[6] John Major, *The Autobiography*, (London: Harper Collins, 1999) 269

[7] *House of Commons Debates*, 18/12/1991, Vol. 201, col. 277

[8] *The Best Future for Britain*, Conservative Party Manifesto, 1992

[9] See David Baker, Andrew Gamble and Steve Ludlam, "Whips or Scorpions? The Maastricht Vote and the Conservative Party", *Parliamentary Affairs*, 46:2 (1993): 151-166.

[10] Major,364

[11] *Ibid.*,365

[12] *House of Commons Debates*, 4/11/1992, vol. 213, col. 284-285

[13] *Ibid.*, 22/7/1993, vol. 229, col. 520.

[14] Major, 581

[15] John Major, "Raise your eyes, there is a land beyond", *The Economist*, September 25, 1993

[16] *House of Commons Debates*, 1/3/1995, Vol. 255, cols. 1068-1069

[17] See Russell Holden, *The Making of New Labour's European Policy*, (Basingstoke: Palgrave, 2002).

[18] *House of Commons Debates*, 4/11/1992, vol. 213, col. 308.

[19] *Ibid.*, 22/7/1993, vol. 229, col. 535).

[20] Peter Riddell, *The Unfulfilled Prime Minister: Tony Blair's Quest for a Legacy* (London: Politico's, 2005) 131

[21] See Tony Blair, "Committed to Europe, Reforming Europe" speech in Ghent, February 23, 2000. See also Blair, "Britain's role in Europe", speech to the European Research Institute, Birmingham, November 23, 2001

[22] Blair, "Change: A Modern Britain in a Modern Europe", speech in The Hague, January 20, 1998.

[23] Blair, "Speech to the French National Assembly", March 24, 1998.

[24] Blair, "Britain's role in Europe".

[25] Blair, "Change"

[26] Blair, "Britain's role in Europe",

[27] Blair, "Change"

[28] Blair, "Speech to the Polish Stock Exchange", October 6, 2000.

[29] Blair, "Britain's role in Europe".

[30] Blair, "Speech at the Foreign Office Conference", January 7, 2003.

[31] (Blair, "A Clear Course for Europe", speech, November 28, 2002.

[32] *Ibid.*

[33] Blair, "Speech to the Polish Stock Exchange".

[34] Anand Menon, "Britain and the Convention on the Future of Europe", *International Affairs* 79:5 (2003): 963-978.

[35] *House of Commons Debates*, 21/5/2003, vol. 405, col. 1005

[36] *Ibid.*, 20/4/2004, vol. 420, col. 157

[37] Blair, "speech to the Lord Mayor's Banquet", November 10, 2003.

[38] Blair, "Speech on the Future of Europe", Oxford, February 2, 2006.

[39] Peter Riddell, "Europe", in *The Blair Effect 2001-2005*, edited by Anthony Seldon and Dennis Kavanagh. Cambridge: Cambridge University Press, 2005.

[40] Agnès Alexandre-Collier, Bernard d'Hellencourt and Pauline Schnapper, eds. *Le Royaume-Uni et l'Union Européenne depuis 1997*. Dijon: Editions Universitaires Dijonnaises, 2007.

[41] William Hague, "Speech to the Second Congress for Democracy", July 9, 1999.

[42] Hague, "Speech to the Conservative Party Conference, October 5, 2000

[43] Iain Duncan Smith "Speech to the British-Swiss Chamber of Commerce", May 19, 2003.

[44] Menon, *op. cit.*

[45] Michael Howard, "Speech to the Conservative Party Conference", October 5, 2004.

[46] Andrew Roth, "Michael Howard: the First Jewish Prime Minister?" *Political Quarterly*, 75:4 (2004): 362-366.

[47] David Cameron, "The EU–A New Agenda for the 21st Century", speech at the Movement for European Reform, March 6, 2007.

[48] *House of Commons Debates*, 4/11/1992, vol. 213, col. 316

[49] Liberal Democrats, Manifesto 1997

[50] *House of Commons Debates*, 9/9/2003

CHAPTER FOUR

CHANGING POLITICAL DISCOURSES ON THE SINGLE CURRENCY? THE CONSERVATIVES AND LABOUR SINCE 1992

CARINE BERBÉRI

"Yet, we always come back to the same dilemma: in or out of Europe. To be in or not to be in, that is the question. In the end, we have always chosen to be in. Any British government, governing for the true national interest, always comes back to the same place. It is not weakness, or the beguiling embrace of European allies; it is stark reality, good old-fashioned British pragmatism that brings us there. Europe matters politically and economically. Influence and partnership in Europe is essential to the British national interest."[1]

Analysing the political discourses of the Conservatives and Labour on the single currency implies examining the statements made at each level of the two main parties, and particularly the viewpoints noticeable in the Cabinet/Shadow Cabinet, and in the Conservative and Labour parliamentary parties. This is all the more important as European monetary initiatives, whether they refer to the European Monetary System (EMS) or to Economic and Monetary Union (EMU), have been rather problematic and divisive issues in Britain. As shown by the above-mentioned quote, British governments have been rather reluctant to join them, hesitating a lot and generally refusing to join at the outset. This was rather surprising since British governments in the twentieth century had all generally been attracted by the idea of fixed exchange rates rather than by that of floating exchange rates. Even Labour governments had continued to prefer fixed exchange rates despite their difficulties in maintaining the value of sterling.[2] From the start, these European monetary initiatives have also given rise to a debate within the two main political parties. On the right of the political spectrum, the arguments of Conservative opponents have generally been political—EMU would entail an unacceptable loss of sovereignty and would lead to fiscal union—but also economic—a single currency would never be launched because it was based on an unachievable timetable and flawed convergence criteria—whereas proponents have considered the single currency as a natural extension of the single market, which would put an end to exchange rate instability and uneven inflation. On the left of the political spectrum, opponents have stressed that EMU would prevent governments from using policy instruments to tackle long-term unemployment and would transfer power to unelected institutions whereas proponents have insisted on the economic benefits a single currency would deliver and have highlighted that standing aside would leave Britain isolated in Europe.

   This article is aimed at analysing the political discourses of the two main political parties in the 1992-2008 period, focusing on their rhetoric once they were in power. More precisely, it will try to determine whether the new tone adopted by the Labour governments since May 1997 has contrasted starkly with that of the previous Conservative government and has brought about a real change. Indeed, one should not forget that neither the Tories under the leadership of John Major nor Labour under the premierships of Tony Blair and Gordon Brown have decided to join monetary union. Between April 1992 and May 1997, the Major government was quite reluctant to support any move towards EMU, following a wait and see policy and taking no steps to prepare for the possibility of a single currency. This was possible insofar as the Maastricht Treaty included an opt-out clause on the third stage of the programme towards monetary union, allowing Britain to choose if and when it wanted to join the single currency. Since May 1997 the Blair and Brown governments have also constantly postponed a referendum on the single currency, and have not called into question the opt-out clause negotiated by the Conservatives, even though Labour had hinted before the 1997 General Election that they would adopt a more positive tone than their predecessors.

   This article will consequently try to contrast the political discourses of the Conservatives and Labour on this issue, examining first their traditional discourses on European monetary initiatives between 1979 and 1992. Then, it will focus on the rhetoric used by each party when they were in power—first, the Major government until May 1997, then the Blair and Brown governments—so as to determine if the Labour governments have really adopted a new kind of discourse on the single currency.

1. Background: the traditional discourses
of the Conservatives and Labour on European
monetary initiatives (1979-1992)

Between 1979 and 1990, the Conservative governments headed by Margaret Thatcher followed a very cautious or even hostile policy on European monetary plans, which was reflected in their rhetoric. After criticizing Callaghan's refusal to join the Exchange Rate Mechanism (ERM) of the EMS in 1978, Margaret Thatcher remained undecided when she came to power, stating that sterling would enter the ERM when "the time was ripe", when the right economic conditions were met. Three conditions in particular had to be respected—the UK inflation rate had to match that of other European member states, the British economy had to be strong, and clear steps had to be taken by other European countries, especially by France and Italy, to liberalize capital movements:

> Although Britain's membership of the exchange rate mechanism of the European monetary system was not an issue at this Council, I reaffirmed our intention to join the ERM, but we must first get our inflation down. We shall look for satisfactory implementation of other aspects of the first phase of the Delors report, including free movement of capital and abolition of foreign exchange control.[3]

Thatcher was rather opposed to British membership of the ERM for two main reasons: she did not want decisions on exchange rate movement to be determined by the Bundesbank, and she wanted to control inflation thanks to a monetarist policy, which was incompatible with excessive intervention to support the pound within the ERM.[4] Consequently, the decision to join the ERM in 1990 was taken against her inclination, Thatcher declining to continue to resist sterling joining the ERM and acting under pressure from her new Chancellor of the Exchequer, John Major.[5] At that time, she could no longer refuse to enter the ERM and stand up to her new Chancellor owing to three main political reasons: her growing hostility to the European project had exposed deep divisions in the Conservative Party; the introduction of the poll tax in the late 1980s had led to huge public protest; and her authority within the Conservative Party had been shaken by the departure of Nigel Lawson, her former Chancellor, who had resigned because of his disagreement with the Prime Minister about the policy to be adopted on the ERM.[6]

Since 1979 British Conservative governments had also opposed movement to monetary union, considering that the creation of a single currency and a European Central Bank (ECB) would threaten Britain's national identity and parliamentary sovereignty, and would inexorably lead to political integration. Their statements had a very critical tone:

> ....if I [Margaret Thatcher] were [governor of an independent central bank], there would be no European central bank accountable to no one, least of all national Parliaments. The point of that kind of Europe with a central bank is no democracy, taking powers away from every single Parliament, and having a single currency, a monetary policy and interest rates which take all political power away from us. As my right hon. Friend the Member for Blaby (Mr. Lawson) said in his first speech after the proposal for a single currency was made, a single currency is about the politics of Europe, it is about a federal Europe by the back door.[7]

Instead, the Conservative governments supported the idea of a "hard ecu", which would have run alongside the national currencies before becoming a single currency, but this plan was rejected by the other European governments.[8] In 1991 the Major government consequently chose to negotiate an opt-out for sterling instead of supporting moves towards EMU:

> Our insistence that there should be no imposition of a single currency is well known: by that we mean that we cannot commit ourselves now to entry at a later date as a result of the treaty. We are therefore insisting that there must be a provision in the treaty giving us the right, quite separately from any European Council decision, to decide for ourselves whether or not to move to stage 3. That decision can be taken only by this House.
> That means that, even if the requisite majority of member states decide to embrace full economic and monetary union with a single currency and a single central bank, Britain will not be obliged to do so. Whether to join—not just when to join—will be matters of separate decision by Government and by Parliament. Nothing in the treaty that I sign will bind us now to the decision that we must take then.[9]

As to the Labour Party, it had first been hostile to European monetary plans, but it progressively adopted a more positive tone, wishing to work constructively within Europe and to support its initiatives from 1983 onwards. This shift in attitude, which was initiated by Neil Kinnock and then reinforced by John Smith, became quite obvious from the end of the 1980s (1988/89) and was also reflected in its rhetoric. From then on, the Labour Party advocated entry to the Exchange Rate Mechanism praising the stability it would give to Britain, as highlighted by leader Neil Kinnock in a debate on the completion of the single market of the European Community:

> Our only choice is whether to participate constructively in order strongly to influence the change or to be dragged along behind it, as we are being dragged along behind the European monetary system. We are in it, but not of it. The result is that we bear all the pressures of having a currency measured against the deutschmark, without having any of the benefits of stability and credibility for the currency that could be secured by participation in the exchange rate mechanism. I do not counsel that we go in without conditions... It is essential to negotiate proper conditions and we should negotiate them now.[10]

Four conditions particularly had to be met: sterling would have to enter at a rate and on conditions ensuring the competitiveness of British goods, there would have to be more effective collaboration between the central banks of the EU countries, an EU-wide trade policy contributing to balance of payments stability for individual members, and a coordinated EU-wide growth policy.[11]

From that moment on, Labour also favoured the creation of EMU even if their support depended on several conditions, such as a more accountable European Central Bank, real convergence in the economic performance of member states, or a significant enhancement of the EU regional policies.[12] Consequently, the Labour Party vehemently criticized the opt-out negotiated by the Conservatives in 1991, considering it left Britain isolated in Europe:

> It is a statement from a double opt-out Government who have isolated Britain on the most vital issues of economic and monetary union and the social charter... That is abdication, not negotiation... Isolation means sacrificing essential influence over the process of European monetary union; it means shadowing the creation of others and ultimately accepting conditions determined by others; it means throwing away all chance of getting the European central bank to Britain.... That is how the Government are putting Britain into the economic, financial, industrial and employment second division in Europe.[13]

The following years confirmed this evolution in favour of European monetary initiatives. In the mid-1990s, Labour had clearly become the more pro-European of the two major political parties.

Consequently, comparing the discourses of the Conservative and Labour Parties between 1979 and 1992 seems to bring to the fore differences on the single currency issue since the Labour Party had clearly become more enthusiastic about the EMS and monetary union than the Conservatives in the early 1990s even though the latter had finally decided to join the ERM under the influence of political factors.

2. The parties' discourse on the single currency since April 1992

2.1 The increasingly sceptical discourse of the Tories

2.1.1 Choosing between "never" and "some time, maybe"[14]

John Major's victory in the 1992 General Election did not lead to a change in the discourse of the Conservatives on the single currency. As already mentioned, Britain had an opt-out clause for sterling. Therefore, the Major government maintained its wait-and-see attitude, considering that it could not make the right decision for the UK until it knew the precise economic and political conditions of its creation for example, which members would be eligible to participate in it, or the economic performance of these countries. In their 1992 manifesto the Conservatives had made this idea quite clear, insisting on the need to make sensible decisions and refusing an "automatic commitment" to join EMU:

> A union will only come about by 1997 if a substantial majority of Community members agree it should. It would only include those members who were judged to have met specified conditions. And it would only come about if a majority of members were judged to have done so.
> But the Treaty goes on to say that monetary union will come about automatically in 1999, for all who meet the conditions. We did not want to exclude ourselves from membership; but we could not accept such an automatic commitment. By the end of this decade the EC's membership will have changed; the economic performance of many of its members may have changed. We cannot tell who the members of such a union might be. We therefore secured the freedom to make a proper judgement on events.[15]

Despite this cautious stance, the Conservative government had also stressed its willingness to take part in the discussions concerning the third stage of the programme of monetary union, wishing to use its place at the negotiating table to shape its arrangements and to make Britain's voice heard so as to ensure that EMU would not damage Britain's interests. More precisely, it had insisted on the crucial importance of the five convergence criteria to guarantee there were not too sharp divergences in economic performance between European member states:

> The Treaty negotiated at Maastricht laid down the process under which the Community can, if its members meet certain economic conditions, create a monetary union with a single currency for some or all of them. Together

with Germany we fought for tough criteria. We believe a monetary union would collapse, with damaging consequences, if it were imposed on economies that were too diverse.[16]

If the Tories' discourse on the single currency had first been very cautious, it gradually evolved into an increasingly sceptical direction, particularly after Britain's exit from the ERM. A shift was noticeable late in 1993. In an article published in *The Economist* on September 25th, the Prime Minister wrote that monetary union would certainly not happen, adopting a very critical tone:

> The plain fact is that economic and monetary union is not realisable in present circumstances... I hope my fellow heads of government will resist the temptation to recite the mantra of full economic and monetary union as if nothing had changed. If they do recite it, it will have all the quaintness of a rain dance and about the same potency.[17]

These doubts were reiterated in 1995: not only did the Prime Minister now state that European countries would not be able to meet the economic conditions for a successful single currency by the end of the century, but he also added that, even if a small group of European nations adopted the single currency before then, it was almost inconceivable that Britain would join them.[18] The Conservative government argued against a possible fudging of the rules which would enable monetary union to go ahead in 1999 even though most EU members did not meet the strict conditions laid down in the treaty. They insisted that the five economic criteria and economic convergence, rather than the constraints of a political timetable, should be the most important factors determining the launch of the single currency: "Convergence is necessary before economic and monetary union could be a practical economic step, apart from its political or other desirability."[19] In addition, the Prime Minister now admitted that the single currency had "serious political and constitutional implications":

> Let me reiterate the changes that need to be made [to join EMU]. They are: locking exchange rates, agreeing a single currency, abolishing domestic currencies, making the Bank of England independent and passing control of interest rates and monetary policy as a whole to an international bank, on which this country would be represented as one among many... In addition to that, we should accept the possibility....that a unified monetary policy would require a far greater alignment both of spending and of tax rates.... The House knows.... that I am wary of a single currency for those economic reasons—wary of its economic impact and of the serious political and constitutional implications.[20]

This evolution was illustrated by the 1997 election manifesto which struck a more sceptical tone than that of 1992. Thus, the Conservatives stated that it was quite unlikely that the single currency would be introduced on January 1st, 1999. Furthermore, they explained that Britain would not be part of a hastily created monetary union, and that the Maastricht criteria should not be fudged:

> For a single currency to come into effect, European economies will have to meet crucial criteria. On the information currently available, we believe that it is very unlikely that there will be sufficient convergence of economic conditions across Europe for a single currency to proceed safely on the target date of January 1st 1999. We will not include legislation on the single currency in the first Queen's Speech. If it cannot proceed safely, we believe it would be better for Europe to delay any introduction of a single currency rather than rush ahead to meet an artificial timetable. We will argue this case in the negotiations that lie ahead.
>
> We believe it is in our national interest to keep our options open to take a decision on a single currency when all the facts are before us. If a single currency is created, without sustainable convergence, a British Conservative government will not be part of it.[21]

Finally, the 1997 manifesto included the promise of a referendum on the single currency during the course of the next Parliament if a Conservative government decided to join it. Such a referendum would be held after the Cabinet had concluded that it was in Britain's interest to join and that this decision had been sanctioned by Parliament.[22]

2.1.2 Reasons: the ERM exit and internal party tensions

Two main reasons could account for the increasingly sceptical discourse of the Conservative Party on the single currency from 1992 to 1997: the suspension of the pound's membership of the ERM, and the increasing tensions brought about by the single currency within the ranks of the Conservative Party.

Firstly, sterling's ejection from the ERM in September 1992 had a knock-on effect on the policy followed by the Conservatives on monetary union and on their rhetoric. In September 1992, after almost two years of membership, the ERM faced an acute financial crisis. Although the Conservative government tried to do its best to protect the value of sterling within the ERM, it could not restore stability on the financial markets.[23] On September 16th, John Major had to announce that sterling's membership of the ERM had to be suspended. This event led to a change in the Conservatives' rhetoric about this system. From now on many Conservatives criticized it, considering that such a system could not work since several other countries had been forced to withdraw from the ERM or to devalue their currency following the international financial crisis. They consequently called for a review of the whole way in which the ERM worked, highlighting that there were fault-lines in the system. This was exemplified by several statements made by Conservative MPs the following days. John Watts, for example, insisted on new intervention procedures:

> We would certainly not rejoin the system [ERM] as it stands; and the fault lines to which he [the Prime Minister] has referred were clearly the events of recent weeks.... It seems to me that the very least necessary modification would be a requirement for asymmetry of obligations on member currencies.... A currency that is under pressure should not bear all the responsibility for maintaining its parity. There should be an equal and symmetrical obligation on a currency that is strengthening against its central rate to take action to deal with that. That is an essential component if there is to be any prospect of this country rejoining the ERM.[24]

Obviously, such a stance jeopardized Britain joining the single currency one day insofar as, in theory, sterling had to re-enter the ERM to be allowed to be part of EMU (one of the five Maastricht criteria). Moreover, sterling's withdrawal from the ERM cast doubts on the success of a single currency—according to some Conservative MPs, like John Townend, the failure of the ERM to deliver showed that the aim of monetary union was not viable:

> The main casualty of last week was the ERM. It has failed to deliver. It has been shown that the aim of monetary union and a single currency as set out in the Maastricht treaty is a dead duck.[25]

From that moment on, the Conservative government hardened its position on the ERM, becoming more Eurosceptic and insisting that there was no question of sterling's return to the ERM until the system had been reformed, until the flaws had been put right, even though the Conservative Euro-enthusiasts insisted on keeping open the option of rejoining the ERM.

Secondly, during the 1992-1997 period, John Major was compelled to adopt a more critical discourse about monetary union owing to the intra-party tensions on the single currency. If these divisions were already noticeable before September 1992, the pound's ejection from the ERM tore open the party divide over Europe and the single currency. From then on, the Euro-sceptics became more vehement and increasingly criticized the wait-and-see policy of the government on EMU, calling into question the "opt-out" clause and demanding that Britain should retain sterling.[26] Consequently, John Major was compelled to adopt a conciliatory tone aimed at appeasing the Euro-sceptics–whom he feared most–without antagonizing the Euro-enthusiasts, so as to preserve a semblance of party unity.[27] Nevertheless, this more sceptical discourse did not put an end to the internal dissent within the Conservative Party, tensions even became all the more obvious as Conservative members–whether they were frontbenchers or backbenchers–made public comments on this issue on many occasions.

In fact, three different types of discourses on European monetary issues were noticeable within the Conservative Party: the official stance, as expressed by John Major, the view of the Euro-sceptics and that of the Euro-enthusiasts. The Euro-sceptics, who included Michael Howard (Home Secretary), Peter Lilley, John Redwood (Secretary of State for Wales) or Michael Portillo, were particularly strong since they were the largest group (accounting for about 60% of Conservative MPs).[28] Their opposition to the single currency was mainly based on political and constitutional reasons: the single currency would lead to the permanent transfer to an unelected ECB of control over domestic economic policy. This would involve a crucial loss of power/sovereignty:

> That is what most of us on the Government Benches want to see continuing. We want a Chancellor setting interest rates with the Governor of the Bank of England and being accountable to the House for his decisions. The provisions set out in the Maastricht treaty would not allow that process of accountability to continue. The establishment of a European central bank clearly takes the relevant powers away from the Chancellor. The European constitution could not be clearer. It could not be clearer also from reading that constitution that monetary union is not a purely technical and economic matter. Instead, it is of fundamental constitutional importance. It creates a central bank that is unaccountable.[29]

Besides, it would mean that Britain would no longer be able to devalue its currency if its industrial costs exceeded those of its European partners. Therefore, EMU would lead to a progressive extension of the European Union's control over Britain's fiscal policy since it would result in large disparities in the unemployment rates of its member states (which would involve large budgetary transfers between European countries):

[A single currency] would remove the safety valve of the currency; there would not be the opportunities for mass migration that have enabled the United States to cope with economic developments; there would not even be the opportunities for the population movements that have taken place in the United Kingdom. Instead, economic disparities across Europe would increase. Prosperity would not develop evenly; massive transfer payments would have to be made across the regions.[30]

Westminster would consequently lose the right to set the level of interest rates, and to determine spending and taxation.[31] Owing to these constitutional implications, the Conservative Euro-sceptics' camp concluded that the idea of a single currency should be rejected right away since the UK would never accept the destruction of parliamentary sovereignty. In 1994 62% of Conservative MPs considered that sovereignty could not be pooled.[32]

As far as the Euro-enthusiasts were concerned, they accounted for about 30% of Conservative MPs and included for example Michael Heseltine (Deputy Prime Minister from 1995 onwards) or Kenneth Clarke (Chancellor of the Exchequer from 1993 onwards). They remained rather unobtrusive from 1992 to 1997, not wishing to weaken the Prime Minister even more and maybe impressed by the vehement protests of the Euro-sceptics. They encouraged John Major to keep open the option for Parliament to say "yes" or "no" to joining the single currency, considering that monetary union would provide a more stable environment:

I want us not to lose the prospect of a single currency…. There is too much mincing of words on that subject. I want the security of that prospect—for myself, my children and my country. Anyone who considers what has happened to the pound—not just since the war, but before it—will have some idea what I am getting at and will also know the sophistication of the pure speculation which present structures, I am afraid permit.[33]

According to them, standing aside would also marginalize Britain in the EU:

It seems likely that there will be a cohesion of the five, six or seven countries at the centre of Europe into a bloc—and indeed, into a single currency. If so, when our economy is strong enough I would be doubtful whether it would not be in the British national interest to align ourselves with those countries and join in. The dangers of getting left behind are huge.[34]

Apart from these main reasons, two other factors might have contributed to the Major government's sceptical discourse on the single currency: the Euroscepticism of the British and of the British press. Indeed, since the early 1990s British people had been rather reluctant about the idea of a single currency, opposing Britain joining by a majority of two to one. In the mid-1990s, the British particularly showed little enthusiasm for the single currency, maybe influenced by the policy followed by the Major government.[35] As to the press, most British newspapers (*The Times*, *The Daily Telegraph*, *The Daily Mail*, *The Sun*....) were hostile to monetary union and published articles highlighting the dangers of a single currency at every opportunity.

2.2 New Labour's discourse on the euro: "prepare and decide"

2.2.1 A formal discourse based, above all, on the meeting of economic conditions

In early 1997 New Labour[36] had hinted that they would adopt a more positive tone than the Conservatives towards Europe and the euro. Nevertheless, their 1997 election manifesto was quite cautious since it explained that any decision about the UK joining the single currency would only be taken after "a hard-headed assessment of Britain's economic interests" and that it would be quite unlikely that the UK would adhere to monetary union at its launch:

> Any decision about Britain joining the single currency must be determined by a hard-headed assessment of Britain's economic interests..... But there are formidable obstacles in the way of Britain being in the first wave of membership, if EMU takes place on 1 January 1999. What is essential for the success of EMU is genuine convergence among the economies that take part, without any fudging of the rules. However, to exclude British membership of EMU forever would be to destroy any influence we have over a process which will affect us whether we are in or out.[37]

Furthermore, the manifesto insisted on a triple lock (three pre-conditions), which would determine Britain joining the single currency: the Cabinet would first have to agree, second Parliament, and third, the British would have to give their approval in a referendum. In fact, Labour had decided to soften their rhetoric and adopt a more cautious discourse so as to appease British voters and to keep their party united. As they had been excluded from national government since 1979, they were not ready to jeopardize a possible victory by adopting too positive a policy on the euro.

Once elected, New Labour took two important measures which could herald a change in discourse on the euro. On the one hand, it appointed David Simon, BP (British Petroleum) Chairman and a convinced pro-European as Minister for Trade and Competitiveness in Europe. On the other hand, it gave the Bank of England "operational independence" in monetary policy: from now on, it would be the Bank of England, and not the Chancellor, which would set key short-term official interest rates.[38] If this move was described as a way to ensure that monetary political decisions would no longer be dominated by short-term political considerations, it also allowed Great Britain to comply with some of the provisions of the Maastricht Treaty (stage two of the timetable to EMU asked member states to make their central bank independent from policy-makers).[39]

However, New Labour maintained a cautious line of action on the euro. On October 27, 1997 in the House of Commons, Chancellor of the Exchequer Gordon Brown set out the official policy of the government. He explained that in principle, the government was in favour of joining the single currency if the latter was successful and if five economic tests were satisfied:

> If, in the end, a single currency is successful, and the economic case is clear and unambiguous, then the Government believes Britain should be part of it..... So we conclude that the determining factor as to whether Britain joins a single currency is the national economic interest and whether the economic case for doing so is clear and unambiguous.[40]

The five tests set by the Chancellor were the following: (1) there should be sustainable convergence between the business cycles and economic structures of the UK and the rest of the euro-zone countries, (2) there should be sufficient flexibility in the UK and in continental Europe to adapt to change and other unexpected economic events, (3) joining EMU should create better conditions for businesses to make long-term decisions to invest in Britain, (4) it should have a beneficial effect upon Britain's financial services industry, (5) it should promote higher growth, stability, and a lasting increase in jobs. Nevertheless, since these five conditions were not satisfied for the time being, Gordon Brown clearly said that the United Kingdom would not be able to join monetary union on January 1st, 1999:

> British membership of a single currency in 1999 could not meet the tests and therefore is not in the country's economic interests. There is no proper convergence between the British and the other European economies now.[41]

Moreover, he stated that it would be quite unlikely that Britain would join the euro during the lifetime of this parliament (1997-2001) insofar as it would be difficult to examine in such a short time scale if British nations could benefit from adhering to EMU and if they had demonstrated a period of sustainable convergence:

> There is no realistic prospect of our having demonstrated, before the end of this parliament, that we have achieved convergence which is sustainable and settled rather than transitory..... Therefore, barring some fundamental and unforeseen change in economic circumstances, making a decision, during this Parliament, to join is not realistic.[42]

Consequently, the official discourse of the Blair governments on the single currency was essentially based on the meeting of five economic criteria. As Tony Blair had made it quite clear in several statements, for Labour, EMU was not inconsistent with the nation-state: " ...unlike the Conservatives, there is no insuperable constitutional or political objection to it [the single currency]" / "There is no insuperable constitutional barrier to our joining."[43] Even if he admitted that the single currency would bring about significant constitutional and political changes, he thought that the British had to overcome the fears aroused by the increasing globalisation of the economy:

> I do not dismiss the constitutional or political issues. They are real. Monetary union is a big step of integration. But so was the Single European Act. And the EU itself.
> In finance and business the world is more and more integrated. It is moving closer together. And if joining a single currency is good for British jobs and British industry, if it enhances British power and British influence, I believe it is right for Britain to overcome these constitutional and political arguments and the fears behind them.[44]

Despite their refusal to enter the single currency on January 1st, 1999, New Labour kept the option of joining open. In his statement on October 27, 1997, Gordon Brown explained that in the meantime the United Kingdom would have to prepare for entry, i.e. to put in place measures that would allow for eventual membership. Thus, the British nations would be ready to enter EMU should New Labour decide to do so:

> We should therefore begin now to prepare ourselves so that, should we meet the economic tests, we can make a decision to join a successful single currency early in the next Parliament. At present, with no preparation, it is

not a practical option. We must put ourselves in the position for Britain to exercise genuine choice.[45]

This cautious discourse based on the meeting of economic tests and on a "prepare and decide" policy has been maintained and confirmed ever since. First, New Labour has taken numerous steps to help British companies to prepare for the possibility of a single currency and to make them aware of the changes introduced in the euro-zone, particularly in the 1997-2004 period. Preparations have included: a wide range of publications—such as the National Changeover Plan announced by Tony Blair in his statement to the Commons in February 1999, advertising campaigns, annual or biennial surveys to assess the preparations made by Britain's small and medium-sized enterprises, business seminars, regional forums or the setting-up of a website (the euro preparations website).[46] In addition, an organisational structure to take forward preparations across the economy has been put in place.

Second, New Labour has tried to build a pro-European consensus in Britain to change the national mood towards the EU and the euro. Thus, a great number of speeches in favour of the EU and of Britain's role in the EU have been made by the Labour Prime Ministers, and by Tony Blair more precisely, or by the successive Foreign Secretaries and Ministers for Europe between 1997 and 2001. Similarly, the Blair and Brown governments have insisted on the importance of economic reform in the EU to ensure the success of the euro and that of Britain's participation in the euro-zone:

> The single currency alone won't make Europe prosperous. The single currency plus fundamental reform in labour, capital and product markets and in our welfare systems, can do so. Economic reform is crucial, not just to the success of Britain's participation in the euro, but to the euro itself.[47]

Third, New Labour has adopted a very cooperative discourse, promising for example that the launch of the euro would be a success:

> …there can be no doubt that the most significant event of our Presidency is the launch of EMU. We want it to succeed, and we will work hard to make its launch successful.[48]

Thus, during the British Presidency of the EU in the first half of 1998, the Blair government took part in the preparations for the launch of the euro, and presided over the decision on which countries would join EMU in 1999.

Finally, in June 2003 the Blair government undertook an assessment of the five tests to examine whether the five economic tests had been met and whether Britain could join the euro. Such a decision had been announced on February 7th, 2001. At Prime Minister's Questions that day, Tony Blair had replied to William Hague, the Conservative leader, that New Labour would complete an assessment about whether the five tests had been met within two years of the start of the next Parliament, which meant before June 2003.[49] On June 9th, 2003 New Labour published its detailed conclusions: since only one of the five tests was met–that concerning financial services–Britain could not join the single currency. Nevertheless, even though entry into EMU was delayed, the Blair government still refused to close the option of joining. This was confirmed by Gordon Brown who announced major reforms to help achieve sustainable and durable convergence and flexibility, and meet the five tests:

> So we conclude the financial services test is met. We still have to meet the two tests of sustainable convergence and flexibility. Subject to the achievement of sustainable convergence and sufficient flexibility, the tests for investment and employment would be met. So I am today announcing major reforms, right for the British economy, reforms which will be implemented over the next year and will greatly assist the process of achieving sustainable and durable convergence and the flexibility necessary for Britain to succeed sustainably within the euro zone and realise its potential for trade and investment.[50]

These reforms included, for example, the introduction of a new target for domestic inflation,[51] new arrangements for British fiscal policy and further reforms in the housing market, in labour, capital and product markets to comply with the two tests of sustainable convergence and flexibility tests, the two most important tests for the Chancellor. In fact, according to Brown, the British housing market was the main reason why Britain was not ready to join the euro. Indeed, Britain's housing market is more sensitive to interest rate changes than that of other EU countries. First, the real house price growth has been stronger in the UK than in the larger euro zone countries over the past few years. Second, mortgage debt in the UK (60% of GDP) is well above the EU average and the system of mortgage finance is dominated by short-term, floating-rate loans.[52] This means that if Britain joined the euro, its interest rates would fall to the European level–British interest rates being generally higher than those of other countries because of the volatility of the housing market and its potential for higher inflation. The Chancellor of the Exchequer consequently feared that this could lead to large swings in the housing market and in the UK economy, and more precisely to an increase in demand, which would boost house prices in Britain, as noticed in some euro area countries, like Spain and Ireland:

> The issue in housing, where we are more interest rate sensitive, is....the fact that to deliver stability in Britain the combination of house price inflation and volatility....has generally led to interest rates higher than other countries. Indeed most stop-go problems that Britain has suffered in the last 50 years have been led or influenced by the housing market. The volatility of the housing market and potential for higher inflation is a problem for stability that we are determined to do more to address to produce greater stability and reduce the risks of inflation....[53]

This would be all the more dangerous to the stability of the British economy as the British government would no longer be able to lower interest rates. Indeed, within the euro zone, Britain would only be allowed to cut public expenditure or to increase taxes.[54] In June 2003 the Labour government announced that they would take another look at the euro issue in next year's budget, i.e., in March 2004, and would report on progress in all these areas of reform:

> We will report on progress in the Budget next year. We can then consider the extent of progress and determine whether on the basis of it we make a further Treasury assessment of the five tests which—if positive next year—would allow us at that time to put the issue before the British people in a referendum.[55]

Although a referendum on the euro has been postponed since October 1997, New Labour has never excluded the possibility for Britain to join the single currency, as illustrated by its 2005 election manifesto:

> On the euro we maintain our common-sense policy. The determining factor underpinning any government decision is the national economic interest and whether the case for joining is clear and unambiguous. The five economic decisions must be met before any decision to join can be made.[56]

Nevertheless, one should admit that the Labour governments have today become far more cautious and even silent on the single currency issue. Contrary to what had been announced, New Labour has not pursued a consistent programme in favour of entry since June 2003, and no further assessment of the five tests has occurred. Besides, Tony Blair's promise to organise a referendum on the EU constitution in 2004 made the prospect of a referendum on the euro even less likely.[57] Relevantly enough, during the 2005 election campaign, Tony Blair himself admitted that euro entry was off the agenda for the foreseeable future. Since Gordon Brown succeeded Tony Blair in June 2007, he has never called this viewpoint into question, asserting in July:

> I think everybody knows that we made a difficult decision on the euro, it wasn't a decision that we made in principle against the euro, but we believed it was not either the right time or the right circumstances in which either Britain or for that matter the rest of Europe can benefit from British membership of the euro. We continue to review that but I think it is right to say in the present circumstances we are not proposing to either have a major new assessment of the euro or to join the euro at this stage.[58]

How can we explain such a cautious discourse, which is all the more surprising as Labour had promised a more positive tone than that adopted by the Conservatives before May 1997, and as a higher level of economic convergence was noticeable between the British and continental European economies during the 2001-2003 period?[59]

2.2.2 An informal and unstated discourse determined by political considerations

In fact, the official discourse adopted by Labour on the euro would only be a smoke screen, a shield for the governments to hide behind, in order to ensure that the single currency issue is not detrimental to the party's interests and does not dominate every hour and week of the governments. Indeed, as most economists, researchers and two of Tony Blair's advisers have shown, the five economic conditions defined by Gordon Brown are rather vague and likely to be interpreted in various ways.[60] As early as 1997, an expert of the House of Commons Treasury select committee had criticized these tests, highlighting their flexibility:

> The Chancellor's tests are so loosely defined that anyone will be able to say that they have either been passed or failed according to the dictates of political expediency.[61]

Consequently, the five tests would probably have been determined to make it possible for the Blair and Brown governments to join the euro when they think it is the most appropriate, i. e. when they think they can fight a winnable referendum, when the political context is the most favourable. This means that since May 1997 a correlation of political factors would have deterred the Blair and Brown governments from holding a referendum on the euro and from adopting a really enthusiastic discourse on the single currency.

Firstly, New Labour wanted to remain in power as long as possible (after 18 years of continuous Conservative government) and consequently wanted to prevent the euro from prejudicing Labour's chances of election/re-election. As Tony Blair had made it quite clear, he did not want a second General Election to be fought on international/European issues : "Tony doesn't want all this to get in the way of a second term... he is more concerned about fighting the election on domestic issues."[62] New Labour was all the more willing to do so as it had spent 18 years in opposition, as explained by Labour MP, Phyllis Starkey, during Labour's first term in office:

> ... all the members of the party and not only Labour MPs and members of the Cabinet are determined to do everything possible to ensure that the Labour government is re-elected, wins a second full term in power (which had never happened before), and even succeeds in winning a third general election. Not that we love power even though this is the aim of all politicians, but we want to be in a position to completely restructure Britain according to our wishes and aspirations. One single term would be too short to allow us to fulfil this purpose, the Conservatives would come back to power and destroy everything we have achieved.[63]

Secondly, postponing a referendum on the single currency to an unspecified date has allowed New Labour to kill off the rumours about possible entry which had been spread by the British media, and more particularly by the British press, from September 1997 onwards.[64] It was all the more important to take a clear-cut decision on this issue as most British newspapers are opposed to the euro.

Thirdly, the Blair and Brown governments have not been encouraged to adopt a more enthusiastic discourse on the euro by the reluctant attitude of the British electorate, still weighted heavily against the single currency.[65] Indeed, between 50 per cent and 60 per cent of the British have remained consistently opposed to the euro during the Blair and Brown governments. Two main factors may explain the steady rejection of the single currency in Britain: the refusal of the Labour governments to make a pro-EMU case and the unlikeliness of a referendum on the euro in the near future.

Fourthly, the more euro-sceptical discourse of the Tories has deterred the Blair and Brown governments from being too favourable to this idea. Since May 1997 the Conservatives have abandoned Major's wait-and-see policy and taken a tougher stand on the euro. Thus, the Conservatives led by William Hague ruled out membership until 2007, i. e., the lifetime of two parliaments. The three leaders who succeeded him–Iain Duncan Smith, Michael Howard and David Cameron–did not call this policy into question and continued to oppose giving up the pound.[66]

Finally, the tensions brought about by the euro within the Labour Party have prevented the Labour governments from really increasing their pro-euro rhetoric. Indeed, the single currency issue has brought to the fore various types of discourses–on the frontbenches and the backbenches of the Labour Party–even if most MPs favour monetary union and if fewer tensions can be noticed within New Labour than within the Conservative Party. If we focus on the May 1997-June 2007 period, the euro mainly gave rise to tensions between Tony Blair and Gordon Brown in the Cabinet. Thus, Tony Blair was far more enthusiastic about the single currency than Gordon Brown:

> We have declared our support in principle for UK membership, though stressed the necessary conditions that have to be met for us to join. The intention is real. The conditions are real. I have a bold aim: that over the next few years Britain resolves once and for all its ambivalence towards Europe. I want to end the uncertainty, the lack of confidence, the Europhobia. I want Britain to be at home with Europe because Britain is once again a leading player in Europe.[67]

In fact, Blair's support was mainly subject to political reasons. He considered Britain should join the single currency to remain a leading power on the European stage and to establish his own place in history.[68]

On the contrary, Gordon Brown was far more cautious. Although he had first been favourable to EMU entry, thinking it was not in Britain's interest not to be part of this initiative and that joining the euro would allow his party to gain economic credibility, he changed his mind once he became Chancellor of the Exchequer.[69] From then on, Gordon Brown gave the greatest importance to the five economic tests he had set out in 1997: Britain should not adhere to the euro as long as these conditions had not been met. In his opinion, the key factor was whether joining was in Britain's economic interest so as not to repeat the mistakes made by the Conservatives when they had joined the ERM–at the wrong rate and at the wrong time–in 1990:[70]

> With the tests met, Britain in the euro can enjoy the benefits I have outlined—greater trade, investment and employment. If we entered with the tests not met at the wrong exchange rate then—just as with the ERM in 1992—we could see unemployment rise, public service investment fall and

growth stall. The discipline of the five tests is to ensure there will be no repeat of the experience of the ERM when Britain joined at the wrong rate and at the wrong time without either convergence or flexibility and the potential benefits could not be realised.[71]

More broadly speaking, his cautious discourse on the single currency could be explained by his willingness to secure the economic stability on which his credibility and that of New Labour now rested.[72]

Within the Labour Party, viewpoints on the single currency can be categorised into three camps: the Euro-enthusiasts, the pragmatists and the Euro-sceptics. The first grouping, the Euro-enthusiasts, would like Britain to be part of EMU for several economic and political reasons. According to them, the euro would deliver numerous benefits, such as lower transaction costs for business and consumers, diminished exchange-rate volatility, increased price transparency, greater cross-border trade, or a more stable environment for economic growth:

> Let us consider the positive case for the single currency....The single currency is first and foremost about tackling currency speculation and the instability that flows from it, which can be tremendously damaging to a country's economy.... Among the [other] benefits are reduced transaction costs, and the European Commission estimates that the UK would save about £3 billion a year. Price transparency is another advantage. When we enter the euro, we will be able to make genuine comparisons between prices, ending the nonsensical situation in which a Ford Fiesta costs 50 per cent more in Britain than in Portugal, for no justifiable or logical reason.[73]

Britain would also have a greater potential to influence European and global monetary policy:

> If we are not part of the formal process within economic and monetary union, there is a danger that, in the long term, political discussions and developments that may impinge on this country will go ahead, and we shall not be part of them to the extent that we could be if we joined the 11 who are in economic and monetary union, as well as being one of the 15 members of the European Union.[74]

The Euro-enthusiasts would consequently like the Labour governments to be less cautious and to hold a referendum on the single currency as soon as possible.[75]

The Euro-sceptics, a minor group within the Labour Party, mainly focus on political ideas relating to Britain's sovereignty and to democracy/accountability:

My objections to the single European currency are not economic—although plenty of criticisms may be levelled in that regard—but essentially political. The single European currency is basically a political project about the creation of a European super-state.... I have always wondered why the supporters of Maastricht are so enthusiastic about transferring power from elected institutions to unelected bankers sitting in Frankfurt or Bonn who are accountable to absolutely no one. Why is it such a great victory for the democratic process that power over interest rates should be concentrated in the hands of a few unelected, unaccountable people sitting in a board room somewhere?[76]

They consider that a British government would lose the policy instruments to address low levels of investment and the ability to tackle long-term unemployment once it is part of EMU:

I am fearful about losing our own currency because we would lose control of macro-economic policy, which is of fundamental importance to ensuring that we can retain full employment and growth in living standards and that we can manage our own economy in the way that we want, according to the democratic dictates of our population.[77]

According to them, EMU would ultimately lead to a European super-state and to fiscal union. Highlighting the economic problems of several euro-zone countries, such as France and Germany, they are also critical of the deflationary bias of EMU which has damaging effects on growth and employment because of the priority given to inflation.[78]

Finally, the pragmatists, who are the most numerous within Labour ranks, support the cautious stance of the governments. According to them, the timing of Britain's entry into EMU and the meeting of the five tests are crucial so as not to repeat the mistakes made by the Tories in 1990.[79] However, they think it is inevitable and desirable that the UK should join the single currency—by staying out of the euro, Britain risks economic and political isolation:

There is also a significant danger in delay. Although I accept the Government's rigorous assessment of the five economic tests and the economics of whether we should join at this point, our economy will suffer if we delay for too long.....there will be a gradual and slow deterioration of our economic strength, viability and competitiveness... Delay....would also be a problem for a political reason. The European Union faces dramatic change in every aspect of its workings, from the operation of the Council of Ministers to that of the European Central Bank....it will be difficult for us to win arguments about how the growth and stability pact and the ECB should operate, and about transparency within the ECB, unless we declare our hand and say that we intend to join the euro.[80]

These political considerations explain why today Britain has not decided to adhere to the single currency and why New Labour has adopted such a cautious discourse. Recently three other factors might also have contributed to influencing its rhetoric. Firstly, the refusal to join monetary union seems to have been justified by Britain's economic figures: the UK economy has grown faster than those of the euro-zone countries since 1997. Secondly, under the premiership of Tony Blair, the conduct of the Iraq war created a less favourable context to promote Britain joining the single currency: on the one hand, it undermined the trust of the British and of a great number of Labour MPs in the Prime Minister, on the other hand, it brought to the fore deep disagreements between the UK, France and Germany. Thirdly, since France and the Netherlands voted against the European Constitution in May and June 2005, the EU crisis has not encouraged New Labour to open up a constructive debate on the single currency in the UK.

3. Changing discourses on the single currency?

This paper shows that differences remain when we compare the discourses of the Conservatives and Labour on the single currency.

Firstly, the discourse of the Labour governments, and more precisely of the Blair governments, on the single currency has been much more positive and constructive than that of the Major government. Between 1992 and 1997, the Conservatives were very critical of EMU and they particularly adopted a more sceptical tone after "Black" Wednesday, refusing to take any measures to prepare Britain for the possibility of a single currency. In contrast, New Labour's approach and tone have been more positive. Thus, the Blair governments participated fully in the launch of the single currency during the British Presidency of the EU, took numerous steps to help Britain and British companies to prepare for entry, and tried to build a pro-European and pro-euro consensus in Britain. Since Gordon Brown succeeded Tony Blair, he has remained rather silent on this issue and maybe seemed less positive but in July 2007 he clearly said he was "pro-European" and insisted on the importance of economic reform in the EU.[81] More time would be needed to define the rhetoric of the Brown government on the single currency.

Secondly, New Labour has had a clearer and more coherent discourse on the single currency: so far this issue has exposed fewer divisions in the

Labour Party than in the Conservative Party. If some tensions could sometimes be noticed, they were at least less obvious than those existing under Major since the Blair and Brown leaderships have done their best to limit dissent within the party. Thus, few debates on the euro have been organized in the Cabinet or in Parliament since 1997. The latest debate took place on July 10th, 2003 following the publication of the conclusions of the five tests. On that occasion, most of the Labour MPs who were allowed to speak were pragmatists.[82] Despite these internal tensions, one should note that only a minority of MPs are opposed to the euro within the Labour Party, and that most Labour parliamentarians support the cautious attitude of the Blair and Brown governments.

Thirdly, the discourses of the Conservatives and Labour on the euro have implied two different lines of action even if they have both officially insisted on the meeting of economic conditions and on economic convergence. Regarding the Conservatives, they laid stress on the importance of the Maastricht criteria, but they were eager above all to preserve Britain's national autonomy and parliamentary sovereignty. Therefore, even if the economic conditions had been met, it is highly unlikely that the Major government would have decided to support Britain joining monetary union at its launch, especially as the Conservatives were still badly scarred by the humiliating experience of sterling's ejection from the ERM. This interpretation has been confirmed by the evolution of the Conservatives' rhetoric on the euro since 1997: since their election defeat, they have adopted a more sceptical discourse on this issue, and declared their outright opposition to a single currency. By contrast, the Labour governments have been much more favourable to Britain entering monetary union and their intention to join has been real, and was particularly genuine during the first two Blair governments (as already mentioned, Labour have become rather silent on this issue since 2004). Thus, they have played down the constitutional issues, insisting that for Labour there were no overriding constitutional obstacles to Britain joining the euro–as shown by their decision to hand control of interest rates over to the Bank of England in May 1997. If their official discourse has been subject to the meeting of five economic conditions, their informal discourse has been quite different since it has been based on the will to wait for the right political context to hold a referendum. Consequently, the Labour Party's position has been more flexible and their policy options more open since they could have made a decision to join the single currency at any time.

In spite of these differences, one cannot say that the Blair and Brown governments have differed markedly from the previous Conservative government. A change in tone has been noticeable but the more positive and constructive discourse has not led to any concrete commitment in favour of the single currency. In fact, the discourses of the Conservatives and Labour on the single currency have been determined by the same factors. As regards the Major government, its rhetoric was much influenced by the Euro-sceptical wing of the Conservative party, particularly vehement after Britain's exit from the ERM. Regarding the Blair and Brown governments, they have adopted a very cautious discourse owing to several factors, such as the intra-party tensions on the euro, the Euroscepticism of the electorate and of the British press, election/re-election concerns, or the more Euro-sceptical attitude of the Tories. In both cases, the party leaderships tried to adopt a conciliatory tone in order to placate internal dissent and to keep their party united. Their discourse was consequently essentially determined by domestic political factors, by the domestic context, rather than by economic reasons–which can seem rather paradoxical concerning such an issue as the single currency.

Conclusion

In conclusion, one cannot say that the discourses of the Major and the Blair and Brown governments on the single currency were similar even if both resulted in Britain's exclusion from monetary union. Not only have the Labour governments adopted a more constructive and clearer discourse but their intention to join has also been real: they would have joined the euro if it had been to the political advantage of New Labour to do so; this was particularly true during the first two Blair governments. Nevertheless, since the 1980s the discourse of all British governments on the single currency has been influenced/determined by the same factors, by the same domestic obstacles, i.e., internal dissent, the Euroscepticism of the British electorate and of the British press..... This explains why British governments have never been able to adopt a very enthusiastic tone towards this issue. British governments will only be willing to promote European interests when they coincide with those of Britain and those of their political parties: they will never be ready to jeopardize the survival/credibility of their parties by adopting too positive a discourse on European monetary initiatives.

Bibliography

Austin, Tim. *The Times Guide to the House of Commons–May 1997.* London: Times Book, 1997.

Baker, David and Seawright David. "The British Conservative and Labour Parties and Europe: Euro-positive, Eurosceptic or Euro-exit?" Colloquium (*Le Royaume-Uni et la construction européenne*) organised by the University of Orléans (France), November 24-25, 2000.

Berbéri, Carine. *Le Parti travailliste et les syndicats face aux questions monétaires européennes.* Paris : L'Harmattan, 2005.

Conservative Party. "The Best Future for Britain." *1992 General Election Manifesto.* 1992.

Denman, Roy. *Missed Chances: Britain and Europe in the 20th Century.* London: Cassel, 1996.

Driver, Stephen and Martell Luke. *New Labour.* Cambridge: Polity, 2nd ed., 2006.

Forster, Anthony. *Euroscepticism in Contemporary British Politics. Opposition to Europe in the Conservative and Labour Parties since 1945.* London: Routledge, 2002.

Gamble Andrew and Kelly Gavin. "The British Labour Party and Monetary Union." *West European Politics*, 23(1) (2000): 1-25.

Garnett, Mark and Lynch Philip. *The Conservatives in Crisis. The Tories after 1997.* Manchester: Manchester University Press, 2003.

Geddes, Andrew. *Britain in the European Union.* Tisbury: Baseline, 2nd ed., 1999.

George, Stephen. *An Awkward Partner–Britain in the European Community.* Oxford: Oxford University Press, 1989.

HM Treasury. *Third report on Euro Preparations.* November 1999.

—. "Housing, consumption and EMU." *EMU study.* 2003.

House of Commons Library. *The euro: background to the five economic tests.* Research Paper 03/53, 4 June 2003.

—. *The Euro-zone: The early years & UK Convergence.* Research Paper 02/45, 16 July 2002.

—. *The Euro-zone: Year One.* Research Paper 00/34, 27 March 2000.

Labour Party (NEC). *Labour in Europe.* 30 October 1991.

Labour Party. "Meet the Challenge. Make the Change, A New Agenda for Britain." *Final Report of Labour's Policy Review for the 1990s.* 1989.

New Labour. "Because Britain deserves better." *Labour Manifesto.* May 1997.

—. "Britain forward not back." *Labour Party Manifesto.* 2005.

Peston, Robert. *Brown's Britain*. London: Short Books, 2006.

Pym, Hugh and Kochan Nick. *Gordon Brown–The First Year in Power*. London: Bloomsbury, 1998.

Radice, Giles. *Offshore. Britain and the European Idea*. London: I. B. Tauris, 1992.

Robinson, Geoffrey. *The Unconventional Minister. My Life Inside New Labour*. London: Michael Joseph, 2000.

Scott, Derek. *Off Whitehall. A View from Downing Street by Tony Blair's Adviser*. London: I. B. Tauris, 2004.

Seldon, Anthony. *The Blair Effect. The Blair Government 1997-2001*. London: Little, Brown, 2001.

Sergeant, John. *Maggie: Her Fatal Legacy*. London: Macmillan, 2005.

Seyd, Patrick, Whiteley Paul and Parry John. *Labour and Conservative Party Members 1990-1992: Social Characteristics, Political Attitudes and Activities*. Aldershot: Dartmouth, 1996.

Stephens, Philip. *Politics and the Pound–The Tories, The Economy and Europe*. London: Papermac, 1997.

Thatcher, Margaret. *The Downing Street Years*. London: Harper Collins, 1993.

Whitton, Timothy. *Le New Labour: Rupture ou continuité?* Rennes: Presses Universitaires de Rennes, 2000.

Young, Hugo. This Blessed Plot. Britain and Europe from Churchill to Blair. London: Papermac, 2nd ed., 1999.

Notes

[1] Tony Blair, "Making the case for Britain in Europe", speech to the London Business School, 27 July 1999. (http://www.guardian.co.uk/)

[2] One should not forget that Labour governments were associated with most devaluations of the pound in the twentieth century and Labour's inability to avoid devaluation in 1931, 1949, 1967 and 1976 really harmed its reputation for economic competence.

[3] *House of Commons Debates*, 29/6/1989, vol. 155, col. 1180.

[4] Philip Stephens, *Politics and the Pound* (London: Papermac, 1997) 50.

[5] John Sergeant, *Maggie* (London: Macmillan, 2005) 97-98; Margaret Thatcher, *The Downing Street Years* (London: Harper Collins, 1993) 722. Even if different interpretations of this event can be noticed, it seems that Margaret Thatcher could no longer resist John Major's wish to go into the ERM at that time.

[6] Although Margaret Thatcher had refused to be part of the ERM since 1979, Nigel Lawson had argued for British membership (to ensure greater monetary stability in the EU).

[7] *House of Commons Debates*, 22/11/1990, vol. 181, col. 451.

[8] If found more attractive by market forces than national currencies, the hard ecu would have replaced the national currencies and become a single currency.

[9] John Major, *House of Commons Debates*, 20/11/1991, vol. 199, col. 272.

[10] *House of Commons Debates*, 21/11/1989, vol. 162, col. 17.

[11] Labour Party, *Meet the Challenge. Make the Change*, 14.

[12] Labour Party (NEC), *Labour in Europe*, October 30, 1991, 6-12.

[13] Neil Kinnock, *House of Commons Debates*, 11/12/1991, vol. 200, cols. 862-3.

[14] Hugo Young, *This Blessed Plot*, (London: Papermac, 2nd ed., 1999) 459.

[15] "The Best Future for Britain", *1992 Conservative Party General Election Manifesto*.

[16] *Ibid.*

[17] *The Economist*, September 25, 1993 (quoted by Roy Denman, *Missed Chances: Britain and Europe in the 20th century*, 273).

[18] Stephens, *op. cit.,* 322; "Fighting to the finish", *The Economist*, February 11, 1995, 37-38.

[19] *House of Commons Debates*, 12/12/1994, vol. 251, col. 618.

[20] *Ibid.*, 1 March 1995, vol. 255, cols. 1068-1069.

[21] "Conservative Manifesto" in Tim Austin, ed., *The Times Guide to the House of Commons–May 1997* (London: Times Book, 1997) 356.

[22] John Major had begun to think about this idea during the autumn of 1994, but the decision to hold a referendum on the single currency was only taken in April 1996.

[23] One should mention that the pound had been locked into the system at probably too high a rate against the German currency-a central rate of DM2.95 had been fixed-and this was catastrophic for sterling: the Conservative government found it quite difficult to maintain sterling's parity in mid-1992, particularly after the Danish electorate had voted in June to reject the Maastricht treaty. Indeed, this event which called into question the progress to EMU also endangered the stability of the ERM and the established ERM parities.

[24] *House of Commons Debates*, 24/9/1992, vol. 212, col. 42.

[25] *Ibid.*, col. 74.

[26] Stephens, *op. cit.*, 300-301.

[27] These internal tensions could not be ignored by the leadership of the party owing to the Conservatives' reduced Commons majority after the 1992 General Election. Even after John Major had decided to resign as leader of the Conservative Party on June 25, 1995 and won the new leadership election, his victory was not decisive enough to enable him to disregard the pressures from the sceptics for a more sceptical line over the single currency.

[28] Patrick Seyd *et al.*, *Labour and Conservative Party Members 1990-1992*, (Aldershot: Dartmouth, 1996) 11; David Baker *et al.*, "The British Conservative and Labour Parties and Europe: Euro-positive, Eurosceptic or Euro-exit?" in *Le Royaume-Uni et la construction européenne*, Colloquium (*Le Royaume-Uni et la construction européenne*) organised by the University of Orléans (France), November 24-25, 2000, 126-127.

[29] Barry Legg, *House of Commons Debates*, 13/2/1995, vol. 254, col. 743.

[30] *Ibid.*, 9/12/1993, vol. 234, cols. 551-2. (Barry Legg)

[31] Stephens, *op. cit.*, 311.

[32] David Baker *et al.*, *op. cit.* , 121.

[33] Peter Temple-Morris, *House of Commons Debates*, 24/11/1992, vol. 214, col. 790.

[34] Ray Whitney, *House of Commons Debates*, 24/9/1992, vol. 212, col. 83.

[35] See "Major's right", *The Economist*, July 1, 1995, 30-31, or the ICM polls (www.icmresearch.co.uk).

[36] Since 1994 (since Tony Blair's election as leader of the party) the Labour Party has been known as "New Labour" to highlight the modernisation of Labour Party policy.

[37] New Labour, "because Britain deserves better", *Labour Manifesto*, May 1997, 37-38.

[38] The Chancellor would continue to set the inflation target, but the Monetary Policy Committee of the Bank would have responsibility for setting interest rates to keep inflation to that target (i. e. within 1% either side of 2.5%). Gordon Brown, "Chancellor's Statement to the House of Commons on the Bank of England", *House of Commons Debates*, 20/5/1997, vol. 294, cols. 508-511.

[39] Further legislation would yet be necessary at a later stage to give the Bank the full independence required by EMU.

[40] Gordon Brown, "Chancellor's Statement on EMU", *House of Commons Debates*, 27/10/1997, vol. 299, col. 584.

[41] *Ibid.*, col. 586.

[42] *Ibid.*

[43] Speech by Tony Blair to a Lunch for French Business organised by "Les Echos", Paris, 15 November 1996. Tony Blair, "A modern Britain in a modern Europe", speech to the Annual Friends of Nieuwspoort Dinner, The Ridderzaal, The Hague, Netherlands, 20 January 1998. (http://www.number-10.gov.uk/)

[44] Tony Blair, "Blair's Euro Statement", *House of Commons Debates*, 23/2/1999, vol. 326, col. 179.

[45] Gordon Brown, "Chancellor's Statement on EMU", *House of Commons Debates*, 27/10/1997, vol. 299, col. 587.

[46] http://www.euro.gov.uk

[47] Tony Blair, "Blair's Euro Statement", *House of Commons Debates*, 23/2/1999, vol. 326, col. 183.

[48] Tony Blair, "A modern Britain in a modern Europe", Speech to the Annual Friends of Nieuwspoort Dinner, The Ridderzaal, The Hague, Netherlands, 20 January 1998. (http://www.number-10.gov.uk/)

[49] *House of Commons Debates*, 7/2/2001, vol. 362, col. 918.

[50] Gordon Brown, "Statement by the chancellor on UK membership of the single currency", *House of Commons Debates*, 9/6/2003, vol. 406, cols. 414.

[51] The Retail Price Index excluding mortgage interest payments was replaced by the Harmonized Index of Consumer Prices, a better measure which is used by most other countries in Europe.

[52] More than 60% of British mortgages are variable rate and the rest are on short-term fixed rates.

[53] Gordon Brown, "Statement by the chancellor on UK membership of the single currency", *House of Commons Debates*, 9/6/2003, vol. 406, col. 411.

[54] HM Treasury, "Housing, consumption and EMU", *EMU study*, 2003, p. 2, p. 4. Faisal Islam, "Getting on with Europe like a house on fire", *The Observer*, May 25, 2003.

[55] Gordon Brown, "Statement by the chancellor on UK membership of the single currency", *House of Commons Debates*, 9/6/2003, vol. 406, col. 415.

[56] New Labour, "Britain forward not back", *2005 Labour Party Manifesto*, 84.

[57] In October 2007 Gordon Brown finally refused to hold a referendum on the EU treaty, saying that the debate would be conducted in Parliament.

[58] See, for example, the Downing Street Press Conference of July 23, 2007. (http://www.number-10.gov.uk/)

[59] During this period, the difference between Britain's short-term interest rates and those of the euro zone had narrowed (falling from 3.7% in 1997 to 0.75% in 2001). Besides, the UK had met four of the five convergence criteria laid out in the Maastricht Treaty, whether they referred to price stability, general government deficit, public debt or long-term interest rates. The only criterion it did not meet was that concerning ERM membership.

[60] See, for example, Derek Scott (Blair's former top economic adviser), *Off Whitehall*, (London: I. B. Tauris, 2004) 17. This was also mentioned by Stephen Wall, the Prime Minister's Europe Adviser, at a colloquium in Paris ("Le Royaume-Uni et l'Union Européenne depuis 1997", *Colloquium organised by Paris III University on June 9-10, 2006*).

[61] Quoted in Andrew Geddes, *Britain in the European Union*, (Tisbury: Baseline, 2nd ed., 1999) 65.

[62] Quote from a Labour insider (mentioned in Hugh Pym and Nick Kochan, *Gordon Brown*, (London: Bloomsbury, 1998) 136.

[63] Translated from French. See: Phyllis Starkey, "New Labour de l'intérieur" in Timothy Whitton, ed., *Le New Labour: Rupture ou continuité ?*, (Rennes: Presses Universitaires de Rennes, 2000) 40.

[64] Hugh Pym and Nick Kochan, *op. cit.*, 134-146.

[65] Derek Scott, *op. cit.*, 3. Hugo Young, "If Tony goes for the euro, Gordon will back him", *The Guardian*, November, 22, 2001.

[66] See for example: Philip Lynch, "The Conservatives and Europe, 1997-2001" or Ian Taylor, "The Conservatives, 1997-2001: a party in crisis?" in Mark Garnett and Philip Lynch, eds., *The Conservatives in Crisis*, (Manchester: Manchester University Press, 2003) 146-163, 229-247.

[67] Tony Blair, "The new Challenge for Europe", Speech at a ceremony to receive the Charlemagne prize, Aachen, Germany, 13 May 1999. (http://www.number-10.gov.uk/)

[68] Andrew Rawnsley, "Haven't we been here before?", *The Observer*, July 29, 2001. Scott, *op. cit.*, 219.

[69] Philip Stephens, "The Treasury under Labour" in *The Blair Effect*, edited by Anthony Seldon, (London: Little, Brown, 2001) 201.

[70] Hugh Pym and Nick Kochan, *op. cit.*, 139. Geoffrey Robinson, *The Unconventional Minister*, (London: Michael Joseph, 2000) 123-124.

[71] Gordon Brown, "Statement by the chancellor on UK membership of the single currency", House of Commons Debates, 9/6/2003, vol. 406, col. 409.

[72] Robert Peston, *Brown's Britain*, (London: Short Books, 2006) 188.

[73] Bill Rammell, *House of Commons Debates*, 21/7/1998, vol. 316, cols. 997-8.

[74] Mike Gapes, *House of Commons Debates*, 11/6/1998, vol. 313, cols. 1256-7.

[75] See: "Euro referendum", *Early Day Motion 1301*, 14 May 2002; "British membership of the Euro", *Early Day Motion 903*, 24 March 2004.

[76] John Cryer, *House of Commons Debates*, 25/5/1999, vol. 332, cols. 205-206.

[77] Kelvin Hopkins, *House of Commons Debates*, 10/7/2003, vol. 408, col. 1470.

[78] See: "Performance of the euro", *EDM 514*, January 14, 2003; "Performance of the euro", *EDM 1080*, 14 April 2003; "Performance of the euro", *EDM 834*, 4 March 2005.

[79] Andrew Gamble and Gavin Kelly, "The British Labour Party and Monetary Union", *West European Politics*, 23(1), 2000, 14-15.

[80] Chris Bryant, *House of Commons Debates*, 10/7/2003, vol. 408, cols. 1451-2.

[81] See the Downing Street Press Conference of July 23, 2007. (http://www.number-10.gov.uk/)

[82] *House of Commons Debates*, 10/7/2003, vol. 408, cols. 1469-1471.

CHAPTER FIVE

THE CHANGING AMERICAN DISCOURSE ON GENDER AT THE UNITED NATIONS

FATMA RAMDANI

Introduction

In the United States, between 1980 and 1992, the lobbying exercised by two different special interest social movements, the American feminist movement and the social conservatives of the Christian Right[1], had a tremendous impact on the platforms of the Democratic and Republican parties. As far as the gender issue is concerned, these two parties have since then adopted diametrically opposite positions. The 1992 presidential campaign exemplified this political divide by staging the sustained mobilization of pro-life and pro-choice groups.[2]

At around the same time, the United Nations were organizing a series of international conferences. Two conferences in the 1990s, the third population conference in Cairo in 1994, and the fourth women's conference in Beijing in 1995 are of special interest for the purpose of this article because they embody the exportation of the American political and ideological divide into the United Nations. Since these two conferences, the American liberal Left and conservative Right, through the help of their respective alliances, have been waging a rhetorical fight in the global arena by playing on the frequently ambiguous terms used at the UN. Their ultimate goal is to convey and give more legitimacy to their respective ideologies on gender issues, both at national and international levels.

To better understand the influence of the United States in the gender discourse at the United Nations, a historical perspective on population and development issues is essential. An analysis of the discourse promoted by the American Left under Clinton at the two conferences mentioned above will constitute the second part of this article. It will mainly be demonstrated what factors and actors enabled such a discourse and how the concepts advocated by the liberal Left at these conferences marked the emergence of the activism from the Christian Right in the international arena. Since Cairo and Beijing, the American Christian Right has adopted a new discourse on feminism and women's rights which is in total opposition with the discourse promoted by a more moderate American Right in the mid-seventies.

Historical perspective

Development issues have become increasingly prominent on the UN agenda since the 1960s. Through the impetus of the United States, the United Nations launched the UN decades of development. The United Nations conferences on population and on women were organized within this development framework. Starting in the early seventies, under the impetus of the American Republican administration, UN members came to realise that women were a key factor in their development solutions.

At the first United Nations conference on population, in Bucharest in 1974, the United States tried with much difficulty to get a consensus on population issues. Concerned about the adverse effects of overpopulation on the environment, on international peace and world development, the United States advocated an urgent curb on population growth. The discourse they tried to promote was that rapid population increase constituted a serious impediment to development. Family planning programmes were urgently needed to solve the population problem.[3] In Bucharest, the United States' basic position was that population programmes were not a substitute for development but were a proper and integral part of development.[4] The NSSM 200, a report mandated by President Nixon to the National Security Council in 1974, linked American economic and security interests to population issues.[5] American demographers, who had already been influential in promoting population control at the United Nations, had helped to set up the UNFPA (United Nations Fund for Population Activities) in 1969. In 1974, they had finally succeeded in convincing their government to adopt a neo-Malthusian approach to population issues. However at Bucharest, the American discourse on these population issues was fiercely attacked by developing countries. The G77 group, the then majority bloc in the United Nations, demonstrated its new political strength by developing a new discourse. This increasingly powerful political bloc asserted that population problems were not a cause but a consequence of underdevelopment. The leader of the Indian delegation stated that development was the best contraceptive, whereas the Chinese delegate pointed out that "the primary way of solving the population problem lies in combating the aggression plunder of the imperialists... and particularly the superpowers."[6] However, we can consider that the United States marked a slight victory since they managed to persuade some third-world countries to adopt population control policies.

One year later, in 1975, the first United Nations women's conference organized in Mexico helped the United States to promote and impose their vision of population and development issues. This conference provided them with a two-fold opportunity. It mainly enabled them to give international legitimacy to their family planning programmes. It also helped them counter-attack the vision promoted by the G77, who viewed the establishment of a new world order as a prerequisite for the equality of women. In Mexico, by underscoring the shared problems of women in the world, the United States aimed to embark the G77 in their population and development discourse. The American message at the first United Nations conference on women was that population issues, the status of women, and their integration were inextricably linked.

> Equality without development means shared misery and frustration. Development without equality may mean a worsened situation for many women. ... And the full, equal participation of women in the development process can make a difference between success and failure of development itself.[7]

In Mexico, the Republican administration of Gerald Ford made women's equality an essential tool of American foreign policy. On January 9, 1975, when signing Executive Order 11832 establishing the National Commission on the Observance of International Women's Year[8], President Ford stated that the promotion of women's status was dedicated to the achievement of the highest potential for each human being. All the American speeches for the conference conveyed the same message: that women's rights were essential for the settling of international problems.

> The integration of women in development is a direction, an affirmative action which touches on the overall question of international economic and political stability.[9]

In Mexico, the United States managed to advance their agenda one step further. By using family planning as a strategy to raise women's status and thus achieve development, they were also successful in promoting the population policies they had been advocating since the mid sixties.

Family planning, whether in terms of women's ability to space pregnancies
or limit excessive births, is a major means towards fuller participation in
economic, social, and political life.[10]

At this first United Nations conference on women, the United States'
co-sponsored a resolution entitled "Family Planning and the full
integration of women in development" which gained the support of the
133 countries attending the conference. The world plan of action, which is
the official conference document setting a number of guidelines to
improve the status of women at national and international levels, was
adopted by consensus in its entirety. Except for some reservations from the
Vatican, even paragraph 142 of this world plan of action of Mexico[11]
which stipulated that "individuals and couples should have access, through
an institutionalized system, to the information that will enable them to
determine freely and responsibly the number and spacing of their
children...," did not trigger any controversy.

Undoubtedly, in the mid-seventies, the improvement of the status of
women helped the American Right under President Ford to promote its
population and development discourse in the UN arena. Such a stance was
facilitated by a group of activist Republican feminists, such as Jill
Ruckleshaus (Presiding Officer of the National Commission on the
Observance of International Women's Year) or Margaret Heckler
(Republican House Representative from Massachusetts and Chairwoman
of ERAmerica) who acted as official delegates at the Mexico conference.
These Republican women activists on women's issues managed to lobby
and to get the endorsement of their administration on key issues, like
reproductive rights and the ratification of the ERA (Equal Right
Amendment).[12] It is also worth noticing that some of the strongest
supporters of family planning were not only Republicans, but were right-
to-life Republicans who believed that family planning programmes were
the answer to the tragic need for abortion.[13] Thus, in the mid-seventies, the
Republican party under President Ford was at the centre of the framing of
gender policies in the United Nations.

Twenty years later, the United States was again exercising a leadership
role in the framing of the population discourse at the United Nations, in
particular at the third world population conference in Cairo in 1994 and at
the fourth United Nations conference on women in Beijing in 1995. Under
the Democratic presidency of Bill Clinton, new concepts such as
reproductive health, access to safe abortion, women's empowerment and
gender mainstreaming were integrated into the world plan of action
stemming from these conferences. For the Democratic administration, the
world would never be the same after Cairo.[14] So as to better analyse the

discourse advocated by the American liberals in the UN arena in this post Cold War era, a brief overview of the underlying socio-historical factors which helped the emergence of such a discourse is needed.

The American Left's discourse in the United Nations

In the United States, in the 1992 presidential elections, the gender gap contributed to Bill Clinton's victory. Twelve years of conservative policies under the Reagan and Bush presidencies had constituted a continuous threat to women's rights. The non-ratification of the ERA, the appointment of conservative Supreme Court judges and the progressive erosion of the Roe *vs* Wade case were some of the many examples of this. The backlash reached its peak during the 1992 election campaign when Pat Robertson vilified women and demonized feminists as witches at the Republican convention in Houston in August.[15] A majority of women favoured Bill Clinton's pro-choice agenda; that and his plan for welfare reform provided him victory with an 8 point advantage.[16]

At the international level, two other factors must also to be taken into account as far as women's status was concerned. First, the neo-liberal economic policies combined with the structural adjustments had frequently had adverse effects on the status of women. These two factors contributed to putting a heavier burden on women both in the North and the South, making the feminization of poverty a reality of this post Cold War era. Secondly, the abuses of human rights through the quantitative-targeted population policies, such as compulsory abortion or sterilization policies, brought the health hazard consequences for women to the fore.[17]

In 1994, the United Nations organized the third conference on population and development. As the first major international conference on population issues since the beginning of the Clinton administration, this conference was seized as the opportunity to present American priorities and directions. As the sole remaining superpower, the Democratic administration pledged a strong commitment to promote an international consensus around stabilizing population growth and called for a comprehensive approach built around three priorities: development, environment, and women's rights. In this post Cold War era, population growth and its adverse effect on the environment and on women's health, as well as the alleviation of poverty were the top priorities set by the Clinton administration. Its position was that the experience of the past ten years had brought the world to a realization that the only way to bring about equality, development and peace was to empower women by integrating them into the mainstream where they could work in partnership with men in all levels and structures of societies.[18] President Clinton's UN agenda embraced a two-fold challenge which consisted in tackling the problems neglected during the Cold War era and in legitimizing the pro-choice issue in the international arena. The involvement of American NGOs in the framing of American policy at the United Nations was used as the ultimate tool to promote the approach advocated by the Democratic administration on population issues. The involvement of American civil society would also help the United States export its model of democracy to the rest of the world.

A holistic approach to population issues

Under President Bill Clinton, population policies were articulated through a holistic approach to women's needs and rights. Two main areas of concern were underscored. Population issues embraced a human rights perspective, with special attention given to women's health. The message conveyed at Cairo PrepCom3 (preparatory committee for the conference) by Timothy Wirth, the then American Under Secretary of Global Affairs was revealing:

> Women's empowerment, rights and well-being are central to achieving population and sustainable development goals, and are top priorities for the Clinton administration.

Reproductive health and sexual health issues, including HIV/AIDS and other sexually transmitted diseases, reproductive rights, unsafe abortion, unwanted pregnancies, condom and contraceptive use were main components of the life-span health approach advocated by the Clinton administration. These were also considered as key components of global security and social well-being. To justify such an agenda, the administration relied upon a set of statistics to show the urgency of the effects of global issues on American security: the tripling of global population by the next century, the global pandemic of AIDS, the 500,000 women who died due to inadequate access to maternal health-care, contraception and safe abortion.[19] As Hillary Clinton stated in the message she delivered at the fourth United Nations conference on women in Beijing in September 1995, investing in the health of girls and women was as important as investing in the development of free markets and trades.

So let us now draw some preliminary conclusions. Just like President Ford twenty years earlier, President Bill Clinton was strongly committed to population issues. Both President Ford in 1975 and President Clinton in 1995 thought that population issues urgently needed to be addressed. Both put a particular emphasis on women's rights. Without women's empowerment, no sustainable development could be achieved. One noticeable difference, however, is that President Clinton's stance was articulated on a more comprehensive approach and gave particular attention to women's well-being. Such was the message conveyed by Hillary Clinton in her speech "Women's rights are human rights and human rights are women's rights" at Beijing in 1995:

> ... if women are healthy and educated, their families will flourish. If women are free from violence, their families will flourish. If women have a chance to work and earn as full and equal partners in society, their families will flourish. And when families flourish, communities and nations will flourish.

Women's rights and needs were then viewed as key solutions to population and development issues. However, the Clinton administration went one step further than the Ford administration as regarding the abortion discourse. In 1975, in Mexico, the American women delegates talked about legalized abortion as a back-up solution to contraceptive methods. They advocated that women, under proper medical advice, should have the right to obtain safe abortion. This would help them not to be subjected to the trauma and risk of clandestine abortions. Almost twenty years later, the abortion discourse was seized upon by the Executive branch itself. In March 1994, the US State Department sent a cable to all diplomatic and consular posts directing them to approach host governments to present American views. This cable stated without any ambiguity that: "The United States believes that access to safe, legal and voluntary abortion is a fundamental right of all women."[20]

Actually, it should be pointed out that just three days after his inauguration, on January 22, 1993, through an executive order, President Clinton overturned the so-called Mexico City policy initiated by Reagan at the second United Nations conference on population in Mexico in 1984. Restrictions that prohibited some family planning organizations from receiving American funding because of abortion-related activities, were thus lifted.[21] President Clinton also promised to reinstate funding for the UNFPA, the key UN population agency. In addition, he asked for an additional $100 million dollars for the American population assistance programmes. Strong support of reproductive choice, including access to safe abortion, was the cornerstone of President Clinton's policy for Cairo. The problem of unsafe abortion was a key health problem and needed to be addressed. Illegal and unsafe abortion was referred to as a human tragedy. Also by citing American teen pregnancy rates and the prevalence of sexually transmitted diseases and their combined impact on women's health, the Clinton administration insisted upon the need to enhance adolescent education about sexuality. Because the Clinton administration wanted to promote its vision on population issues and wanted to put special emphasis on this ideological shift, the American stance on abortion was made clear as of PrepCom2: "Our position is to support reproductive choice, including access to safe abortion."[22]

The American Left's conception of population policies under Bill Clinton consisted in equating access to abortion and sex education to respect for human rights, to every individual's dignity and worth. One can thus infer that such a stance seemed to translate principles into reality. By linking family planning policies to a human rights frame, the United States mainly aimed to show the world that the United States' population programmes condemned all forms of coercion, and thus shielded itself from any accusation of imperialistic motives. During his speech at Cairo, Vice President Al Gore, the American delegation leader, clarified his country's position. While the American Constitution guaranteed women's choice to abortion, the United States was neither seeking to establish a new international right to abortion, nor did they believe that abortion should be promoted as a method of family planning. If we have a closer look at the stance promoted at Cairo by the Clinton administration, we are struck by the commonality with the message conveyed twenty years earlier by the Ford administration.

> I want to be clear about the US position on abortion so that there is no misunderstanding. We believe that making available the highest quality family-planning and health-care services will simultaneously respect women's own desire to prevent unintended pregnancies, reduce population growth and the rate of abortion.

Al Gore's speech echoed President Clinton's message on June 29 when he addressed the National Academy of Sciences in Washington DC.

> Now, I want to be clear about this. Contrary to some assertions, we do not support abortion as a method of family planning... Our own policy is that this should be a matter of personal choice, not public dictation. And, as I have said many times, abortion should be safe, legal and rare.

Both President Clinton and Vice President Al Gore were in fact sending a message to Pope John Paul II, who through an intensive media campaign had embarked on turning the Cairo and Beijing conferences into abortion conferences. Pope John Paul II and other Church leaders feared that the United Nations, through the United States, were aiming to destroy the family and spread a culture of death.[23] They blamed the United States, through American feminist lobbies, for wanting to impose Western-style sexual life styles on the rest of the world, and in particular on developing countries.[24] Indeed, the special observer status of the Holy See enabled Vatican delegates to attend all the preparatory process for Cairo. These Vatican delegates witnessed the contribution of feminist NGOs who successfully lobbied their government delegations to broaden the scope of the population debate so as to include reproductive rights and health issues. President Clinton's promotion of access to safe, legal and rare abortion only reflected the concerns of American and international feminist health organizations. The Clinton administration recognized that NGOs had helped the administration develop its understanding of the quality of care approach.[25] The NGOs' ideas, expertise and their connections to people in every corner of the world had helped the American administration to adopt this new stance on population issues.

NGOs as partners and negotiators

The work of many NGO participants, most of whom had been working hard to make the reality of women's lives part of their government's priorities, culminated in the Cairo world plan of action. The Cairo platform translated into the inseparability of population and sustainable development, the need for gender equity and equality, and the importance of meeting the totality of people's reproductive health needs, including family planning. Women's NGOs succeeded in establishing in UN documents that women's issues were the world's issues. The United States in particular championed the cause of NGOs in the United Nations process and worked in partnership with NGOs from start to finish. This partnership was viewed as necessary to efficiently tackle the policies and actions necessary to remove the obstacles to empowerment that women faced and thus to achieve development. From the very beginning of the preparatory process for Cairo and Beijing, the American Democratic administration emphasized repeatedly and persuasively the need for greater NGOs access to UN conferences.[26] As a result, 1,254 NGOs were accredited to the Cairo conference. These NGOS could attend all the preparatory committees, were offered the opportunity to present their views, to speak at plenary sessions, and were free to circulate their proposals for changes and additions among delegations. At PrepCom2, Timothy Wirth, then Counselor to the US State Department, already stated that:

> We must recognize that women are taking leadership around the world on
> their own behalf and for the benefit of their families, their communities
> and their countries. They know what they need, and they must be equal
> partners in programs and policies.

To better face the concerted backlash generated by the Holy See and the
steady mobilisation of the social conservatives of the Christian Right, one
of the key priorities set by the Clinton administration for Beijing was to
prevent any backsliding from the rights guaranteed at previous
conferences.[27] To maintain the gains acquired at Cairo, key American
prominent feminist leaders, like Bella Abzug (Women's Environment and
Development Organization, WEDO) or Adrienne Germain (International
Women's Health Coalition, IWHC) were given special status in the
American policy framing. Bella Abzug acted as an advisor to the
American delegation and Adrienne Germain attended the Cairo and
Beijing conferences as an official delegate. Giving women access to the
negotiating process constituted an efficient pressure tool on conservative
forces. Already in 1992, Bella Abzug, who was the Executive Director of
WEDO, had initiated a Women's Caucus, an international feminist
lobbying group. She drafted a pledge by almost 200 women's NGOs from
every region of the world. This pledge was used as an advocacy tool
aiming to call on government to the integration of gender perspectives in
all governmental bodies and policy making processes.[28]

In addition, through the impetus of IWHC, in January 1994, feminist
organizations issued a twenty-one-point Rio Statement of "Reproductive
Health and Justice: International Women's Health Conference for Cairo
94", in which around 215 women from 79 countries elaborated strategies
and activities to ensure that women's perspectives and experiences were
considered and acted upon at Cairo. This statement called on national
governments and international agencies to reshape their policies to ensure
women's health and rights were integrated in the international population
discourse. Feminists had argued that women needed a level of control over
their reproductive roles, as often their status in society was connected to
their child bearing and rearing—activities that took the bulk of their
productive years.[29]

So when in the final days of the four-week Beijing PrepCom3 in April
1995, 40 per cent of the Beijing platform for action, including language
already agreed to at previous conferences, was bracketed, the Women's
Caucus reacted promptly. When the Holy See and an alliance of
conservative governments in favour of outlawing abortion required that
the word "gender" be bracketed until a definition that accommodated a
traditional view of women could be agreed upon at the forthcoming

conference, the Women's Caucus drafted a protest statement "Take the Brackets Off Women's Lives" signed by hundreds of women's NGOs. At the April 3 plenary session of PrepCom3, Bella Abzug was allowed to read the protest statement signed by hundreds of women's NGOs. Describing the attempt to censor the word gender as "an insulting and demeaning attempt to reverse the gains made by women", Bella Abzug said that the word gender expressed the reality that women's and men's roles and status were socially constructed and subject to change. She continued by stating that:

> We will not be forced back into the biology is destiny concept that seeks to define, confine and reduce women and girls to the physical sexual characteristics. ... We will not go back to subordinate roles...[30]

Undeniably, the Clinton administration used the United Nations to better impose its population policy. As they included leaders from feminist organizations who could negotiate the language of the UN documents, the United States gave feminist organizations a prominent role in the shaping of American policy in the United Nations. As Timothy Wirth stated before the US Senate, America could thus offer the world one of its best assets: the promotion of the American model of democracy.[31] The executive branch and women's NGOs worked hand in hand so as to give more legitimacy to their claims and ideology. Articulating their claims in the international arena had a double-edged sword effect, however. Indeed, by targeting a larger audience, the discourse articulated by the American liberal Left also reached dissenting voices on the American Right. The Cairo and Beijing Platforms for Action helped these dissenting voices from the Right to eventually organize and mobilize in the international arena. The American conservative Right has since Cairo and Beijing imposed a new discourse on gender, a discourse which is still valid under the George W. Bush presidency.

The discourse promoted by the American conservative Right in the United Nations

The Vatican mobilisation at Cairo, and especially John Pope II's call to all heads of states, made American social conservatives, and in particular pro-life and pro-family NGOs, realize that the United Nations could turn out to be the appropriate forum to counterattack the secular radical feminist agenda they had been trying to combat since the legalization of abortion in 1973 and during the Equal Rights Amendment ratification campaign. The high-profile position of the Vatican at Cairo was a clarion call for Catholics, Protestants and Mormons on the right.[32] Because many members of these American religious denominations were frightened by the progress feminists made during the Cairo process, they considered it necessary to become involved in the international arena. The Pope's call which conveyed their values received an immediate positive response and announced a new era in the American policy framing in the United Nations.

> Even more serious are the numerous proposals for a general recognition of a completely unrestricted right to abortion. ... Indeed, reading this document–which, granted, is only a draft–leaves the troubling impression of something being imposed: namely a lifestyle typical of certain fringes within developed societies, societies which are materially rich and secularized. (The Pope was then referring to the draft version of the Cairo plan of action).[33]

By cooperating with their counterparts in Congress which had a Republican majority in November 1994, and with President George W. Bush since January 2001, these social conservatives from the Right set up a three-fold programme within the United Nations. Their priorities were to combat secular feminist liberalism,[34] give international visibility to their domestic concerns and advance a sustained international pro-family and pro-life agenda. It can thus be asserted that Cairo and Beijing marked the American conservative revolution within the United Nations.

The focus now will be on two concepts–reproductive health and gender. It will be shown how the social conservatives, through the rebuttal of the feminist discourse in its most specific items, built a new discourse at the other end of that promoted by the Ford administration more than twenty years earlier. Its play on the ambiguity of UN talk, its resort to metaphorical and hyperbolic rhetoric and its international network-building are the strategies around which American social conservatives have successfully established their ideology in the United Nations, an ideology which is still prevailing in the international arena. This ideology already existed and was espoused by a number of developing countries.

The publicity around the Vatican's action in Cairo, through its special permanent observer status, aroused the social conservatives' interest in the wording of the United Nations Conferences' world plans of action. The guidelines set up in these word plans of action were then thoroughly scrutinised by the American Christian Right and equated to the agenda promoted at the national Houston feminist conference in 1977 by radical feminist leaders, like Bella Abzug, Betty Friedan and Gloria Steinem.

These women embodied American second wave feminism[35] which prompted the founding of a set of conservative NGOs at the national level and gave rise to what is called the "first conservative revolution" in the United States. President Reagan's victory gained partly through the endorsement of the Christian Right marked a new era in the Republican programme around gender issues.

According to James Dobson, Cairo and Beijing were just stages for the same revolutionaries to make even more outrageous plans for the family. Having Bella Abzug as a special adviser to the American delegation to United Nations conferences was then seen by social conservatives as an overt assault. Referring to the Cairo process, James Dobson writes: "It looked as though the Clinton administration and the radical feminists would spread their revolutionary ideas around the World".[36] He presents American feminist NGOs involved in the preparatory process of Beijing as extremists and expresses his terror at their schemes: "The more I learn about what these radical feminists want to impose on the human family, the more appalled I am ...."

Austin Ruse, Director of the Catholic Family and Human Rights Institute (C-FAM) explains the mobilisation of his organization in the United Nations as an urge to fight the Beijing Platform for Action he considers as being one of "the most radical and dangerous documents you can imagine."[37] Beverly LaHaye from Concerned Women of America argues that in the name of equality, development and peace, the Beijing conference is *"a tax-payer funded promotion of abortion, lesbianism and other left-wing crusades."*[38] This recalls the charges voiced during the preparatory process of the Beijing conference by the social conservatives in Congress. They then considered that the conference was a "waste of taxpayers" money... with a left-wing ideological agenda."[39] They objected to American taxpayers having to pay one-third of the 14 million-dollar conference budget.

Many social conservatives see UN conferences as sneaky ways to bypass the American constitutional process, which requires a majority in both Houses of Congress. By obtaining new gains through consensus at UN conferences, they argue that feminists can then better advance their radical agenda by putting pressure on the federal bureaucracy to implement their policies. The Family Research Council (FRC) claims that their organization got involved in the United Nations because they feared that concepts such as reproductive health were euphemisms for an international right to abortion. It seemed undeniable to them that the Cairo and Beijing world plans of action were just ploys used by radical feminists to introduce a set of norms which over time would become customary international law.[40]

American social conservatives considered that the time was ripe for them "to provide balanced, pro-family input and effectively educate the United Nations' system on moral, religious and other value-based issues."[41] They see their new mission as to counter the one-sided lobbying of American radical feminists, who pressure the United Nations into adopting legal norms that pose serious threats to family stability, parental rights and religious liberty. They also believe that these norms do not represent the ethical religious and cultural values of the majority of the citizens of the United States.

Reproductive health

The American Christian Right considers that pushing for safe abortion as a fundamental universal human right is inconceivable. The unsafe abortion concept is seen as a dangerous and false. Any abortion, including the so-called safe abortion, causes serious physical, emotional and psychological damage to women.[42] Abortion, safe or not, legal or not, takes the life of a human being. The American Christian Right asserts that the human rights' concept is a fallacy, as it denies both the third article of the Human Rights Declaration which stipulates that everyone has the right to life, and the fifth amendment to the American Constitution which states that no person shall be deprived of life. One can therefore argue that despite its disrespect for the United Nations, which it considers to be a dangerous "one-world government", the American Christian Right accepts UN language when it accomodates its values. Another example of this is its reference to the Convention of the Rights of the Child, which makes special provision for parents' rights and responsibilities concerning education and upbringing. Indeed, the American Christian Right also rejects sex education for adolescents, which is seen as a direct attack on parental authority. It claims that such education borders on anti-family propaganda. It is also viewed as promoting promiscuous sexual behaviour and a higher number of births out-of-wedlock. Such a stance enables social conservatives to justify the abstinence programmes they have been promoting at the national level.

In addition, as it considers the foetus as a human being from the point of conception, the American Christian Right compares abortion victims to war victims. A right to abortion is equated to a 21st century genocide. The use of metaphorical suggestions seeks to make an impression on the audience and to appeal to emotions. The polarisation around the abortion issue takes the dimension of religious warfare, a third world war, the cultural and ideological war mentioned by Pat Buchanan in his keynote speech at the August 1992 Republican National convention in Houston, Texas.

> There is a religious war going on in our country for the soul of America. It is a cultural war, as critical to the kind of nation we will one day be as was the Cold War itself.

In 1975, at the first United Nations conference on Women in Mexico, the Ford administration gave priority to the ratification of the ERA and reproductive choice. Women's equality and reproductive rights through access to family planning were seen as prerequisites for development and relevant solutions to demographic explosion. Family planning was then considered the answer to the tragic need for unsafe abortion. Thirty years later, under the George W. Bush presidency, family planning is equated to abortion-access on demand. What began during the Reagan years as a tentative step into the international arena with the goal of curtailing abortions has grown into a major political success under the administration of George W. Bush. With President Bush's arrival at the White House, the American Christian Right has gone one step further in imposing its ideology in the United Nations. On the day following his arrival at the White House, President George W. Bush cut Clinton's policy short and reinstated the Mexico City Policy set up under Reagan at the second World Population Conference at Bucharest in 1984 . His deep conviction is that "... taxpayer funds should not be used to pay for abortions or advocate or actively promote abortion, either here or abroad." On the same day, the National Right to Life Committee applauded the restoration of the Mexico City Policy. For this organisation, the annihilation of the Mexico City Policy by President Clinton, was seen as a "pro-abortion crusade to promote the killing of unborn children, a crusade colliding with the cultural and religious values of many developing countries." In March 2005, Ellen Sauerbrey, the American delegate to the UN Commission on the Status of Women said that the United States did not support abortion in their American health assistance programmes.

In addition, it is worth noticing that the power of the purse gives the United States considerable influence over many international programmes. In 2003 and again in 2005, the American House of Representatives blocked $500 million in international family planning funds destined for the United Nations Population Fund (UNFPA), claiming that the funds would go to China's one child-one-family population policy.[43]

The gender issue

American social conservatives are critical of the Cairo and Beijing world plans of action for disparaging women's central role, that of motherhood. A scrupulous quantitative and semantic analysis of the Beijing platform for action underlines the negative portrayal of motherhood. When the social conservatives from the Right mobilized during the Beijing preparatory process, they pointed out that the thirteen occurrences of the word mother only referred to negative references dealing with single mothers or mothers with the HIV virus. They drew special attention to the word family, in its singular form, which is used only to mention battered women or lack of shared responsibilities in housework. They objected to the many references to the word families used in its plural form, fearing that such a concept promoted lesbianism. They were mainly concerned with the 200 occurrences of the gender concept that Bella Abzug defended so vehemently in the final days of PrepCom3 in April 1995. For social conservatives, such occurrences demonstrate the effective lobbying of radical feminist leaders, trying to impose a theoretical radical gender perspective, in which gender roles are socially constructed rather than inherent and God-given.[44] They are convinced that the hidden notion behind the gender issue is the idea of imposing new normative sexual behaviour. They fear that feminists want to impose their radical scheme which defines a spectrum of five genders (female and male heterosexuals, female and male homosexuals and trans-bisexuals).[45] They thus push for a clear definition of gender as the biological classification of male and female, which are the two sexes of the human-being.

American social conservatives reject the theoretical notion of socially constructed gender because such notion implies that religion is a barrier to women's rights. It also argues that this concept is dangerous because by denying the natural differences between man and woman, it constitutes a direct attack on traditional female roles and marriage. The concept of shared responsibilities within the family is considered as a direct threat to the traditional patriarchal family, by forcing the husband to do the dishes and change diapers. Social conservatives reject the idea that the husband-wife relationship is a mere power play. The concept of gender as a new ideology - a class struggle between man and woman, and the oppression of woman by man and family - is to be rejected. Indeed, they consider that the reproductive role of women is of significant importance to the traditional patriarchal family, to future generations, and to society as a whole. As a consequence, they also equate this concept to the modern and international version of the Equal Rights Amendment and can thus blame it for failing to protect housewives and mothers. In view of the fact that the United States is not listed among the 185 signatories of CEDAW (Convention on the Elimination of all Forms of Discrimination Against Women), an international treaty adopted in 1979 by the UN General Assembly and pushed for under the Clinton administration, one can thus infer that the social conservatives have successfully imposed their discourse relating to the gender issue in the United States

Strategies: from observers to insiders

A national ally: President George W. Bush

Since the Cairo and Beijing conferences, advancing an alternative view of gender and equality in the international arena has become the central focus point of the American Christian Right. Its strategies have proven to be very effective in injecting a new discourse on gender issues in the United Nations. Indeed, social conservatives from the Right have mobilised around an internationally resonant theme, the sanctity of the family, and created alliances between different national denominations, Catholics, Protestants and Mormons. They have also built networks with other pro-family countries, including Islamic countries like Libya, Iran or Syria, which they view as allies to give more weight to their cause.

In 2000, at Beijing+five, Austin Ruse orchestrated the first international conservative mobilisation in the UN arena. He sent a call to his followers, assigning them a biblical mission, using language international religious warfare between the forces of good and evil. "You will work alongside Catholics, Evangelicals, Jews, Muslims and Mormons... We are the children of Abraham arising to fight for faith and family."[46] At that event, American social conservatives, though still in minority, made themselves visible through intimidation campaigns (like surrounding feminist activists and praying for them) and symbolic protests. Delegates distributed flyers, wore red buttons reading "motherhood" and blue buttons reading "Family". They walked about with bibles in their hands and even prayed during some panels.[47]

A few months later, in 2001, President Bush's access to the White House marked the second step in the American Christian Right's mobilization and influence in the United Nations. Social conservatives from the Right were given room in the official delegations and could in turn insert new language. By acting as negotiators and advisors, by hiring young, professional lawyers, American social conservatives' ultimate goal has been to clarify the opaque UN talk. Indeed, defying the Cairo and Beijing platforms has become the major tactic used by the Bush administration at the United Nations. The removal of words like "services", a catchword to express abortion in the American Christian Right's eyes, are attempts to weaken UN recommendations on the right to health.[48]

International networking

By exercising lobbying within UN corridors, American social conservatives have managed to consolidate their alliances with friendly states. Just two years after the Beijing conference, the World Family Policy Center started organizing a series of World Congresses on Families (Prague in 1997, Geneva in 1999, Mexico in 2004 and Warsaw in 2007). The culmination of these conferences resulted in a milestone document for the American Christian Right, the Doha Declaration in 2004. Indeed, ten years after Cairo, on November 29-30, 2004, to commemorate the 10th Anniversary of the 1994 Year of the Family, the American Christian Right successfully managed to coordinate its international efforts through the organization of an international family conference. This conference was attended by more than a thousand delegates in Doha, in Qatar. In 2004, the American Christian Right took the lead in organizing a series of regional conferences around that event. Among the main American sponsors, key pro-life and pro-family organizations, like Catholic Family and Human Rights Foundation, the Family Research Council, the World Family Policy Center, and Brigham Young University coordinated the preliminary discussions, conferences and dialogues. Much of the surveys circulated in Doha relied on social sciences research conducted by American conservative think tank groups. They all aimed to emphasize the consequences of radical feminism on the disintegration of the family unit. American social conservatives could then confirm that the Cairo and Beijing conferences were concerned with lifestyles and not facts.

The Doha Declaration's approval at the General Assembly in December 2004 showed, how in a very relatively short period, in fact in less than ten years, the American Christian Right had managed to figure out how to influence UN policy. It had taken around twenty years for the international feminist movement to achieve the same goal. Austin Ruse explains the consensus rules in a couple of words:

> We don't need them all; we need only a few [member states]... We establish a permanent UN pro-family bloc of twelve states. And upon these we lavish all of our attention.[49]

By aiming to clarify the ambiguous UN talk, the Doha declaration definitely helped the social conservatives impose the discourse advocated since its mobilisation at Beijing. At the December 2004 General Assembly, Assistant Secretary of Health and Human Services Wade Horn spoke on behalf of the United States, noting that "the state's foremost obligation is to respect, defend, and protect the family." Going beyond Article 16 (3) of the Universal of Declaration of Human Rights, which states that family is "the natural and fundamental group unit of society, the Doha Declaration acknowledges that the family is the bedrock of society and "the fundamental agent for sustainable development."[50] This declaration has its limitations. The concept of reproductive health is still enshrined in UN documents and still serves as a reference tool. This probably can partly account for a new strategy adopted by American social conservatives: the defense of developing countries.

Western "imperialism" or defence of developing countries

To enlarge their international base, American social conservatives have taken up the defense of developing countries. As Republican representative Chris Smith once declared "Anti-life strategies which rely on deception and hyperbole...are now being deployed with a vengeance in the developing world." For those who think like him, the new struggle at the United Nations is to save poor countries from being held hostage by radical feminists who have been using the United Nations to impose their ideology.

Another noticeable shift from 1975 to 1995 is the perception of American population assistance programmes. At both Bucharest and Mexico, bilateral American population programmes, distributed through USAID, the American independent agency for foreign economic aid, were compared by developing countries to imperialistic tools and racist measures to assert the supremacy of rich and industrialised countries over poor countries.[51] In 1995, Congress held hearings because American social conservatives, from both inside and outside Congress itself, called for a boycott of the Beijing conference. Ironically, during these hearings, these American social conservatives reiterated the same charges against the American government as the ones put forward by developing countries twenty years earlier. Latin American NGOs testified that American population programmes were mainly enforced in countries listed in the NSSM report.[52] Social conservatives could then argue in turn that population policies aimed to maintain an unequal balance between the South and the North.

The American Christian Right has been conveying the message that American foreign aid is subtle intimidation and blatant corruption of poor countries. The United States is reproached for trading food and loans for liberal values and is thus violating democratic principles by forcing their will upon the poorest countries. [53] Social conservatives from the Right argue that family planning programmes are first and foremost campaigns to impose a radical feminist agenda, a Western imperialist lifestyle.[54] They are convinced that radical American feminists want to replace religious beliefs with a new secular culture.

Concerned Women of America[55] considers that the Beijing Platform for action uses deceptive and subtle verbiage to describe a liberal agenda in terms that would be readily acceptable to many countries and individuals.[56] CWA members attending the Beijing conference accused American delegates at the conference of having pressured developing countries into accepting some wording. They claim that they witnessed American delegates threatening to end American aid if their pro-feminist UN agenda was not supported. Just like the Vatican, the social conservatives stress the need to really tackle development issues. Indeed, since the emergence of the population and development UN discourse, the Vatican has always endeavoured to link the population discourse to a broader context of poverty struggle and global inequality. Just like the Vatican, the American Christian Right draws particular attention to the sexual agenda promoted in Cairo. It is critical of the fact that only nine pages out of the 100-page Cairo official document deal with development issues. It tries to show that this flaw demonstrates that the recommendations set in Cairo are just linguistic exercises to try to hide efforts to destroy traditional moral beliefs on an international level. Consequently, the American Christian Right considers that the population bomb propaganda is just a myth which promotes fallacious data and which denies more recent studies carried out by a new generation of demographers.

> Overpopulation has been used as a Trojan Horse by the Left to advance their assault on the right to life, religious faith and traditional morality.[57]

As a preliminary conclusion, it can be said that social conservatives from the American Right have used exactly the same strategies as American feminists to infiltrate the international organization and impose their discourse: agenda framing, mobilising and networking around a common issue. Mobilising in the United Nations can help them to increase their organizations' political power and grass-roots base in the United States. They can then give more legitimacy to their national claims.

President Bush, just as President Reagan did at the second population conference in Mexico in 1984, has offered them international visibility.

Conclusion

The 1974-1995 United Nations conferences on population and women showed two diametrically opposite visions of gender issues from the American Right and Left. They are also a good illustration of the complete shift of the discourse advocated by the American Right, notably the Republican party, which had been the leading proponent of women's rights in the international arena in the mid-seventies, just before the dawn of the first national conservative revolution marked by the arrival of Ronald Reagan at the White House in 1980.

In the post Cold-War era, the American Left under Bill Clinton took hold of the concepts advocated by the American moderate Right of the mid-seventies on gender issues. However, the liberals infused these issues with a much stronger feminist perspective, and linked women's empowerment, rights and well-being, and in particular women's reproductive health and sexual rights to the population discourse. Concepts like reproductive health have since then been considered by the American Christian Right as euphemisms to prompt the international legalisation of abortion. By becoming involved in the United Nations and playing on the ambiguous UN talk, the aim of the American social Right is to counterattack the feminist agenda. In the United Nations, the Republican administration is no longer fighting for the ratification of the Equal Rights Amendment. It has been promoting an "Equal Right for each innocent life"[58] and has placed family values at the center of its agenda.

This shift in the American discourse on gender issues shows how the UN conferences' world plans of action, though not binding, can turn out to be genuine and effective pressure tools both on the national and international level. By using the United Nations as an alternative space to give more legitimacy to their claims and ideologies, the ultimate goal for both the American Left and Right is to make their national agendas progress. Edward Luck's words in his book entitled *Mixed Messages* (1999) are relevant here. Referring to what most Americans think of the United Nations, he states that:

> What matters, in their view, has less to do with what the organization does around the world than how its words and deeds might affect the outcome of US domestic policy struggles.[59]

Bibliography

Primary Sources

Background Paper for Agenda Item 10, World Conference For International Women's Year, "Various Charges Directed Against US Population Program Assistance to Developing Countries", folder "International Women's Year Conference U.S. Positions Book (1)-(2)", US Statements and Report (2) Files, Box 25, Gerald R. Ford

"Clinton Removes Conditions on AID Family Planning Grants, January 22, 1993", *Foreign Bulletin Policy*, May-June (1993): 48

Committee on International Relations. House of Representatives, "United Nations Fourth World Conference on Women", *Hearings before the Subcommittee on International Operations and Human Rights, July 18, Aug. 2, 1995*, 104th Congress, First Session (Washington DC: US GPO, 1996): 1-261

Position Paper, Item 11, World Conference for International Women's Year, "Population, the Status of Women, and the Role of Women in Development, folder "International Women's Year Conference U.S. Positions Book (1)-(2)", US Statements and Report (2) Files, Box 25, Gerald R. Ford

"United Nations World Conferences", *Hearing before the Committee on Foreign Relations, United States Senate,* 104th Congress, Second Session, June 4, 1996, (Washington DC: US GPO, 1984): 1-96

"US Policy on Population Assistance", *Hearing before the Subcommittee on Census and Population of the Committee on Post Office and Civil Service, House of Representatives,* 98th Congress, Second Session, July 25, 1984, (Washington DC: US GPO, 1984)

US Department of State, "Overview of the Draft Platform For Action as Negotiated at the Final Preparatory Conference for the Fourth World Conference on Women, United States Actions and Priorities", June 1995.
http://dosfan.lib.uic.edu/ERC/intlorg/conference_women/950601.html (26 May 26, 2005)

US Department of State, "The President's Interagency Council on Women, Report to the President from the United States Delegation to the United Nations Fourth World Conference on Women, Beijing, 1995", October 25, 1995.
http://secretary.state.gov/www/picw/archives/oct95.html,   (February 23, 2006)

Wirth, Timothy E. "Statement to the Second Preparatory Committee for the International Conference on Population and Development, United

Nations, New York City, May 11, 1993". *US Department of State Dispatch*, vol. 4, no 22 (May 1993): 397-398

Secondary Sources

Archibald, George. "Defense of Mothers By Senate Wins Praise, Foreign Delegates to Conference Thrilled", *The Washington Times,* August 5, 1995

Bernstein, Carl, and Marco Politi. *His Holiness: John Paul II and the Hidden History of our Time.* London: Doubleday, 1996.

Burk, Martha. "Is Bill Clinton A Feminist?", *The Nation,* 256:5, (February 8, 1993): 154-157

Buss, Doris, and Didi Herman. *Globalizing Family Values: The Christian Right in International Politics.* Minneapolis: University of Minnesota Press, 2003

Butler, Jennifer. "300 Religious Right Participants Attend Beijing PrepCom", June 2001. www.globalpolicy.org/ngos/00deb/beij5-2.htm (29 September 2006)

Chamberlain, Pam, "The Globalization of an Agenda, The Right Targets the UN with its Anti-Choice Politics", *The Public Eye Magazine,* Spring 2006,
www.publiceye.org/magazine/v20n1/chamberlain_globalization.html (3 February 2008)

Crouse, Janice Shaw "Feminism and the Family", World Congress of Families III, March 2004,
www.worldcongress.org/wcf3_spkrs/wcf3_crouse.htm   (February   3, 2008)

CWA (Concerned Women of America), "Feminist Assault on Reasonnables", *The Phyllis Schlafly Report,* 30:5, December 1196, www.eagleforum.org/psr/1996/dec96/psrdec96.html   (November   18, 2005)

CWA (Concerned Women of America), "Feminist Movement on Fast Forward", December 26, 1997,
www.cwfa.org/articledisplay.asp?id=977&department=CWA&categor yid=family (6 April 2006)

Demeney, Paul. "Bucharest, Mexico City, and Beyond", *Population and Development Review,* 11:1 (March 1985): 99-106

Druelle, Annick. "Right-Wing Anti-Feminist Groups at the United Nations, (June 2000): 1-40,
http://netfemmes.cdeacf.ca/documents/Anti-Feminist%20Groups-USLetter.pdf

"FRC Objects to Beijing Conference, A Statement from a Pro-Family Perspective*", *PRNewswire*, August 2, 1995

Finkle, Jason, L. and Barbara B. Crane. "The Politics of Bucharest: Population, Development, and the New International Economic Order", *Population and Development Review*, 1:1 (Sept, 1975): 87-114

Finkle, Jason and Alison McIntosh. "The Cairo Conference on Population and Development: A New Paradigm?", *Population and Development Review*, 21:2 (June 1995): 223-260

IWHC (International Women's Health Coalition), *Reproductive Health and Justice, International Women's Health Conference for Cairo '94, January 24-28, 1994, Rio de Janeiro*, New York: IWHC, 1994

—. "Bush's Other War: The Assault on Women's Sexual and Reproductive Health and Rights", www.iwhc.org/resources/bushsotherwar/index.cfm (July 4, 2006)

Luck, Edward. *Mixed Messages: American Politics and International Organzation, 1919-1999*. Brookings Institution Press: Washington DC, 1999.

Permanent Observer Mission of the Holy See to the United Nations. *Serving the Human Family, The Holy See at the Major United Nations Conferences*. New York City: The Path to Peace Foundation, 1997

"Pro-Family Leader Calls Upon Upcoming UN Women's World Conference Anti-Family, Anti-Women; Focus on the Family to Send Delegation", *PRNewswire*, (July 14, 1995): 1-10

"UN Ambassador Testifies Conference on Women is Crucial; CWA: Madeleine Albreight does not represent Most Women", *PR Newswire,* August 2, 1995

Sen, Gita, Adrienne Germain and Lincoln Chen, eds., *Reconsidering Population Policies: Health, Empowerment, and Rights,* Boston: Harvard University Press, 1994

WEDO (Women's Environment and Development Organization), "Women's Conference Document Dispute", *News and Views*, .8:1-2 (June 1995): 1-16

Notes

[1] I define the social conservatives of the Christian Right in this article as a political movement composed of several religious denominations (Protestants, Catholics and Mormons) acting both in the United States and in the United Nations around an anti-abortion and pro-family agenda. They started becoming a very powerful political force in the 1980s and have since then deeply changed the Republican party agenda on gender issues.

[2] Pro-life and Pro-choice groups are two opposed movements. Pro-life activists are opposed to abortion and maintain that a fetus is a human-being and has thus a right to live. Pro-choice activists contend that the decision of having a child rests upon a woman's choice as it affects her body and health. They do not object to abortion in some circumstances (when the health or life of a mother is in danger or even as a back-up solution when contraception fails).

[3] Jason L. Finkle and Barbara B. Crane, "The Politics of Bucharest: Population, Development, and the New International Economic Order", *Population and Development Review*, 1:1 (Sept, 1975): 90

[4] US Statement by HEW Secretary Weinberger at the Plenary Meeting of the United Nations World Population conference at Bucharest on August 20, 1974

[5] The report NSSM200 was completed and classified confidential in December 1974.

[6] Paul, Demeney, "Bucharest, Mexico City, and Beyond", *Population and Development Review*, 11: 1 (March 1985): 99-100

[7] Statement by Patricia Hutar, Head of the American delegation at Mexico, June 20, 1975, Plenary Session

[8] The main function of the National Commission on the Observance of International Women's Year was to promote the national observance in the United States of International Women's Year and to serve as a coordinating body between the United Nations and the United States.

[9] Statement by Charles Percy, June 23, 1975, Seminar Open Forum on Development Assistance at the NGO forum in Mexico.

[10] Position Paper, Item 11, World Conference For International Women's Year, "Population, the Status of Women, and the Role of Women in Development", 3 (G. Ford Library Archives)

[11] The world plan of action is the official document of the conference. It is a prescriptive outline or blueprint of steps that governments are recommended to implement at the national, regional and international levels.

[12] The Equal Rights Amendment is the name of a proposed amendment to the American Constitution and adopted by American Congress in March 1972. Intended to guarantee equal rights regardless of sex, it was first introduced in Congress by Republicans in 1923. In 1980, President Reagan broke with Republican tradition on the issue and did not support the ERA. The amendment failed ratification following the mobilisation of the Christian Right who favoured protectionist measures for women. Although the ratification period was extended, only 35 states ratified the amendment. Thirty-eight signatures were needed for the ERA to become the 28th Amendment of the American Constitution.

[13] Congressional Hearing, "US Policy on Population Assistance", *Hearing before the Subcommittee on Census and Population of the Committee on Post Office and Civil Service of Representatives*, 98th Congress, 2nd Session, July 25, 1984, (1984): 20

[14] Jason Finkle, Alison McIntosh, "The Cairo Conference on Population and Development: A New Paradigm?", *Population and Development Review*, 21:2 (June 1995): 224

[15] Martha, Burk, "Is Bill Clinton A Feminist ?", *The Nation*, 256:5, February 8, 1993, 54

[16] 45 % of women voted for Clinton against 37 % for Bush, whereas 41 % men voted for Clinton against 38 % for Bush

[17] Gita Sen, Adrienne Germain, and Lincoln Chen, eds. *Reconsidering Population Policies: Ethics, Development and Strategies for Change*, (Boston: Harvard University Press, 1994) 6

[18] US Department of State, "Overview of the Draft Platform For Action as Negociated at the Final Preparatory Conference for the Fourth World Conference on Women, United States Actions and Priorities", June 1995, <http://dosfan.lib.uic.edu/ERC/intlorg/conference_women/950601.html>

[19] Timothy Wirth, "Statement to the Second Preparatory Committee for the International Conference on Population and Development", United Nations, New York City, May 11, 1993

[20] Jason Finkle , McIntosh, Alison., op. cit., (1995): 246

[21] "Clinton Removes Conditions on AID Family Planning Grants, January 22, 1993, *Foreign Bulletin Policy*, (May-June, 1993): 48

[22] Timothy Wirth at PrepCom2, *op. cit.*, (May 11, 1993)

[23] United States Cardinals and Conference President's Letter to President William Clinton on the Cairo Conference, May 29, 1994, in Permanent Observer Mission of the Holy See to the United Nations, *Serving the Human Family, The Holy See at the Major United Nations Conferences,* (New York City: The Path to Peace Foundation, 1997) 787-790

[24] Carl Bernstein and Marco Politi, *His Holiness: John Paul II and the Hidden History of our Time*, (London: Doubleday, 1996), 552

[25] Personal interview with Sarah Covner, 1995 Special Assistant to the Secretary, Department of Health and Human Services, in July 2006 in New York

[26] The President's Interagency Council on Women, "Report to the President from the United States Delegation to the United Nations Fourth World Conference on Women, Beijing, 1995, (October 25, 1995), 6

[27] George Archibald, "Defense of Mothers By Senate Wins Praise, Foreign Delegates to Conference Thrilled, *The Washington Times,* August 5, 1995

[28] WEDO, "Women's Conference Document Dispute", *News and* Views, 8:1-2 (June 1995): 6

[29] IWHC, *Reproductive Health and Justice, International Women's Health Conference for Cairo'94, January 24-28, 1994, Rio de Janeiro,* (New York: IWHC, 1994), 4-7

[30] WEDO, *op.cit.*, (June 1995): 9

[31] Statement of Timothy Wirth before the Committee on Foreign Relations United States Senate, March 25, 1993

[32]Doris Buss, and Didi Herman, *Globalizing Family Values: The Christian Right in International Politics.* (Minneapolis: University of Minnesota Press, 2003)

[33] Letter of His Holiness Pope John Paul II to the World's Head of State, Vatican, 19 March 1994, in Permanent Observer Mission Of The Holy See To The United

Nations, *Serving the Human Family, The Holy See at the Major United Nations conferences*, (New York City: The Path to Peace Foundation, 1997) 200-201
[34] Janice Shaw Crouse, "Feminism and the Family", World Congress of Families III, March 2004,
www.worldcongress.org/wcf3_spkrs/wcf3_crouse.htm (3 February 2008)
[35] Second wave feminism refers to feminist activities from the mid-sixties. The book published by Betty Friedan *The Feminine Mystique* as well as the civil rights movement prompted American women to struggle for their rights. Their main claims were the Equal Rights Amendment and reproductive rights.
[36] Letter sent by James Dobson to more than 2 million American households to express his serious concerns about the Beijing conference (in *NPRNewswire*, July 14, 1995)
[37] Jennifer Butler, "300 Religious Right Participants Attend Beijing PrepCom", June 2001, www.globalpolicy.org/ngos/00deb/beij5-2.htm
[38] "UN Ambassador Testifies Conference on Women is Crucial; CWA : Madeleine Albreight does not represent Most Women", *PR Newswire,* August 2, 1995
[39] Senate majority leader Dole quoted in *Washington Times*, August 31, 1995
[40] Personal interview with Bill Saunders, Human Rights Counsel at the Family Research Council, in August 2006
[41] World Family Policy Center, About WFPC,
www.worldfamilypolicy.org/about.htm (February 3, 2008)
[42] Congressional Hearings, "United Nations Fourth World Conference on Women, July 18, Aug. 2, 1995" (Washington DC: US GPO, 1996): 63
[43] Pam Chamberlain, " The Globalization of an Agenda, The Right Targets the UN with its Anti-Choice Politics", *The Public Eye Magazine,* Spring 2006,
www.publiceye.org/magazine/v20n1/chamberlain_globalization.html
[44] Congressional Hearings, "United Nations Fourth World Conference on Women", *July 18, Aug. 2, 1995, op. cit.,* (1996) 74
[45] "FRC Objects to Beijing Conference, A Statement from a Pro-Family Perspective*", PRNewswire*, August 2, 1995
[46] Butler, *op. cit.*
[47]Annick Druelle, "Right-Wing Anti-Feminist Groups at the United Nations, (June 2000): 13, http://netfemmes.cdeacf.ca/documents/Anti-Feminist%20Groups-USLetter.pdf
[48] International Women's Health Coalition, "Bush's Other War: The Assault on Women's Sexual and Reproductive Health and Rights",
www.iwhc.org/resources/bushsotherwar/index.cfm (4 July 2006)
[49] Austin Ruse as quoted in Jennifer Butler, *op. cit.*
[50]William Saunders, "The Doha Declaration: An International Consensus in Favor Of Marriage And The Traditional Family" (document given by William Saunders at the Family Research Council in Washington, August 2006)
[51] Background Paper for Agenda Item 10, World Conference For International Women's Year, "Various Charges Directed Against US Population Program Assistance to Developing Countries", 3

[52] Congressional Hearings, "United Nations World Conferences", June 4, 1996, (Washington DC: US GPO, 1984): 52

[53] *Ibid.*, 43

[54] *Ibid*, 92

[55] Concerned Women of America is a conservative Christian feminist group founded in 1979 in response to the liberal activities of NOW, the National Organization of Women. It was then one of the leading conservative organisations who lobbied for the defeat of the ERA. With 600,000 members in the mid-nineties, Concerned Women of American claimed to be the largest feminist organization in the US.

[56] Concerned Women of America, "Feminist Movement on Fast Forward", December 26 December 1997, www.cwfa.org/articledisplay.asp?id=977&department=CWA&categoryid=family

[57] Congressional Hearings, "United Nations World Conferences", June 4, 1996, (Washington DC: US GPO, 1984): 50

[58] This is the slogan which has been used by pro-life groups at marches organized each January to protest against the Roe v Wade Supreme Court decision which legalized abortion in the United States in 1973.

[59] Edward Luck, *Mixed Messages: American Politics and International Organization, 1919-1999* (Washington DC: Brookings Institution Press, 1999), 120

PART II:

RELATIONS WITH FORMER COLD WAR PLAYERS

CHAPTER SIX

"FREEDOM, DEMOCRACY AND THE RULE OF LAW": THE DEBATE IN GREAT BRITAIN AROUND THE RETURN OF HONG KONG TO CHINA, 1992-1997

LORI MAGUIRE

On 30 June 1997, Hong Kong, Britain's last major colony, returned to China, marking the effective end of the long history of the British Empire.[1] But the word "return" tells us a great deal about how Hong Kong's fate differed from that of other imperial possessions. All the others had become "independent" and U.K. policy had been to ensure that they received preparation and training in establishing a political system that reflected British values–even if that system did not always last long. Chris Patten, the last governor of Hong Kong, described this process in both admiring and ironic tones:

> Overall, nevertheless, it is not a bad story: men and women infused with the values of 19th century liberalism trying to do their best, installing democracy, training civil servants, policemen and soldiers, establishing independent courts, entrenching civil liberties. In one country after another, the whole constitutional module was wheeled out one sultry southern night, mounted on its launching pad, and, as the midnight hour struck and the brass bands played a baptismal anthem, blasted off into outer space.[2]

But this one-size-fits-all module could not work in the case of Hong Kong for it was being "returned"; there was a "handover" to China–a nation not renowned for its record on human rights. Paradoxically, the civil service, police and independent courts already existed, as did a very real demand for democracy on the part of the population but there were very real fears that these elements would not survive the handover.

Unlike a number of other colonies, Hong Kong had never preoccupied British domestic opinion very much. As John Darwin has noted: "Neither politicians of the day nor historians since have been tempted to argue that possession of Hong Kong was incompatible with Britain's European destiny or the achievement of economic and social modernisation at home."[3] Very little academic work on Hong Kong appeared in the U.K. before the 1980s, and it was largely ignored in the United States and elsewhere.[4] So it only figured significantly in British political discourse at the end of its time as a colony.[5] Debate in Britain about the handover centred on two areas. First, the question of democracy and human rights which preoccupied much of the press and most lawmakers. The other major subject of debate was that of immigration. Because the people of Hong Kong worried about their future under Chinese rule, many of them sought to leave. As the familiar colonial power, Britain was the first choice for many of these and this fact would shape British discourse and policy on the question. Interestingly enough, there was very little difference between the parties on either of these two subjects. With very few dissenting voices, they all agreed on the need to support the reforms of Chris Patten. And, once again with few dissenting voices (but one of these was Michael Howard, Home Secretary from 1993 to 1997) basic agreement existed on immigration policies. Patten summarised the situation in his memoirs:

> If Britain was to deny any moral obligation to Hong Kong that raised issues of race (and this was the real purport of its policy on nationality and passports), it clearly recognized its duty to defend Hong Kong's bonds to the economic and political values that had shaped it and that defined its difference from the rest of China. From the outset in 1982 of its negotiations with China on Hong Kong's future, Britain made plain its commitment to the maintenance of capitalism and freedom in the territory.[6]

Although there was a difference in emphasis between the parties, almost everyone agreed that Britain's last major act of decolonization should be conducted with dignity and honour–which meant bequeathing to Hong Kong a legacy of "freedom, democracy and the rule of law", as Chris Patten put it–whatever China's objections might be.[7]

To begin with, let us briefly examine the history of the return of Hong Kong. Although the United Kingdom had an internationally recognised title to Hong Kong Island and the Kowloon Peninsula, most of the rest of the territory was held under a 99 year lease from China, which expired in 1997. During the premiership of Thatcher, the government realised that they had to tackle the issue of the future of Hong Kong. Given the relative strength of Britain and China at the time, the former had no choice but to negotiate and try to get the best deal possible for its colony. By this time, Deng Xiaoping had embarked on his economic reforms and many people in the West were optimistic about the future of China. They hoped that, as the economy developed so would political liberty. Indeed, the British were, on the whole, satisfied with the Joint Declaration, signed in 1984, that enshrined the concept of "one country, two systems"–Hong Kong would be part of China but as a special administrative region for fifty years and would enjoy considerable independence. This principle was given shape in the Basic Law, promulgated in 1990, which became the constitutional document of Hong Kong after its transfer.

In June 1989 the Chinese government violently repressed pro-democracy demonstrators at Tiananmen Square. The event traumatised much of the population of Hong Kong who, quite understandably, worried about their own future. Numerous protests took place there and strong calls for democracy developed in the colony. Indeed, London had been singularly lax in introducing self-government into Hong Kong: few people possessed the right to vote and all of the colony's governors had been civil servants appointed by London without local consultation. Of course, the British could justify this democratic deficit: chiefly because of their fear of how the Chinese government would react. Still, the British government had declared in 1984 that they would "build up a firmly-based, democratic administration in Hong Kong in the years between now and 1997" but in reality did little about this.[8] Added to this, as we shall see, a major reform of British citizenship in 1981 had deprived most people in the colony of full British nationality and thus the right of abode in the United Kingdom. By the late 1980s, this, plus the governmental reluctance to put into effect democratic reforms, had caused many people in Hong Kong to lose confidence in London. In such circumstances, most British leaders felt they had to make an attempt to remedy these deficiencies and try to provide some form of future protection to Hong Kong. John Major, recently appointed Foreign Secretary and soon-to-be Prime Minister, described the situation as follows:

> Before Tiananmen Square it was possible to be optimistic. After it, trust was shattered. A mood of near despair gripped the territory. Its stock exchange fell 30%, and business investment was held back.[9]

For this reason, Major decided to keep a previously scheduled meeting with Qian Qichen, the Chinese Foreign Minister, a few weeks after the massacre, as he felt that cancelling it would only hurt Hong Kong. He received criticism in the British press for this which, like most of the Western media, became more hostile to China after Tiananmen Square.

In September 1991, Major, now Prime Minister, became the first important Western leader to visit Beijing since the massacre. He did so to discuss the construction of a new airport in Hong Kong which the Chinese had been blocking. The visit also received much criticism in the British media and its only tangible result was a "Memorandum of Understanding" on the new airport which, it was hoped, would clear Chinese obstacles to its construction.[10] Furthermore, at around the same time, on 17 September, Legislative Council elections were held in Hong Kong and the democrats got 16 of 18 seats while no pro-China candidate won. However, Governor Wilson failed to appoint any of the victorious democrats to the Executive Council, which functioned as his cabinet. Although only 39.2% of voters actually cast their ballots, the result showed much support for democracy and the governor looked out of touch.[11] These factors all seem to have weighed on Major who decided, with the accord of Douglas Hurd, the Foreign Secretary, to replace the current governor with a heavyweight politician. He made the announcement that this change would occur after the next election. Furthermore, Sir Percy Cradock, the government's major adviser on Hong Kong, was pensioned off. London had clearly signalled a significant change in the direction of its policy.

Many in the press saw this as a direct result of Major's visit: he had gained little from the Chinese and only embarrassed himself, and had come to the conclusion that there was little to be gained from attempting to placate China. Hurd, however, has downplayed the importance of the visit in the policy change. As we have already seen, many other factors weighed in the decision. Indeed, it reflects ideas that Hurd already held. In his book, *The Arrow War: An Anglo-Chinese Confusion, 1856 to 1860*, written in 1967, he described the Chinese as possessing an "assumption of superiority". In the nineteenth century, Western nations had dealt with this by obliging the Chinese, sometimes through the use of force, to treat them as equals.[12] He does not seem to have found any advantage in following Cradock's belief in placating China. Hurd felt that Great Britain's honour was at stake. In December 1989 the Foreign Secretary announced that:

> This is just about the last chapter in the story of this country's empire. I am rather keen… that the last chapter should not end in a shabby way.[13]

Previously, the strong concentration on seeking accommodation with the Chinese government had meant that the aspirations to self-government of Hong Kong's population had been neglected. This had not caused instability in earlier years when the colony had been poor and most residents had focused on improving their economic position. But with wealth and education they desired some say in their own government. Most British people felt that, as a democratic country, they had to make an effort to show respect for what were their own fundamental values. They had failed earlier to introduce democracy and self-government into Hong Kong but in their last hours of governance–and especially after the shock of Tiananmen Square–they felt it necessary to push through reforms and to be seen as responsive to the local inhabitants. As Major said:

> It was right that as Hong Kong changed, its constitution should change too. Throughout the 1960s and 1970s the colony had a low-cost manufacturing base, with no demand for political reform. By the 1990s it was a prosperous, educated financial centre of global importance, and expectations were far greater. The citizens of Hong Kong were now eager for political reform, and it would have been wrong to deny it, although the changes we implemented had to be within the terms of the Joint Declaration.[14]

In this policy the British government had the full support of the other parties. So the discourse on Hong Kong during this period is remarkably one-sided.

After the Conservative victory in the 1992 elections, Major and Hurd chose to appoint Chris Patten as the last governor of Hong Kong. Patten, a former cabinet minister, rising star in the Conservative party and close personal friend of the Prime Minister, had lost his seat in the 1992 election. He was, thus, a governor with considerable political weight and one with strong ideas about his job. Patten was given the mission of reassuring the populace of Hong Kong about the handover as well as increasing democracy there. Hurd informed Parliament in May 1992:

> The new governor will find the political development of Hong Kong high on his list of priorities. With his advice, we shall need soon to start putting in place arrangements for the 1995 elections to the Legislative Council. As the House knows, we will raise with the Chinese the need for a faster pace of democratisation... We want–this is familiar ground to the House–to promote the political development of Hong Kong in a way that is capable of enduring beyond 1997–a through train. Reconciling these two requirements will be one of the main tasks in Hong Kong over the next year or so.[15]

Hurd had no illusions about the difficulty involved. When asked earlier about the impediments to introducing universal suffrage in Hong Kong, he had replied simply: "That it will come to an abrupt end in 1997."[16]

Patten became a governor unlike any previous one. He refused the governor's formal dress (which he described as making one look like "a recently deceased hen") and went around in a plain suit.[17] Being a politician, he also worked the crowds and made a point of leaving Government House to meet ordinary people and see conditions in Hong Kong for himself. By autumn 1992 he had prepared his proposals to extend democracy and gave them the maximum of publicity in the world press. He clearly wished to draw the eyes of the world on Hong Kong. China was furious. In the past, agreements had been worked out quietly, behind the scenes, between the two governments. Although China had been given advance notice, they had not been consulted and so immediately rejected the changes.

Patten's proposals were modest enough and probably did not violate either the Joint Declaration or the Basic Law but he pushed both as far as he could. Furthermore, Patten clothed his proposals in the rhetoric of democracy and did his best to attract the attention of the world's press–especially that of the United States–to Hong Kong. Jonathan Dimbleby stated that: "Patten's goal, commonplace in Western democracies, but hitherto untested in Hong Kong, was to charm the media into unwitting complicity with his efforts to woo public opinion, and thereby protect his flank from potential critics within the foreign-policy establishment in Britain and the business community in Hong Kong."[18] Patten clearly realized the key economic role played by the colony which enjoyed significant business and investment interests, not only from Great Britain and China, but from the United States, Canada, Australia, Japan and the European Union. Furthermore, because of recent large-scale emigration, there were large numbers of its citizens in the first three of these countries where they could exercise pressure in domestic politics.[19] Patten certainly succeeded in getting international attention and received near universal praise in the Western media for his proposals. The American press in particular flocked to the colony. Larry King actually broadcast a special edition of his CNN show from there with Patten present. *Newsweek* published an article on Patten entitled "The 'God of Democracy'".[20] *Time, Business Week, U.S. News and World Report, The New Yorker* and major newspapers all featured articles on the subject. Patten also made numerous trips abroad to explain his position. At around the same time as he was presenting his proposals, the United States Congress also decided to act and voted the United States-Hong Kong Policy Act. Among other things, it outlined how the U.S. would relate to Hong Kong after the handover: Hong Kong would be treated as a distinct entity on its own and all previous agreements would continue. The law also expressed backing for democracy and human rights and required the Secretary of State to report regularly on conditions in Hong Kong relating to U.S. interests. These later reports generally espoused the process of democratisation.

After the Chinese had expressed their hostility, they turned to trying to hurt Hong Kong economically in order to show their own power. For the first month or so, Chinese threats had little impact on investor confidence but in mid November the Hong Kong stock market began to decline and this trend continued. As *The Economist* explained: "The market has fallen by 23% in less than three weeks.... falling markets–property is likely to go down next–step up the pressure on Mr. Patten and undercut his support in the colony."[21] A number of Hong Kong businessmen certainly urged the governor to give in but, on the whole, public opinion in both the colony and Britain remained firm. *The Financial Times* succinctly explained why:

> Worrying as its threats may be, however, they do not constitute an argument for changing course. For one thing, they are still largely rhetorical. In saying that it will, after the handover, reverse reforms and refuse to honour contracts, Beijing is underlining that, notwithstanding the Sino-British deal on Hong Kong's future, it will be in charge and will do as it pleases. The hope must be that in practice its policies will be shaped by an economic self-interest based on the status quo in Hong Kong. For another thing, Mr Patten's ideas for improving democratic accountability still enjoy–so far as can be gauged–overwhelming support from the Hong Kong people. His proclaimed object is to ensure that they have a say in their destiny. So long as they, and their representatives in the colony's Legislative Council, continue to express the wish for greater political freedom, that is what he should be striving to provide, even if the price is friction with China and instability.
>
> Nothing in recent events has undermined Mr Patten's judgment that trying "in a modest way" to accommodate the Hong Kong people's aspirations is the best way to promote political stability.[22]

Many felt that, by attracting the eyes of the world on Hong Kong, Patten had made it more difficult for the Chinese to destroy its freedoms. As Malcolm Rifkind, who later replaced Hurd as Foreign Secretary, put it: "There will be great global interest in what happens and the Chinese government will need to reassure the entire international community that the welfare of Hong Kong will be properly safeguarded."[23] Of course, the British insisted on placing the onus for the failure to reach an agreement on the Chinese. Patten publicly called on China to make its own proposals and, when they failed to do so, complained about the difficulty of playing tennis "unless the ball comes back over the net".[24] Hurd also stressed this:

The Governor's proposals represent our judgment of the right way forward for Hong Kong, but we have said from the start that we are open to alternative ideas, from the people of Hong Kong or from the Chinese side. We have had a wide range of suggestions from people in Hong Kong. The Chinese side have opposed the proposals without offering anything in their place. Since last October, we and the Governor have been urging the Chinese side to discuss those electoral issues with us in order to reach an understanding. We are ready to enter such discussion without preconditions. We want to see as much continuity as possible in Hong Kong's electoral arrangements before and after 1997... We cannot and do not accept what some Chinese officials have said in the past few days–that the role of people from Hong Kong in discussions about Hong Kong's future should be downgraded.[25]

Hurd was clear: the blame lay squarely with the Chinese. The British were simply standing up for the rights of the people of Hong Kong and trying to ensure that they had a role in determining their own future.

A number of MPs, especially in the Conservative party, saw policy on Hong Kong in almost mystical terms and they frequently used words like "mission". The Conservative MP, Timothy Renton, chairman of the all-party Hong Kong parliamentary group, described his view of Patten's role: "The mission was to leave a legacy of a very well-founded democracy in Hong Kong from 1 July 1997 onwards." Note also his use of the word "legacy" another important term which focuses on Britain and on Britain's involvement. The stress is clearly on Britain's honour–in her own eyes and in that of the world's–and on the survival of its values and this became an important theme, primarily of the Conservatives. David Howell, chairman of the Select Committee on Foreign Affairs insisted that: "The issue at the forefront of our relations with China, and which has understandably been the subject of most comments today because it blocks our longer-term vision, is Hong Kong and how we can do the right thing and fulfil our duty from Hong Kong's point of view."[26] For Nigel Waterson: "The only realistic bulwark in favour of Hong Kong, to protect it after 1997, is the rule of law. That is the lasting legacy of this country in Hong Kong."[27] The former journalist, Lady Olga Maitland concluded that when 1997 comes: "We should feel proud that we have more than honoured our obligations. We shall have strived to the end... We shall leave Hong Kong with pride and honour."[28] This line of reasoning, though, was not limited to the Conservatives. The Labour peer Lord Dubs talked of Britain's "enormous responsibility to do the right thing by the people of Hong Kong".[29] And no less a figure than Robin Cook insisted that: "It is important to show that we have discharged our obligation to the people of Hong Kong that we will surrender sovereignty of the territory of Hong Kong without surrendering the liberty of the people of Hong Kong."[30]

Certainly one must see much of this rhetoric in the context of a long history of British discourse on Empire. By the late eighteenth century, many had come to see imperialism in a paternalist light; not only should the Mother Country benefit from her colonies but the colonies should themselves gain from the system. William Pitt the Younger told Parliament in 1784 that there was a need "to render that connection a blessing to the native Indians". This theme grew in the nineteenth century and many argued that what Britain offered its colonies was a superior economic and political system. This idea was perhaps most famously expressed by the writer Rudyard Kipling who contended that Western nations had a duty to bring their superior civilization to less-developed countries. He called this "the White Man's Burden". Imperial masters had to improve the life of colonial inhabitants; they had "To seek another's profit/And work another's gain". They had to "Fill full the mouths of Famine/And bid the sickness cease". The debate on Hong Kong follows this tradition but generally avoids taking a patronising tone towards the people of the colony, who are widely recognised as sophisticated and educated. It also helped that a genuine demand for democracy existed there. Therefore, Britain was honour-bound to do its best to give them her traditions. Since the UK was not granting independence to Hong Kong but returning it to a nation known for its political repression, they also had a duty to ensure that the colony would have some protection in the future—a protection that they could not guarantee themselves—and, therefore, the need for international recognition of the importance of the question. Certainly there is a self-congratulatory air to much of the discourse. Pride in the imperial past had not totally died, at least among the Conservatives, as can be seen from Edward Leigh, scion of a gentry family and descendant of Henry VII:

> This may be an historic occasion—the last occasion on which the House debates the future of a major British colony. This is the last of the debates—conducted over perhaps half a millennium—that have affected the fate of millions of people around the world. Before he [Malcolm Rifkind] finishes his speech and hauls down the flag of empire, will he pay tribute to the many men and women who created something that was special, not only in its extent, but as a great example in world history of good government and justice?[31]

Rifkind, now Foreign Secretary, was happy to do so, talking about the "historic achievement" of the Empire, "the provision of the rule of law and democratic government, and a massive increase in prosperity for all territories".[32] John Redwood, the Eurosceptic who challenged Major for the party leadership in 1995, went even further, suggesting that the government should levy a "success fee" on the colony so that China would not benefit so much from Britain's good work.[33] Many Conservatives seem to have felt that the "White Man's Burden" had been fulfilled and that democracy was virtually a British invention. Of course, the Labour Party showed markedly less enthusiasm for imperial praise. Robin Cook even suggested that the main reason for Patten's popularity was his social policy: "The programme that he has pursued in Hong Kong could be written as an illustration in a textbook of social democracy."[34]

Many people argued that Hong Kong must retain freedom and the rule of law in order to keep its economic prosperity and that, in fact, the Chinese would only hurt themselves by curtailing its liberty. Baroness Dunn, who was of Chinese origin herself and had been one of the most senior politicians in the colony, serving on both the Executive and the Legislative Councils, stated that: "One of Hong Kong's main attractions to investors is its reputation as a free, fair and clean place to do business."[35] The Liberal Democrat peer, Lord Thomson of Monifieth, former Commonwealth secretary, went even further:

> The inter-dependence in Hong Kong of its various facets–the integrity of the Civil Service, the inviolability of the commercial law system, the academic freedom of the universities, its citizens' right to travel–all hang together. They form a seamless web essential to the continuation of Hong Kong's economic success. As Hong Kong's seven million people generate a GDP nearly a quarter of that generated by China's one billion plus population, any damage to Hong Kong's economy as a world trading city will do massive damage to the whole Chinese economy. That is by far the best argument to Chinese self-interest in living up to its commitment to "one country, two systems", under the Joint Declaration.[36]

The warning–echoed by many others–was clear: China should tread softly in Hong Kong or risk destroying both the goose and its golden egg. The press also echoed this argument. *The Times*, for example, in an article entitled "Bone-Headed China" wrote that: "Businessmen will not wait until June 30, 1997 to decide whether they are confident that the rule of law will continue to be impartially upheld. Some are already moving the legal domicile of their companies elsewhere."[37] As *The Economist* put it: "China's economic ambitions depend on a prospering Hong Kong."[38] Chris Patten followed this line of reasoning. He later explained in an interview with the Institute of International Studies at Berkeley that:

I thought British interests were pretty clear. Britain had to be seen to withdraw honourably from its last colonial responsibility, even though what it was obliged to do, by history, would appear to a lot of people to be dishonourable... the handing over of a free society to a society which was not free. I always reckoned that honor and short-term interest and longer-term interest, in every sense, went hand-in-hand. If we weren't to behave honourably, for example, it would help to produce political instability, which would be extremely bad for the economy in Hong Kong. Britain had a large stake in that economy; a lot of firms on the Hong Kong stock market, a lot of British firms, and big investments of three billion also. Huge commercial stake in Hong Kong's continuing success. So I never saw what some [of] my business critics argued–a distinction between trying to do what was right and what was, in every sense, in Britain's interest–its commercial interest and its political interest as well.[39]

So Britain's economic interests and her sense of honour led her in the same direction.

The term "one country, two systems" had obvious implications for Taiwan and many believed that China needed to show it could respect freedom if it wanted to have any chance of getting back this even greater prize. The independence of Taiwan, although not internationally recognized, was, and is, protected by American military strength. If China wished to avoid World War III, it would have to convince the Taiwanese to join them voluntarily. As Patten noted in his memoirs: "Taiwan will watch closely what happens further down the coast: can "one country, two systems" work in the former colony, and if it cannot do so there, the Taiwanese will ask, how could it possibly work for them?"[40] So, once again, it was in China's own long-term, and particularly economic, interest to keep freedom and the rule of law in Hong Kong.

Very few dissented from Patten's policy and he enjoyed the support of all the major parties. Many Labour M.P.s took a keen interest in the fate of Chinese dissidents and frequently asked questions about them. People like Jeremy Bray of the Labour Party, who had been born in Hong Kong, confessed that:

A question faced the Opposition when the Chris Patten whom we knew so well appeared as a somewhat belated knight in shining armour in Hong Kong, seeking ingeniously to squeeze the last ounce of democracy out of the arrangements that he found had already been made there, even at the risk of upsetting Chinese friends in Beijing. I was in Shanghai at the time, and I must confess my reaction was to cheer.[41]

He expressed quite clearly here his support for government policy and admiration for Patten. In April 1995, Robin Cook, Shadow Foreign Secretary, stressed the cross party nature of the policy:

> We do not approach the debate in a party political spirit. I hope that I do not disappoint the House when I say that I do not intend to make this a partisan occasion. It is a subject that we should try to pursue with the least party political disagreement between us, and with the fullest unity on a national basis.[42]

He went on to underline the human dimension of the question and the anxiety felt in Hong Kong over the handover. Tiananmen, he argued perceptively, had pushed China and Hong Kong in different directions:

> The events of Tiananmen square had a profound effect on the views of people resident in Hong Kong, and appear to have had a profound effect on the rulers of China as well. One of the issues with which we must now grapple is that those events appear to have left the rulers of China perhaps more hostile to democratic reform and more nervous about the impact on the rest of China of the political processes in Hong Kong.... There is a paradox in the fact that the events of five years ago have made progress towards democratic rights in Hong Kong more pressing, but have also made it more difficult to obtain the agreement of the Government of China.

In November 1996, Cook told Parliament that, if a Labour government came to power in May 1997, there would be no change on policy towards Hong Kong.[43] As we shall see, Cook would follow a more moderate line towards China after becoming Foreign Secretary but, while the colony remained British, he and the Labour Party resolutely supported the Conservative government's policies, as did the Liberal Democrats.

This, of course, did not mean that there was no opposition in Britain to Patten's policies, only that this disagreement did not follow party lines. Many businessmen who had investments in the colony voiced their hostility. Obviously, most of those who had constructed the earlier policy, and in particular the Joint Declaration resented the change and predicted dire consequences. The strongest critic of the government's policy was undoubtedly Sir Percy Cradock who had been one of the major architects of the handover. He wrote a number of articles in the press that scathingly attacked Patten's policy. In his memoirs he went as far as to suggest it had an irrational and even racist base:

> The episode [the Patten governorship] might be seen as an irruption of irrational forces, a reminder of the still unexhausted reserves of prejudice

and emotion on both sides arising from a long, painful and too often uncomprehending relationship. It is also possible to see British policy as an example of nostalgia in action, an attempted reversion to times when Britain was in a position to impose solutions. Others may see the failure to read Chinese intentions as only another example of that chronic inability to put ourselves in the shoes of the other side which has manifested itself in our European as much as our Far Eastern dilemma.[44]

There is an element of truth here for, as we have seen, many of the comments on Hong Kong resembled earlier imperial discourse. But there is also something spiteful about many of Cradock's comments. Others insisted that Patten's policies were aimed more at pleasing the U.S. and the British press than at ensuring the future of Hong Kong.[45]

Within Parliament, the main dissident was the former Conservative Prime Minister, Edward Heath who took an extremely pragmatic view of the question, notably stressing the importance of cultivating and increasing British economic interests with China:

> I take the example of China, which has a rapid rate of expansion of between 8.5 per cent and 12.5 per cent. We are not establishing ourselves in those markets as we should be. When the Governor of Hong Kong said that when Hong Kong returns to China on 1 July next year, we shall still have responsibility for looking after Hong Kong, he could not have chosen a better way of upsetting Beijing and affecting the Chinese Government's future attitude towards Hong Kong and towards us. That undoubtedly affects our trading arrangements with Hong Kong. As I know from my discussions with officials in Beijing and elsewhere in China, such comments affect where they place their orders.[46]

His main argument was simple: China was potentially a massive market so do not upset the Chinese government or there will be little or no economic profit for Britain. He also insisted on the limits of British power, which were very real. As he put it: "They [the Chinese] know the power they have, and what they can bring about."[47] Heath also stressed that Britain had been in Hong Kong for a long time and asked the difficult question, why now?

> We have had Hong Kong for nearly 150 years, and what did we do about all those issues? We did nothing. Only when the time came to hand it back did we say that they all should be addressed immediately and in exactly the way we wanted. The House and the Government cannot get away with that. We must be realistic.[48]

And so realism and the economic importance of China were the cornerstones of those who opposed the government's Hong Kong policy. But, as we have already seen, those who supported the policy felt that this was an exaggeration or, indeed, wrong and that Britain's, as well as China's, economic interest lay in supporting Patten's proposals.

Let us now turn to the other major subject of debate–immigration and nationality. Much of this discourse had been settled before this period. The British Nationality Act of 1981 created a British Dependent Territories citizenship for residents of those regions which took away the right of abode in the United Kingdom. Its principal target was obviously Hong Kong. Thatcher justified this by insisting that there was a real danger "that financial confidence would evaporate and that money and in due course key personnel would flee the Colony, impoverishing and destablizing it well before the lease of the New Territories came to an end.[49] There was some truth in her assertion. About one per cent of the population emigrated in 1990 and this figure actually increased in 1992. *U.S. News and World Report* even ran a cover story asking, "Will the last one to leave please turn out the lights?"[50] This mass emigration was certainly something that the Chinese government did not want either.

Further complicating the situation was the plight of the Vietnamese boat people. After the Vietnam War ended in 1975 with the reunification of the country under a communist government, hundreds of thousands of people decided to leave. Over the next two decades nearly 200,000 took refuge in Hong Kong and most of them spent years in refugee camps there.[51] Dealing with these refugees placed a considerable strain on the colony's resources. In 1988, the Hong Kong government announced a plan to screen the arrivals to see if they were genuine refugees or simply looking for economic improvement. Those deemed to fall in the latter category would be repatriated. There was much criticism of this plan in the British press as well as in the American press and government. Douglas Hurd justified his decision in his memoirs:

> The Americans, whose hostile policy towards Vietnam was one reason for the country's poverty and the outflow of boat people, began to object on humanitarian grounds to what we intended. Despite this, I decided in December 1989 that we must begin to fly even unwilling Vietnamese home from Hong Kong. There were by then 57,000 boat people in Hong Kong. This seemed the only way of deterring larger numbers from risking the voyage. We also needed to put paid to the stories current in Vietnam that once in Hong Kong the boat people would be generously treated and perhaps offered a golden life across the Pacific in California.[52]

Britain took about 15,000 of these immigrants but there was hostility among many people to taking more.

Policy towards immigration from Hong Kong changed slightly after the Tiananmen massacre and Thatcher herself insisted on legislation in 1990 to give 50,000 key civil servants and business people and their families British passports. The expressed hope was that this would reassure them and that they would therefore stay in Hong Kong. Although Patten, in October 1995, publicly called for the government to grant full British nationality to all Hong Kong citizens, a general consensus prevailed among the parties against such a policy. Immigration discourse, then, tended to focus on certain small groups who were perceived as being especially deserving or as facing particular difficulties. One of these was the wives and widows of British servicemen who had fought to defend Hong Kong during the Second World War. According to Major there were only about 29 of these and it struck many as particularly ungenerous of the Home Office to block such a small number from receiving full citizenship. The Labour peer, Lord Dubs called it "a disgrace to us as a country".[53] The Prime Minister finally made the announcement granting this during his visit to Hong Kong in 1996. Many, though, criticized the fact that–instead of making this a government bill–it was only a Private Member's bill. On the 8th of May 1996, V-E Day, the Conservative Tim Renton, with bipartisan support, introduced the bill to grant these women full British citizenship which quickly passed both houses of Parliament and received the Royal Assent. The question was resolved but it left a bitter taste for some. Sir Peter Lloyd, a former Conservative minister of state at the Home Office, summed up the feelings of many: "Although the substance was conceded, with an undertaking that they could come to the UK whenever they wanted, the desire for citizenship was insensitively and pointlessly denied for years."[54]

Another group on which there was a near consensus was that of the non-Chinese ethnic minorities who numbered around 7000 people. Primarily of Asian descent, they had often been settled in Hong Kong for several generations and most of them worked for the British military forces. As such, they had earlier signed a document renouncing any earlier nationality they might have possessed. They had British National (Overseas) citizenship which meant that, once Hong Kong returned to China, they would have no right of abode anywhere in the world. Nor could they receive Chinese nationality like the other inhabitants of Hong Kong since Chinese citizenship was based on ethnicity.

Both Patten and the Legislative Council of Hong Kong called on the government to grant them British nationality. To illustrate the widespread support for such a measure, the ultra-conservative Sir Teddy Taylor, member of the anti-immigration Monday Club, raised the question in the House of Commons in July 1993 and called on the government to grant citizenship to these people. He stated that:

> My real interest stems from my belief that Britain is in danger of flouting its inescapable duty to a group of citizens whose rights are being ignored and whose future will be unstable and constitutionally deprived unless we do something. It would be terrible if we told these 5000 people that they belong nowhere–that they are nationals of nowhere–especially as they have served Britain so well in the past.[55]

In 1993 Lord Bonham-Carter, publisher and first chairman of the Race Relations Board, introduced a bill into the House of Lords to grant this nationality but this was defeated in the House of Commons because of government opposition. But numerous people continued to lobby the government. This resulted in John Major stating on 4 March 1996 that: "Her Majesty's Government will guarantee admission and settlement should they come under pressure to leave Hong Kong".[56] This did not, however, solve the problem and lobbying continued. In December 1996, with the return of Hong Kong a little over six months away, the Eurosceptic 21st Baron Willoughby de Broke, Conservative peer, introduced another bill. In his speech he criticized the government guarantee:

> That statement implicitly recognises that that group is a special case, but I fear that the guarantee is seen in Hong Kong as having little value. For what is that pressure? Who is to decide it? Will that be decided in Hong Kong or in the remote comfort of a Whitehall office? This looks like an administrative and moral swamp, employing objective criteria that the Government refuse to define, leaving 5000 individuals uncertain of their eligibility. But, what is most important, that policy will result in the need for each person to put his or her case individually, exposing himself or herself to further discrimination if their specific circumstances do not fall into the, as yet, undetermined definition of "under pressure".
> In addition, that policy completely misses the point. That community does not want to rush into the UK. All it is asking for is a full British passport so that its status in Hong Kong will not be an anomaly that exposes it to discrimination and a subjective interpretation of their status. Ministerial assurances, however well-intentioned, are in this case just not good enough.[57]

For Willoughby de Broke, it came down, once again, to a question of honour: "Therefore, if only for political reasons, let us resolve this issue which could blight our record and reputation in Hong Kong and tarnish our colonial legacy."[58] Another Conservative, David Howell, told the House of Commons that the government's failure to grant citizenship to this group left "an overall feeling–an aroma–of meanness".[59] Sir Patrick Cormack, also a Conservative, used the term "moral obligation" to describe the situation and told the House of Commons that: "Moral obligations are real. What is morally wrong is never politically right. I think that we made a mistake in not granting passports."[60] The distinguished barrister, Sir Ivan Lawrence, yet another Conservative, could not understand "Why the United Kingdom Government are deliberately making it appear that they do not want to be seen to be magnanimous."[61] The question of honour was developed in more detail by the Conservative businesswoman, Baroness O'Cathain who spoke of Britain's "responsibility":

> We are talking about non-ethnic Chinese living in Hong Kong whose ancestors, let us recall, were taken to Hong Kong by the British founding fathers of the colony in the 1840s. About 2,000 Indian troops were there when the British flag was first raised in Hong Kong. They did not choose to go there; they were taken there by us. Since that time many of them have suffered as a result of their "British" nationality. They are regarded by the ethnic Chinese as British. During the Second World War some were taken to Japanese prisoner of war camps because they were perceived to be British. This House has great knowledge of the deprivation and the sheer horrors that occurred in those prisoner of war camps. We should remember that. They suffered alongside British prisoners. Their loyalty to the Crown was never in question. More of them served in the British Armed Forces. Again, their loyalty was never in question. And more of them gave sterling service to this country in the voluntary support services... Surely we in turn should show loyalty to them.[62]

Clearly, many right-wing Conservatives were still using an imperial discourse and the issue for them was one of *noblesse oblige*. Their vocabulary reflects this belief, for they talk of "duty" and "loyalty". The British government has a duty to recognise and reward the past loyalty of the ethnic minorities. Major later said that there were many people in his own party who supported the government position but there is no sign of this in the records of parliamentary debate.[63] The other parties supported Willoughby de Broke's bill and, indeed, there is not an enormous difference in their arguments. Paddy Ashdown of the Liberal Democrats, for example, called the government's treatment of the non-ethnic minorities "disgraceful".[64]

The Labour peer and celebrity lawyer, Lord Mishcon asserted that: "We shall lower the Union Jack on 30th June; please may it be done with honour."[65] In the previous month, Robin Cook, Shadow Foreign Secretary, announced his own and his party's support for granting them full citizenship. The arguments he used differed little from those put forward by the Conservative peers, although his language was less emotional:

> The Labour party has written to the Prime Minister urging him to extend British citizenship now to that small group of people. Such a step would honour our obligation to them, because of their past contribution to our colony, and remove any uncertainty about their rights in future. I assured the Government that Labour would co-operate in facilitating the passage of such legislation. I repeat that offer.

He went on to say that "if a general election produces a Labour Government, we will be prepared to legislate to extend citizenship to the small Asian community of Hong Kong."[66] Cook recognized that this would be difficult in the short time between 1 May and the handover unless the Conservatives cooperated with him.

Amazingly enough, the only participant in the House of Lords debate to speak against granting nationality was the government spokesperson and her only argument was to say that the government did not think such a bill necessary. The only real opposition, in fact, appears to have come from Michael Howard, the Home Secretary. Baroness Dunn attacked him directly:

> On 15th July 1993, by a vote of 60 to 48, this House called upon the Government to give them full British citizenship. Those who supported the Motion spoke from all sides of the House and included two previous Governors of Hong Kong and a former Minister responsible for Hong Kong.
> None of this has moved the Home Secretary. He has argued against granting full British citizenship on three main grounds: first, that this is not a special case; secondly, that giving them full citizenship would require legislation which it would be difficult to get through Parliament; and, thirdly, that existing arrangements give them sufficient protection.
> None of these objections stands up to scrutiny.[67]

Lord Dubs, went even further:

> My understanding is that the Bill is widely supported in this House and in the other place; it is supported by the present governor of Hong Kong and two previous governors; it is supported by the Chinese Government, LegCo and the bulk of public opinion itself. Who is against it? I know that

the Government of this country speak with one voice. But if one looks behind that voice, there is reason to believe that there are many voices in government who would urge that this Bill be supported. I know the Minister cannot comment on that, but my understanding for some time has been that the only thing that stands in the way of the passage of this Bill is the Home Office... I suppose there is one other argument–let us be frank– an election is coming. Is the Home Secretary nervous lest he be accused of being soft on immigration?[68]

It became clear that the bill was likely to pass in the House of Commons in spite of government opposition. Howard finally decided to give in and on 4 February 1997 announced that non-ethnic minorities would be given full British citizenship. The Home Office then almost completely rewrote Willoughby de Broke's bill, introducing requirements like the need for residence in Hong Kong before the date of his announcement and making it obligatory to register to become British subjects instead of having an automatic process. Willoughby de Broke accepted the changes graciously and with good humour:

One of the favourite expressions of the late Deng Xiaoping was, "It matters not what colour your cat is as long as it catches mice." So although the amendment before your lordships will substantially alter the original Bill, I am satisfied that even though the cat is a different sort of cat–a blow-dried, shampooed-and-set cat–it will still do its job and catch mice.[69]

At midnight on 30 June 1997, amidst the pouring rain, Hong Kong became a special administrative region of China. The event received massive coverage in the world press. After the handover, British policy became much more conciliatory towards China. In May 1995 Robin Cook made his first visit to Beijing. According to John Kampfner, he decided then that Labour's approach to China would differ from Chris Patten's.[70] Indeed, as Foreign Secretary, Cook would establish a policy of constructive engagement with China. As such, Britain did not back the annual resolution at the United Nations Commission on Human Rights which criticized China. During a 1999 visit to the U.K. by the Chinese President, the Labour government was criticised for using strong arm tactics to hide protesters. Cook also announced in January 1998 that he was "too busy" to meet a leading Chinese dissident, now resident in the United States, Wei Jingsheng. When Wei returned on a second visit, Cook felt obligated to meet him but, due to an apparent mix-up, the press arrived too late and no photos were taken.[71] Essentially Cook followed the E.U. line on China–to such an extent that it was often difficult to distinguish a separate British policy.[72]

Let us try now to evaluate the success or not of British policy. Major later wrote that Patten's actions eventually had the result of making the Chinese more amenable–notably on finally reaching an agreement on the new airport.[73] Major also insisted that the dispute had little or no effect on trade with China for exports to there doubled during Patten's term of office. Still, China refused to accept the Patten reforms of 1992. As they had promised, they dissolved the elected Legislative Council and replaced it with a hand-picked Provisional Legislative Council. The Shanghai-born millionaire businessman, Tung Chee-hwa became Hong Kong's Chief Executive. He also had been chosen by Beijing and possessed almost no political experience. In 2001 the popular Deputy Chief Executive Anson Chan, who had earlier assisted Patten, resigned under pressure from Beijing. The following year the Hong Kong administration tried to introduce an anti-subversion law, called Article 23. After widespread protests, the bill was withdrawn and, eventually, in 2005, Tung himself resigned. At the time of writing, the press remains free and the judiciary largely independent. Although democracy has not been achieved, civil liberties continue and the people of Hong Kong seem determined to defend them, frequently protesting in the streets. So perhaps Patten's gamble paid off. Britain did leave its last colony with a sense of honour and the colony has retained most of its old freedom (although it might have done so anyway). Let us, therefore, give the last word to Patten:

> Was the consequence fatal for Hong Kong?... The condition of Hong Kong in 1997 answered that question better than I could ever have done. We had stood up for Hong Kong, belatedly honouring the promises made to it about freedom, democracy and the rule of law. Where were the fatalities? Had the roof fallen in on us?... Here was Hong Kong in the summer of 1997, richer than we could ever have believed possible, with a good government guaranteed its passage through the transition, with an independent judiciary enjoying the same guarantee, with a rich fabric of civil society, and with no disorder on the streets. The demonstrations, when they occurred, were politely directed against China, not Britain.[74]

Bibliography

Ash, Robert, et.al., eds. *Hong Kong in Transition: The Handover Years*. London: Macmillan, 2000.

Brown, Judith and Rosemary Foot, eds. *Hong Kong's Transitions, 1842-1997*. Basingstoke: Macmillan, 1997.

Chang, David Wen-wei & Richard Chuang. *The Politics of Hong Kong's Reversion to China*. Basingstoke: Macmillan, 1998.

Ching, Frank, ed. *Hong Kong: 1997 and Beyond.* Hong Kong: Far Eastern Economic Review, 1997.

Cohen, Warren & Li Zhao, eds. *Hong Kong under Chinese Rule: The Economic and Political Implications of Reversion.* Cambridge: Cambridge University Pres, 1997.

Cradock, Percy. *Experiences of China.* London: John Murray, new ed., 1999.

Craig, Neil & Jo. *Black Watch–Red Dawn: The Hong Kong Handover to China.* London: Brassey's, 1998.

Dimbleby, Jonathan. *The Last Governor: Chris Patten and the Handover of Hong Kong.* London: Little, Brown & Co., 1997.

Flowerdew, John. *The Final Years of British Hong Kong: The Discourse of Colonial Withdrawal.* Basingstoke: Macmillan, 1998

Herschensohn, Bruce, ed. *Hong Kong at the Handover.* Oxford: Lexington Books, 1999.

Hurd, Douglas. *Memoirs.* London: Little, Brown, 2003.

Kampfner, John. *Robin Cook.* London: Phoenix, 1998.

Little, Richard & Mark Wickham-Jones, eds. *New Labour's Foreign Policy: A New Moral Crusade.* Manchester: Manchester University Press, 2000.

Major, John. *John Major: The Autobiography.* London: Harper Collins, 2nd edition, 2000.

Patten, Chris. *East and West.* London: Macmillan, 1998.

Reynolds, David. *Britannia Overruled: British Policy and World Power in the Twentieth Century.* Harlow: Pearson, 2nd edition, 2000.

Roberti, Mark. *The Fall of Hong Kong.* New York: John Wiley & Sons, 2nd edition, 1996.

Seldon, Anthony with Lewis Baston. *Major: A Political Life.* London: Phoenix, 1997.

Stuart, Mark. *Douglas Hurd: The Public Servant.* Edinburgh: Mainstream Publishing, 1998.

Thatcher, Margaret. *The Downing Street Years.* London: Harper Collins, 1993.

Tsang, Steve. *Hong Kong: Appointment with China.* London: Tauris, 1997.

Notes

[1] I would like to thank Barbara Cartwright and my husband, Henri Zuber, for their help with this article.

[2] Chris Patten, *East and West* (London: Macmillan, 1998) 12.

[3] John Darwin, "Hong Kong in British Decolonisation" in *Hong Kong's Transitions, 1842-1997*, ed. Judith Brown and Rosemary Foot (Basingstoke: Macmillan, 1997) 117

[4] Robert Ash, et. al., eds., *Hong Kong in Transition: The Handover Years* (London: Macmillan, 2000) 188

[5] And even then in only a limited way. A relatively small number of MPs attended the major parliamentary debates on Hong Kong.

[6] Patten, 29

[7] *Ibid.*, 82

[8] Richard Luce, *House of Commons Debates*, 5/12/1984, 6th Series, vol. 69, col. 471

[9] John Major, *John Major: The Autobiography* (London: Harper Collins, 2nd edition, 2000) 119-20

[10] Although the Chinese continued for years to debate the terms of the Memorandum and delayed support for the project.

[11] David Chang and Richard Chuang, *The Politics of Hong Kong's Reversion to China* (Basingstoke: Macmillan, 1998) xvi. They ascribe the lack of voter participation either to apathy or to a belief that the election would have no effect on Hong Kong's future government.

[12] Mark Stuart, *Douglas Hurd: The Public Servant* (Edinburgh: Mainstream Publishing, 1998) 345-6.

[13] *House of Commons Debates*, 20/12/1989, 6th Series, vol. 164, col. 368

[14] Major, 506. Steve Tsang has shown how the colonial government of Hong Kong, by the 1980s, came closer than any purely Chinese government ever had to fulfilling Confucian ideals. Paradoxically, by this time it was not enough and as Major said, a real demand for democracy had arisen. See Steve Tsang, "Government and Politics in Hong Kong: A Colonial Paradox" in Brown and Foot.

[15] *House of Commons Debates*, 8/5/1992, 6th Series, vol. 207, col. 285

[16] *Ibid.*, 5/2/1992, 6th Series, vol. 203, col 283

[17] Patten, 52

[18] Jonathan Dimbleby, *The Last Governor: Chris Patten and the Handover of Hong Kong* (London: Little, Brown & Co., 1997) 90

[19] For more on this see Brian Hook, "National and International Interests in the Decolonisation of Hong Kong, 1946-97" in Brown and Foot.

[20] S. Strasser, *Newsweek*, November 23, 1992, 42-3

[21] "Patten's Chinese Torture", *The Economist*, December 5, 1992, 63

[22] "Dragon's Wrath", *The Financial Times*, December 2, 1992

[23] *House of Commons Debates*, 12/6/1996, vol. 279, col. 294

[24] "Beijing vs. Patten", *The Economist*, October 31, 1992, 15

[25] *House of Commons Debates*, 15/3/1993, vol. 220, col. 21

[26] *Ibid.*, 27/4/1995, vol. 258, col. 1028

[27] *Ibid.*, 27/4/1995, vol. 258, col. 1060

[28] *Ibid.*, 27/4/1995, vol. 258, col. 1066

[29] *House of Lords Debates*, 27/4/1996, vol. 571, col. 1198

[30] *House of Commons Debates*, 14/11/1996, vol. 285, col. 538

[31] *Ibid.*, 14/11/1996, vol. 285, col. 527

[32] *Ibid.*, 14/11/1996, vol. 285, col. 527

[33] *Ibid.*, 12/3/1997, vol. 292, col. 341

[34] *Ibid.*, 14/11/1996, vol. 285, col. 530

[35] *House of Lords Debates*, 24/4/1996, vol. 571, col. 1208

[36] *Ibid.*, 24/4/1996, vol. 571, col. 1215

[37] *The Times*, December 28, 1995, 15

[38] "Beijing vs. Patten", *The Economist*, October 31, 1992, 15

[39] Conversation with Christopher Patten 8 April 1999, Conversations with History, Institute of International Studies, University of California at Berkeley, http://globetrotter.berkeley.edu/conversations/Patten/patten99-con3.html

[40] Patten, 92

[41] *House of Commons Debates*, 27/4/95, vol. 258, col. 1024

[42] *Ibid.*, 27/4/95, vol. 258, col. 1002

[43] *Ibid.*, 14/11/96, vol. 285, cols. 533-4

[44] Percy Cradock, *Experiences of China* (London: John Murray, new edition, 1999) 297-8

[45] See "Sheriff Patten Comes to Town", *The Economist*, November 14, 1992, 63

[46] *House of Commons Debates*, 30/10/96, vol. 284, col 686

[47] *Ibid.*, 27/4/95, vol. 258, col. 1009

[48] *Ibid.*, 27/4/95, vol. 258, col 1012

[49] Margaret Thatcher. *The Downing Street Years* (London: Harper Collins, 1993) 260

[50] E. MacFarquahar, *U.S. News and World Report*, August 21, 1989, 36-7

[51] Alastair Goodlad, House of Commons Debates, 18/10/1993, vol. 230, col. 125

[52] Douglas Hurd, *Memoirs* (London: Little Brown, 2003) 478

[53] *House of Lords Debates*, 24/4/1996, vol. 571, col. 1197

[54] *House of Commons Debates*, 28/10/1996, vol. 284, col. 364

[55] *Ibid.*, 9/7/1993, vol. 228, col. 647

[56] *House of Lords Debates*, 12/12/96, vol. 576, col. 1212

[57] *Ibid.*, col 1212

[58] *Ibid.*, col. 1214

[59] *House of Commons Debates*, 14/11/96, vol. 285, col. 519

[60] *Ibid.*, 14/11/96, vol. 285, col. 551

[61] *Ibid.*, 14/11/96, vol. 285, col. 560

[62] *House of Lords' Debates*, 12/12/96, vol. 576, col. 1220-1221

[63] Major, 507

[64] *House of Commons Debates*, 15/11/95, vol. 267, col. 40

[65] *House of Lords Debates*, 12/12/96, vol. 576, col. 1218

[66] *House of Commons Debates*, 14/11/96, vol. 285, col. 537

[67] *House of Lords Debates*, 12/12/96, vol. 576, col. 1222

[68] *Ibid.*, 12/12/96, vol. 576 cols. 1227-8

[69] *Ibid.*, 13/3/97, vol. 579,, col. 495

[70] John Kampfner, *Robin Cook* (London: Phoenix, 1998) 218

[71] For more on this see Kampfner.

[72] For more on this see Angela Bourne and Michelle Cini "Exporting the Third Way in Foreign Policy: New Lab, the EU and Human Rights Policy" in *New Labour's Foreign Policy: A New Moral Crusade*, ed. Richard Little and Mark Wickham-Jones (Manchester: Manchester University Press, 2000)

[73] Major, 506

[74] Patten, 82

CHAPTER SEVEN

THE US DEBATE ON CHINA POLICY, 1992-2007: FROM ENGAGEMENT TO "CONGAGEMENT"?

JULIETTE BOURDIN

When Bill Clinton was elected President of the United States in 1992, the consensus on China policy had already been broken by the Tiananmen crackdown in 1989 and by the end of the Cold War in the early 1990s. As years went by, China became increasingly the focus of attention because of its remarkable economic rise, and also because of the serious diplomatic crises and the growing economic interdependence which marked Sino-American relations throughout Bill Clinton's and George W. Bush's presidencies.

Sino-American relations were further complicated by their historical legacy. In 1972, Richard Nixon put an end to a two-decade long diplomatic break by visiting the People's Republic of China (PRC), on which occasion both countries agreed on the "One China Policy"—that is to say that Washington acknowledged that Taiwan was a part of China, but insisted on the "peaceful settlement" of the Taiwan question. The opening up to China was then possible and accepted because of the Cold War, and Washington decided to play the "China card" to counterbalance the Soviet Union within what Henry Kissinger defined as a "Strategic Triangle." Although this *Realpolitik* was pursued in the following years, Congress reacted to the White House opening up to Beijing, right after the normalization of Sino-American relations in 1979, by voting the Taiwan Relations Act which reinforced Taiwan's protection.

Despite some difficulties, US-China relations gradually improved in the 1980s, until the 1989 Tiananmen crackdown abruptly put an end to the era of good feeling. If the executive had previously enjoyed much independence in determining its China policy, then other actors—such as Congress, the lobbies, the media, and public opinion—entered the debate and wanted to have a say in the matter. In addition to the impact of the Tiananmen crackdown, the collapse of the Soviet Union and the end of the Cold War made the very foundation of Sino-American relations disappear and thus constrained the US to question its China policy.

From the early 1990s onwards, the debate on China became decisively complex, because the heritage of the Cold War and the Tiananmen crackdown made it difficult for the US to find a consensus on which China policy the country should follow. It was further complicated by the broad range of actors who would often present competing viewpoints. This explains how issues which seemed to have little in common at first sight— such as the American trade deficit with China, the defence of human rights (including freedom of religion), the Taiwan issue, intellectual property rights protection, etc—would finally intermingle. It also shed light on the difference of opinion, particularly between Congress and the White House, or between labour unions and pro-business lobbies.

The globalization process clearly contributed to complicating the debates on China, for the mere reason that the interdependence which grew deeper every year between the Chinese and the American economies made it more difficult for Washington to take drastic decisions. As a matter of fact, it was precisely because the US realized that it was losing room for manoeuvre that the debates became more heated, mostly under the influence of the "China threat" theorists who advocated a new kind of containment of China.

Although the issues which were raised were finally relatively similar, especially in terms of economic policy, the Clinton and the Bush presidencies revealed certain differences, for the nature of the debate changed after China's entry into the World Trade Organization (WTO) and after the terrorist attacks of September 11, which both occurred in 2001. Broadly speaking, the United States seemed to hesitate between promoting the doctrine of engagement or that of containment, and this very vacillation actually found its expression in the creation of the neologism "congagement" which started to spread from 2000 onwards. In fact, given this hesitation and the lack of consensus about China-related issues, in the end Washington would generally act pragmatically when dealing with China.

The Clinton Years: towards a Strategy of Engagement

In the first place, it is necessary to evoke the Tiananmen crackdown and the end of the Cold War which developed under George Herbert

Bush's presidency, for these events greatly influenced the way China was perceived and also explained why the debate changed afterwards.

One of the reasons why the Tiananmen crackdown—which killed hundreds and injured thousands of Chinese demonstrators on the night of June 3-4, 1989—had such an impact in the US was because the images of the military repression were broadcasted on television. The Americans were as horrified by the violence of the crackdown as they had been enthusiastic about the Chinese students' so-called demands for democracy.

All Congressmen were appalled, and they reacted at once to condemn the massacre, claiming that the White House should immediately break off diplomatic relations with Beijing and impose an embargo and sanctions on the PRC. Democratic Representative Stephen J. Solarz bluntly declared:

> We have to make it clear that the United States will not continue to conduct business as usual with a government that engages in the wanton slaughter of its own people. ... And I have to say that if the president doesn't take the initiative in changing American policy in this regard, the Congress will do it for him.[1]

It was thus very difficult for George Herbert Bush to pursue *Realpolitik* without becoming himself the target of all the critics, and despite his calls to maintain a long-term view of US relations with China, he was constrained to answer in part the claims from Congress. As James Mann summed it up, "Beforehand, members of Congress had played a relatively submissive role. After the Tiananmen crackdown, Congress became much more assertive and was often the dominant factor in determining policy."[2] And the consensus would be all the more difficult to reach since China became one of the main targets of those who made the promotion of human rights or the defence of Taiwan their key issues.

The images of the slaughter had an enormous impact on American public opinion which henceforth viewed China mainly through the prism of the 1989 images of an authoritarian regime, just as a poll conducted a decade later demonstrated.[3] Actually, the media would contribute to this bad image, not only because they would echo the criticism from Congress and from anti-China lobbies, but also because they would themselves offer rather caricatural images of China on which they cast a very critical, distrustful eye.

With the passing years, China became a matter of controversy—sometimes to the point of evoking the rhetoric of McCarthyism—which toughened opinions and often fuelled domestic policy debates in the US. This was particularly obvious during the Clinton presidency because of the harsh rivalry between Congress and the administration. As Morton

Abramowitz deplored some years later, "Tiananmen made good relations with Beijing bad domestic politics again."[4]

Because it fell within the framework of the Cold War, the normalization of US-China relations had been justified by the necessity to counter the Soviet Union which represented a threat to both the United States and China. But when the USSR collapsed—proclaiming America's "victory by default", the base on which Sino-American relations had developed within the "Strategic Triangle" collapsed as well. Moreover, while so many communist regimes disappeared, the PRC survived and resisted the protests from within. Now, its continued existence seemed to make the last communist giant an anachronism in the world political landscape, and it also challenged the new world order which was not defined by world bipolarity any longer, but was—as the 1990-91 Gulf War demonstrated—dominated by what is often called the "Pax Americana." The United States thus seemed bound to question its China policy, not only because concessions to China could not be justified by the Cold War anymore, but also because all eyes turned on China when searching for America's next potential rival.

In the light of the circumstances, many considered that the US did not have to accommodate a communist regime they disapproved of, and this was precisely the argument that Democratic candidate Bill Clinton used to criticize George Herbert Bush in the 1992 presidential campaign:

> In China, the President continues to coddle aging rulers with undisguised contempt for democracy, for human rights, and for the need to control the spread of dangerous weapons technologies. Such forbearance on our part might have been justified during the Cold War as a strategic necessity, when China was a counterweight to the Soviet Union. But it makes no sense to play that China card now, when our opponents have thrown in their hands.[5]

It was also because of the Tiananmen crackdown that "moral" issues gained momentum in the United States. Clinton used these moral issues in his campaign program, and tried to please public opinion and Congress by declaring that, if elected, he would defend human rights and encourage democracy throughout the world. Yet, this emphasis on the defence of democracy and human rights would reveal itself a double-edged sword, because, although it was appealing to many, it would be much more difficult to apply it concretely in a coherent or simply realistic China policy.

Bill Clinton's First Term: a Policy of "Pragmatic Neo-Wilsonianism"?

During his first term, Bill Clinton's China policy was characterized by a certain tactlessness, which was partly due to his inexperience and lack of interest in foreign affairs. In order to keep its campaign promise not to "coddle the butchers of Beijing," the Clinton administration started by conditioning the renewal of the Most-Favored-Nation (MFN) status to effective progress in human rights in China. Yet, this policy—which National Security Adviser Anthony Lake defined as "Pragmatic neo-Wilsonianism"[6]—proved a disaster, for Beijing refused to give in to the American requirements. The problem was that the Clinton administration both overestimated America's capacity to impose its rules and underestimated Beijing's capacity to resist them.

After Secretary of State Warren Christopher's mortifying trip to China in March 1994, during which the Chinese leaders made clear that they would not make any concession to the US, the Clinton administration was criticized and ridiculed for having fallen into its own trap. In view of Beijing's inflexibility, Clinton could please neither human rights activists if he decided to delink MFN and human rights, nor the business community if he refused to extend Most-Favored-Nation status to China. Clinton finally decided to backtrack and officially delinked human rights from MFN renewal on May 26, 1994.

Obviously, it would have made no sense refusing to renew MFN status to China when the latter had been granted it even after the Tiananmen crackdown. In fact, this policy was inapplicable not only because China's economy was on the rise and much less fragile than it was in 1989, but also because the American business community had been increasingly investing in China. [7] After this humiliating episode, the Clinton administration decided to act more in accordance with its campaign slogan "It's the economy, stupid," and adopted a more sober China policy, thus abandoning neo-Wilsonianism to retain only pragmatism.

Yet, the 1994 mid-term congressional elections gave the Republican Party a comfortable majority in Congress, and the tug-of-war between the Clinton administration and Congress would make it particularly difficult to open the dialogue with Beijing without being the target of sharp criticism, just as it would make foreign and domestic policies easily overlap on the China issue. It also furthered the two-headed policy that America could develop towards China, with Congress listening to Taipei, and the administration managing relations with Beijing. For instance, in 1995, Taiwanese President Lee Teng-hui asked to be granted a visa to visit his alma mater, Cornell University, and Congress agreed to the Taiwanese leader's request by a quasi unanimous vote (396-0 in the House of Representatives, and 97-1 in the Senate). [8] This put the Clinton administration in a very embarrassing position, for Clinton could not veto such an overwhelming vote by Congress, but he also had to convince Beijing that he still stuck to the One China Policy. After Lee Teng-hui's unambiguous declarations at Cornell University about the de facto sovereignty of the "Republic of China in Taiwan," Beijing immediately recalled its ambassador to the US and answered the provocation with a series of missile tests in the Taiwan Strait first during the summer of 1995, and then before the Taiwanese presidential elections in early 1996. Washington could not but respond to the PLA missile threats and sent USS Nimitz and USS Independence to the Taiwan Strait. After Lee Teng-hui's re-election, tensions finally receded, but this had definitely been a test for both countries.

The first consequence of the 1995-96 Taiwan Strait Crisis was that China was viewed again with much suspicion, in particular by the "China threat" advocates. The second one was that the Clinton administration realized that it had to give much more thought to its China policy, not only because relations with China had taken a dangerous path, but also because, on a larger scale, many factors had already started to affect the debates on China: the process of globalization, China's economic rise, the increasing interdependence between the American and the Chinese economies, and the American trade deficit with China, all became growing concerns because of their domestic socio-economic repercussions. It was in this context that Bill Clinton presented his strategy of "engagement" towards China:

> Our engagement policy means using the best tools we have, incentives and disincentives alike, to advance core American interests. Engagement does not mean closing our eyes to the policies in China we oppose. We have serious and continuing concerns in areas like human rights, non-proliferation, and trade. When we disagree with China, we will continue to defend our interests and to assert our values. But by engaging China, we have achieved important benefits for our people and the rest of the world. [9]

Three days before, Warren Christopher had paved the way by declaring that "Here at home, we must mend the consensus, frayed since Tiananmen," for, in view of the very heated debates that had been taking place on the China issue, the administration was perfectly conscious that this strategy of engagement would not be welcome by everyone, especially in Congress:

We reject the counsel of those who seek to contain or isolate China. That course would harm our national interests, not protect them. Demonizing China is as dangerously misleading as romanticizing it. American policy toward China has been most successful when we have acknowledged that country's great complexity, recognized that change requires patience as well as persistence, and respected China's sovereignty while standing up for our own values and interests.[10]

Despite a profound redefinition of its China policy, the Clinton administration would still be confronted with the opposition of Congress, and the new "engagement policy" would have to face a series of crises throughout Clinton's second term. Moreover, a new controversy involving China disturbed American domestic politics again, when rumours about PRC financial contributions to Clinton's re-election campaign started to circulate in 1996. Henceforth, the "Chinagate" scandal would come up regularly and last until the end of Clinton's presidency.[11]

Bill Clinton's Second Term:
the Doctrine of "Engagement"

During his re-election campaign, Clinton reoriented much more his discourse on economic matters, arguing that economic prosperity should be the conveyor of the values advocated by America, as he explained in 1996:

That's why we have supported commercial liberalization in China—the world's fastest-growing market. Just as democracy helps make the world safe for commerce, commerce helps make the world safe for democracy. It's a two-way street.[12]

No sooner was Clinton re-elected than his administration pronounced itself in favour of China's entry into the World Trade Organization.

In 1997, the Asian financial crisis which started on July 2—the very day after the handover of Hong Kong—gave China the occasion to appear as a responsible partner, since it quite unexpectedly cooperated with Washington and agreed not to devalue its currency so as to curb the spread of the financial crisis. Clinton thanked Beijing's leaders for their collaboration when President Jiang Zemin made an official State visit to the US (October 26–November 2, 1997). Jiang's visit was, per se, an important event, for it was the first time that a Chinese leader was received with all the honours at the White House since the Tiananmen crackdown; but that was also why it was intrinsically dangerous for the administration.

After both leaders expressed their wish to establish a "constructive strategic partnership," Clinton anticipated the likely attacks of the anti-China lobbyists by stating, during the joint press conference, that he believed that on the issue of human rights "the policy of the [Chinese] Government is on the wrong side of history."[13] This statement was greeted with praise by the media and allowed Clinton to prevent his opponents from criticizing him. As a matter of fact, suspicion had been gaining momentum on both sides of the Pacific: in China, the 1996 bestseller *China Can Say No* both denounced America's imperialism and expressed China's increasing nationalism, while the "China threat" theory was spreading in the American public debate as anti-China books became more numerous and as the Chinagate scandal developed.[14]

Between 1998 and 2000, the improvements in the dialogue between the White House and the Chinese executive were then subject to the domestic crisis which affected the US. As he was weakened at home by the Lewinsky scandal which started in early 1998, Clinton became more active in his foreign policy which was, nevertheless, kept under close scrutiny. Congress severely criticized Clinton's 1998 official State visit to China (June 24-July 3, 1998), and the House of Representatives actually voted the House Resolution 454 on the symbolic day of June 4th to disapprove of Clinton's decision to attend the PLA parade in Tiananmen Square (305-116), as Republican Representative Gerald B. H. Solomon vehemently declared:

> ... in a few weeks, the President of the United States will condone that terrorist act by the Communist Chinese regime, place those internationally recognized human rights on the back burner, and throw those cherished American values into the trash can by being formally received by the Butchers of Beijing right in that very place where the massacres occurred! For years, ... I have been appalled and aghast at the depths of shamelessness to which this administration has sunk in its cowardly but relentless effort to appease the government of Communist China, but this decision by President Clinton is the topper.[15]

During his visit, Clinton seemed to move away from the strategic ambiguity on the Taiwan question when he stated: "We don't support independence for Taiwan, or two Chinas, or one Taiwan, one China. And we don't believe that Taiwan should be a member in any organization for which statehood is a requirement."[16] Congress strongly disapproved of Clinton's "Three-Noes Policy" on the Taiwan issue, and the Senate retaliated a few days later with the unanimous vote (92-0) of the 107 resolution which reaffirmed America's historic engagement towards

Taiwan. The House of Representatives also voted overwhelmingly (390-1) a similar resolution shortly afterwards. Actually, the more the American domestic scene was shaken, the more relations with China were strained, because the "China argument" was often used in the Republicans' anti-Clinton crusade.

In 1999, tensions rose between the two countries and led once more to a climate of mistrust and to heated debates which reached their climax in early 2000 with the unpredictable vote in Congress of granting China Permanent Normal Trade Relations (PNTR). It started with Zhu Rongji's visit to the US in April 1999. The Chinese Premier wanted to reach an agreement with the US and came with extraordinary concessions so as to speed up China's entry into the WTO. Although the concessions were both unexpected and particularly favourable to the US, the Clinton administration feared that Congress might refuse the agreement. Thus, despite its own engagement policy and its official position in favour of China's entry into the WTO, the White House tried to obtain still more concessions, until negotiations finally reached a deadlock. Given the concessions he was ready to make, Zhu Rongji was not only humiliated by the American refusal, but he was also politically weakened in Beijing.

Soon afterwards, tensions worsened with the bombing of the Chinese embassy in Belgrade on May 8, which was immediately followed by violent anti-American protests throughout China. The climate was already particularly ominous when the report written by Representative Christopher Cox on US-China commercial and military relations was published on May 25, 1999. Echoing the rhetoric of McCarthyism, the Cox Report accused China of espionage, and claimed that the Chinese secret services had been stealing for several decades technological plans and information to build sophisticated thermonuclear weapons. It went as far as maintaining that China's aim was to target the United States militarily, and that a very active spy network was present at all levels and in all circles throughout the country.[17]

Although it was difficult to promote a strategy of "engagement" while US-China relations were at their nadir, it became all the more important for the administration to reach an agreement with China since Clinton would soon enter the last year of his second term. It was finally reached on November 15, 1999, and the Clinton administration officially declared it welcomed China's entry into the WTO, while the Chinese agreed that the US could protect its domestic market against possible surges of Chinese products. However, this hard-earned agreement could be ratified only if Congress consented to grant China Permanent Normal Trade Relations status; now, opinions on China had kept toughening, in particular among those who considered China as America's new enemy.

The Climax of the PNTR Debate

The PNTR debate fundamentally questioned the very nature of US-China relations, and the economic issue of China's entry into the WTO soon became a political, if not a strategic issue. This debate, which took place between January and June 2000, gathered all the ingredients that plainly revealed the lack of consensus about China in America. Given the unpredictability of the vote in Congress, more and more actors entered the debate to tip the scales, and for the pros and cons, China was perceived either as an opportunity or as a threat to America's prosperity and interests. In fact, the more the debate raged in the US, the more opinions became radical, until domestic and foreign affairs overlapped once again.

The continuous tug-of-war between the Clinton administration and Congress largely expressed itself during this ultimate trial of strength over Clinton's China policy. As a matter of fact, the House of Representatives started the debate indirectly by voting the Taiwan Security Enhancement Act on February 1st, which sent an obvious message to both the Chinese leaders and the White House, which announced that it would veto the act if the Senate approved it. But as Taiwan was then in the middle of the presidential election campaign, Beijing forcefully declared that it was ready to use force if the negotiations on the return of Taiwan to the mainland dragged on. Thus, the debate on PNTR rapidly gave way to security issues.

A trial of strength took place among interest groups, and more specifically between labour unions and pro-business lobbies who both invested millions of dollars in publicity campaigns. On the one hand, labour unions—in particular the AFL-CIO and the Teamsters—opposed PNTR just as they had fought against the North American Free Trade Agreement (NAFTA). They were concerned about the globalization of the economy and China's economic rise, and denounced the negative effects upon American jobs. In mid-April, labour unions rallied around the slogan "No Blank Check for China" and managed to gather more than 15,000 demonstrators on Capitol Hill.[18] Labour unions eventually joined forces with environmentalists and human rights activists, as they had during the WTO ministerial conference held in Seattle in November 1999.[19] In this respect, the debate went beyond the China issue itself to challenge the very nature of economic globalization.

On the other hand, pro-business lobbies—among which the US Chamber of Commerce and the Business Roundtable—were also extremely active in weighing in on the debate, for they feared Congress might reject PNTR. They considered that the Chinese market offered promising prospects for American companies, and they ceaselessly repeated that the potential market of 1.3 billion consumers could not but favour American exports and guarantee high growth rates. When they saw that the debate was moving from purely economic issues to "moral" ones such as human rights and environment protection, pro-business lobbies did not hesitate to turn trade with China into a "moral issue." They even presented themselves as the guarantors of the respect of liberties and fundamental rights, arguing that the development of trade would be a way—if not the only way—to lead China to democratize and protect human rights. For instance, the Business Roundtable financed several TV advertisements, among which two videos pictured Reverend Kim Kwong Chan who stated that "Trade is a powerful force to help spread religious and democratic values."[20]

Important public figures, such as former Presidents Gerald Ford, Jimmy Carter and George Herbert Bush, and former Secretaries of State Kissinger, Haig, Shultz, Baker, Eagleburger, and Christopher, also gave their support to the bill and advised Congressmen to go beyond partisanship.

By mid-April, Democratic Representative Sander Levin, who was supported by Republican Douglas Bereuter, tabled an amendment to the bill to convince those who reluctantly considered granting China PNTR for "moral" reasons. Their proposal was to create a commission that would allow the US to monitor human rights in China and to limit import surges of Chinese products. But, above all, the fact that certain key figures such as the Dalai Lama, Taiwanese President Chen Shui-bian, or Tiananmen demonstrator Dai Qing, were favourable to China's entry into the WTO did have a great influence on many congressmen.

Finally, on May 24, the vote was won with a rather comfortable majority (237-197), but the hour-long debate preceding it was symbolic of how divided the representatives had been on the issue. Like many others, Democratic Representative Charles Rangel testified:

> Truly, this is a very contentious issue. Members have deep-seated feelings.
> I do not remember anything being lobbied so hard by the administration,
> by the private sector, the Chamber of Commerce and unions, and certainly
> our constituents."[21]

The debate was characteristic of how Congress considered China, because, although opinions could range from the most severe denunciation of communist rule to the mere hope of seeing future democratic improvements, the fact is that none of the representatives expressed a positive opinion of the Chinese government. Moreover, whether they voted for or against PNTR, almost all representatives voiced their concerns about human rights protection, the impact on American jobs and national security, and they basically disagreed on how to answer these problems.

About two-thirds of the representatives followed party lines: despite their continuous opposition to Clinton and their strong support to Taiwan, most Republican representatives supported PNTR because they went along with the pro-business lobbies and generally promoted economic liberalization. They, too, saw China's potential market as an opportunity for American exports and companies, and they also considered that China's integration into the WTO would force China to open up and democratize.

As far as the Democrats were concerned, the majority of their representatives were not favourable to PNTR because they sided with the labour unions' position on the matter. In fact, with the elections in the House of Representatives scheduled for the following November, the Democrats were in a rather uncomfortable position, for the labour unions threatened not to renew their votes for the Democrats if ever they approved PNTR. The Democrats put forward the repeated attacks on human rights and fundamental freedoms and, as for economic issues, they retorted that China had never respected the agreements signed with her trading partners, and that the US should protect American workers.

In the pro-PNTR camp—among which 73 Democrats, most explained that engaging China was a better course than isolating it, first because increasing trade would serve the cause of human rights and democracy by spreading American values throughout China, and secondly because it would be safer in terms of national security. Even conservative Republican Tom DeLay justified his vote by claiming that "Granting PNTR to China is a critical component of a strategy driven by our one, clear objective: destroying communism."[22]

In the opposite camp, most Democrats claimed that China should not be rewarded until it truly protects labour and human rights, and that the US should remain committed to its moral mission throughout the world, as Robert A. Borski argued:

> The Chinese government uses executions and torture to maintain order, persecutes religious minorities and imprisons dissidents who dare to speak

out for democracy. At a bare minimum, China's human rights record must
improve if we are to treat it as an equal partner. ...
If Congress approves PNTR, we forever relinquish any leverage we have
to improve Chinese behavior. ...
But I believe that America stands for something more than the almighty
dollar. As the world's sole superpower and strongest democracy, we have a
moral responsibility to stand up for those who struggle against tyranny. We
are the only nation capable and willing to bring about democratic change in
China. And we can use our economic power to exert that leverage.[23]

If Borski's words summed up the general opinion of anti-PNTR
Democratic representatives, others also denounced the manoeuvres of big
business, whose alleged goal was to relocate production and exploit the
cheap Chinese labour.

However, it should be noted that the anti-PNTR group presented quite
a contrasting picture, because most of the Republicans who opposed the
bill were mainly concerned with national security. They pictured China, as
Dana Rohrabacher did, as "America's number one potential enemy in the
years ahead,"[24] and even made historical references to World War II, Nazi
Germany, or the Cold War against the Soviet Union to prove their point.
According to them, granting China PNTR would jeopardize national
security, since this agreement would help the Chinese military build-up by
an inflow of US dollars, as Duncan Hunter explained:

Well, whichever side of this debate one is on, everyone here has to
concede American dollars are arming Communist China today. ...
Many [Americans] fought in wars for which we were unprepared; that is a
tragedy of the 20th century. But the greater tragedy, which could be the
tragedy of the 21st century, could happen if this country, having fought and
bled and sacrificed to dissolve the Soviet empire, through a massive
infusion of cash produces, by our own hand, another military superpower,
and if the cemeteries of this country one day hold the bodies of Americans
in uniform killed with weapons purchased by American trade dollars.[25]

Quite characteristically, many representatives justified their vote
according to the interests of their home states, and even a geographical
division could also be roughly drawn from this vote. The states where the
vote was largely won were the export-oriented and agricultural states
(Arkansas, California, Iowa, Kansas, Kentucky, Louisiana, Nebraska,
Oklahoma, Texas, Washington). Indeed, the prospect of an increase in
agricultural exports proved a weighty argument, as was the case in Texas
where 25 (among whom 14 Democrats) out of 30 representatives voted for

PNTR. As Democratic Representative Skelton (Missouri) put it plainly, "China is the last major untapped market for American agriculture."[26]

On the other hand, the states where representatives voted massively against PNTR were the northern and eastern states whose economy is based mostly on the industrial and service sectors, and where labour unions are well-established (Connecticut, Massachusetts, Michigan, New Jersey, the two Carolinas, Pennsylvania, Rhode Island, West Virginia). Republican Robin Hayes explained that he opposed the measure because "For the tens of thousands of textile employees in North Carolina's 8th Congressional District, this agreement continues down the road of trading away their jobs to cheap products."[27]

Domestic policy and foreign affairs clearly intermingled in the course of the debate, and Robert Sutter's analysis proved true once again, that is to say that some interest groups "have been less interested in changing China policy than in using China-related issues for U.S. partisan political reasons."[28]

Overall, Congress reluctantly granted China PNTR. Indeed, Congress had been in charge of voting the renewal of MFN status to China until then, and normalizing economic relations made Congress lose this handy tool to check the administration's China policy. Many Congressmen also considered that the US would thus abandon the only weapon it had to pressure China on issues such as human rights, the environment, or Taiwan. Actually, Congress was so reluctant to let go of this possibility that, as early as October 2000, it instituted the US-China Economic and Security Review Commission which has reported annually on China since then. The creation of this new commission was simply another way for Congress to win back lost ground on the China case.

Since Tiananmen, Congress had always tried to appear as the moral conscience of the nation, and implicitly suggested that the legislature, contrary to the executive, would not act out of base motives of economic self-interest. And yet, even though Congress had often voted symbolic measures to criticize either the administration or the Chinese government, it had systematically renewed MFN status for China. Actually, it is highly probable that some undecided representatives finally rallied to the "yes" vote because they did not want to be held responsible for harming the American economy or for provoking a dangerous deterioration of Sino-American relations.

Last but not least, the PNTR debate reached a climax because the very question of accepting or refusing China's entry into the WTO would speak volumes about how Americans considered China and whether they decided to "engage" or "contain" China. Afterwards, the nature of the debate could not but change, for the US would henceforth wonder about how to protect its interests within this new configuration. In a way, by granting China PNTR, the US acknowledged China's place in the new international order both economically and diplomatically, and it also closed, to some extent, the decade-long debate on human rights that had followed the 1989 Tiananmen crackdown.

George W. Bush: a Strategy of "Congagement"?

As many observers have pointed out, the Clinton years were a rather exceptional period in American history, because, strategically speaking, the US remained without any major rival in the 1990s, and it enjoyed a long period of economic prosperity within the process of globalization that Washington furthered through its undisputed leadership. Thus, the US focused on the next potential threat that China seemed to embody, and in view of this most favourable context, actors such as Congress could turn China into a controversial issue without taking too many risks.

The Bush years presented quite a different picture. The election of George W. Bush was accompanied by the arrival of many neo-conservatives who considered that the "China threat" was to be answered by a new form of containment, and the first months of George W. Bush's presidency, indeed, pictured a relationship based on an increasing mutual mistrust. However, after the terrorist attacks of September 11, the priority was not to defy China any longer but, on the contrary, to appease tensions and seek Beijing's cooperation in the so-called "War on Terrorism." Although the relationship followed a calmer path, motives for tension progressively arose again, notably because the China threat theorists did not fundamentally change their opinions about the PRC.

Before 9/11: the Spectre of a New Cold War

As soon as he was nominated by the Republican Party in the 2000 presidential campaign, George W. Bush differentiated himself from Clinton by declaring that "China is a competitor, not a strategic partner. We must deal with China without ill-will—but without illusions."[29] Bush was influenced by the so-called "Blue Team"—which is composed of defence intellectuals, neo-conservative congressmen, Pentagon hawks, conservative journalists, pro-Taiwan lobbyists, etc—who saw China as a threat to American interests. George W. Bush thus gave US-China relations something of a Cold War stance and pictured China as the USSR of the twenty-first century.

During the presidential campaign, Condoleezza Rice—who was then Bush's foreign policy adviser—described the priorities of the future Republican administration and declared that the US should take advantage of the historic occasion of being the one and only superpower since the end of the Cold War to shape its foreign policy according to the "national interest." Now, according to Rice, America's interest was to prevent the emergence of rival powers, and China was unsurprisingly at the top of the list:

> It is important to promote China's internal transition through economic interaction while containing Chinese power and security ambitions. Cooperation should be pursued, but we should never be afraid to confront Beijing when our interests collide.[30]

Condoleezza Rice's policy echoed the "congagement" strategy advocated by Zalmay Khalilzad in an article published by the influential think tank the RAND Corporation in 1999. According to Khalilzad, neither engagement, nor containment was an appropriate strategy vis-à-vis China, insofar as too many uncertainties reigned over China's future and over the Chinese leaders' real objectives. The US should adopt a more flexible strategy that would allow switching policies, depending on whether China would prove friendly or hostile towards the US. For this reason he offered a strategy whose neologism borrows from the Cold War "containment" strategy and from Clinton's "engagement" policy:

> Since neither prevention-containment nor engagement serves U.S. interests, a different strategy is appropriate. The best strategic option must accomplish three things: preserve the hope inherent in engagement policy while deterring China from becoming hostile and hedging against the possibility that a strong China might challenge U.S. interests. Such a strategy could be called "congagement." It would continue to try to bring China into the current international system while giving equal attention to deterrence and preparing for a possible Chinese challenge to this system while seeking to convince the Chinese leadership that a challenge would be difficult to prepare and extremely risky to pursue.[31]

In fact, the neo-conservatives' rhetoric proved more categorical on the strategy that they wanted to set up. In this respect, the Pentagon's annual reports to Congress on China's military power are illuminating on how the PRC has been perceived by the American military.[32] Although they have acknowledged that China is still backward militarily and although their reports are mainly based on estimations and assumptions, they have affirmed, in substance, that the People's Liberation Army wants to modernize and turn China into a military superpower that would ultimately threaten American interests. In other words, the mere fact of China's potentiality makes it an obvious target for the Pentagon.

Just as Condoleezza Rice said that the military should serve as a coercive instrument to defend the national interest, the neo-conservative think tank Project for the New American Century published a manifesto on the necessity of "Rebuilding America's Defenses" in September 2000, in which they also argued that the American military power should be a top priority so as to prevent the emergence of any rival and, therefore, perpetuate the "Pax Americana" into the twenty-first century. They bluntly explained that "at present the United States faces no global rival. America's grand strategy should aim to preserve and extend this advantageous position as far into the future as possible."[33] More precisely, they asserted that the US military defence should be rethought according to the challenge of China's rise in power, and that the focus of strategic competition is no longer Europe but East Asia.[34] In fact, the neo-conservatives tried to use the "China threat" argument in order to justify a military reinforcement, until the 9/11 terrorist attacks provided ample justification to convince Congress to vote the increase in the defence budget.

Indisputably, the Bush administration chose to harden its policy, which was illustrated by the rather undiplomatic words addressed to Beijing. Controversial issues such as human rights, China's compliance with the WTO rules, the National Missile Defense shield, or the Taiwan question were again on the negotiating table when Vice-Premier Qian Qichen made his visit to Washington. The course of events during the first months of 2001 also convinced the administration to adopt a tougher policy vis-à-vis China, particularly after the collision between a US surveillance aircraft and a Chinese fighter jet near Hainan Island on April 1, 2001. The Chinese held the American crew in detention, analyzed meticulously the military-aeronautical technology of the American aircraft, and waited until April 12—that is, after they obtained official excuses from Washington—before they agreed to release the crew. A few days later, after the US retaliated by announcing new arms sales to Taiwan, President George W. Bush even declared in a TV interview that the US would do "whatever it took to help Taiwan defend herself" against a PRC attack, and he allowed Taiwanese President Chen Shui-bian to go to the US in May 2001. This was a blunt, drastic move away from the "One China Policy" which all former presidents, once elected, had followed since the 1972 Shanghai Communiqué. As could be expected, Beijing vehemently warned that it would defend its territorial integrity at all costs.

So, only a few months after Bush took office, US-China relations were again at their nadir, and the warlike rhetoric from both sides of the Pacific was such that the possibility of an open war between the two countries could not be totally ruled out. Until the summer of 2001, everything seemed to announce a new Cold War as the Bush administration increasingly presented China as America's new enemy, when the September 11, 2001 attacks radically disrupted the international scene. Suddenly, China was not part of Washington's immediate priorities any longer and, consequently, also disappeared from the news headlines.

The Consequences of 9/11

Immediately after 9/11, Washington's priority was no longer to battle in the WTO or to provoke China about Taiwan, but to gain Beijing's support on many fronts—North Korea, Central Asia, the Middle East—or at least to secure Beijing's neutrality. In a sudden reversal of the situation, China was presented as an important partner in the "War on Terrorism," and as early as October 2001, during the Asia-Pacific Economic Cooperation forum organized in Shanghai, George W. Bush's rhetoric was markedly more conciliatory:

> China is a great power. And America wants a constructive relationship with China. ...
> Today's meetings convinced me that we can build on our common interests. Two great nations will rarely agree on everything; I understand that. But I assured the President that we'll always deal with our differences in a spirit of mutual respect. We seek a relationship that is candid, constructive and cooperative.[35]

In fact, Beijing soon gave its official support to the "War on Terrorism," and this strategic swing could also be observed in the much more frequent official visits made by both George W. Bush and Jiang Zemin to their respective countries. Not only did the US need China's cooperation in its "War on Terrorism," but it also needed its mediation to deal with North Korea, since the latter was included, along with Iraq and Iran, in the so-called "axis of evil."

As long as the US-led offensives against Afghanistan and Iraq monopolized its attention, Washington chose to maintain the status quo ante in its relations with China. Even the question of Taiwan did not bring up new controversies, and the relations between Taipei, Beijing and Washington were even particularly smooth—that is, after Washington made Chen Shui-bian understand that any unilateral action to move away from strategic ambiguity or to declare Taiwan's independence would be firmly condemned.[36] In other words, Washington implicitly came round to the One China Policy, and Beijing took advantage of the less warlike stance in the bilateral dialogue to pursue its own goals and establish a better relationship with the US, whose market is vital to China's exports and economic growth.

The other important changes that 9/11 brought about was that the "China threat" theory was forgotten for a while and, consequently, the drastic shift in priorities led most actors who had participated in the PNTR debate not to bring up the subject of China. And yet, this did not mean that the hawks and the anti-China lobbyists remained inactive, as the first report of the US-China Economic and Security Review showed, since it echoed both the views of the supporters of the engagement strategy and those of the China threat theory.[37] But the fact that China no longer made the headlines as it had until 9/11 demonstrated that the nationwide debate had calmed down or, at least, that the White House had more leeway to manage its China policy. It should also be noted that Bush did not have to face a hostile Congress as Clinton had, and that the globalization process was not questioned so much anymore, simply because those who opposed the neoliberal nature of globalization were hardly heard after 9/11.

Characteristically, the presence of a third threat made the US and China try and establish a much more cooperative relationship, and the improvements in the bilateral dialogue led Secretary of State Colin Powell to draw the following conclusion in 2004:

> Sino-American relations got off to a bad start in this administration when a certain American airplane made an unscheduled visit to Hainan Island in April 2001. Today, however, U.S. relations with China are the best they have been since President Richard Nixon first visited Beijing more than 30 years ago.
> ... neither we nor the Chinese believe that there is anything inevitable about our relationship any longer—either inevitably bad or inevitably good. Instead, we now believe that it is up to us, together, to take responsibility for our common future. The NSS [National Security Strategy] put it directly: "We welcome the emergence of a strong, peaceful, and prosperous China." We also seek a constructive relationship. Indeed, we welcome a global role for China, so long as China assumes responsibilities commensurate with that role. China's leaders know all this. Neither false fear about the future nor the overhang of Cold War enmity prevents us from cooperating where our interests coincide.[38]

Although Sino-American relations were then characterized by a more open dialogue, this did not mean that the two countries would not face contentious issues. As a matter of fact, the US continued to follow the so-called strategy of "congagement."

An Increasing Economic Interdependence

When China officially entered the World Trade Organization in 2001, the debate in America shifted to whether China would play by the rules or not. Although it welcomed China's entry into the WTO, Washington did not disarm and used either its own coercive instruments or the WTO Dispute Settlement Body to protect its interests. However, the US has always preferred to reach agreements bilaterally, as the multiplication and the reinforcement of China-related commissions have demonstrated: the United States Trade Representative (USTR) Report to Congress on China's WTO Compliance has been published annually since 2002; from 2003 onwards, the USTR has been associated with the Department of Commerce in the annual meetings of the US-China Joint Commission on Commerce and Trade; and this trend was furthered when President Bush and President Hu Jintao announced in September 2006 the creation of the US-China Strategic Economic Dialogue which added to the existing commissions and forums, but also implied a more active presidential participation on the basis of biannual meetings.

Among the contentious issues which have continued to fuel the debate in the US, the problem which has been regularly brought up is the US trade deficit with China. In 1992, the trade deficit was only 18.3 billion dollars, but it kept increasing to such an extent that China finally became the commercial partner with which the US had its biggest deficit in 2000 (83.8 billion dollars). After China's entry into the WTO, it reached a total of 256.2 billion dollars in 2007.[39] However, the US commercial deficit with China has often been used as a political argument in domestic debates.

This gaping trade deficit also explains why the US has ceaselessly pressured China to respect intellectual property rights (IPR), for America wants to get the expected profits from its "knowledge economy." As early as 1994, China was on the US "Priority Watch List" of the Special 301 for IPR infringements, and was monitored even more closely from 1997 onwards with the Special 306 Monitoring—which concerns only China and Paraguay. Lobbies such as the International Intellectual Property Alliance have been particularly active in Washington, and again, in 2005, the USTR Special 301 report announced that China was back at the top of the list for lack of improvement in IPR protection.[40]

In recent years, the US also denounced the undervaluation of the Chinese currency (the renminbi) and accused China of benefiting from an excessively low currency that was said to aggravate the trade deficit and to provoke the loss of American jobs. The renminbi was pegged to the US dollar and its exchange rate had remained the same since 1994 (¥ 8,277 to the US$). But when the drop in the US dollar in 2002 brought about that of the renminbi, the US complained and demanded a revaluation of the Chinese currency. On September 25, 2003, during a congressional session in which the "China threat" theory came back again, the US-China Economic and Security Review Commission gave the results of its inquiry and accused the Chinese government of voluntarily maintaining its currency 15% to 40% under its true value and of manipulating its currency through the acquisition of US dollars—which was estimated at 120 billion every year. According to the commission, the undervaluation of the renminbi contributed to relocating production in China and, therefore, to undermining American industry's competitiveness. The commission strongly advised the Treasury to immediately enter into negotiations with the Chinese authorities so as to put an end to this unfair competition.[41] In early 2004, the National Association of Manufacturers and the Fair Currency Alliance—which was later replaced by the China Currency Coalition—also lobbied both the administration and Congress to plead their cause.[42] But in this debate, it seemed that, once more, China was used so as to blame someone for the deterioration of the American economy which, particularly in 2002-2003, suffered from a downturn in economic growth and a drop in the US dollar. It resembled a political manoeuvre, for accusing China of unfair competition could divert public attention from the domestic problems and from the politicians' mismanagement. Above all, this controversy showed that the debate on China could be easily rekindled, and also that the "China threat" theory had not vanished.

As a matter of fact, the problem has been much complicated by the growing financial interdependence, for, paradoxically, China buys large amounts of US Treasury bonds which, in return, allows the US to buy the cheap Chinese products it needs to meet consumer demand:

> The result is a historically unusual relationship in which the rising power, developing China, provides both exports (second-leading supplier) and loans (second-leading foreign holder of government debt) to the superpower, the industrialized United States.[43]

On the one hand, this very interdependence has given both countries less latitude to take drastic measures that would also affect their own economy, but on the other hand, it has also allowed them to try and apply a strategy of "economic deterrence." In this respect, the US has still been in a more powerful position than China, for the latter absolutely needs to have access to the American market; yet, China has definitely reinforced its capacity to discourage the US from retaliating.

In 2006, China's gross domestic product (GDP) was ranked sixth in real GDP, but it was ranked second, close behind the US, when calculated in purchasing power parity. The perception of China's power—and above all its potential—has weighed on how Washington has conceived its relations with China: the Clinton administration tried to see to it that China would respect the world trade rules, so that its integration into the world economy would not be detrimental to the US; the Bush administration's strategy was relatively different, insofar as it did not want to harm the American economy by containing China economically, but it dreaded the idea that China's economic rise could give Beijing the means to become America's new rival.

To a certain extent, the US-led war in Iraq seems the expression of the strategy of "congagement." Indeed, the US and China have become the top world oil consumers, and China's booming oil demand has been worrying the US.[44] Now, in view of the vital necessity to have access to energy resources for economic and military needs, many observers have considered the war in Iraq as a means to check China's rise. In fact, this was precisely what the report "Rebuilding America's Defenses" advocated in substance in 2000, and Beijing is convinced that the US has invested in the Middle East militarily, diplomatically and economically, so as to control this most coveted resource and, therefore, to make use of this weapon against China, if need be.[45] So, despite some improvements in the Sino-American dialogue, mutual suspicion has remained and there is no doubt that China can easily make a come-back in the headlines in America.

Conclusion

Since the Tiananmen crackdown, Sino-American relations have become increasingly complex and China has been more and more often at the heart of the debates in the United States. Not only does China represent the last communist giant in the post-Cold War era, but its economic rise is such that many fear that China may replace America as the world's leading economic power and, therefore, may have the capacity to reinforce its military power in the process. Although there has been a consensus on the idea that China is a challenge to the US, the consensus on how to answer this challenge has been hard to reach, and all the more so since not only are the actors numerous, but they also diverge greatly in their perceptions of China. In other words, the US has hesitated between promoting a strategy of "engagement" and applying a new form of "containment."

If domestic and foreign affairs often mix in the US, this trend has been particularly obvious as far as China is concerned, because its symbolic power—be it negative or positive—has often been used by many different lobbies as an argument in American domestic debates. In this respect, the differences between the Clinton years and the Bush years are quite obvious, for the domestic constraints and the international context radically changed, first with the end of the Cold War in the early 1990s, which explained why the US paid much closer attention to China, and then with the terrorist attacks of September 11, 2001, which made the US and China unexpectedly come together in the "War on Terrorism." Indeed, characteristically, Sino-American relations are less strained when the focus of attention is diverted by an external threat.

Yet, although their relations improved, at least diplomatically, contentious issues remained, particularly in the economic field, such as the gaping US trade deficit with China, the problem of intellectual property rights infringements, the undervaluation of the Chinese currency, etc. But because of their growing economic and financial interdependence, the two countries have had much less room for manoeuvre without taking risks of affecting their own economy. Likewise, the question of Taiwan's status remains a potentially explosive issue between the United States and China, and suspicion on both sides is unlikely to recede in the near future. But it seems that an increasing number of actors finally favour the so-called strategy of "congagement," because, although the most radical China threat theorists consider that China's rise in power should be contained, they also realize that economic interdependence is such that containing China could be detrimental to America's own economy and that it calls for a very pragmatic China policy.

China's outstanding economic growth has contributed to disrupting the international chessboard and has made the United States worry about its capacity to compete with China in the long run and about China's ambitions on the international scene. Now, given that many in the US consider that China's mere potential makes it one of the most probable rivals to America's interests in the 21st century, there is, therefore, absolutely no doubt that China will continue to fuel debates in the United States. Whether China is considered as a "strategic partner" or as a "strategic competitor," in both cases the keyword which defines US-China relations is definitely the term "strategic."

Bibliography

Primary Sources

AFL-CIO. "No Blank Check for China Rally, U.S. Capitol Washington, D.C." 12 April 2000 http://www.aflcio.org/ (January 10, 2001).

Bush, George Walker. "China and Russia—Powers in Transition." November, 19, 1999 http://usinfo.state.gov/journals/itps/0900/ijpe/pj52bush.htm (September 20, 2004).

—. "U.S., China Stand against Terrorism—Joint Press Conference with Jiang Zemin in Shanghai." October 19, 2001 www.whitehouse.gov/news/releases/2001/10/20011019-4.html   (20 September 2004).

Business Roundtable. TV advertisements broadcasted on American TV networks between January and May 2000. www.brtable.org (January 10, 2002).

Christopher, Warren. *In the Stream of History. Shaping Foreign Policy for a New Era*. Stanford: Stanford University Press, 1998.

Clinton, Bill. *Between Hope and History: Meeting America's Challenges for the 21st Century*. New York: Times Books, 1996.

—. *The Clinton Foreign Policy Reader: Presidential Speeches with Commentary*. Edited by Alvin Z. Rubinstein, Albina Shayevich, and Boris Zlotnikov. Armonk: M.E. Sharpe, 2000.

—. "Joint Press Conference by President Clinton and President Jiang Zemin." October 29, 1997 www.clintonpresidentialcenter.org (September 14, 2004).

—. "Remarks by the President and the First Lady in Discussion on Shaping China for the 21st Century, Shanghai, PRC." June 30, 1998 http://clinton4.nara.gov/WH/New/China/19980630-3597.html (May 20, 2002).

Human Rights Watch. "China's Accession to the WTO and Human Rights, Testimony before the House Committee on International Relations." May 10, 2000 www.hrw.org/campaigns/china-99/china-testimony-051100.htm (January 13, 2002).

Powell, Colin L. "A Strategy of Partnerships." *Foreign Affairs* 83:1 (2004): 22-34.

Project for the New American Century. "Rebuilding America's Defenses: Strategy, Forces and Resources for a New Century." September 2000 www.newamericancentury.org/publicationsreports.htm (January 15, 2006).

Rice, Condoleezza. "Promoting the National Interest." *Foreign Affairs* 79:1 (2000): 45-62.

US Census Bureau. "Trade with China, 1985-2007." www.census.gov/foreign-trade/balance/c5700.html (January 25, 2008).

US-China Economic and Security Review Commission. "2002 Annual Report," www.uscc.gov (February 20, 2005).

—. "China's Industrial, Investment and Exchange Rate Policies: Impact on the United States." *Congressional Hearing*. September 25, 2003 www.uscc.gov (January 9, 2006).

—. "China's Energy Needs and Strategies." *Congressional Hearing*. 30 October 2003 http://www.uscc.gov (October 25, 2005)

US Department of Defense. "Annual Report to Congress: Military Power of the People's Republic of China." Annual Report since 2002 www.dod.mil/pubs/china.html.

US House of Representatives. H.R. 454. "Sense of Congress that the President Should Reconsider Decision to Be Formally Received in Tiananmen Square by People's Republic of China." *Congressional Record*. 105th cong., 2nd sess. 1998. 144, no.71 (June 4, 1998): H4112-H4123.

—. "Cox Report." May 1999 http://www.house.gov/coxreport/ (December 2, 2002).

—. H.R. 4444. "Providing for Further Consideration of H.R. 4444, Authorizing Extension of Nondiscriminatory Treatment (Normal Trade Relations Treatment) to People's Republic of China." *Congressional Record*. 105th cong., 2nd sess. 2000. 146, no.66 (May 24, 2000): H3652-H3747.

—. "Oil Diplomacy: Facts and Myths behind Foreign Oil Dependency." *Congressional Hearing*. June 20, 2002 http://www.foreignaffairs.house.gov/archives/107/80291.pdf (May 30, 2004).

US Trade Representative. "Report to Congress on China's WTO Compliance." Annual Report since 2002 http://www.ustr.gov.

—. "Special 301 Report Finds Progress and Need for Significant Improvements—Results of China OCR Released, China Elevated to Priority Watch List." April 29, 2005 http://www.ustr.gov (August 30, 2007).

Secondary Sources

Abramowitz, Morton I. *China: Can We Have a Policy?* Washington, D.C.: Carnegie Endowment for International Peace, 1997.

Bernstein, Richard, and Ross H. Munro. *The Coming Conflict with China.* New York: Vintage Books, 1997.

Deng, Yong, and Thomas G. Moore. "China Views Globalization: Toward a New Great-Power Politics?" *Washington Quarterly* 27:3 (2004): 116-136.

Downs, Erica Strecker. *China's Quest for Energy Security.* Santa Monica: Rand, 2000.

Gertz, Bill. *Betrayal: How the Clinton Administration Undermined American Security.* Washington, D.C.: Regnery Publishing, 1999.

—. *The China Threat: How the People's Republic Targets America.* Washington, D.C.: Regnery Publishing, 2002.

Hufbauer, Gary Clyde, Yee Wong, and Ketki Sheth. *US-China Trade Disputes: Rising Tide, Rising Stakes.* Washington, D.C.: Institute for International Economics, 2006.

Khalilzad, Zalmay. "Congage China." *RAND Corporation,* Issue Paper 187, (1999): 1-8 http://www.rand.org/pubs/issue_papers/IP187/ (April 15, 2007)

Mann, James. *About Face: A History of America's Curious Relationship with China, from Nixon to Clinton.* New York: Vintage Books, 2nd ed., 2000.

Sutter, Robert G. *U.S. Policy toward China: An Introduction to the Role of Interest Groups.* Lanham: Rowman & Littlefield Publishers, 1998.

Tien, Charles, and James A. Nathan. "The Polls-Trend: Ambivalence towards China." *Public Opinion Quarterly* 65:1 (2001): 124-138.

Notes

[1] *Washington Post,* June 5, 1989

[2] James Mann, *About Face: A History of America's Curious Relationship with China, from Nixon to Clinton.* (New York: Vintage Books, 2nd ed., 2000) 372

[3] Tien and Nathan, "The Polls-Trend: Ambivalence towards China," 125.

[4] Abramowitz, *China: Can We Have a Policy?* 7.

[5] *Associated Press,* April 1, 1992

[6] Anthony Lake, "From Containment to Enlargement—Speech of Assistant to the President for National Security Affairs, at Johns Hopkins University, Washington, D.C.," September 21, 1993, *in* Clinton, *The Clinton Foreign Policy Reader,* 21-22.

[7] Mann, *About Face,* 285.

[8] Christopher, *In the Stream of History,* 287.

[9] Clinton, "Remarks by the President to the Pacific Basin Economic Council," May 20, 1996, in Clinton, *The Clinton Foreign Policy Reader,* 117-118.

[10] Christopher, "American Interests and the U.S.-China Relationship," May 17, 1996, *in* Christopher, *In the Stream of History,* 434.

[11] The term "Chinagate" came to refer to other scandals, such as alleged nuclear espionage on behalf of the PRC. Mann, *About Face*, 349-350.

[12] Clinton, *Between Hope and History*, 36.

[13] Clinton, "Joint Press Conference by President Clinton and President Jiang Zemin," October 29, 1997.

[14] For instance, Bernstein and Munro, *The Coming Conflict with China* (1997), or *Washington Times* journalist Bill Gertz, *Betrayal: How the Clinton Administration Undermined American Security* (1999), and later *The China Threat: How the People's Republic Targets America* (2002).

[15] US House of Representatives, H.R. 454, June 4, 1998: H4112.

[16] Clinton, "Remarks by the President and the First Lady in Discussion on Shaping China for the 21st Century," June 30, 1998.

[17] US House of Representatives, *Cox Report*, May 1999.

[18] AFL-CIO, "No Blank Check for China Rally," April 12, 2000.

[19] Human Rights Watch, "China's Accession to the WTO and Human Rights," May 10, 2000.

[20] Business Roundtable, TV advertisements broadcasted on American TV networks between January and May 2000.

[21] US House of Representatives, H.R. 4444, May 24, 2000: H3670.

[22] *Ibid.*, H3717.

[23] *Ibid.*, H3721.

[24] *Ibid.*, H3673.

[25] *Ibid.*, H3709.

[26] *Ibid.*, H3741.

[27] *Ibid.*, H3693.

[28] Sutter, *U.S. Policy Toward China: An Introduction to the Role of Interest Groups*, 2.

[29] Bush, "China and Russia—Powers in Transition," November 19, 1999.

[30] Rice, "Promoting the National Interest," 57.

[31] Khalilzad, "Congage China," 6.

[32] US Department of Defense, "Annual Report to Congress: Military Power of the People's Republic of China."

[33] Project for the New American Century, "Rebuilding America's Defenses," ii.

[34] *Ibid.*, 2

[35] Bush, "U.S., China Stand Against Terrorism," October 19, 2001.

[36] Bush, "President Bush and Premier Wen Jiabao Remarks to the Press," December 9, 2003.

[37] US-China Economic and Security Commission, "2002 Annual Report."

[38] Powell, "A Strategy of Partnerships," 31.

[39] US Census Bureau, "Trade with China, 1985-2007."

[40] USTR, "Special 301 Report Finds Progress and Need for Significant Improvements," April 29, 2005.

[41] US-China Economic and Security Review Commission, "China's Industrial, Investment and Exchange Rate Policies: Impact on the United States," September 25, 2003, iii.

[42] Hufbauer, et al., *US-China Trade Disputes*, 13-14.
[43] Deng & Moore, "China Views Globalization: toward a New Great-Power politics?" 132.
[44] US House of Representatives, "Oil Diplomacy: Facts and Myths behind Foreign Oil Dependency," 20 June 2002; US-China Economic and Security Review Commission, "China's Energy Needs and Strategies," October 30, 2003.
[45] Downs, *China's Quest for Energy Security*, 44-45.

CHAPTER EIGHT

LIFTING "THE VEIL OF HOSTILITY": DISCOURSE ON RUSSIA BY BRITISH AND AMERICAN POLITICAL LEADERS

LORI MAGUIRE

Russia, as the dominant power in the USSR, was the great enemy of the Cold War and the primary target of Cold-War rhetoric in both Britain and the United States. From the "iron curtain" speech by Churchill in 1946 to the "evil empire" discourse of Reagan in 1983, Russia received the central focus of Cold War oratory which, simply put, tended to focus on fear and hostility. Mikhail Gorbachev's assumption of the reins of power in 1985 and his policies of *glasnost* and *perestroika* began a re-evaluation of attitudes towards Russia which now appeared less threatening to the West. In 1991 the Soviet Union collapsed and eventually split into 15 different countries with the reformer Boris Yeltsin President of Russia. Neither the British nor the American governments had foreseen this development and both had problems adjusting to it. The West reacted ambivalently and, at times, with indifference to this radical change and to the economic plight of the former Soviet Union. We shall trace here the evolution of discourse by political leaders in both the United States and the United Kingdom from the fall of the Soviet Union in 1991 to the election of Dmitry Medvedev as President of Russia in 2008. We shall see that, although both nations expressed great hope about the future of Russia, fear, hostility and criticism were never far, and had a propensity to dominate discourse at the end of the period. Indeed, one is frequently struck by the continuation of Cold War rhetoric rather than a break from it.

When the Soviet Union fell apart in 1991, the then American President, George H.W. Bush, showed remarkably little interest in the development and in the future of its former members. Indeed, in several areas the British reacted faster than the Americans. They invited Gorbachev, the first time a Russian leader had been so honoured, to the

1991 G-7 Conference which they hosted in London and later, in 1998 when the British next hosted it, the group officially became the G-8. British leaders believed that the West had to help stabilize Russia–in spite of the apparent lack of interest of the Bush administration. As the Labour Defence spokesman, Gerald Kaufman explained:

> The West bears its own heavy responsibility for what has taken place. At the G-7 summit six months ago, Mikhail Gorbachev was treated like a mendicant. Seeking aid for his country, he was sent home empty-handed and humiliated.[1]

A key idea here was Russia's feeling of humiliation as a fallen superpower–a feeling that Britain, an ex-superpower herself, might understand and sympathize with. The general consensus in the U.K. held that something had to be done to show Russia that she was still respected and played a major role in the world. The fact that John Major, British Prime Minister from 1990 to 1997, had invited Gorbachev to the conference showed already that the Conservative government felt the need to help Russia and involve it in Western institutions. In February 1994 the then Foreign Minister, Douglas Hurd, wrote in his diary: "It's this sense of being ignored which really damages, and could be fatal to Yeltsin if we go on doing that."[2] Major echoed this idea in his memoirs, writing: "To disregard Russia when she was weak might not be forgotten when she was strong once again."[3] Britain had a real opportunity–or so its leaders felt–to influence Russia, gaining its gratitude and friendship and thus help the U.K. in its quest to continue playing a major role on the world scene. Kauffman stated this clearly:

> The question now for the international community is not what can be done to restore the old stability–that is not possible–but how to create a new and lasting stability. With the United States still dominant, but economically weak and ready to accept others sharing its hegemony, there is an unprecedented opportunity for the United Kingdom to give a lead not as a superpower but as a catalyst. Britain can count in the world. There is an agenda waiting to be implemented and Britain can help to formulate that agenda.[4]

If America would not give the lead then the United Kingdom, although weaker, could still use its influence to get Western nations to help–which might reap important benefits, notably in an extension of British influence, later.

Of course, Russia had been the main security threat to Britain, and to Europe in general, since the end of World War II; Many British people felt that giving financial assistance to Russia would help stabilize the country. Their goal was to integrate the former enemy into European institutions (as had been done with Germany after World War II), lead it towards democracy and, thereby, hopefully, remove the U.K.'s predominant security risk. In this they were not alone for, in spite of the apparent indifference of the first Bush administration, many Americans felt the same way–most notably the former President, Richard Nixon. On 11 March 1992, Nixon gave a widely noticed speech in which he called for more assistance to Russia:

> Yeltsin is the most pro-Western leader in Russian history. Under those circumstances, then, he deserves our help. Charity, it is said, begins at home, and I agree. But aid to Russia, just speaking of Russia specifically, is not charity. We have to realize that if Yeltsin fails, the alternative is not going to be somebody better – it's going to be somebody infinitely worse. We have to realise that if Yeltsin fails, the new despotism, which will take its place, will mean that the peace dividend is finished, we will have to rearm, and that's going to cost infinitely more than would the aid that we provide at the present time.[5]

Here we see what will become one of the major themes of both American and British discourse in the 1990s: help Yeltsin or risk returning to the worst days of the Cold War with a new, even more expensive arms race and threats to Western security. Nixon succeeded in his immediate goal: the Bush administration did propose an aid package. But interestingly enough, one of the persons who listened most carefully to this speech was the future Democratic candidate for president, Bill Clinton and stabilizing Russia became one of the major foreign policy goals of his administration. Not long after his election, on 1 April 1993, Clinton spoke at length about Russia to the American Society of Newspaper Editors, re-echoing Nixon's ideas:

> Nothing could contribute more to global freedom, to security, to prosperity than the peaceful progression of this rebirth of Russia. It could mean a modern state, at peace not only with itself but with the world... The success of Russia's renewal must be a first-order concern to our country... Our ability to put people first at home requires that we put Russia and its neighbors first on our agenda abroad.[6]

Put simply, you cannot have both guns and butter and, if Americans want a better life, they need to cut military spending. The greatest threat to American security since World War II had been the Soviet Union which had now disintegrated. Russia, the heart of the former empire remained, though. Clinton's reasoning followed the same path as the British: stabilize Russia to remove it as a potential menace. Clinton proposed a "strategic alliance" not with Russia itself, significantly, but with "Russian reform": the heart of the nation itself still remains suspect but Russian reformers can lead it, if they have the necessary resources, to beat in harmony with the West. The symbol of this reform was Boris Yeltsin and very quickly this alliance took on the aspect of a personal relationship with virtually unconditional support for the Russian President. Yeltsin, it was argued, had to remain in power because, if he did not, worse was waiting.

In his April 1993 meeting with Yeltsin in Vancouver, Clinton promised extensive economic assistance and, at first, the U.S. Congress went along with this.[7] In that same year a $2.5 billion aid package to the ex-Soviet Union was voted with over $1.6 billion for Russia. But the money was not necessarily earmarked for the most important areas nor was it always well spent as corruption flourished. 1993 also saw Yeltsin's stand-off with the Russian Parliament that ended in the military shelling the building. Although Yeltsin called elections soon afterwards and had been firmly supported by both Major and Clinton, critical voices began to gain strength. The revelation, in February 1994, that CIA agent Aldrich Ames had worked as a spy for the Soviet Union and had continued to do so for Russia further soured relations, notably in Congress.

The lead-up to the 1994 congressional elections saw increasing criticism of Clinton by Republican leaders and polarisation between the parties. Clinton had made Russia one of the centrepieces of his foreign policy and so it was particularly vulnerable to attack–especially since the deficiencies of the new Russia were so obvious. Added to this, the Republicans especially had a long Cold War tradition of anti-Russian rhetoric which easily resurfaced. Senator Bob Dole, leader of the Republicans in the Senate, talked of "the reassertion of Russian imperialism" and called for "a fundamental reassessment of United States policy toward Russia."[8] According to Senator Richard Lugar, another Republican: "We are not partners with Russia. We are tough-minded rivals."[9] The confirmation hearings for Strobe Talbott as Deputy Secretary of State in February 1994 showed clearly the growing partisanship in the Senate. Senator Slade Gorton of Washington, for example, attacked Talbott saying: "But after the cold war was won, Mr. Talbott insisted that only the inherent weakness of the Soviet system was responsible for our victory and that President Reagan's military buildup was unnecessary."[10] Gorton appeared to be saying that Talbott should not be approved by the Senate because the Democrats did not accept the Republicans' interpretation for the fall of communism. Trent Lott of Mississippi, future

Senate majority leader, also attacked Talbott for having written against
Reagan's policies and went even further. He saw Talbott as "soft on the
former Soviet Union" and sung the virtues of American ideals and
American strength:

> With the end of the cold war, America and her ideals should be triumphant.
> The international sphere has never been a Garden of Eden, but America,
> sure in its resolve and rightness, and steeled by its victory over
> communism, should now have a sturdier hand and influence in the world.
>
> Yet we are floundering. Part of the problem is that this administration is
> unsure of our country's rightness. Thus, you have this multilateralism
> fetish. The United States has been carrying water for the United Nations
> because we are not willing to play the quarterback ourselves. We have
> threatened force and not used it. We have promised intervention and then
> we have cowered… There is the danger that our allies and, even worse, our
> enemies think our resolve is only bluster and that we are weak and we are
> blind.[11]

Lott clearly saw foreign policy in Manichean terms with America cast as
the personification of goodness. The United States' great virtue made it the
proper leader of the world but Clinton had betrayed this by compromising
American purity through multilateralism. For Lott, America must not
corrupt itself by acting through the UN but maintain its independent purity
and make others behave properly, if necessary through force. Lott insisted
later in his speech that "the Soviet Union was an illegitimate regime and
was an evil empire". Talbott, then was guilty of moral relativism and even
of a betrayal of American ideals for, according to Lott, he "took the former
Soviet Union to be legitimate and morally equivalent to our own system,
which it was not."[12] In some sense, then the Russians deserved what they
had got and the United States should not worry about their feelings or
hesitate to assert its power on the world scene.

It was only a short trip from here to comparisons with another conflict
frequently portrayed in terms of good and evil: the Second World War.
Senator Gorton already used the word "appeasement" in the Talbott
confirmation hearings and its use continued among Republicans. Many
portrayed Bill Clinton as a modern Neville Chamberlain, leading the
nation to the indignity of a new Munich. The comparison usually occurred
in relation to the treatment of eastern European nations and of former parts
of the Soviet Union. Representative Gerald Solomon of New York told the
House of Representatives in September 1994: "the Clinton administration
is preparing to sell out Russia's neighbors for the sake of appeasing
Russia."[13] He went on to add:

> It is morally unthinkable that we would sell these people out again... In 1938, Munich. In 1945, Yalta. In the 1970's détente. Every time we have ceded Russia or Germany hegemony over these areas, disaster has followed.[14]

There is undeniably some truth here for Eastern Europe and former countries of the Soviet Union had legitimate security needs. They still smarted from earlier Russian domination and had no wish to see it return so they looked to the West for security and assistance. These concerns had to be addressed and Eastern Europe stabilized–preferably as democracies. The obvious way to do this was through NATO and the EU–but Russian opposition had to be dealt with. Added to this, many of these countries had large immigrant communities present in the United States who voted in elections and members of Congress would be highly sensitive to this. Still, it seems that many people found it difficult to break out of the traditional rhetoric of the Cold War.   In fact, a close look at the rhetoric of those who supported aid to Russia and those who attacked it reveals few fundamental differences. Both see Russia as a major security threat; they disagree, however, about how to deal with it. The major divergence was that those who thought like Clinton believed that Russia could change for the better (that an alliance with Russian reform could transform that nation) while those who opposed his policies did not believe alteration possible. Furthermore, on the Republican side especially, the rhetorical links with the neo-conservatives and the justifications for the Iraq War are also obvious and one may wonder if years of listening to such oratory did not presuppose many members of Congress to vote in favour of that conflict.

Of course, the association with the Second World War did not work only one way and could be used to justify assistance to Russia. At the time of the financial meltdown, Representative Tom Lantos, Democrat from California, told the House:

> Not too many decades ago, in the bemired Republic of Germany, as hyperinflation took hold, fascism followed, and so did the Second World War. It is in our prime policy interests to attempt to stabilise the Russian economy.[15]

It was difficult to miss his message that a dictator like Hitler could come to power in Russia and that this could lead to war (or worse). Added to this were signs of rising anti-Semitism in Russia which, according to one Democratic Representative was "dangerously reminiscent of pre-Nazi Germany".[16]

Steve Horn from California saw parallels with World War I. He followed the principal interpretation that the Allies had won the war only to lose the peace through the injustices of the Versailles treaty:

> We must not assume that as victors of the cold war we can impose any conditions we wish on the losers. The allies made that mistake at the end of the First World War. We had won the war in 1918, and we lost the peace in 1919 by forcing on a vanquished Germany a Treaty of Versailles that every thoughtful person knew was completely unreasonable, harsh, and ultimately unsustainable. The result was not a lasting peace but a temporary truce between two great world wars. We must not repeat that mistake.[17]

Once again we see the logic of helping Russia now or facing worse later. Otherwise they might find themselves involved in another, worse conflict. Interestingly enough, Steve Horn was a Republican Congressman, albeit a moderate one, and this is one of the rare departures, in an increasingly partisan House, from party rhetoric.

For Horn, and others who thought like him, Russia had to become involved in the major Western institutions. We have already seen that Major pushed for Russian participation in the G-7. That was settled relatively quickly and easily. The Russian relationship with European institutions and NATO was more complicated. In 1995, the European Union signed partnership and cooperation agreements with Russia and Ukraine. This accord required ratification by all member states, including, of course, Great Britain. The agreements sought to foster political dialogue at all levels between Russia and the EU and place their relations on the same level as those between the United States and the EU. They also purposed to establish closer trading links, with the possibility of free trade in the future. When first signed, the accords were relatively uncontroversial but the first Chechen war broke out in November 1994 and attitudes changed. David Davis, Minister of State at the Foreign Office, was quite clear about the impact of Chechnya:

> The agreement with Russia was signed amid great optimism about the prospects for Russia's relations with the west. Events in Chechnya have cast a cloud over that relationship. Some people have said that the west should punish the Russians by withdrawing co-operation. We believe that would be a mistake. The west cannot, and does not, turn a blind eye to what is going on in Chechnya, but we shall not help our powers of influence over the Russian Government by closing off all avenues of co-operation.[18]

Once again we see this idea that "punishing" Russia would only lead to disaster. Later in the debate, Davis made an interesting admission:

> We in the House have an objective: to ensure that our western institutions are used to engage Russia so that it acts according to internationally accepted norms of behaviour... Events in Chechnya show us all that Russia has a long time to go before meeting the standards that we expect, but my hon. Friends are wrong if they think that we do not take the position seriously. What we are debating, in fact, is not that, but the method whereby we can ensure that the Russian Government's behaviour improves.[19]

Note the dominant theme here: Russia must belong to Western institutions not because it subscribes to Western standards of behaviour and thus deserves to be there but because membership will push Russia towards these standards. Russia must not be punished but it must be educated. Like Germany and Japan after World War II, Russia is to be brought into these institutions, although not ready for them, in the hope that this will unite Russia to the Western democracies, make it progress towards their standards and defuse it as a threat. There is something patronising about this attitude: to some extent, Russia was being spoken of as a naughty child who needed to be taught proper behaviour. It is perhaps not surprising to see that, while the European Parliament held up ratification of the agreements because of the Chechen war, they finally entered into force in 1997.

As in America one can also find a continuation of Cold War rhetoric. Christopher Gill, for example, argued against the agreements with Russia:

> I am opposed to agreements with the former Soviet Union because I do not share the evident view of the Foreign Office that the leaders of the former Soviet Union can be trusted. On the contrary, there is ample evidence to suggest that the Russians are pursuing a devious strategy that is designed to lock the western powers into complex arrangements and then to dominate them.[20]

Notice how he refers to "the former Soviet Union" instead of Russia. This rhetorical device reinforces his thesis that nothing has really changed and that hostility and reason for fear remain. Obviously, events like the Chechen war gave force to these arguments although they appear to have been less common in Britain than in the United States. This was possibly linked to the fact that such opinions tended to occur on the right. In Britain at this time the Conservatives were in power so it would have meant criticizing their own party while in America Russian policy was used as an issue by Republicans in Congress to attack a Democratic president.

The Chechen War also had an impact on Russia's application to join the Council of Europe. Russia first applied in 1992 and in the following years made significant progress towards acceptance. David Atkinson, a British MP, headed the Non-member Countries Committee of the Council whose task was to evaluate candidates. He explained in Westminster, in the same debate cited earlier, that, although there were obvious problems with Russian democracy, the Council had been "prepared to turn a blind eye" and "invite it into full membership". Chechnya changed all this:

> Russia's action in Chechnya, however, put paid to that, and rightly so. We have now suspended our consideration of Russia's application until we are satisfied with the response to the terms of the resolution that we passed on 2 February... the principal concern behind our resolution was that Russia had demonstrated for all to see, even while it was pressing to join the Council of Europe, that it was prepared to ignore the entire purpose of the Council of Europe's existence – that never again should force be used to resolve disputes.[21]

According to Atkinson, Russia was acting against the basic direction of European history since the end of World War II by using force against Chechnya. Examination of Russian candidature was thus suspended and only restarted in September 1995 after meetings with both Russian and Chechen leaders. Finally, after the December parliamentary elections in Russia, the rapporteurs who included Atkinson, decided to recommend Russian membership to the Parliamentary Assembly of the Council. His lack of enthusiasm was evident:

> Should we decide to invite Russia to join, for which it has been pressing since 1992, we know that that will be a political judgment, made in the clear realisation that Russia has not yet reached our standards of membership, but that it is more likely to achieve those standards as a full member than if we were to keep it out in the cold.
> Should we decide that we cannot compromise our standards to such an extent in the case of the largest country in Europe, we risk unknown consequences for Russia, Europe and the rest of the world.[22]

So here we return to the argument that punishing Russia would only hurt the West. Note the reference to Russia being "out in the cold" which contains clear reminiscences of the Cold War. In some sense he is implying that the Cold War had not really ended and would not end until Russia was fully integrated into Europe. Atkinson went on to state that:

"Full membership will encourage the forces of democracy and reform in Russia, both in Parliament and in government", which sounds very similar to many of the Clinton administration's pronouncements. Atkinson also talked, in terms that Russia probably would have found patronising, of encouraging its progress towards "our European standards"–echoing the idea that Russia had to learn proper behaviour. He also stressed the fact that Russian individuals would have the right to petition the European Court in case of abuses.

Certainly, at the back of Atkinson's mind was the rise of Vladimir Zhirinovsky, the ultra-nationalist whose party, the Liberal Democratic Party of Russia, came first in the 1993 parliamentary elections. Atkinson believed that:

> Should a reactionary, fascist or ultra-nationalist candidate be elected as Russia's next president in June, it will not be so easy for Russia to withdraw from the clear international legal commitments of full membership, amid all the publicity that such an unprecedented move would encourage. I would expect such a withdrawal to end Russia's association agreement with the EU and its partnership agreement with NATO, as well as to create problems for itself within the OSCE.[23]

In other words, a clear movement backwards and towards hostility and fear. So, once again, the main argument is not enthusiasm or praise of Russia but fear of what Russia might become. Atkinson emphasized this further by saying that a rejection of Russia's application would be "a slap in the face" for Yeltsin and other reformers. Here again we see the focus on specific personalities and on maintaining them in power. Like the Clinton administration, Atkinson and those who think like him in Europe want to do everything possible to strengthen Yeltsin for the June 1996 election from fear of the alternative. In the end, Russia became a member of the Council of Europe in February 1996, just a few months before the election but, as we shall see, Russia has had a rocky relationship with the Council.

Even more controversial were all the questions involving the future of NATO. Although some argued that the end of the Cold War made NATO unnecessary, most political leaders in the West wanted to keep it alive. In terms of the Russian debate, we shall consider two issues that dominated NATO: first, its enlargement towards Eastern Europe (which Russia obviously opposed) and, second, the need to establish a peaceful working relationship with Russia.[24] The two are obviously related to each other. United States Senator Sam Nunn pointed out how difficult it would be to reconcile these two objectives: "Are we really going to be able to convince the East Europeans that we are protecting them from their historical threats that usually boils down to Russia–while we convince the Russians that NATO enlargement has nothing to do with Russia as a potential military threat?"[25] Not surprisingly, the main argument against NATO enlargement, in both Great Britain and the United States, was the potential hostility it might cause in Russia. In the same speech, Nunn asserted that, although Russia might not be able to respond by seriously increasing its conventional forces over the next few years, the danger was still real:

> If, however, the more nationalist and more extreme political forces gain the upper hand by election or otherwise, we are likely to see other responses that are more achievable, and also even more dangerous to European stability. For example, while Russia would take years to mount a sustained military threat to Eastern Europe, it can within weeks or months exert severe external and internal pressures on its immediate neighbors to the west, including the Baltic countries, and including the Ukraine. This could set in motion a dangerous action-reaction cycle... We will not be doing anyone in Europe a favour if, by taking certain action regarding NATO expansion, we end up giving an edge in the political process to the most extremist elements in Russia.[26]

At the same time, it did not seem fair to allow Russia, as many people put it, to have a "veto" over NATO expansion. Many argued that not extending NATO because of Russian opposition might be interpreted, as Senator Lugar put it, as encouraging the Russians in "any empire-restoration tendencies".[27] Others emphasized that it was wrong to focus on Russia and forget Eastern Europe and the other parts of the former Soviet Union. Senator John McCain complained that the Clinton administration aid programmes left "other former Soviet Republics waiting for the table scraps left over from our generous assistance to Russia."[28] Senator Gorton went even further:

> Our current policy not only ignores the security of nations clearly dedicated to democracy, free markets and the West; it encourages Russian nationalism. In effect, we have given Russian nationalism a veto on the enlargement of NATO membership. Given this deference, what else will Russia soon be demanding?[29]

Eastern Europe and the former Soviet republics had their own legitimate security needs and these had to be taken into account and not just subjugated to America's Russian policy.

For this reason the Clinton administration and the British governments of the time decided to proceed with NATO enlargement, although slowly and with constant reassurances to Russia. The first step was the North Atlantic Cooperation Council which was created in 1991. In 1994 the Partnership for Peace was launched which developed individual bilateral relations between NATO and its "partners" which included Russia. Senator Claiborne Pell, a Democrat, hailed this as "another significant milestone in the dismantlement of the Iron Curtain".[30]   Pell went on to explain that Partnership for Peace seeks to avoid drawing new lines in Europe" with the goal of an "undivided Europe". Senator Lugar, however, derided this as "not a sustainable premise, unless the West is willing to accept both the Russian definition of 'partner' and their definition of 'Russian geographical space'". He saw something more sinister in Russian participation:

> For the Russians, participation in Partnership for Peace is a means of derailing NATO enlargement and revitalization of solidifying their interpretation of Russia's rights and interests in the "Near Abroad".[31]

In 1997 the North Atlantic Cooperation Council was succeeded by the Euro-Atlantic Partnership Council (EAPC) and the NATO-Russia Permanent Joint Council established. For Clinton this was a major step forward: "The NATO-Russia Founding act we have just signed joins a great nation and history's most successful alliance in common cause for a long-sought but never before realized goal: a peaceful, democratic, undivided Europe."[32] He went on to summon up the ghost of World War II and the alliance between Russia, the United States and the United Kingdom:

> Half a century ago, on a continent darkened by the shadow of evil, brave men and women in Russia and the world's free nations fought a common enemy with uncommon valor. Their partnership forged in battle, strengthened by sacrifice, cemented by blood, gave hope to millions in the West and in Russia that the grand alliance would be extended in peace. But in victory's afterglow, the freedom the Russian people deserved was denied them. The dream of peace gave way to the hard reality of Cold War, and our predecessors lost an opportunity to shape a new Europe, whole and free.
> Now we have another chance. Russia has opened itself to freedom. The veil of hostility between East and West has lifted. Together we see a future of partnership too long delayed that must no longer be denied.[33]

Not everyone shared Clinton's idealistic belief that the dream of World War II had come true and this led to criticism that he was giving Russia a "veto" over NATO. Madeleine Albright, the Secretary of State, denied this in considerably less optimistic terms: "The NATO-Russia Founding Act gives Russia no opportunity to dilute, delay or block NATO decisions." She went on to say that "NATO's allies will always meet to agree on every item on their agenda before meeting with Russia" and that "the relationship between NATO and Russia will grow in importance only to the extent Russia uses it constructively."[34] This went forward at the same time as NATO expansion into Eastern Europe with the Czech Republic, Poland and Hungary accepted as members. While some worried that Russia was getting too much power, others sought to reassure Russia about enlargement–and even to assert that it could help Russia. Senator Alfonse D'Amato, Republican of New York insisted that:

> An Eastern Europe without NATO could become a black hole of unrest, poverty, ethnic conflict, and extremism of the worst kinds. This would likely attract overt and covert Russian intervention in the affairs of the states in this area, pulling Russia into rebuilding its military machine and deploying it westward, and triggering United States and allied reaction... An Eastern Europe without NATO would threaten Russia's security by preventing Russia from changing its thinking about NATO and about European political and economic relations, preventing constructive changes in Russian policy, and delaying or blocking Russia's full integration into the community of nations.[35]

The Kosovo crisis, however, caused Russia to suspend its participation in these NATO groups until 1999, then resumed slowly over the next few years. Relations worsened, however, over problems with Georgia and Ukraine, especially in 2008.

Another major subject of discussion with regard to Russia was the dread of nuclear proliferation. The dissolution of the Soviet Union left a number of former republics in possession of nuclear weapons and the goal of both Britain and the U.S. was to destroy as many as possible and centralise the rest in Russia. Even if this were achieved, many commentators pointed out, it would not guarantee security for the situation in Russia itself was highly volatile. The British Defence Minister, Tom King, signalled his worries on the subject as early as January 1992:

> When we debated related issues in November, the Soviet Union existed – now it does not. There was then a central control over the nuclear arsenal and assurances by President Gorbachev, Foreign Minister Shevardnadze, who had returned to government, and Marshal Shaposhnikov. We were also given what I suppose must be the shortest lived assurance of all time by General Lobov when he visited this country. When asked who was in

charge of nuclear weapons, he said that he was, and two days later he was sacked. All those personalities and figures have gone.[36]

The painful death of the Soviet Union left its once all-powerful military-industrial complex in a terrible crisis. King explained that many in the army found themselves homeless and without regular food supplies–to such an extent that they were trading fuel for food. King summarized the situation, saying: "The sense of alienation and desperation that exists not only in the officer corps, but throughout the armed forces, represents a very serious development."[37] The Labour spokesman, Gerald Kaufman, stated the problem even more clearly:

> A world power balance which lasted for 46 years has ended. A superpower has vanished. Alarming incertitudes have arisen. The danger of nuclear proliferation through the seepage of weapons and of scientists is immensely disturbing.[38]

Everyone agreed that the current leaders of Russia were not a threat but that they did not have full control over the situation. David Howell, another member of the British Parliament, spelled out the consequences of this development even more plainly:

> We have no guarantees at all of the huge complex which has to lie behind an effectively maintained system of control over a vast arsenal of nuclear weapons, some new, some old, some well maintained, some deteriorating, some under close guard near Moscow, and some perhaps lost away under guard or perhaps not under adequate guard in faraway places. We have no guarantee that the politico-technical system required to control all that exists any more. In fact, it is almost certain that it does not exist.[39]

Added to this was the fear that economic penury would lead scientists and military to sell their knowledge and weapons to the highest bidder–probably either a so-called "rogue state" like, Iran, Libya, Iraq or North Korea, or a terrorist group. One member of Parliament worried about an "Islam bomb", as he called it, coming about.[40]

This worry was even more pronounced in the American Congress. Action had been taken to deal with this problem fairly quickly. In 1991 attempts were already being made by people in both houses of Congress to attach an aid programme for the Soviet Union to the yearly defence authorization bill. The initial attempt failed but in December of that year Bush signed a bill authorizing the President to use up to $100 million in defence funds for humanitarian assistance and up to $400 million for denuclearization. The latter provision is known as the Cooperative Threat

Reduction Initiative (CTRI) or, more popularly, the Nunn-Lugar program. In February 1993, the United States and Russia agreed to the Megatons and Megawatts Agreement whose goal was to convert highly enriched uranium (HEU) from Russian nuclear warheads to low enriched uranium (LEU) for commercial nuclear reactors in the United States.[41] The START II Treaty, which limited nuclear weapons in both nations, was signed by the first President Bush, was ratified by both the U.S. Senate and the Russian Duma but never went into effect and was superseded by the SORT Agreement of 2002.

But despite these efforts, which achieved some notable successes, fears remained and they centred on two main areas. First, worries about the lack of central control over Soviet-era weapons and scientists continued. In 1995, Senator Sam Nunn, chairman of the powerful Armed Services Committee and one of those responsible for the CTRI, warned:

> Russia is a vast reservoir of weaponry, weapons material, and weapons know-how, thousands of people in Russia and throughout the former Soviet Union have the knowledge, the access, and the strong economic incentives to engage in weapons traffic... there are literally thousands of scientists in Russia that know how to make weapons of mass destruction, that know how to make high technology weapons that can shoot down aircraft in the air including passenger liners, that know how to make missile technology to deliver these weapons of mass destruction across borders, and even across continents. They have this knowledge, but several thousand of them at least do not know where their next paycheck is coming from. They do not know how they are going to feed their families, and they are in great demand around the world from both terrorist groups and from rogue Third World countries.[42]

Reasoning like this tended to lead the speaker to support continued aid to Russia. But as mentioned earlier, there was another source of anxiety and that was Russia's sales of nuclear reactors and other potentially dangerous products such as fighter aircraft and submarines, to Iran. As the moderate Republican Senator Olympia Snowe said:

> I am submitting a resolution expressing the sense of Congress that the Russian Federation should be strongly condemned for continuing with a commercial agreement to provide Iran with much technology which would assist that country in the development of nuclear weapons, and that such an agreement would make Russia ineligible for United States assistance under the terms of the Freedom Support Act.[43]

As we can see, emphasis on this tended to lead the speaker to oppose continued aid to Russia. It is interesting to note that, in the end, the Clinton administration did sanction a number of Russian companies in 1998.

Fears only grew after it was learned that in 1995, the routine launching of a Norwegian weather rocket to study the Northern lights–about which Russia had been informed according to standard procedure–had provoked a nuclear war scare in the latter country that had placed the country in combat mode.[44] The letter from Norway on the rocket had been misplaced in Russia and had never reached the radar crews. Yeltsin, without appropriate information, decided on his own that the Americans were not attacking and so refused a counter launch. The episode, once the Americans discovered it, reinforced doubts about the control and command of Russian nuclear weapons. Republican Curt Weldon, a Russian studies specialist, expressed genuine panic in his analysis of the episode:

> Russia is in such a paranoid state that it put its entire strategic offensive force on alert because of Norway's launch of a weather rocket meant that Russia was within 60 seconds of an all-out attack in response to a Norwegian weather rocket which they had been previously notified of.[45]

Russia's economic meltdown in the summer of 1998 further increased worries. The Democratic Senator, Joseph Biden of Delaware, explained at the time:

> The reason that an economy only the size of Holland is having such a profound impact on the rest of the world is because of the military danger that its collapse would cause. If the Russian economy collapses and causes societal and political instability, there are 15,000 nuclear weapons there that could fall into the hands of unreliable and perhaps unstable leaders in a fractured country.[46]

Indeed, one might, once again, wonder if years of listening to debates and warnings about the danger of nuclear proliferation, in particular to certain Islamic countries, did not predispose the U.S. Congress and the British Parliament to believe that Saddam Hussein still had weapons of mass destruction in 2003 and so make them more inclined to vote in favour of the invasion of Iraq.

The Norwegian weather rocket and the economic meltdown in Russia also reinforced the arguments of those who wanted an anti-missile defence in the United States. The National Missile Defense Act of 1999 called for the deployment of such a system. The main arguments put forward in its favour, however, focused on nuclear proliferation rather than on Russia. Senator Joseph Lieberman of Connecticut went so far as to insist that:

> The countries we are developing this defense against are rogue nations, subnational groups that may attempt to inflict harm, intimidate us, leverage us to extract compromises on our national security from our leadership–not Russia.[47]

Opponents to the anti-missile defence pointed out that it would demand U.S. withdrawal from the ABM Treaty of 1972 or at least a substantial modification of it. Sandy Berger, Clinton's National Security Adviser at the time, stated his belief that: "The ABM Treaty remains a cornerstone of strategic stability, and Presidents Clinton and Yeltsin agree that it is of fundamental significance to achieving the elimination of thousands of strategic nuclear arms under these treaties."[48] In other words, it would send the wrong message to the Russians and give a bad impression about American sincerity in its relations with that country. The Duma had not yet ratified the START II Treaty and the administration and its supporters worried that this would give them a further excuse for delaying ratification.

Senator Jesse Helms of North Carolina dismissed these arguments in characteristic fashion:

> The United States has already paid a dozen ransom notes to Russia in an effort to secure START II's ratification – to no avail. This latest price demanded by Russia is simply too high... The truth is that Russia's strategic force level are going to plummet far past the levels mandated by START II regardless of whether there is any agreement in force. The strategic missiles Russia (then the Soviet Union) deployed in the 1980s are reaching the end of their useful life, and cannot be replaced. Russia has neither the money nor a reason to replace them.[49]

This represents a somewhat different assessment for Helms considers Russia to be of little interest since, he feels, it can no longer seriously threaten the United States. It can, therefore, be disregarded. This is one aspect of the humiliation of Russia that the British so worried about. In the end, citing the effect of the September 11th attacks, George W. Bush's government announced the withdrawal the United States from the ABM Treaty in December 2001.[50]

In 2000 George W. Bush became President of the United States and he and his advisers had a less friendly attitude towards Russia. During the campaign, Bush did not show a great deal of interest in foreign policy. His then foreign policy adviser, Condoleezza Rice, wrote an article in early

2000 in *Foreign Affairs* in which she talked of "Russia fatigue" and argued that there was "no longer a consensus in America or Europe on what to do next with Russia". She believed that: "Russia's economic future is now in the hands of the Russians... In the meantime, U.S. policy must concentrate on the important security agenda with Russia."[51] For her, this seemed to mean primarily changing or getting rid of the ABM Treaty. Like many Republicans, Rice also heavily criticized the Clinton administration's policy of large amounts of monetary aid to Russia. Both Rice and Bush felt that this had done little good for the economy and had, indeed, stimulated corruption. When Bush became President he downgraded Russian questions, continued the expansion of NATO, showed some support for the Chechens and talked about cutting funds for the dismantling of nuclear weapons. In line with Rice's article, he also sought a revision of the ABM Treaty.

The year 2000, of course, also saw the election of Vladimir Putin as President of Russia. Interestingly enough, Tony Blair moved quickly to establish close relations with him. He was the first Western leader to meet Putin in March 2000, although Putin was still only Acting President. The Russian President repaid Blair's early attention in 2003 by becoming the first Russian leader to pay a state visit to Britain since 1874. Blair's government held an initially positive impression of him. One of the Foreign Secretary's advisers said of Putin:

> He was essentially a liberal moderniser by instinct who may at times be inclined to use slightly authoritarian methods to restore order at the end of what had been a pretty chaotic period of Russia's history under Boris Yeltsin.[52]

On the other hand, it was only in June 2001 that Bush and Putin met for the first time. The day before, in a speech at Warsaw University, Bush gave a preview of what he would tell Putin. There was little original in his rhetoric for he called on Russia to move closer to Europe and stressed that, while NATO expansion would continue, it was no threat to Russia:

> Tomorrow I will see President Putin, and express my hopes for a Russia that is truly great–a greatness measured by the strength of its democracy, the good treatment of minorities and the achievements of its people. I will express to President Putin that Russia is a part of Europe and, therefore, does not need a buffer zone of insecure states separating it from Europe. NATO, even as it grows, is no enemy of Russia... America is no enemy of Russia. We will seek a constructive relationship with Russia, for the benefit of all our peoples.[53]

He went on to talk about the importance of freedom, notably of speech, press and religion, asserting that "greater prosperity and greater security lies in greater freedom". When Bush and Putin did meet, Bush found that he liked the Russian leader, making this rather strange comment about him:

> I looked the man straight in the eye. I found him to be very straightforward and trustworthy. We had a very good dialogue. I was able to get a sense of his soul.[54]

Interestingly enough, Bush found Putin showed some flexibility on the ABM Treaty which may have increased his positive impression.

The attacks of 11 September 2001 brought Great Britain and the United States closer to Russia and the rhetoric of both countries noticeably warmed towards their former Cold War rival at this time. Putin immediately called Bush to offer his help and, indeed, provided a great deal of assistance in Afghanistan as well as supporting anti-terrorism resolutions in the U.N. Nor did Russia object to the establishment of American bases in Uzbekistan and Tajikistan. The British talked of "a sea change" in relationships between NATO and Russia since 11 September and the tone became somewhat more nuanced on Chechnya: "We talk to the Russians at every opportunity about human rights, but we recognise they have a legitimate right to protect their citizens against a terrorist threat which we know is linked to Osama bin Laden.[55] As Putin would wish, the campaign against bin Laden and the Russian campaign in Chechnya were being linked together. Later, the Minister for Defence, Geoffrey Hoon, praised Russian support as "exceptional" and argued that there was "a unique opportunity to enter into a new security relationship with Russia".[56] In the United States much appreciation was expressed for Russian assistance. Congressman Weldon even talked of buying more Russian oil so as to make America less dependent on Middle Eastern sources.[57]

Of course, not everyone was convinced that Russia had truly changed and become an ally. There was much debate about Russia's motives and many felt that Putin's new friendliness was simply a cynical attempt to escape criticism over Chechnya. Rice herself remained rather noncommittal in her appraisal of the situation:

> I do think that all of the time that we've spent in discussions with the Russians, all of the time that they've spent with us, that we are understanding better each other and what our constraints and demands

are. But I would not jump to any conclusions about precisely how this is all going to come out or when there's going to be an agreement.[58]

The administration did, however, move toward Russia's position on Chechnya and decided to maintain aid but they proceeded with plans to amend or withdraw from the ABM Treaty. Although Putin expressed his displeasure, he agreed to live with it and the United States withdrew in December 2001. Perhaps the high point of good relations came in May 2002 when Bush and Putin signed a major new arms control treaty and the NATO-Russia Council was created. Bush told the German Parliament, the Bundestag, at the time:

> The Council gives us an opportunity to build common security against common threats. We will start with projects on non-proliferation, counterterrorism, and search-and-rescue operations. Over time, we will expand the cooperation, even as we preserve the core mission of NATO. Many generations have looked at Russia with alarm. Our generation can finally lift this shadow from Europe by embracing the friendship of a new democratic Russia.[59]

In November of that year, Bush even talked of "my friend, Vladimir Putin".[60]

Of course, the warm attitude did not last very long. Russia did not support the United States and the United Kingdom on Iraq, and, indeed, expressed strong opposition to the invasion, threatening a veto in the U.N. Security Council. In private, Putin showed great hostility to the Americans, according to Alastair Campbell:

> He said the US had created this situation. In ignoring the UN they had created danger. They were saying here may be rules, but not for us. Time and again he made comparisons with the situation he faced in Georgia, used as a base for terrorists against Russia. "What would you say if we took out Georgia or sent in the B-52 bombers to wipe out the terror camps?" And what are they planning next–is it Syria, Iran or Korea? "I bet they haven't told you," he added with a rather unpleasant curl of the lip… He said the Americans' enemy was anyone who didn't support them at the time.[61]

Interestingly, though, both the British and the Americans tended to concentrate their attacks on the French rather than on the Russians. Blair gave a major speech to Parliament on 18 March 2003 in a bid for support (which he received) and put the blame for the failure to get a UN resolution squarely on the French:

Last Monday, we … very nearly had the majority agreement. … Yes, there were debates about the length of the ultimatum, but the basic construct was gathering support. Then, on Monday night, France said that it would veto a second resolution, whatever the circumstances. Then France denounced the six tests. Later that day, Iraq rejected them. Still, we continued to negotiate, even at that point.

Last Friday, France said that it could not accept any resolution with an ultimatum in it. On Monday, we made final efforts to secure agreement. However, the fact is that France remains utterly opposed to anything that lays down an ultimatum authorising action in the event of non-compliance by Saddam.[62]

Blair uses the word "France" four times in this short extract, always in relation to negative words: "veto", "denounced", "not accept", and "utterly opposed". By putting the blame on the French meant that Blair could avoid any harsh criticism of Russia or China–nations which he obviously considered more threatening.

Relations worsened after the "colour revolutions" that took place, first in Georgia (the "rose revolution" of late 2003), then in Ukraine (the "orange revolution" in 2004) and finally in Kyrgyzstan (the "tulip revolution" of 2005). These events brought to power pro-Western governments in all these countries. In particular the United States enthusiastically supported them and Russia opposed them, often giving support to anti-Western parties in those countries. Bush welcomed the new Georgian President, Mikheil Saakashvili to the White House only a month after he took office and praised the rose revolution enthusiastically:

The Rose revolution? It was an historic moment. It was a moment where the people spoke. It was a moment where a government changed because the people peacefully exercised their voice and raised their voice. And Georgia transitioned to a new government in an inspiring way…. The possibility of people taking charge of their own lives and transforming society in a peaceful way is a powerful example to people around the world who long for freedom and long for honest government.[63]

Senate Resolution 472 congratulated the people of Georgia for "their commitment to democracy, peace, stability, and economic opportunity" and affirmed their support for "the sovereignty, independence, territorial integrity, and democratic government of Georgia."[64] Even more enthusiasm was expressed for the other colour revolutions, particularly in Ukraine. Since 2003, Georgia and Ukraine have become the focal point for tensions between Russia and the West.

In particular, Anglo-Russian relations have declined precipitously since 2003. The *Second Report on Global Security: Russia* by the Select Committee on Foreign Affairs of the U.K. Parliament outlined three reasons for this: Britain's attempts to promote democracy and human rights in Russia; its close relationship with the U.S. and, most importantly, the existence of a large Russian émigré community there.[65] The report states quite clearly that:

> The most serious source of tension in the UK-Russia bilateral state-to-state relationship arises from the growing Russian émigré community in the U.K., now thought to number perhaps 400,000. The Russians who live in the U.K. include a number of individuals who left Russia for political reasons or who are otherwise at odds with President Putin's rule. The continued protected presence of these individuals in the U.K. acts as a permanent irritant to the bilateral relationship.[66]

These émigrés include Akhmed Zakayev, a Chechen separatist leader who since November 2007 has claimed to be Prime Minister of the Chechen government in exile. Although Moscow requested his extradition, British courts refused it and he was granted asylum in Britain. Boris Berezovsky is another high profile figure, one of the so-called "oligarchs" who enjoyed a privileged position in Yeltsin's time. In 2000 he quarrelled with Putin and moved to the U.K. Three years later Russia demanded his extradition for fraud but he was granted political asylum. A number of executives from the Yukos oil company have also taken refuge in Britain in spite of Russian demands for extradition. The most famous case, however, is that of Alexander Litvinenko, a former KGB agent who took refuge in the U.K. in 2000 where he attached himself to the circle around Berezovsky. On 1 November 2006 he fell ill after meeting with two Russians, Andrey Lugovoy and Dmitry Kovtun. Over the next three weeks the world watched the dramatic decline and death of Litvinenko from poisoning by polonium-210. In a deathbed statement Litvinenko accused Putin of being responsible for his murder. British police eventually charged Lugovoy with involvement in his murder but Russian authorities refused to extradite him. In July 2007 David Miliband, the Foreign Secretary, announced a number of measures in response, including the expulsion of four Russian diplomats. The Opposition fully supported these measures as did most members of Parliament, although a few, such as Andrew MacKinlay of the Labour Party protested, saying: "I am deeply concerned about the House's mood which sems to be anti-Russian, regardless of the fact that we sometimes treat the Russians very arrogantly, and that they have people who they perceive should be facing their courts in London, protected by our system."[67] Most, however, agreed with Denis MacShane, also of Labour, who praised "the first fight back by any European Foreign Minister against Russia's bullying".[68]

Lugovoy's election to the Russian Duma later only worsened relations as did Russian moves against the British Council. In January 2008 Miliband lashed out against Russia:

> Russia has failed to show any legal reasons under Russian or international law why the British Council should not continue to operate. It has also failed to substantiate its claims that the British Council is avoiding paying tax... Instead of taking legal action against the British Council, the Russian government have resorted to intimidation of its staff. I am confident that the whole House will share the anger and dismay felt by this Government at the actions of the Russian Government. We saw similar actions during the cold war but thought, frankly, they had been put behind us... We are in a Catch 22, because although the Russian authorities keep on denouncing what they call the "illegal activities" of the British Council they never say what the illegal activities are, and it is very difficult for someone to prove that they are not doing something illegal if they are not charged with doing something illegal.[69]

Once again we see a reference to the Cold War and the fear that it was returning. Miliband also stated that the Russian government had made clear that these attacks were linked to the Litvinenko affair. The conflict spread to the United States in March when two brothers with dual Russian and American citizenship were charged with industrial espionage, although this was not the first case of American citizens being so accused. In July, after a BBC report about the Russian government's involvement in the Litvinenko murder, a British diplomat was also accused of spying. Far from having gained the gratitude of Russia, as she had hoped earlier, Britain found herself having extremely poor relations with that nation.

Of course all of this is related to the more general denunciation of the deteriorating human rights situation in Russia. In 2004 Andrew Tyrie of the Conservative Party said of Putin:

> Domestically, he is taking powers to control the judiciary. He is crushing democracy in the provinces by removing elections for provincial governors, confiscating assets and eroding property rights. Free speech is being suppressed in parts of Russia and, in the name of anti-terrorist measures, we now have a sanction for the widespread and systematic use of torture, particularly in Dagestan and Chechnya.[70]

He went on to cite Churchill's "iron curtain" speech–another example of the returning (if it had ever really disappeared) Cold War dimension to rhetoric.

A few months later David Atkinson, still reporting on Russia for the Council of Europe, although it was now a member, revealed his exasperation:

> I am under considerable pressure from our Russian colleagues to recommend that Russia should no longer be subjected to the humiliation of such detailed scrutiny, or "outside interference" as the ultra-nationalists describe it. I am told that... I should now recommend the end of my detailed monitoring of its commitments to encourage President Putin to pursue his reforms against the darker forces that threaten Russia today and it is also said, encourage him to attend the Council of Europe's third summit on 16 and 17 May in Warsaw.[71]

Atkinson refused to recommend the end of the monitoring of Russia. Relations were also tense with the European Court of Human Rights with nearly a quarter of the complaints it received coming from Russian citizens. Atkinson went on to condemn Russian conduct in Chechnya and the "near abroad":

> Russia continues to interfere in the internal affairs of other member states that were formerly part of the Soviet Union, contrary to its commitment to abandon a policy of having a zone of special influence... The personnel, arsenal and equipment of the 14th Russian army remains in Transnistria, thus contributing to a divided Moldova. Russia maintains an active presence in Abkhazia in Georgia and encourages separatism by issuing dual passports to its citizens. That is not peacekeeping, but a long-standing policy of divide and rule, which is unacceptable in today's Europe... We continue to make it clear to our Russian colleagues that as long as civilians disappear or are kidnapped and the military act with impunity, without being held to account we cannot accept the claim that life in Chechnya is returning to normal.[72]

Furthermore, numerous human rights groups as well as British MPs and members of the U.S. Congress signalled the increasing loss of religious liberty in Russia. Signs of anti-Semitism in Russia were also attacked in all these forums. In particular, the repeated assassinations of journalists outraged opinion in Western countries. In July 2004 the U.S. citizen, Paul Klebnikov, editor of the Russian version of *Forbes* magazine was shot to death while investigating corruption and suspect business practices in Russia. In 2006 Anna Politkovskaya was murdered after numerous articles criticizing human rights abuses by the Russian government especially in Chechnya and there were many other cases which either did not come to trial or had secret, often suspended trials or reached the verdict of suicide. In June 2007 the House of Representatives tabled a resolution condemning this situation. Congressman Chris Smith, Republican of New Jersey, who co-sponsored the resolution, explained:

> My resolution addresses the violence of the murder of independent journalists, and the lie in the claim that their murders have been seriously investigated. Solzhenitsyn said of Communist Russia, in our country, the lie has become not just a moral category, but a killer of the state. We have to ask ourselves and ask Mr. Putin, was this terrible statement also true of post-Communist Russia?[73]

Once again we notice the return of references to Russia in the Cold War. His implication was clear: Russia was moving back towards the authoritarianism it had had under communism. Senator Barack Obama of Illinois shared these worries and strongly condemned irregularities in the Russian parliamentary elections of 2007:

> Well before the campaign even began, several Russian political parties and politicians were banned from participating in the election. During the campaign, President Putin and his party, United Russia, enjoyed virtually unlimited positive television air-time on Kremlin-controlled networks, while opposition parties had their ads removed and their campaign materials confiscated. The Russian authorities have prevented opposition parties from campaigning fairly, imprisoning opposition leaders, intimidating activists, and preventing them from making their case to Russia's voters. Russian voters have reported that they have been pressured to vote for the Kremlin's party, United Russia, by employers and local officials. In Chechnya, 99.2 percent of voters allegedly turned out to vote and 99.3 percent of these voters allegedly cast their ballot for United Russia. Several other regions have reported similar results for Putin's party, making a mockery of this vote as a free and fair election. Yesterday's elections were the least free and fair in the 16 years of Russia's modern history as an independent country.[74]

In the last sentence we see, once again, this idea of regression: Russia is returning to authoritarianism.

Perhaps even more important to the Western powers was that Russia, which has one of the world's largest reserves of oil and gas, increasingly seemed a threat in the energy domain. At the end of 2005 Russia demanded that Ukraine should pay market prices for gas as of 1 January 2006 which would have meant a massive and sudden increase. Ukraine insisted that the country would need a phase in period as it could not, overnight as it were, pay such a large augmentation. Since the two countries failed to reach an agreement, Russia cut off gas to Ukraine in the new year and Ukraine, then, siphoned off gas from Russian pipelines to the E.U. causing drops in supply there. A year later a second incident occurred involving Belarus. Both episodes were widely interpreted as politically motivated and a Russian assertion of power in the "near abroad". They shook confidence in the West about Russia's reliability as an energy supplier. Although the United States was not immediately concerned by events, the House of Representatives voted a resolution stating, among other things, "Russia has repeatedly demonstrated its willingness to use its role as supplier of oil and gas to exert political pressure on other countries, such as Georgia, Ukraine, and Belarus, among others"[75] Britain, although not very dependent on Russian energy, was, as a European power, more directly concerned. Alan Johnson, Secretary of State for Trade and Industry, insisted that: "We need to ensure not just in this country but throughout the European Union, that the dominance of Russia does not become a real problem in future, as it was for Ukraine over Christmas."[76] Like many in Congress, other British MPs, not only the unrepentant cold warriors, drew more ominous conclusions from the episode. The distinguished barrister Vera Baird of the Labour party said:

> The whole of Europe, which relies on Russia for a quarter of its supply, was forced to realise that there are serious limits to the length of the spoon that can be used when supping with President Putin. Clearly he will readily use his abundance of hydrocarbons for political purposes, in this instance to punish the western-leaning Ukraine for considering joining NATO and the EU and to force them back into Russian hegemony.[77]

Few tried to defend Russia or mentioned that the dispute was over raising prices to market levels.

In February 2008, Senator Jeff Sessions, Republican of Alabama, made a list of all the ominous signs coming from Russia: its cutting off of gas supplies; cyber attacks against Estonia; its support for Georgian separatists and anti-Western elements in Ukraine and Kyrgyzstan; its increasing military budget; its testing of new nuclear weapons and its continuing sale of enriched uranium to Iran. In particular he attacked Russian opposition to the construction of a missile defence system in Poland and the Czech Republic, which he stated, did not threaten Russia. Instead he warned that America "has to wake up and be able to understand that Russia, fuelled by all this new oil money and an increasingly autocratic regime under Mr

Putin, is not a healthy partner."[78] Condoleezza Rice, Secretary of State, was more nuanced in her evaluation of Russo-American relations:

> Our relationship with Russia has been sorely tested by Moscow's rhetoric, by its tendency to treat its neighbors as lost "spheres of influence," and by its energy policies that have a distinct political tinge. And Russia's internal course has been a source of considerable disappointment, especially because in 2000 we hoped that it was moving closer to us in terms of values. Yet it is useful to remember that Russia is not the Soviet Union. It is neither a permanent enemy nor a strategic threat. Russians now enjoy greater opportunity and, yes, personal freedom than at almost any other time in their country's history. But that alone is not the standard to which Russians themselves want to be held. Russia is not just a great power; it is also the land and culture of a great people. And in the twenty-first century, greatness is increasingly defined by the technological and economic development that flows naturally in open and free societies. That is why the full development both of Russia and of our relationship with it still hangs in the balance as the country's internal transformation unfolds.[79]

In the period since the end of the Cold War, rhetoric about Russia has not changed fundamentally, with fear and hostility still dominating. Although both Britain and the United States initiated a policy of economic assistance to Russia after the collapse of the Soviet Union and spoke favourably of certain Russian leaders, they did so to a large extent from fear of more antagonistic forces gaining power there. Few people spoke positively about Russia itself or of Russian culture. The dominant attitude expressed was rather patronising, insisting that Western values were superior and that Russia had to learn proper behaviour. Certainly, as the war in Chechnya shows, there was a great deal of justification for this mind-set. But Putin was not entirely wrong in pointing out a very real hypocrisy in both Britain and America, for while they criticized Russian actions in Chechnya they later invaded Iraq without UN authorization. After the 9/11 attacks, Putin did provide important support to both nations, notably in Afghanistan (although he undoubtedly did so from calculations of Russian advantage). It was only after the invasion of Iraq in 2003 that his rhetoric towards the West became more aggressive–and this in turn provoked more hostility against Russia in the West. The democratic deficiencies of Russia and its human rights abuses are indisputable (notably the repeated assassinations of journalists and other opponents of the regime) and its behaviour in the Caucasus region more than alarming. Much of the rhetoric in the West is, therefore, justifiable. yet, one is tempted to wonder if the patronising attitude of both the U.S. and the U.K. since the end of the Cold War–their conviction in the superiority of their values–did not provoke a real hostility in Russia–especially after the Iraq War convinced many in that nation that much of it was hypocrisy.

Bibliography

Berman, William. *From the Center to the Edge: The Politics and Policies of the Clinton Presidency*. London: Rowman & Littlefield, 2001.

Bush, George W. *The George W. Bush Foreign Policy Reader*. Edited by John Dietrich. London: M.E. Sharpe, 2005

Campbell, Alastair. *The Blair Years: Extracts from the Alastair Campbell Diaries*. Edited by Alastair Campbell and Richard Stott. London: Hutchinson, 2007.

Clinton, Bill. *The Clinton Foreign Policy Reader*. Edited by Alvin Rubinstein, Albina Shayevich and Boris Zlotnikov. London: M E Sharpe, 2000

—. *My Life*. New York: Knopf Publishing, 2004

Cohen, Stephen. *Failed Crusade: America and the Tragedy of Post-Communist Russia*. New York: Norton, 2000

Cox, Michael. *U.S. Foreign Policy after the Cold War*. London: Pinter, 1995

Dumbrell, John. *American Foreign Policy: Carter to Clinton*. Basingstoke: Macmillan, 1997.

Dumbrell, John with a chapter by David Barrett. *The Making of US Foreign Policy*. Manchester: Manchester University press, 2nd ed 1997

Fraser, Cameron. *US Foreign Policy after the Cold War: Global Hegemon or Reluctant Sheriff?* London: Routledge, 2nd edition, 2005

Gardner, Hall. *Dangerous Crossroads: Europe, Russia and the Future of NATO*. Westport, Conn: Praeger, 1997

__. *Surviving the Millenium: American Global Security, the Collapse of the Soviet Empire and the Question of Peace*. Westport, Conn: Praeger, 1994

Goldgeier, James & Michael McFaul. *Power and Purpose: US Policy toward Russia after the Cold War* Washington, D.C.: Brookings Institute, 2003

Hyland, William. *Clinton's World: Remaking American Foreign Policy*. Westport, Conn: Praeger, 1999.

MacLean, George. *Clinton's Foreign Policy in Russia: From Deterrence and Isolation to Democratization and Engagement*. Aldershot, Hampshire: Ashgate, 2006

Major, John. *John Major: The Autobiography*. London: Harper Collins, 1999

Rosner, Jeremy, "American Assistance to the Former Soviet States in
    1993-1994". In *After the End: Making U.S. Foreign Policy in the Post
    Cold War World*, edited by J.M. Scott. London: Duke University Press,
    1998
Scott, James, ed. *After the End: Making US Foreign Policy in the Post-
    Cold War World*. London: Duke University Press, 1998
Seldon, Anthony with Lewis Baston. *Major: A Political Life*. London:
    Phoenix, 1992
Seldon, Anthony with Peter Snowdon and Daniel Collings. *Blair
    Unbound*. London: Simon & Schuster, 2007.
Stuart, Mark. *Douglas Hurd: The Public Servant, an Authorized
    Biography*. Edinburgh: Mainstream Publishing, 1998.

Notes

[1] Gerald Kauffman, *House of Commons Debates*, 14/1/1992, vol. 201, col. 830

[2] Mark Stuart, *Douglas Hurd: The Public Servant, an Authorized Biography*. (Edinburgh: Mainstream Publishing, 1998) 335-6

[3] John Major, *John Major: The Autobiography* (London: Harper Collins, 1999) 501

[4] Kauffman, *op.cit.*

[5] Quoted in Bill Clinton, *The Clinton Foreign Policy Reader*, ed. Alvin Rubinstein, Albina Shayevich and Boris Zlotnikov (London: M E Sharpe, 2000), 44.

[6] Bill Clinton, Address to the American Society of Newspaper Editors, 1/4/1993, in *Presidential Public Papers: Bill Clinton, 1993, Book 1, January 20 to July 31 1993* (Washington, D.C.: USGPO, 1994) 375

[7] For more information on this see James Goldgeier and Michael McFaul. *Power and Purpose: US Policy toward Russia after the Cold War* (Washington, D.C.: Brookings Institute, 2003)

[8] Bob Dole, *Congressional Record*, 17/3/1994, S3128

[9] Richard Lugar, Speech at American Spectator Washington Dinner Club,, 7 March 1994, in *Congressional Record*, 17/3/1994, S3129

[10] Slade Gorton, *Congressional Record*, vol. 140, 22/2/1994, S1563

[11] Trent Lott, *Congressional Record*, vol. 140, 22/2/1994, S1580

[12] *Ibid*

[13] Gerald Solomon, *Congressional Record*, 16/9/1994, H24678

[14] *Ibid.*

[15] Tom Lantos, *Congressional Record*, 15/9/1998, H7786

[16] Jan Schakowsky, *Congressional Record*, 23/3/1999, H 1537

[17] Steve Horn, *Congressional Record*, 18/3/1997, H1109

[18] David Davis, *House of Commons Debates*, 8/6/1995, vol. 261, col. 357

[19] *Ibid.*, col. 373

[20] *Ibid.* col 368

[21] David Atkinson, *House of Commons Debates,* 8/6/1995, vol. 261, cols. 363-4

[22] Atkinson, *House of Commons Debates,* 10/1/1996, vol. 269, col.

[23] *Ibid.,* col 175

[24] A third question, that of the ex-Yugoslavia, will not be considered in any detail here as there is a separate chapter on it.

[25] Nunn, *Congressional Record,* 10/10/1995, S14846

[26] *Ibid.,* S14847

[27] Lugar speech *op. cit.*

[28] McCain, *Congressional Record,* 22/2/1994, S1561

[29] Gorton, *op. cit.*

[30] Claiborne Pell, *Congressional Record,* 23/6/1994, S7482

[31] Lugar speech, *op cit.* "Near Abroad" is the translation of a Russian term for the other republics of the former Soviet Union

[32] Bill Clinton, "Remarks at a Signing Ceremony for the NATO-Russia Founding Act", Paris, 27 May 1997, *Presidential Public Papers, Bill Clinton: 1997,* Book 1, January 1-June 30, 1997 (Washington, D.C.: USGPO, 1998) 657

[33] *Ibid* p. 658

[34] Madeleine Albright, statement before the Senate Foreign Relations Committee, 7/10/1997, *Congressional Record,* S 10784

[35] Alphonse D'Amato, 20/5/1997, *Congressional Record,* S 4763

[36] Tom King, *House of Commons Debates,* 14/1/1992, vol. 201, col. 818

[37] *Ibid.,* col 820

[38] Gerald Kaufman, *House of Commons Debates* , 14/1/1992, vol. 201, col. 829

[39] David Howell, *House of Commons Debates* 14/1/1992, vol. 201, col. 858

[40] Sir Patrick Duffy, *House of Commons Debates,* 14/1/1992, vol. 201, col. 844

[41] For more on this project see George MacLean, *Clinton's Foreign Policy in Russia* (Aldershot: Ashgate, 2006)

[42] Sam Nunn, *Congressional Record,* 10/10/1995, S 14846

[43] Olympia Snowe, *Congressional Record,* 25/5/1995, S 7528

[44] For more on this see David Hoffman, "Cold-war Doctrines Refuse to Die–False alert after '95 rocket lunch shows fragility of aging safeguards" *The Washington Post,* March 15, 1998

[45] Curt Weldon, *Congressional Record,* 4/9/1997, H 6913

[46] Joseph Biden, *Congressional Record, Senate,* 10/9/1998, S10191

[47] Joseph Lieberman, *Congressional Record, Senate,* 15/3/1999, S2635

[48] Sandy Berger to Carl Levin, 3 February 1999, in *Congressional Record, Senate,* 15/3/1999, S 2629

[49] Jesse Helms, *Congressional Record,* 15/3/1999, S2633

[50] The text of the withdrawal statement is at http://www.state.gov/t/ac/rls/fs/2001/6848.htm

[51] Condoleezza Rice, "Campaign 2000 : Promoting the National Interest" *Foreign Affairs* 79:1 (January-February 2000): 58

[52] David Clark, special adviser to Robin Cook, statement to Select Committee on Foreign Affairs, Second Report on *Global Security: Russia,* 25 November 2007, HC 51

[53] George W. Bush, "Future of Europe", speech at Warsaw University, 15 June 2001 in *Public Papers of the Presidents: George W. Bush, 2001: Book 1, January 20-June 30 2001* (Washington, D.C.: USGPO, 2003) 679-80

[54] Quoted in Jane Perlez, "Cordial Rivals: How Bush and Putin expressed some flexibility" *The New York Times,* June 18, 2001

[55] Ben Bradshaw, Parliamentary Under-Secretary for Foreign and Commonwealth Affairs, *House of Commons Debates, 30/10/2001,* vol. 373, col. 741

[56] Geoffrey Hoon, *House of Commons Debates,* 14/1/2002, vol. 378, col. 9

[57] Curt Weldon, 5/6/2002 *Congressional Record,* H 3220

[58] Quoted in Bob Kemper, "U.S. Hints at Progress in Missile Talks" *The Chicago Tribune,* November 2, 2001.

[59] George W. Bush, speech at the Bundestag, Berlin, 23 May 2002, in *Public Papers: George W. Bush, Book 1, January 1-June 30, 2002* (Washington, D.C.: USGPO, 2004) 855-6

[60] George W. Bush, speech at the NATO summit, Prague Hilton, Prague, 20 November 2002, in *Public Papers: George W. Bush, 2002, Book 2, July 1-December 31 2002* (Washington, D.C.: USGPO, 2005) 2102

[61] Alastair Campbell, entry for 29 April 2003, *The Blair Years: Extracts from the Alastair Campbell Diaries,* ed. Alastair Campbell and Richard Stott, (London: Hutchinson, 2007) 693-4. Putin would make similar statements publicly in February 2007 at a speech in Munich.

[62] Tony Blair, *House f Commons Debates,* 18/3/2003, vol. 401, col. 764

[63] George W. Bush, joint press conference with Mikheil Saakashvili, 25 February 2004 at www.whitehouse.gov/news/releases/2004/02/20040225-1.html

[64] *Congressional Record,* 18/11/2004, S 11512

[65] *Op.cit.* See chapter 4, paragraph 96. Dr. Alexander Pravda told the committee that "Moscow sees Britain as very close to the U.S. yet of little use as a source of influence on Washington."

[66] *Ibid.,* chapter 4, paragraph 97

[67] Andrew MacKinlay, *House of Commons Debates,* 16/7/2007, vol. 463, col. 29

[68] *Ibid.,* col 30

[69] David Miliband, *House of Commons Debates,* 17/1/2008, vol. 470, col. 1095

[70] Andrew Tyrie, *House of Commons Debates,* 24/11/2004 vol. 428, col. 161

[71] David Atkinson, *House of Commons Debates,* 24/3/2005, vol. 432, col. 1056

[72] *Ibid.,* col. 1057

[73] Chris Smith, *Congressional Record,* 18/6/2007, H 6612

[74] Barack Obama, *Congressional Record,* 3/12/2007, S 14697

[75] House Resolution 500, 11/7/2007, H 7620

[76] Alan Johnson, *House of Commons Debates,* 16/2/2006, vol. 441, col. 1552

[77] Vera Baird, *House of Commons Debates,* 2 May 2006, vol. 445, col. 942

[78] Jeff Sessions, *Congressional Record,* 8/2/2008, S 812

[79] Condoleezza Rice, *Foreign Affairs*: 87:4 (July-Aug 2008), 3-4

CHAPTER NINE

BRITISH POLITICAL DISCOURSES ON THE CRISIS IN THE FORMER YUGOSLAVIA

ANN LANE

The Yugoslav wars provided the context and circumstances in which the major actors in international affairs considered the validity of the post-Second World War rules governing intervention in the internal affairs of states.[1] If the proposition that war as an activity provides direction at a time when structure fails is accepted, then the wars generated by the ethnic and national conflicts of the Yugoslav peoples which emerged once the Cold War framework which had sustained Yugoslavia since 1945 had been removed can be regarded as providing the opportunity for a reconsideration of the circumstances in which the international "community" could intervene in third party conflict and the role of military power in serving those objectives.

The political debate in the United Kingdom about intervention in the former Yugoslavia necessarily turned on these very issues. British tradition has been to make policy through cases, based on a pragmatic acceptance that Britain must respond to events rather than seek to drive policy agendas internationally. Britain's responsibilities were defined primarily in institutional terms as the holder of a unique set of memberships, a point which Douglas Hurd made to the House of Commons on 1 November 1991.[2] Britain, he observed, was "at the centre of events. No other country belongs to NATO, the [European] Community, the Commonwealth, the Group of Seven and the United Nations Security Council." For these reasons it was an axiom of British foreign policy that the country play a part in the resolution of the conflict occasioned by Yugoslavia's dissolution. The manner of such involvement was uncertain, however. Whereas the issues at the centre of the Gulf and the Falklands conflicts had been straightforward, the problems of Yugoslavia were neither morally nor intellectually clear cut. The result, as Douglas Hurd recalled later, was "fog and frustration" or as the literature would have it "pusillanimity".[3]

Political debate about the appropriate response for Britain to Yugoslavia's violent dissolution was similarly fractured and complex. The immediacy of the media involvement rendered considered and consistent policy-making especially difficult. Proximity to the Cold War and the complicated nature not just of Britain's involvement with the region but of that of the major actors which came to form the six-nation Contact Group exacerbated these difficulties. The turbulence brought to the principal international institutions as a result of the Cold War's abrupt ending added further layers of complexity to the politics that bedevilled the diplomacy. These factors provided if not the substance of political discourse on Yugoslavia in the 1990s, then at least the framework for it.

This essay seeks to take an overview of the political discourses that surrounded policy-making towards the successive crises created by Yugoslavia's dissolution between June 1991 and the conclusion of Operation *Allied Force*, the air campaign against the Serbian government of President Milosevic, on 9 June 1999. For the purposes of analysis the essay will look firstly at the nature of British interests in former Yugoslavia as well as the factors constraining British foreign policy more generally before moving on to consider the political debate that ensued and the way in which this impacted on the role played in the conflict by the principal institutions–namely the EC/EU, NATO and the UN. The main line of argument is that the Yugoslav conflicts of the early 1990s strengthened significantly the political will among New Labour politicians to recast British foreign policy around its traditional foundation as a military actor, in which role its pre-eminence had little challenge in the institutions that gave it ongoing presence in world affairs. The only difference was that it would not be legitimised by reference to values broadly defined as adherence to the rule of law and a preoccupation with humanitarian concerns. These circumstances rendered Britain "uniquely central to developments", but the nature of the conflict, which was about affairs within the boundaries of a sovereign state meant that Britain could not "impose peace on the peoples and republics of Yugoslavia–nobody can …".[4]

British interests in the Balkans had deep origins which could be traced back to Serbia's struggles against Ottoman domination for independence.

Serbia's experiments with constitutional monarchy in the early 20th century and its role as an ally during the First World War, created links between the Yugoslav state and the British establishment which surfaced again in the debates that endured until Yugoslavia's dissolution.

The absence of consensus at the centre of the British government about what was happening in the former Yugoslavia was obvious from the earliest stages of the conflict. The official view of the problem is best captured, perhaps, by the views of the then foreign secretary, Douglas Hurd, who argued that Britain had no substantial commercial or strategic interests in the region.[5] Understanding the conflict, at least in its early stages, in terms of nationalism, he argued that there were three main points on which UK foreign policy should focus: firstly, to help resolve conflicts and direct the force of nationalism into containable channels that do not flood the whole landscape; secondly to help countries emerging from dictatorship towards democracy and better government, all the time keeping in mind the background that our main task is the protection and promotion of British interests. And thirdly, that Britain needed to improve, update and strengthen the international institutions to which it belonged and which were crucial in those first two tasks.[6] Percy Cradock, then head of the Joint Intelligence Committee (JIC) apparently summarised this line of argument for the Prime Minister in September 1991, following the crisis generated by Slovenian and Croatian bids for secession. The JIC view held that Britain did not want to get too deeply involved. Cradock later recalled that "As he saw it Britain's interests were not seriously threatened".[7]

John Major, Prime Minister since November 1990, disagreed. While his own account of this period reflects the caution with which he approached foreign affairs in general, he took the view that the region was too much of a tinderbox on the periphery of Europe to be left to solve its own difficulties.[8] Indeed, this argument gets at the issue at the heart of the debate about the motivations of British foreign policy. In this case the issues of self interest–or the possessional goals of foreign policy in which the country's immediate interests are given priority–and the milieu goals derived from the nexus of national and international "community" objectives–were neatly juxtaposed. Britain as a country which struggled itself with an ongoing challenge to the legitimacy of the British state to govern in part of the kingdom, had good reasons to be wary of involving itself too closely in crises rooted in the ethnic tensions of other countries. There were assumptions about the non-involvement of members of the UN P5 in affairs which concerned each other's back yards. This was the argument used persistently by the Russians, particularly about its problems in Chechnya but also in Serbia which it saw, as a Slavic state, as being in some sense its client. However, throughout the Cold War, not just Britain but the West generally and the French and Americans in particular had seen Yugoslavia as a country in which their intervention was perfectly legitimate for a series of reasons rooted largely in the country's geo-strategic importance at the historical juncture where the cultures of Europe and the East mingled and intertwined. A place of communication, of interchange, of migration and exchange at the meeting points of a series of great civilisations was of ongoing interest to all the major actors in international affairs, and remained so once the Cold War corset that had stabilised the region since the Second World War had been removed and the region descended into violence verging on anarchy. While the notions of endemic conflict that abounded in the early 1990s were misleading and unhistorical, the First World War was a recent enough historical experience for renewed conflict, (particularly once it spread to Sarajevo), to strike a resonant cord.[9] For the UK, unique among the European states for being simultaneously a permanent member of the UN Security Council, embedded in the command structure of NATO and a key actor in the European Community, this question was as much about the extent and nature of involvement and how best this should be justified. In was in resolving these issues that the British political debate about Yugoslavia shifted from the relatively straightforward one concerned with the traditional notion of "interests" to one about values.

Much of the contemporary analysis of policy making during this conflict and indeed the criticism of the British government was founded on the apparent obfuscation that seemed to beset the policy process. Even Field Marshal Richard Vincent, Chief of the Defence Staff and from 1993 Chairman of NATO's Military Committee felt strongly enough to compare Western inaction to save Bosnia with appeasement of fascism in the 1930s.[10] Initially debate focused on the appropriateness of the use of force; as the conflict progressed this discussion became intertwined with a transatlantic discourse surrounding the arms embargo that had been imposed by the major actors on all parties in the fighting without discrimination between the apparent aggressors and their supposed victims. This had the effect of empowering the already powerful elements of the former Yugoslavia while penalising the weaker party—in this case, Bosnia—which encouraged the latter to find increasingly ingenious ways of circumventing the embargo, playing effectively on sympathisers particularly within the principal allies on their need for the means of survival in a conflict against a ruthless opponent.[11]

The principal source of confusion initially was the lack of clarity about what was happening compounded by the lack of consensus about the nature of British interests. These confusions emerged forcibly in the House of Commons debate on the Foreign Affairs Select–Committee Report on Bosnia held in early March 1992. There was even a confusion in the debate about the exact contribution of the various elements of the Yugoslav nation and the resistance movements these spawned during the Second World War. For the pro-Serb lobby, the old notion that Serbia was analogous with Yugoslavia was a common assumption. In reality the pattern was much more complicated than this as there were Serbs who fought alongside the multi-ethnic Partisan movement and the Cetnik achievements during the Second World War were by no means uniformly heroic although they were portrayed as such by veterans such as Amery and others, some of whom surfaced to tell their wartime experiences and revise the official narrative of Yugoslav resistance.[12] Bernard Braine and Julian Amery argued for clemency for the Serbs on the basis of historic ties in two world wars as well as out of respect for their ability to fight. This mythology surrounding Serbian fighting potential pervaded the thinking of those both in Parliament and outside it who argued powerfully against military intervention in this period.[13]

During 1992, the debate on the possibility of military action to halt the conflict in Bosnia divided the Conservative Party into four broadly defined camps. Those who recognised no British interest in the Balkans and advocated a policy of inaction; those who thought Britain should at least attempt to deliver humanitarian aid but resist the use of troops so long as these were likely to be opposed on the ground; those who advocated the bombing of Serb forces and finally those who wanted to apply maximum pressure through a bombing campaign and the deployment of ground forces.[14]

Decision-making within the executive was stymied by the existence of a similar range of opinions within the Cabinet itself. As we have seen, the views of Prime Minister and foreign secretary were at variance about the nature of the conflict and Britain's interests in it. Michael Heseltine, then, was supportive of the use of force. The defence secretary, Malcolm Rifkind, was dubious while Michael Portillo and Kenneth Clarke were uneasy. The Opposition meanwhile was unable to formulate a coherent line or indeed offer an alternative policy. In June 1992, Gerald Kaufman, then Shadow foreign secretary, stated his opposition to the use of force:

> The situation is far too confused for forcible intervention from outside to do any positive good. It is certain that force would lead to further unnecessary bloodshed and increase the number of people at risk. I hope that the Government will stand out inflexibly against any suggestions of forcible intervention by the European Community. [15]

Of those in favour of the use of force, Paddy Ashdown, leader of the Liberal Democrats pressed consistently for a more forward-looking policy on the ground while supporting an arms embargo.[16] Ashdown was critical of the government's policy on Bosnia, and in particular what he saw as the Prime Minister's failure to take advantage of the UK's tenure of the EC presidency to lead the Community on the issue:

> The story of the Prime Minister's actions as leader of the European Community–he was not alone in the lack of leadership but had a duty of leadership as President of the EC–will be a story that will look miserable and tortured for the next six months, and the epitaph written on it will be, "Too little and too late."[17]

Ashdown was supported in this by Calum Macdonald and Michael Meacher from the Opposition. Macdonald, for example, argued that sanctions were ineffective, and suggested that more would be necessary:

> Is it not a case of adopting a policy of too little, too late, making the situation much worse and more difficult to deal with? Will the right hon. Gentleman give details of the time scale within which he hopes the sanctions will work? Will he make it clear that there must be a cessation of hostilities by the Serbians within days rather than weeks, failing which, other options will have to be considered?[18]

Several prominent voices from the senior diplomatic community, most notably Anthony Parsons, formerly Britain's ambassador at the United Nations, and John Thompson, favoured direct military intervention.[19] Lord Carrington, in his capacity as EU envoy to former Yugoslavia, suggested preventive deployments following recognition of Bosnia but this was vetoed following receipt in London of a memorandum from Marrack Goulding, then a senior UN officer in charge of peacekeeping operations in New York, advising against UN deployment in Europe. He argued that

UN forces should be reserved for third world conflicts since Europe was well endowed with forces that could have coped with the Former Yugoslavia (FYU).[20]

In the early 1990s, the doctrine of humanitarian interventionism was "arguable but obscure".[21] During the late 1980s, Boutros Boutros Ghali, then Secretary General of the United Nations, had worked on the issue of international interventionism particularly through development of the concept of preventive diplomacy which was based in part on an overt recognition that the UN by itself could not enforce a code of international conduct owing to its lack of military capability. The notion that the UN should work with those countries that had the capability and will to exercise armed force in support of internationally accepted values of both inter and intra state conflict had its origins in the closing years of the Cold War when the increasing weight given to human rights as a means of moral censure about the internal affairs of member states seemed to enhance the UN's authority more generally as an arbiter of what was and was not acceptable conduct by sovereign powers. The contribution this approach made to the final destruction of the legitimacy of the Soviet system had the effect of empowering the UN in the Cold War's wake, and indirectly its members with ongoing claims to military capability as long as they were prepared to use it in concert with UN mandates and diplomacy. The point was not lost on UK policy makers in the context of the crisis in the Balkans.

Proponents of military intervention to stop aggression by Serbia against Croatia and Bosnia, and from 1992-3 by Croatia against Bosnia wanted this to be operationalised through the United Nations. By this route, the legitimacy of using force could be ensured by applying the doctrine of just war. This required that force be applied under a recognised authority, in a cause that could be considered just and only when all other means of finding a solution had failed. Justice in this context meant upholding the rule of law and preventing persecution of the innocent. It was also about upholding the principle of sovereignty. Moreover, the principle of proportionality had to be observed in the application of force in order to sustain the legitimacy of the intervention so that the chances of producing a reasonable settlement could be maximised.

Douglas Hurd pondered the complexities of what he called "interest and conscience" in the autumn of 1992. While the emerging conflicts were not immediately threatening to European or British national security, they were "unacceptable because of the amount of death and suffering they cause, and because of their potential to spread outwards".[22] Some intellectuals had divided the actions contemplated into two categories: areas of interest, of which the Gulf was the best example, and wars of conscience, namely the conflicts in former Yugoslavia, but it is not difficult to see how this is simplistic when set in the context of the events themselves. The recovery of Kuwait was at one and the same time a war of national security and national conscience. Similarly the search for peace and justice in Yugoslavia was both political and humanitarian. Thus he concluded that the central fact about UK security is that it was "indivisible, both geographically and functionally", in other words that matters of national interest and issues of conscience were inextricably linked.[23]

An attempt at codifying the criteria for interventionism was made in April 1993 by Malcolm Rifkind, the Secretary of State for Defence 1992-1995, who set out three criteria for engagement in third party conflict.[24] Firstly, was the conflict in the UK's national interest, given its status as a medium sized power, albeit one with a highly developed sense of international responsibility. National interest, he said, could be defined narrowly from a purely defence point of view as the need to maintain the freedom and territorial integrity of the UK and Dependent Territories and its ability to pursue its legitimate activities at home and abroad. On that basis alone British participation in international peacekeeping would always be highly restricted. However, as he went on to observe, the equation was more complicated than that owing to the difficulties of predicting where conflicts would lead. Additionally, the UK had international obligations, particularly to the UN, in terms of being required to uphold the articles of the UN Charter wherever they were violated.

The second criteria was that of availability. In the early 1990s, UK forces were still engaged in national commitments, especially those in Northern Ireland, but also in the Falklands and elsewhere. Given the progressively shrinking public purse any form of open ended commitment, which engagement in ethnic and national conflict generally portended, was particularly unwelcome. And thirdly, Rifkind argued, the UK needed to find a means of judging whether taking military action was indeed the right solution. Invariably this meant discussion with other countries.

Perhaps the greatest single constraint on UK foreign policy lay in the uncertainties surrounding the Anglo-American alliance. Following the Cold War, UK strategy appeared to bifurcate. While diplomatic effort was directed towards strengthening the common foreign and security pillar of the European Community (EC), and the UK's role in that regard, the defence and security community, whose tenuous faith in the EC had been vindicated by the early inability of that organisation to develop a coherent policy towards the Yugoslav crisis, continued to prioritise the transatlantic connections as the central plank in the UK's post Cold War strategy. "Part of our realism" Douglas Hurd subsequently wrote, "was maintaining the Atlantic Alliance, and that meant keeping our disagreements with the Americans within bounds".[25] The US were strong on policy but confidence in themselves as a military actor which had been shaken so profoundly by Vietnam, and had left them risk-averse, a state of mind that was not to be laid to rest until the nation was galvanised by the events of September 2001. For the United States, the *sine qua non* of policy making regarding military intervention was that they were unwilling to risk casualties in Bosnia until the various factions had signed a peace agreement.[26]

The issue through which this debate was principally conducted was the arms embargo or more accurately the issue of whether or not this should be lifted in order to empower the Bosnians in their various conflicts with the Serbs and Croats. The embargo had been put in place in November 1991 by the UN and the EC with the aim of preventing the conflict spreading. When he first came to office, Clinton had no settled policy on the former Yugoslavia but when Major raised the issue of the arms embargo with both him and President Mitterrand of France on 19 April 1993, Clinton made it clear that he was opposed to air strikes and leant towards lifting the arms embargo on the Bosnian Muslims.[27] At a UK Cabinet meeting a week later, held to discuss the options, the prevailing view was that lifting the arms embargo would not give the Muslims the decisive advantage claimed for it. Major argued that if it was lifted the most likely outcome would be that the Serbs would launch a full-scale offensive with the aim of capturing as much territory as possible before the new weapons came into the equation. The Croats would join the conflict. He subsequently recorded his view that "lift and strike" was founded "on a wilful misreading of the realities".[28] There was scepticism too about the likely efficacy of air strikes, although the option was not ruled out. The Chiefs of Staff had responded to the Prime Minister's enquiry about the feasibility of bombing to protect civilians by advising that it would be impossible due to metereological and geographic features of Bosnia and the highly confused situation on the ground.[29] In any case the Chiefs of Staff were not prepared to consider the use of air power alone. The Gulf

War of 1991 had demonstrated the necessity of using ground troops to achieve a decisive result.

The difficulties in formulating a coherent policy towards the Yugoslav crisis can be understood in context of the debate about the future development of the principal institutions of the international order. Military dependence on the United States had been demonstrated adequately during the Gulf War; the inability of the EC to act as an effective decision making body at moments of crisis had been exposed just a few months after that conflict on the occasion of Slovenia's announcement of its intention to secede from the Yugoslav federation. The UN, to which the UK was the second largest military contributor in this era, had been empowered by the Gulf conflict but its interventions in the Croatian secession crisis of late 1991 and then again in 1992 showed its weaknesses, particularly in doctrinal terms in the context of intra-state conflict. [30]

When the conflict broke out, Britain itself was in the middle of a defence review.[31] The UK's Options for Change exercise conducted within MOD in 1991, turned on the assumption that the threat was reducing and sought accordingly to establish lower military force levels, but with enhanced flexibility and mobility, to meet defence commitments into the next century. The following year the idea of using the military as a political tool appeared in the 1992 Defence White Paper.[32] It envisaged continuation of NATO as a collective self defence alliance but argued that the wider defence role could be conducted by NATO, WEU, the UN or ad hoc coalitions under UN or Commission on Security and Cooperation in Europe (CSCE) auspices'.[33] The Atlantic alliance remained the central plank in defence interests, but given that the Bush administration has committed to reducing US force levels by twenty-five per cent over the following five years, which, in practical terms, raised the spectre of a loss of American willingness to engage with Europe at a time when Europe's ability to cope with the looming difficulties on its periphery was seriously questioned. The lesson that had been learnt from the Gulf War was that there was a pressing need to re-shape the Euro-Atlantic defence relationship into something durable.[34] The conflicts occasioned by Yugoslavia's violent dissolution provided an important opportunity for Britain to assert its influence in shaping the European security agenda. Dame Pauline Neville-Jones, Political Director at the FCO between 1994 and 1996, writes that the decision to send British troops "as part of a UN Force, to Bosnia, was greatly influenced by the fact that at the time the UK held the Presidency of the European Union and felt the need to provide leadership".[35]

During the early 1990s, the UK remained the second largest contributor to the UN with some 4000 personnel committed in six different operations in April 1993. The difficulties of squaring peacekeeping commitments with more routine defence matters in an era when the absence of a coherent and clearly identifiable threat raised the issue of choice about where the weight was placed in the UK defence effort and in what manner was a central preoccupation of the British government in this period. There was also a question about Britain's position as a member of the UNSC which "loomed large in the post cold war environment both in general political terms and from a defence and security perspective". It was this, in Rifkind's view, that imposed both a global perspective on British thinking and arguably too a moral one. Certainly he wrote, it adds greater weight and complexity to the question of why we should or should not take military action. Another pressure came from the increasing demands of the public and international community to "do something" about crisis situations. He cautioned that the application of military force had unpredictable effects and could make situations worse; the aims and objectives of any engagement needed to be spelt out since open-ended commitments carried obvious hazards.[36]

The pattern of policy making during the Major years was characterised by hesitancy and a lack of resolve. However the massacre at Srebrenica in July 1995, more than any other event, changed all that and paved the way for the Blair approach.[37] Britain was drawn into the "humanitarian war" in Kosovo in 1999 as a result of pressures arising from two sets of commitments. Firstly, because of its various roles in the network of multinational and regional institutions in which it seeks to play a leading role. Secondly, as a consequence of the commitments arising from its policy and electoral commitments to promote values such as human rights and to practice as well as preach good international citizenship. New Labour's declared agenda left little room for it to back away from a proactive role in international attempts to resolve the latest Balkan crisis. If Britain was to be a force for good, and sustain its claim to a linkage between foreign policy and the pursuit of good governance and human rights, then it could scarcely stand aside from the developing crisis in Kosovo which from the spring of 1998 indicated that Milosevic's policies in the region amounted to renewed ethnic cleansing. Furthermore, Britain had assumed the presidency of the EU in January 1998, and retained a role in the peace-building process post Dayton through its continuing membership of the Contact Group.[38] Both sets of obligations required that the Blair government, which was relatively inexperienced in international affairs, had to build the confidence of the other leaderships in order to achieve influence.

In some ways the path had already been paved for Blair by the earlier conflict. The Bosnian imbroglio had generated a consensus within British conflict on all sides about the legitimacy of third party intervention where humanitarian issues were at stake. But this consensus was limited to the need to protect the Kosovar Albanians from persecution on the part of the Yugoslav government. The choice of means to achieve this end was the subject of considerable dispute and the way in which force was ultimately used in 1999 was constrained as a result of the need to sustain support for the use of force within Parliament, in the country and amongst the 24-nation coalition. The issues turned firstly on the justifications for the use of force, and the type of force that could and should be used, and secondly from the question of the legitimacy of the use of force and of the use of NATO.

British interests in Kosovo were bound up with the credibility of New Labour's policies in its domestic constituency, as well as with the credibility of the institutions through which Britain exercises its influence, principally the United Nations, the EU and NATO. The Strategic Defence Review (SDR) directed that Britain's armed forces would be utilised to support a combination of strategic and internationalist goals.[39] Strategic interests concerned the management of conflict by readiness to coerce rogue elements through a mixture of strategies involving both deterrence and compellance with regard to actions that would jeopardise the stability of international politics. These interests were concerned with the assessment of the future sources of threat to British interests, such as population displacement, the undermining of the rule of law and democratic governance. Internationalist objectives were concerned with upholding the institutions of the international order, particularly the UN and NATO both of which played important roles in supporting the Contact Group's diplomacy, either through public sanction, and the imposition of economic sanctions, or through issuing threats of force. The credibility of both organisations became an increasingly important factor in political calculations on the part of the Contact Group as a whole and Britain in particular as the crisis deepened. One powerful justification for the use of force in British eyes was the credibility of NATO which had been treated by Milosevic with scorn from the outset. This reasoning was implicit in Robin Cook's presentation of the government's decision to support the military operation to the House of Commons on 25 March 1999 when he justified the use of force both as an outgrowth of having the UK be one of the countries with the capacity to intervene in the face of atrocities but also because "our confidence in our peace and security depend on the credibility of NATO".[40]

Internationalist goals also cover the "values" dimension of New Labour project, particularly the strategies concerning promotion of human rights, good governance on the liberal democratic model and good international citizenship which for New Labour involved preparedness to expend national resources on resolving conflicts which impacted on the shared interests. Kosovo was an opportunity for New Labour to demonstrate the will behind the public statements to assert British leadership by active engagement with the latest Balkan crisis in order to retain its credibility.[41]

A series of sources of constraint can be identified. Most immediately British policy was constrained by what its allies would accept. British policy was more cautious than the US regarding the public declaration of intent to use force at the outset of the crisis, but generally ahead of the other members of the contact group. This issue was fundamental to the evolution both of political and military objectives both during the negotiating process and during the armed conflict itself. When the violence was escalating during the middle of 1998, the UK government which took the lead encouraging the North Atlantic Council to order military planning for possible use of force and to begin manoeuvres in the countries surrounding Kosovo, any suggestion on the part of Blair or his colleague that any means other than peaceful ones would be used would have been out of line with the thinking of Britain's allies.[42]

A second source of constraints was implicit in the character of conflict resolution strategies. Thinking at the time of Kosovo was conditioned by a preference within the international mediators for a liberal integrationist approach, seeking to build consociational settlements which were given form by creating institutions in the conflict zone through which power could be devolved as far as possible to the various communities in dispute. The notion, simply expressed, was that by addressing the sense of insecurity through the devolution of responsibility to minorities, a measure of co-operation and political bargaining between the groups at federal level would replace the circumvention of normal political process occasioned by resort of one side or the other to violence.[43] This policy of making the warring factions live together was seen as preferable to the alternatives of either victory by one side or another, or partition and population exchange or a combination of the two, in so far as it conformed most closely to the principles of the international order. The result of this preference for a liberal, internationalist solution, required that the province be treated throughout as an integral part of the FRY which in turn limited the way in which force could be used and dictated that the international community sustain a lengthy negotiating process.

Domestically, the early phases of the conflict generated little public concern, either politically or in the country at large. Weariness with the Balkan wars of the early 1990s was partly responsible for this uninterest, but the changed political climate which New Labour brought with them which emphasised forward thinking and the forces of modernity, was probably also a factor.

For the most part the left supported NATO action. Clare Short, Ken Livingstone and Michael Foot were vocal supporters. However a small group within the Labour Party, associated for the most part with the left wing Campaign Group, did oppose the intervention.[44] This group argued that by using NATO the UK government was marginalising both the UN Security Council and the House of Commons while ignoring the large public meetings demonstrating against the war. Further, they objected to the demonisation of Serbia by Western governments and the media and maintained that NATO bombing had strengthened Milosevic's position in Serbia. Moreover, the bombings were seen as undoing the work of the humanitarian organisations and others who had worked to develop a consensual approach to political organisation in the region.

Elements of the Conservative Party were also opposed to intervention. Douglas Hogg argued that Britain's strategic interests were not sufficiently threatened to justify involvement in a civil war. In a series of rhetorical questions directed at John Prescott, he made this point clear:

> Does the right hon. Gentleman understand the great sense of dismay that many in the House feel? Does he agree that we have gone to war without there being a sufficient national interest, without there being a clear understanding of the strategic and political objectives, without there being a proper exit strategy and without the authority of the House?[45]

Nicholas Soames argued that the British approach was marginalising NATO, which put him curiously in the same camp as Tony Benn and Lord Healey. Lord Carrington and Alan Clark also raised concerns. Other Conservatives who accepted the need for the use of force were critical of reliance on air power alone which they saw as demonstrating a lack of resolve. Sir Raymond Whitney, for example, argued that:

> Even this Government, having reached this situation, must surely accept that we cannot merely continue with the bombing month after month after month. The Foreign Secretary has given us no idea of when the bombing might achieve any sort of success. There are now only two choices facing NATO Governments. They could call off the bombardment and patch up whatever accommodation they can manage with Milosevic, perhaps hoping that the Russians will come to see it as being somehow in their own interest to play a constructive role. Or they could recognise what they should have understood before they started to threaten the Serbs and before they started the bombing, which is that they will achieve their aims only by backing up the aerial bombardment with the use of land forces.[46]

Of the Liberal Democrats, Paddy Ashdown was highly supportive of Blair's robust stance, as was Menzies Campbell even though he pressed for Blair to persuade the alliance to employ ground forces rather than rely simply on air power.[47] Menzies Campbell clearly stated this in the 19 April 1999 debate in Parliament: "Liberal Democrats have contended that an air campaign alone would not suffice and that military presence on the ground would be essential for the return of the refugees so that they would have the confidence and courage to return to the communities out of which they have been burned, looted and shelled." He added that: "NATO must therefore be willing to impose its will."[48]

The debate about ends and means reached a crescendo in the third week of April 1999. The conflict, which had been planned to last just seventy-two hours was entering its fourth week with little sign that Milosevic was considering conceding to the coalition's demands. These circumstances, which coincided with the fiftieth anniversary of the signing of the North Atlantic Treaty provided the background to Blair's attempt to bring some coherence to the debate on interventionism. Arguably one of the most important foreign policy speeches that Blair made as Prime Minister he articulated what became known as the Doctrine of the International Community on 24 April 1999 at the height of Anglo-

American dissonance on the means to coerce Milosevic.[49] Blair couched his remarks in the just war debate, arguing that:

> This is a just war, based not on any territorial ambitions but on values. We cannot let the evil of ethnic cleansing stand. We must not rest until it is reversed. We have learned twice before in this century that appeasement does not work. If we let an evil dictator range unchallenged, we will have to spill infinitely more blood and treasure to stop him later.[50]

The emphasis then is on, the nature of the Milosevic government's policies in Kosovo and the dangers of "appeasement" an emotive word in the context of UK foreign policy that recalls Neville Chamberlain's attempts to placate Hitler during the late 1930s in order to avoid war. He framed the speech as justification for the demands being made of Milosevic and the use of air power to achieve that end. Blair, however, worried about what would happen if Milosevic could not be stopped solely by air power and wished to have American agreement to prepare for a land war. Clinton, however, refused to give Blair any such assurances. Towards the end of the speech, Blair brought the threads of his argument together, focusing on the coincidence of values and interests. Observing that the apparent absence of a direct threat to the survival of the state had created circumstances in which actions in international affairs were "guided by a more subtle blend of mutual self-interest and moral purpose in defending the values we cherish" he argued that:

> In the end values and interest merge. If we can establish and spread the values of liberty, the rule of law, human rights and an open society then that is in our national interests too. The spread of our values makes us safer. As John Kennedy put it: "Freedom is indivisible and when one man is enslaved who is free?"

The speech showed a considerable progression from Rifkind's speech on the same theme some six years earlier. Blair's five considerations for intervention began with the justice of the cause, whether or not the potential interventionists could be sure of their case in using force. Secondly, and doubtless with his mind on the failed Rambouillet negotiations over Kosovo, whether or not all other means to find a solution had been exhausted. Thirdly, whether military force was likely to succeed. Throughout the conflicts generated by the former Yugoslavia, the perceived efficacy of military power, and the practicalities of backing coercion from the air with ground troops had been a constraint on the major powers and one which Milosevic had understood and exploited from the outset. Similarly with Blair's fourth consideration, preparedness for the long term–or in the early 1990s the lack of it–had helped to stymie British policy, contributing to the ineffectiveness of British diplomacy during the critical early stages. And finally, and most controversially in the context of the debate about the relationship between UK foreign policy and values that New Labour had introduced, whether or not the UK had national interests involved. Blair's statement of principles ended, thereby, with the same point on which Conservative policy on intervention, as defined by Malcolm Rifkind, had opened.

In conclusion, three broad views of the proper role for Britain in these conflicts emerged in political circles in the first half of the 1990s. The post-war consensus on foreign policy was non-existent by this stage and instead of the conventional left-right axis, the debate was fractured on some ill-defined axis which split the major parties into three or more camps. Some thought there was no British interest involved in the region and that the UK should not get involved. Others wanted the UK to assist in delivery of humanitarian aid but not at the expense of casualties among the armed forces. There were those who clamoured for Serbia to be bombed and for the deployment of ground forces. Behind all this was the ever-present spectre of an endless imbroglio and even a military disaster. Britain's confidence in itself as a military actor was not as deep during John Major's premiership as it later became under the direction of Tony Blair. By the late 1990s the conviction politics that characterised the New Labour approach was much more successful in uniting the political sphere behind an interventionist stance. Indeed it could be argued that a new consensus had begun to emerge which held until the complex challenges posed to UK foreign policy by the events of 11 September 2001 created circumstances in which this could unravel.

Bibliography

Bartlett, Will. "'Simply the Right thing to do': Labour goes to war". In *New Labour's Foreign Policy: A new moral crusade?*, edited by Richard Little & Mark Wickham Jones. Manchester: Manchester University Press, 2000.

Baylis, John. *British Defence Policy: Striking the Right Balance*. London: Macmillan, 1989.

Bellamy, Christopher. "Soldier of Fortune: Britain's new military role", *International Affairs*, 68:3 (Jul 1992): 447-8.

Cradock, Percy. *In Pursuit of British Interests. Reflections on British Foreign Policy under Margaret Thatcher and John Major.* London: John Murray 1997.

Gow, Jack. Triumph of the Lack of Will. International Diplomacy and the Yugoslav War. London: Hurst & Co, 1997

Hodge, Carole. *Britain and the Balkans. 1991 until the Present.* London: Routledge, 1996

Hurd, Douglas. *Memoirs.* London: Little Brown, 2003

Kennan, George. "Introduction-The Balkan Crises: 1913 and 1993". In Carnegie Endowment for International Peace, *The Other Balkan Wars: A 1913 Carnegie Endowment Inquiry in Retrospect with a New Introduction and Reflections on the Present Conflict.* Washington, DC: Carnegie Endowment, 1993.

Keohane, Dan. "The Debate on British Policy in Kosovo", *Contemporary Security Policy* (Dec 2000): 78-94

Major, John. *The Autobiography.* London: HarperCollins, 1999.

Parsons, Anthony. *From Cold War to Hot Peace: UN Interventions 1947-1994.* Harmondsworth: Penguin, 1995.

Roberts, Adam. "NATO's 'Humanitarian War' over Kosovo", *Survival*, 41:3 (Autumn 1999): 102-23.

Sabin, Philip. A.G. "British Defence Choices beyond 'Options for Change'", *International Affairs*, 69:2 (1993): 267-87.

Seldon, Anthony. *Blair.* London: The Free Press, 2004.

—. *The Blair Effect 1997-2001.* London: Simon & Schuster, 2002.

—. *Major. A Political Life.* London: Weidenfeld & Nicholson, 1997

Sharp, Jane. *Honest Broker or Perfidious Albion: British Policy in Former Yugoslavia.* London: IPPR, 1997.

Simms, Brendan. *Unfinest Hour. Britain and the Destruction of Bosnia.* Harmondsworth: Penguin, 2001.

Ullman, Richard, ed., *The World and Yugoslavia's Wars.* New York: Council on Foreign Relations, 1996.

Woodward, Susan L. *Balkan Tragedy, Chaos and Dissolution after the Cold War.* Washington DC: The Brookings Institution, 1995

Zimmerman, Warren. *Origins of a Catastrophe.* New York: Random House, 1996

Notes

[1] The analysis, opinions and conclusions expressed or implied in this chapter are those of the author and do not necessarily represent the views of the JSCSC, the UK MOD or any other government agency.

[2] Douglas Hurd, *House of Commons Debates*, 1/11/1991, vol. 198, col. 130.

[3] Hurd, *Memoirs*, (London: Little Brown, 2003), 444-45. The theme of pusillanimity forms the central thesis of James Gow's detailed study of this episode, *Triumph of the Lack of Will. International Diplomacy and the Yugoslav War*, (London: Hurst & Co, 1997). For an alternative critique of UK foreign policy in this period see Jane Sharp, *Honest Broker or Perfidious Albion: British Policy in Former Yugoslavia*, (London: IPPR, 1997).

[4] Douglas Hurd, *House of Commons Debates, op. cit.*

[5] Hurd, *Memoirs*, 444-45.

[6] *House of Commons Debates*, House of Commons Official Report Session 1991-1992, Debate on the Address, 1/11/1991, vol. 198, col 118.

[7] Percy Cradock, *In Pursuit of British Interests. Reflections on British foreign policy under Margaret Thatcher and John Major* (London: John Murray 1997) 157.

[8] John Major, *The Autobiography*, (London: HarperCollins, 1999) 532-49. Anthony Seldon, *Major. A Political Life*, (London: Weidenfeld & Nicholson, 1997) 372-4.

[9] See for example George Kennan, "Introduction-The Balkan Crises: 1913 and 1993", in Carnegie Endowment for International Peace, *The Other Balkan Wars: A 1913 Carnegie Endowment Inquiry in Retrospect with a New Introduction and Reflections on the Present Conflict* (Washington, DC: Carnegie Endowment, 1993) 3-16.

[10] Andrew Marr, "Politicians 'let NATO down' over Bosnia", *Independent*, July 21, 1993, cited in Jane Sharp, *Honest Broker or Perfidious Albion*, 5.

[11] See for example Brendan Simms, *Unfinest Hour. Britain and the Destruction of Bosnia* (Penguin, 2001), 90-134.

[12] Carole Hodge, *Britain and the Balkans. 1991 until present*, (London: Routledge, 1996), 29-31.

[13] *House of Commons Debates*, 5/3/1992, vol. 205, col 471.

[14] Major, *The Autobiography* 539.

[15] Gerald Kaufman, *House of Commons Debates*, 2/6/1992, vol. 208, col. 715

[16] Hurd, *Memoirs*, 467

[17] Paddy Ashdown, *House of Commons Debates*, 20/10/1992, vol. 212, col 323.

[18] Calum Macdonald, *House of Commons Debates*, 2/6/1992, vol. 208, col. 721

[19] "Should we use force in Bosnia?" *The Times*, April 20, 1993; Paddy Ashdown, "Sarajevo. Action Now!", *The Independent*, October 1, 1993; Calum Macdonald et al "Open Letter to John Major", *The Independent,* October 20, 1993. Anthony

Parsons, *From Cold War to Hot Peace: UN Interventions 1947-1994* (Harmondsworth: Penguin, 1995), 220-43; Major, *Autobiography*, 536.

[20] Susan L Woodward, *Balkan Tragedy, Chaos and Dissolution after the Cold War*, (Washington DC: The Brookings Institution, 1995) 188.

[21] Hurd, *Memoirs*, 446.

[22] Douglas Hurd, "Foreign Policy and International Security", *RUSI Journal* (Dec 1992), 1-4

[23] *Ibid.*

[24] Malcolm Rifkind, "Peacekeeping or Peacemaking?" *RUSI Journal* (April 1993) 7-8.

[25] Hurd, *Memoirs*, 467

[26] See Warren Zimmerman, *Origins of a Catastrophe*, (New York: Random House, 1996) 185-221 passim. David Gompert, "The United States and Yugoslavia's Wars" in Richard Ullman, ed, *The World and Yugoslavia's Wars*, (New York: Council on Foreign Relations, 1996) 122-44.

[27] Major, *Autobiography*, 540-41.

[28] *Ibid.*, 542.

[29] *Ibid.*, 541.

[30] Malcolm Rifkind, "Peacekeeping or Peacemaking? *op. cit.*, 1-5

[31] *House of Commons Debates*, 25/7/1991, vol. 195, cols. 470-73. Cuts are detailed in the *Statement of the Defence Estimates, 1991: Britain's defence for the '90s*, CM 1559-I (London: HMSO, Jul 1991).

[32] John Baylis, *British Defence Policy: striking the right balance* (London: Macmillan, 1989). *Statement on the Defence Estimates 1992*, CM 1981 (London: HMSO, 1992) 8-9.

[33] Christopher Bellamy, "Soldier of fortune: Britain's new military role", *International Affairs*, 68:3 (Jul 1992): 447-8. Philip A G Sabin, "British Defence Choices beyond 'Options for Change'", *International Affairs*, 69:2 (1993): 267-87.

[34] Sir Michael Alexander, "NATO's Future Challenges", *RUSI Journal* (April 1992), 13; Richard Mottram, "Options for Change: Process and Prospects", *RUSI Journal* (Spring 1991), 22-27; *House of Commons Debates*, 1/11/1991, vol. 198, col. 181.

[35] Dame Pauline Neville-Jones, "Introduction", Jonathan Eyal, *Documents on British Foreign and Security Policy*, Vol II, (London: TSO, 1997-1998), x.

[36] Malcolm Rifkind, "Peacekeeping or Peacemaking?" *RUSI Journal* (April 1993).

[37] British Diplomacy Oral History Project, Churchill College Cambridge, Sir Roderick Braithwaite, 35. Anthony Seldon, *Blair*, (London: Simon & Schuster, 2004), 392.

[38] The Contact Group, consisting of the United States, the United Kingdom, France, Germany, Italy and the Russian Federation, was established in 1995 and co-ordinated international efforts to bring about a peaceful resolution of the conflict in former Yugoslavia.

[39] Dan Keohane, "The Debate on British Policy in the Kosovo Conflict: An Assessment", *Contemporary Security Policy*, 21:3 (Dec 2000): 78-94.

[40] *House of Commons, Official Report*, 25/3/1999, Col 550. *House of Lords, Official Report*, 25 Mar 1999, Cols. 148-9; Robin Cook, *House of Commons Debates*, 25/3/1999, vol. 328, cols 537-39

[41] Will Bartlett, "'Simply the Right thing to do': Labour goes to war", in Richard Little & Mark Wickham Jones, *New Labour's Foreign Policy: A new moral crusade?*, (Manchester: Manchester University Press, 2000), 131-47; Keohane, *op cit.*

[42] House of Commons, FAC, 4th Report, 1999-2000, para 42.

[43] I am grateful to Dan Keohane, for his discussion of this episode in his article "The Debate on British Policy in Kosovo", *Contemporary Security Policy* (Dec 2000) 83.

[44] Keohane, "The Debate on British Policy in Kosovo", *ibid.*

[45] Douglas Hogg, *House of Commons Debates*, 24/3/1999, vol. 327, col. 489

[46] Sir Raymond Whitney, *House of Commons Debates*, 19/4/1999, vol. 329, col. 615

[47] Keohane, 87.

[48] Menzies Campbell, *House of Commons Debates*, 19/4/1999, vol. 329, cols 588-9

[49] Anthony Seldon, *Blair,* (London: The Free Press, 2004), 397-400; Christopher Hill, "Foreign Policy", in *The Blair Effect 1997-2001*, edited by Anthony Seldon (London: Simon & Schuster, 2002) 341-3; Adam Roberts, "NATO's 'Humanitarian War' over Kosovo", *Survival*, 41:3 (Autumn 1999): 102-23.

[50] Tony Blair, Speech, "Doctrine of the International Community" at the Economic Club, Chicago, 24 Sep 1999, http://www.number-10.gov.uk/output/Page1297.asp accessed September 26, 2005

PART III:

TERRORISM, WAR AND THE MIDDLE EAST

CHAPTER TEN

PEACE *AND* DEMOCRACY?–
THE POST-COLD WAR DEBATE
ON U.S. MIDDLE EAST POLICIES

LARS BERGER

1. Introduction

In the years since the end of the Cold War, the Middle East has become in many ways *the* test case for U.S. policy in a unipolar world. The policies pursued by the world's currently most eminent global power toward one of the world's most penetrated subsystems do not only serve as a vivid example of the prospects and limits of the exercise of hegemonic power. They also reflect the long-standing debate between those who argue in favour of the promotion of political reform and democratization as a central U.S. foreign policy goal and those who support a more cautious approach that centres on what they consider to be more limited "national interests". The following pages will therefore be devoted to the analysis of the debates accompanying these competing approaches toward a region whose strategic and cultural significance puts it at the heart and centre of many U.S. foreign policy interests.

2. The Middle East in U.S. Grand Strategy

The question about the relationship between democratization and other U.S. foreign policy interests forms a central part of the debate on U.S. post-Cold War Grand Strategy. According to Posen and Ross, the latter can best be understood as constituting four ideal-type "visions".[1]

The neo-isolationist approach did not view regional conflicts such as the one between Israel and its Arab neighbours as requiring substantial U.S. involvement and deemed it advisable to leave the quest for its solution to the regional actors themselves.[2] As will be shown below, many critics of U.S. foreign policy toward the Middle East claim that the end of the close relationship with Israel would help defeat the kind of anti-American animosity Islamist terrorist recruiters try to exploit. Such a narrower definition of U.S. interests in the Middle East is also considered as having the additional benefit of withdrawing the United States from its role in the domestic conflicts between the Arab world's "pro-Western" authoritarian regimes and their Islamist opposition. In the end, the world's Islamist challenge could be as unimportant for the United States as "the nationalism of the Quebecois is for Thailand".[3]

Washington's policymakers would thus be free to focus on what Mead termed the Jeffersonian call for the perfection of U.S. democracy.[4] In isolationist thinking the question of whether a link between the Arab-Israeli conflict and democracy promotion in the Middle East exists and what this would mean for U.S. policy would therefore not arise. The conflict itself would not be relevant and democracy promotion would consist of leading by example. While neo-Isolationist Jeffersonian thinking has ceased to exist as a dominant political force in Washington, D.C., a long time ago, the outbreak of political crises in the Middle East continues to bring about repeated allusions to its language.

Critics of neo-Isolationist calls for U.S. withdrawal from the Middle East point out that the United States is not always attacked for what it does, but also for what hostile actors *believe* to have detected in its policies.[5] Also, the acceptance of a link between the status of the Arab-Israeli conflict and the level of anti-Americanism could lead to the conclusion that increased U.S. engagement toward a peaceful settlement might be a more efficient way of fighting regional hostility towards the United States. This line of reasoning finds its strongest support among the adherents of a Grand Strategy of *selective engagement* that focuses on stable relations amongst the most important actors of the international system. The United States would view regional conflicts only through the prism of possible negative implications for the stable relationship with other world powers and the security of the United States as well as the world economy's continued access to the oil resources of the Persian Gulf.[6]

This approach, which Mead termed the *Hamiltonian school* after the nation's first secretary of the treasury, puts particular emphasis on securing U.S. economic interests as exemplified historically by the presidencies of Theodore Roosevelt and George H. W. Bush.[7] Its major proponents with regard to the Middle East are, obviously, representatives of the oil industry and those members of the U.S. military industry who regard the region's Arab regimes as valuable consumers. Together with their regional partners they find their natural access points in the Department of Defence, which is interested in sustaining partnerships that facilitate the fulfilment of its strategic missions in areas such as the Persian Gulf and in offsetting the costs of the development of new weaponry, as well as in the career diplomats of the Department of State, whose professional socialization and regional expertise tend to make them more open to the concerns of Arab governments. The resulting reluctance to follow policies which these "Arabists" perceive as counterproductive has frequently earned them the ire of superiors who share the sometimes conflicting ideological outlook of the respective administration. None other than Francis Fukuyama, who once worked in the State Department's policy-planning staff, remarked that:

> [Arabists are] a sociological phenomenon, an elite within an elite, who have been more systematically wrong than any other area specialists in the diplomatic corps. This is because Arabists not only take on the cause of the Arabs, but also the Arab's tendency of self-delusion.[8]

These business- and military-oriented interests tend to collide with the interest in the secure existence of Israel. Critics such as Jerome Slater thus claim that the "support of Israel has never been in the national interest, *properly understood*".[9] By making this statement Slater adheres to a traditional Realist notion of national interest. However, in doing so, Slater and others put themselves in the position of deciding what the "national interest" of the United States is and, in fact, only put forward the interests of one powerful lobby while, for whatever reason, discarding other lobbies' interests. A contemporary and widely debated example of the irritation Realist thinkers feel over the societal input into foreign policy decisions is the book published by Mearsheimer and Walt on what they broadly term the "Israel Lobby".[10] As perceptive assessments have pointed out, their study suffered not only from a neglect of the input of the above-mentioned oil and defence lobbies, they also offered such a vague definition of who actually constitutes the "lobby" and what could be regarded as its successes that it left their work open to the charge of "incoherent" accounts and "uneven" evidence.[11]

In contrast, liberal critics of this essentialization of the concept of the "national interest" have pointed out that the latter is better understood as the result of the interaction between a broad range of (competing) institutional and societal interests which all shape foreign-policy making in a democracy.[12] In fact, while a large number of organizations and think tanks attempt to channel popular sympathies for the state of Israel into the U.S. foreign policy decision-making process, they all tend to agree on barely more than the most general interest in Israel's secure existence. Especially the polarization of the Jewish communities in the 1990s over the Oslo peace process has resulted in a fragmentation of the "pro-Israeli" political discourse. The leadership of the American Israel Public Affairs Committee (AIPAC), the Zionist Organization of America, Americans for a Safe Israel and think tanks such as the Middle East Forum tend to share the Likud's uncompromising stance toward the Palestinians. Israel's Labour Party and peace movement have their voices heard through Americans for Peace Now, the Israel Policy Forum and the New Israel Fund.[13]

What is remarkable about U.S. foreign policy toward the Middle East during the second part of the 20th century is the fact that while the parallel pursuit of the two interests in the security of Israel and access to the region's oil resources has sometimes caused frictions with allies in the region (the Arab oil embargo of 1973), the U.S. has for the most part been able to achieve both.[14] Yet, it failed to initiate the kind of democratization drives other parts of the world witnessed during and in the immediate aftermath of the Cold War.

This last topic has recently received more attention from adherents of the Grand Strategies of *"Primacy"* or *"Cooperative Security"*.[15] Representatives of both approaches try to turn the thesis of "democratic peace", which stresses structural and cultural causes for the explanation of the empirically observed phenomenon that democracies are more peaceful in their interactions, into a guideline for foreign policy.[16] What sets their treatment of the "democratic peace thesis" apart is the fact that for supporters of *"Primacy"* democratization is part of a drive to realize a "benevolent global hegemony" that forestalls the rise of global and regional competitors.[17] Those who call for a Grand Strategy of "cooperative security" treat democratization as a means of addressing the transnational problems of an interdependent world and perceive the use of U.S. "soft power" as not only a more important, but ultimately a more cost-efficient means of democratization than the unilateral use of "hard power", i.e. military means.[18]

3. Peace precedes democracy–the Clinton administration and the consensus of the 1990s

As a young governor from a relatively remote Southern state, William Jefferson Clinton chose the topic of democratic change as a rhetorical weapon in his 1992 campaign oratory against the sitting President, George H. W. Bush.

> From the Baltics to Beijing, from Sarajevo to South Africa, time after time this President has sided with the status quo against democratic change, with familiar tyrants rather than those who would overthrow them, and with the old geography of repression rather than a new map of freedom. . . My administration will stand up for democracy. We will offer international assistance to emerging fragile democracies in the former Soviet Union, and Eastern Europe, and create a democracy core to help them develop free institutions.[19]

Interestingly enough, Clinton's willingness to distance himself from George H. W. Bush's traditional "Realism" earned him the support of neoconservatives like Joshua Muravchik who at that time were already emerging as spokesmen for the push to topple Saddam Hussein. In particular, Muravchik was incensed by what he considered President Bush's failure to follow through with his promise of a "new world order":

> In his moment of glory, Operation Desert Storm, Bush spoke visionary words about a "new world order". ... any such order rests on the continued advance of democracy, because democracies behave more responsibly and peacefully. But Bush kept democracy off Desert Storm's agenda.[20]

As Muravchik and others would soon realize, Bill Clinton was bound to disappoint them as well. The beginning of his presidency was marked by the confluence of two developments that would shape the course of Middle East politics over the following decade. The signing of the Oslo Declaration of Principles in September 1993, which had been negotiated mostly without U.S. involvement, let hopes prosper for the emergence of a "new Middle East" that would witness the end of old conflicts and the beginning of peaceful coexistence as the first step toward an eventual development along the lines of European integration. Such rosy scenarios not only had to face the challenges of Israeli and Palestinian veto-players, but also the rise of Islamist groups whose political agendas and willingness to resort to terrorist violence posed a direct threat to the stability of the United States' regional partners. Washington's policy-makers would therefore have to weigh the short-term interest in the cooperation of authoritarian Arab regimes, whose domestic deficiencies had facilitated the spread of Islamist groups, and the long-term interest in genuine political reform against each other.

The fact that the regional actors tend to draw a connection between the conflict between Israel and its Arab neighbours and the broader regional context led Laura Drake to caution that the two seemingly separate trends of the legitimacy crisis of most Arab regimes and the U.S.-led efforts in the Oslo process towards regional integration would eventually intersect.

In particular, Drake warned that the widespread impression that the U.S. supported undemocratic regimes in its quest for regional peace would ultimately discredit all diplomatic efforts and lead to the waning of U.S. influence.[21] This challenge was summed up pointedly in a report by the Senate Committee on Foreign Affairs which was published at the beginning of Bill Clinton's presidency:

> The new U.S. Administration, which came into office pledging to shore up international support for democracy and human rights, will find its policies inextricably linked to the question of political Islam. The United States must assess whether and how its programs will effect the political composition and basic security of traditional friends and allies in the region.[22]

Such calls obviously raised the question of whether or not Islamist movements should play a part in the political reform processes in the Arab world. However, this aspect did not receive high-level attention. In line with the Hamiltonian approach that neglects the domestic political setup of countries assisting the United States in its pragmatic and non-ideological pursuit of national interests, the Clinton administration opted in favour of attempts to solve the Arab-Israeli conflict and against the initiation or facilitation of an Arab democratic wave modelled after the post-Cold War Eastern European revolutions.

This was highlighted by the National Security Strategy of 1996, published during the heydays of the Oslo process. Its central concept of "engagement and enlargement" was meant to provide the Clinton administration with a foreword-looking theme for a foreign policy which critics warned had been ignored and lacked focus. Also, its claim that the expansion of the number of democratically ruled countries with a market-economy helped to protect the national security of the United States nicely tied the pursuit of foreign policy interests into the President's domestic agenda.[23] However, the National Security Strategy did not talk about it in terms of U.S. Middle East policy and limited democratization to the successor states of the Soviet Union and its former East European satellites.

> We must continue to help lead the effort to mobilize international resources, as we have with Russia, Ukraine and the other newly independent states. We must be willing to take immediate public positions to help staunch democratic reversals, as we have in Haiti and Guatemala. We must give democratic nations the fullest benefits of integration into foreign markets, which is part of why NAFTA and the GATT ranked so high on our agenda. And we must help these nations strengthen the pillars

of civil society, improve their market institutions, and fight corruption and political discontent through practices of good governance.[24]

While the Clinton administration was very cautious about the notion of a democratizing Middle East, it soon began to focus on stressing its disagreement with the vision of a "clash of civilizations". There, it could follow the direction of a speech in which President George H. W. Bush's last Assistant Secretary of State for the Near and Middle East, Edward Djerejian had already set the tone for all official statements on this issue up until today. He had stressed that for the U.S. government the "Cold War is not being replaced with a new competition between Islam and the West. It is evident that the Crusades have been over for a long time".[25] Robert Satloff, the director of the Washington Institute for Near East Policy, dismissed the latter aspect as a "cultural cliché" and challenged the U.S. government to formulate a position on the question of whether the establishment of sharia-based regimes would constitute a threat to U.S. national interests.[26] While critics of U.S. reluctance to push for democracy in the Middle East agreed with Satloff's observation that Djerejian should have indicated whether the United States would accept an Islamist regime elected in free and fair elections, they still praised the speech as an attempt to "build bridges" to the world of Islam.[27] This position found the endorsement of Robert Gates, who at that time served as Director of the Central Intelligence Agency and would later join George W. Bush's White House as Secretary of Defence. In a testimony before the Democratic-led House Foreign Affairs Committee, he warned that the negative experiences of the Iranian revolution should not let the U.S. perceive Islamism as an inherently anti-Western and anti-democratic phenomenon.[28]

The great lengths to which the Clinton administration went in order to dispel any lingering impression that the U.S. government might share the view of Harvard professor Samuel P. Huntington became evident when National Security Adviser Anthony Lake felt compelled to directly address his thesis:

> Some theorists have suggested that there is no common ground for understanding between the West and the rest–only the prospect of confrontation and conflict. They assert that the United States, as the sole remaining superpower, should lead a new crusade against Islam. In the quest for a new ideology to rally against, they believe, fundamentalism would replace communism as the West's designated threat. The Clinton administration strongly disagrees. There is indeed a fundamental divide in the Middle East, as there is throughout the world, but the fault line does not run between civilizations or religions. Rather, it runs between oppression and responsive government, between isolation and openness, and between

moderation and extremism, and it knows no distinction by race or by creed.[29]

This speech's focus on the distinction between "moderation" and "extremism" was one of the hallmarks of the Clinton administration's rhetoric on the Middle East. It was designed to gather Arab and especially Muslim support for its policies and pre-empt the attempts of hostile actors such as Iraq and Iran to undermine Washington's Arab partners.[30]

One year earlier, Martin Indyk, at that time member of the National Security Council and later Assistant Secretary of State for the Near East and two-time U.S. ambassador to Israel, had also used the venue of the Washington Institute for Near East Policy, which he had helped create after having worked for AIPAC, to spell out the Clinton administration's broader vision for the region. In his speech, Indyk did not only announce the policy of the dual containment of Iraq and Iran, but also called for the establishment of an "informal alliance" between Israel, Egypt, Saudi Arabia, other members of the Gulf Cooperation Council and Turkey whose purpose would be protecting U.S. interests from "extremism" and "radical regimes".[31] Adopting the optimistic scenario of the "new Middle East", Indyk described the President's vision of peace preceding democracy:

> [The President] understands that the Middle East is finely balanced between two alternative futures: one in which extremists, cloaked in religious or nationalist garb, would hold sway across the region, wielding weapons of mass destruction loaded onto ballistic missiles; and the other future in which Israel, its Arab neighbors and the Palestinians would achieve a historic reconciliation that would pave the way for peaceful coexistence, regional economic development, arms control agreements and growing democratization throughout the Middle East.[32]

Interestingly, Paul Wolfowitz, one of the leading proponents of the Iraq War ten years later, lauded the policy of dual containment as "a much-needed break with old notions of depending on a balance between the two to protect security in the Gulf."[33] In what would be a hallmark of neoconservative thinking about the relationship between the regional conflicts in the Gulf and the Levant, he also described any lifting of the sanctions against Iraq with Saddam Hussein still in power as "a terrible setback for stability in the Middle East, including the very promising peace process" since the "accord between Israel and the PLO would not have happened without the peace process launched by President Bush or, even more fundamentally, without the U.S. victory in the Gulf War".[34]

Given the emphasis on seizing Oslo's window of opportunity and the containment of Iraq and Iran, the topic of democracy and human rights protection in the Arab world was relegated to the reports of the State Department's human rights bureau. Under the leadership of Assistant Secretary of State John Shattuck it repeatedly provoked angry Egyptian reactions with its publicly expressed concerns about torture, extrajudicial killings, long-term detentions and restrictions on the freedom of expression.[35]

Djerejian's successor, Robert Pelletreau, supported the notion that a distinction between those Islamists who "preach intolerance and espouse violence" and those who are merely interested in the application of religious beliefs to the challenges of domestic and foreign policy exists.[36] While this statement might be interpreted as leaving open the option of a constructive engagement in the case of eventual Islamist revolution in the Arab Sunni world, U.S. policies were designed to ensure that such a scenario would not materialize. With Cairo at that time being perceived as offering valuable diplomatic support for the U.S. in the Arab-Israeli arena, the domestic stability of the Egyptian regime trumped all other considerations.

This strategic focus found its expression in strong rhetorical support for friendly Arab governments in their struggle with "Islamic extremism" as well as the fact that between 1994 and 2001 one third of all U.S. foreign aid went to Israel and Egypt (USAID). Echoing Indyk's central statement on the Clinton administration's strategic outlook, National Security Adviser Anthony Lake described a comprehensive peace between Israel and its Arab neighbours as the precondition for the fight against the kind of political extremism that tries to exploit the religion of Islam for its own ends. Peace in the region would free the resources necessary to tackle the political, social and economic causes of political extremism.[37] Lake's statement thereby subordinated the domestic political problems of its Arab partners to the common quest for Middle East peace. This allowed the regime in Cairo to detach its diplomatic performance from its (lack of) domestic achievements.

As Laura Drake had predicted, the U.S.'s reluctance to push for political reform forced it to become increasingly involved in the domestic struggle between the authoritarian Arab governments and their Islamist challengers. In 1995, President Clinton used the powers granted by the *International Emergency Economic Powers Act* to declare a "national emergency" with respect to the increasing level of violence targeted at undermining the Israeli-Palestinian peace process. This put him in a position to freeze the financial assets of all persons and entities linked to those organizations that engaged in terrorist attacks in the region. According to President Clinton, the "acts of violence perpetrated by foreign terrorists" in order to disrupt the peace process amounted to a "threat to the national security, foreign policy and economy of the United States".[38] The fact that Clinton not only mentioned those Arab and Jewish terrorist groups that operated within the parameters of the Arab-Israeli conflict, but also those Egyptian groups that only targeted the Egyptian government demonstrated how the domestic stability of Egypt came to be perceived as an essential ingredient of any meaningful attempt at Middle East peace.

4. Peace follows democracy–the Bush administration's approach

4.1. 9/11 and the Arab-Israeli conflict

In a statement on CNN television on 12 September 2001, the young Jordanian King Abdullah II declared that the attacks on New York City and Washington, D.C., would have possibly not taken place had Israelis and Palestinians been capable of bridging their differences during the Camp David summit of summer 2000.[39] His view contrasted sharply with that of President Clinton's former Special Middle East Envoy, Dennis Ross, who denied any link between the status of the Arab-Israeli conflict and the events of 11 September 2001. According to him, Osama bin Laden simply followed in the footsteps of other Middle Eastern actors who, like Saddam Hussein before, had tried to abuse this sensitive topic for their own propagandistic ends.[40] Michael Scott Doran, who would later join President Bush's National Security Council, pointed out that the conflict between Israelis and Palestinians allowed the region's political actors to air their grievances which in themselves are not associated with the political aspirations of the Palestinians.[41]

When Yasser Arafat, in contrast to his pro-Iraqi stance of 1990/91, decided to refrain from embracing a sworn enemy of the United States, Secretary of State Colin Powell praised the Palestinian leadership:

> whose leaders have rejected bin Laden's attempt to hijack their cause for his murderous ends. No, these criminals have no religion, and they have no human cause. Their goal, and the goal of all like them, is to divide and embitter people. They are evil merchants of death and destruction.[42]

The question of U.S. responsibility also coloured the ensuing academic debate. In a book published by the Washington Institute for Near East

Policy, Martin Kramer criticized the U.S.-based Middle East Studies profession for having failed to ring the alarm about the new threat of Islamist terrorism.[43] Daniel Pipes of the Middle East Forum, which shares WINEP's pro-Israeli orientation, but distinguishes itself through a much narrower focus on the hard-line thinking represented by the Likud, declared his emphasis on supposedly unthinkable Islamist threat scenarios as vindicated[44] and warned the U.S. of the long battle ahead:

> ... every fundamentalist Muslim, no matter how peaceable in his own behaviour, is part of a murderous movement and is thus, in some fashion, a foot soldier in the war that bin Laden has launched against civilization ... By recognizing the wide backing of bin Laden's evil for what it is, Americans must begin a process of confrontation with 10 to 15 percent of the vast populations of the Muslim world.[45]

Joel Beinin, former President of the Middle East Studies Association of America, defended his profession against Kramer's and Pipes' criticism. In his view, all those U.S. regional experts unwilling to share George W. Bush's "Manichean worldview" were subject to a campaign "against critical thinking on the Middle East" that found its expression in Daniel Pipes' website Campus Watch which was supposed to monitor "anti-Israeli" statements made at U.S. universities.[46] According to his colleague Alan Richards, the "neoconservative denial" of the social and U.S. policy-related causes of terrorism represented the "American version of the strategy of the 'iron wall'", which the leading revisionist Zeev Jabotinsky had deemed to be the most effective way of protecting the Jewish predecessor to the state of Israel.[47]

Daniel Brumberg presented a possible compromise position with his call to differentiate between the hard core of "Islamist and nationalist ideologues" and the broader, not necessarily politically engaged public. While the former cannot possibly be influenced in their anti-Americanism, the United States could help change the domestic and regional context in such a way as to decrease their influence.[48] This obviously raised the question of whether the United States would be prepared to honestly push for political reform in the Arab world.

The extent to which the Hamiltonian assumptions of the 1990s did not seem to be valid anymore was highlighted by an article former Clinton administration official Martin Indyk published in *Foreign Affairs*, the flagship of Washington's foreign policy consensus. There he admitted that because he had sensed a window of opportunity in the Arab-Israeli conflict, he had pushed back demands within Clinton's National Security Council and from the Department of State's John Shattuck to put the issue of democratization on the agenda of U.S. Middle East policy.[49] However, this "deal" had broken down with Egypt and Saudi Arabia's lack of will or capability to deliver during the Oslo peace process and the fact that on 11 September 2001 their domestic shortcomings turned into a direct national security threat for the United States. In contrast to his "dual containment" speech at the Washington Institute for Near East Policy in 1993, he now declared political reforms in the Arab world to be a "national interest" of the United States.

This sentiment was shared by Richard Haass, the former director of the policy-planning staff at the U.S. Department of State and current chairman of the U.S. Council on Foreign Relations. He offered a similarly honest critique of past U.S. efforts at democracy promotion in the Middle East:

> Muslims cannot blame the United States for their lack of democracy. Still, the United States does play a large role on the world stage, and our efforts to promote democracy throughout the Muslim world have sometimes been halting and incomplete. Indeed, in many parts of the Muslim world, and particularly in the Arab world, successive U.S. administrations, Republican and Democratic alike, have not made democratization a sufficient priority. At times, the United States has avoided scrutinizing the internal workings of countries in the interests of ensuring the steady flow of oil, containing Soviet, Iraqi and Iranian expansionism, addressing issues related to the Arab-Israeli conflict, resisting communism in East Asia, or securing basing rights for our military. Yet by failing to help foster gradual paths to democratization in many of our important relationships–by creating what might be called a "democratic exception"–we missed an opportunity to help these countries become more stable, more prosperous, more peaceful, and more adaptable to the stresses of a globalizing world.[50]

This was even more important given the fact that the question arose whether Arab governments might have to acknowledge responsibility for the fact that Osama bin Laden had such an easy time exploiting the issue of the Arab-Israeli conflict for his own ends. Martin Indyk therefore urged the governments of Saudi Arabia and Egypt to reassess the dominance of anti-Israeli and anti-American voices in their respective countries and criticized what he perceived to be an

> anti-American consensus ... between Islamist fundamentalists on the right, who regarded Americans as infidels; pan-Arab nationalists on the left, who viewed Americans as imperialists; and the regime itself, which found it convenient for the Egyptian intellectual class to criticize the United States and Israel rather than its own government's shortcomings.[51]

According to conservative commentators such as Barry Rubin, the authoritarian governments of the region did not want to see a peaceful conclusion of the Arab-Israeli conflict out of fear that this would increase domestic calls for democratic reform and the protection of civil and human rights. Since most of the Arab intellectual elite adhered to outdated ideologies that were as precarious as their "Soviet equivalents", no change in U.S. public diplomacy or even actual policy could bring about a reduction in the region's dominant anti-Americanism.[52]

At this point the general acceptance of the need to rethink the anti-democratic consensus of the 1990s on the Middle East converged with the Bush administration's decision to sharply break with Clinton's incremental, inclusive, micro-managing approach to the Oslo process and to adopt the Israeli government's position that the latter lacked a "partner in peace" on the Palestinian side. This perception was reinforced when the Israeli navy discovered the Gaza-bound vessel Karine A with 50 tons of Iranian weaponry on board. Arafat's perceived unwillingness to break with a policy of political violence undermined U.S. supporters, mostly to be found within Colin Powell's State Department, of continuing U.S. diplomatic efforts. In April 2001, the AIPAC had already been able to secure the signature of 87 Senators and 209 Representatives under a letter that not only demanded the closure of the PLO's Washington Bureau, but also supported Ariel Sharon's demand that President Bush should refuse to welcome Yasser Arafat at the White House as long as the Palestinian President did not declare an end to violence.[53]

At the end of this continuing disenchantment with Arafat's stance stood President Bush's by now famous Rose Garden speech of June 2002 in which he called for the political renewal of the Palestinian leadership.[54] While his open break with President Clinton's long-time negotiating partner underscored his dramatic turn away from the premises of the 1990s, President Bush added his support for the principle of "land for peace" that was enshrined in UN Resolutions 242 and 338 and thus even became the first sitting U.S. President to publicly support the idea of an independent Palestinian state. By elevating democratic structures to the status of a precondition for a comprehensive peace, President Bush was able to link the Wilsonian call for the region's democratic renewal with Jacksonian hegemonic projects and the Hamiltonian emphasis on the purported centrality of the Arab-Israeli conflict. This led to the interesting twist that George W. Bush turned the 1990s policy of either democracy or peace to one of peace through democracy.

Here, President Bush's words and action began to resemble the recommendations of former Soviet dissident Nathan Sharansky whose book *The Case for Democracy: The Power of Freedom to Overcome Tyranny and Terror* would earn him an invitation to the White House to discuss its theses with President Bush in November 2004.[55] Since the 1990s Sharansky has held various posts in the Israeli government due to his leadership position within the nationalist Russian immigrant party Yisrael Beitanu, which he founded. Having described the establishment of democratic governance among the Palestinians as a precondition for peace with Israel, he told President Bush that he considered his Rose Garden speech to be the "greatest speech" of his lifetime since President Reagan had cast the Soviet Union as the "evil empire".[56] U.S. observers might have detected a possible reason for such enthusiastic praise when they pointed out that in 2002 with the exception of the U.S. call for a freeze in settlement activity in the occupied territories Sharansky's public statements on the need for political reform among the Palestinians closely resembled central passages within President Bush's eventual Rose Garden speech.[57] Disparaging the neo-conservatives favourite bogeymen among the State Department's "Arabists", conservative commentators such as Charles Krauthammer applauded the President's decision to adopt Sharansky's line of reasoning as

> a fundamental rejection of the Oslo conceit that you could impose upon Palestinian society a PLO thugocracy led by the inventors of modern terrorism and then be surprised that seven years later it exploded in violence.[58]

Independent observers such as U.S. Council on Foreign Relations' Henry Siegman pointed out that for quite some time many Palestinians themselves had been issuing calls for the political reform of the Palestinian authority, but had largely been ignored by the Israeli government as well as by the Clinton and Bush administrations. He thus warned against undermining Palestinian reformers by associating the call for reform with what was widely perceived to be Ariel Sharon's rhetorical tool to delay the initiation of diplomatic negotiations and justify the unilateral disengagement from Gaza.[59] In reality, Sharansky barely had any impact beyond the formulation of official rhetoric that resonated with the Bush White House. His opposition to the Gaza withdrawal as "encouraging more terror"[60] and the call for political reform within the Arab world was met with more or less open scepticism within Israel's foreign policy elite. He thus openly complained that "[t]hey see me as a lunatic from a Soviet prison, disconnected from the harsh realities of the Middle East" and that Prime Minister Sharon himself considered his ideas as having "no place in the Middle East".[61]

4.2. The Iraq War and the Greater Middle East Initiative

With democratization increasingly turning into the overarching public rationale for U.S. policy towards the Middle East's two central theatres of conflict, it was not surprising that President Bush continued to link the situation in the occupied territories with the fate of Saddam Hussein's regime. Only days before the start of the war with Iraq, President Bush used a speech at the American Enterprise Institute to stress his expectation that the demise of the old Iraqi regime will ultimately weaken the domestic opponents of Palestinian reformers.[62] At his first appearance at the United Nations after the fall of Saddam Hussein, President Bush declared in September 2003 that "the progress of democratic institutions in Iraq is setting an example others, including the Palestinian people, would be wise to follow."[63]

These ideas fell in line with those voices within the Bush administration that had been propagating a Grand Strategy based on "primacy" since the end of the Cold War.[64] With regard to the Middle East they were supported by prominent academics like Bernard Lewis and Fouad Ajami who in their private conversations with Vice President Dick Cheney had stressed the positive regional effects they expected to originate from Saddam Hussein's fall.[65] In one of his public statements on the issue, Ajami considered a possible negative fall-out of the Iraq war to be "dwarfed" by the "disastrous consequences" of another U.S. failure to topple Saddam Hussein.[66] According to Bernard Lewis, the United States only had the difficult choice between the neo-isolationist complete retreat from the region and the raw hegemonic pursuit of national interests ("Get tough or get out.").[67] Former Director of Central Intelligence, James Woolsey, made it clear that the regimes in Egypt and Saudi Arabia had to understand that

> [w]e want you nervous. We want you to realize that now, for the fourth time in a hundred years, this country and its allies are on the march, and that we are on the side of those whom you most fear. We are on the side of your own people.[68]

Against such thundering rhetoric stood the combined "Realist" scepticism of Washington's traditional foreign policy establishment. In a typical example of Beltway politics, an internal State Department document titled *Iraq, the Middle East and Change: No Dominos* was leaked to the press in the last week before the war. Its authors argued that a precipitous introduction of elections would lead to the establishment of Islamist regimes unless the region's social, political and economic problems were equally addressed.[69] This warning resembled a *Policy Brief* issued by the *Carnegie Endowment for International Peace* in October 2002 which stressed the lack of necessary preconditions for sustainable democratic change in the region. While its authors deemed such a change to be possible, they made it clear that they expected such an undertaking to be a decades-long commitment which could easily lack the required support of the U.S. public.[70] Critics of the aggressive neo-conservative rhetoric about the Iraqi "role model" also remarked that other regional actors might feel compelled to sabotage the U.S.-led reconstruction of post-Saddam Iraq in order to prevent Washington from pushing for further change.[71]

The long-term vision of a democratic redrawing of the mostly authoritarian Middle Eastern political landscape increasingly dominated President Bush's efforts to press a reluctant Congress into appropriating the funds the executive demanded for the pursuit of its policies toward post-Saddam Iraq. In his November 2003 speech at the *National Endowment for Democracy*, the institution which President Reagan had founded twenty years earlier to support the global spread of democracy, President Bush announced that

> [s]ixty years of Western nations excusing and accommodating the lack of freedom in the Middle East did nothing to make us safe–because in the long run, stability cannot be purchased at the expense of liberty.[72]

While liberal Arab commentators like Shafeeq Ghabra, former president of the American University in Kuwait, picked up President Bush's Reaganesque rhetoric by announcing it to be about time to "tear down the Arab wall of authoritarianism"[73], U.S. commentators like Martin Indyk criticized the lack of new programmes or, in the case of the Council on Foreign Relations' Judith Kipper, even went so far as to claim that the questioning of long-standing U.S. positions on the Middle East inherent in the President's "campaign speech" did "not make us safer".[74]

Despite such criticism President Bush stuck to his message of democratization in a speech he gave during a visit to the United Kingdom in late 2003. There he not only thanked the government of Tony Blair for supporting the Iraq war, but also laid out a transatlantic vision for democratic change in the Middle East that featured many of the central arguments of his historic speech he had given only days earlier in Washington, D.C.:

> We must shake off decades of failed policy in the Middle East. Your nation and mine, in the past, have been willing to make a bargain, to tolerate oppression for the sake of stability. Longstanding ties often led us to

overlook the faults of local elites. Yet this bargain did not bring stability or make us safe. It merely bought time, while problems festered and ideologies of violence took hold. As recent history has shown, we cannot turn a blind eye to oppression just because the oppression is not in our own backyard. No longer should we think tyranny is benign because it is temporarily convenient. Tyranny is never benign to its victims, and our great democracies should oppose tyranny wherever it is found.[75]

In order to demonstrate that his focus on democratization was not all about (retrospectively) justifying the war in Iraq, President Bush followed up on his historic November 2003 speech with what came to be known as the *Greater Middle East Initiative*. At its core was the exchange of the promise of Middle Eastern countries to engage in political and economic reforms for U.S. support in their efforts to join the World Trade Organization and establish closer security and military ties with the United States and Europe.[76]

Egypt's authoritarian ruler Hosni Mubarak quickly took the lead in attacking the proposal which had been prematurely leaked to the pan-Arab newspaper *al-Hayat*. He accused the Bush administration of behaving as if the "region, its countries, peoples and societies" would not exist and predicted "chaos" in the event of total political freedom.[77] Saudi Foreign Minister Sa'ud al-Faisal declared in a speech before the European Policy Centre that a democratization drive based on the model of the Helsinki process of the 1970s and 1980s lacked attractiveness since this very process had led to the disintegration of a country and turned the Russians into the "most unfortunate" peoples of the past two decades.[78] At their meeting in February 2004 Mubarak and Saudi Crown Prince Abdullah insisted that reforms could not be imposed "from outside" and had to be in line with "Arab identity".[79]

In the U.S., President Carter's national security advisor, Zbigniew Brzezinski, heavily criticized the circumstances of the eventual official announcement of the initiative:

For starters, the democracy initiative was unveiled by the president in a patronizing way: before an enthusiastic audience at the American Enterprise Institute, a Washington policy institution enamored of the war in Iraq and not particularly sympathetic toward the Arab world. The notion that America, with Europe's support and Israel's endorsement, will teach the Arab world how to become modern and democratic elicits, at the very least, ambivalent reactions. (This, after all, is a region where memory of French and British control is still fresh.) Though the program is meant to be voluntary, some fear that compulsion is not far behind.[80]

In contrast to Brzezinski's assessment, the *Washington Post* editorialized against the critics of the initiative. It portrayed the demands for a solution to the Arab-Israeli conflict to precede any serious attempt at political reform in the Arab world as part of the "decade old rhetoric" that was as empty as the "nationalism and socialism which the regimes in Egypt and Syria are based on".[81] Even Bill Clinton himself advised the region's representatives assembled at the U.S.-Islamic Forum in Doha/Qatar to not let conflict divert attention from the need for political and economic reform.[82]

5. Democracy versus peace–the Bush administration's failure (?)

The beginning of the year 2005 witnessed something of a "perfect storm" with regard to the chances of implementing a democratic reform agenda in the Middle East. In the United States, President Bush had just been re-elected with a historically small margin of victory that could still be construed as demonstrating U.S. popular support, thus providing him with some sort of "political capital" to spend. In the Arab world, the powerful symbolism of the first Iraqi elections in half a century and the election of Mahmoud Abbas as the successor to the late Yasser Arafat seemed to create a new opening for the administration's self-imposed Herculean task of democratizing the region *and* solving the Arab-Israeli conflict.

President Bush therefore declared the spread of freedom to be the central theme of his second term in office and promised to push for the establishment of a democratic Palestinian state by the end of his presidency.[83] The fact that Cairo decided to move against secular opposition leader Ayman Nour only days after Bush's speech was widely regarded as a direct affront by Washington's press corps.[84] It became obvious that the White House shared this assessment when Secretary of State Condoleezza Rice did nothing to stop the spread of speculations that she considered cancelling a joint summit of the G8 and Arab countries in protest of Nour's arrest.[85] Only days later, Hosni Mubarak announced constitutional changes to allow the holding of multiparty elections, even though only weeks before he had predicted negative consequences for the "security and stability" of the country in such an event.[86]

In her forceful speech at the American University in Cairo in June 2005, Condoleezza Rice seemed to echo the sentiment of Egypt's liberal opposition by repeating President Bush's dictum that "sixty years of stability at the expense of democracy" had meant that neither had been achieved and demanded an end to the state of emergency in Egypt.[87] Although her demand for independent local and international election observers was not met, one of her spokesmen would later portray the presidential elections as a "historic step" which would "enrich the political dialogue in Egypt for many years to come".[88] A more sceptical International Crisis Group report described the election as a "false start for reform" since "conditions for a genuinely contested presidential election simply did not exist".[89]

In many respects, Egypt's elections for national assembly would also prove to be disappointing for the United States. Not only did Mubarak's one time liberal challenger Ayman Nour lose his seat against a former member of Egypt's security services; low voter participation of around 25 percent and widespread violence against voters at polling stations in districts where Islamists did well also substantially undermined the election's credibility.[90] In late December 2005, the House of Representatives adopted a non-binding Concurrent Resolution which recognized the "promotion of freedom and democracy" as a national interest of the U.S. and asked the Bush administration to base future inquiries to Congress concerning foreign aid to Egypt on the extent to which Cairo addressed the necessity of lifting the state of emergency, the state monopoly over the printing press, the respect of peaceful demonstration and access for local and international observers to future elections.

The first public statements of the Muslim Brotherhood, who had been able to increase the number of its seats from 17 to 88 in the 454 seat assembly, raised concerns about the potential impact on U.S. Middle East policy. On the one hand, its leader, Mohammed Akef, declared that it would neither "recognize, nor fight" Israel and refrain from any involvement in the political decisions of Hamas, its organizational offspring in the Palestinian territories. On the other hand, however, he praised the "noble resistance" in Iraq with its "noble" methods, described Israel as a soon to disappear "cancer" and the holocaust as a myth.[91]

Despite the Egyptian experience the U.S. government decided to push aside the private warnings of Israeli foreign minister Zipi Livni in December 2005 and to support Mahmoud Abbas' call not to postpone the elections for the Palestinian legislative council. For Secretary of State Rice and her team of counsellors such a postponement would have only worsened Fatah's credibility problem.[92] How surprising Hamas' eventual election victory must have been might be gleaned from a statement Secretary Rice had made during her campaign for electoral reform in

Egypt in the summer of 2005. There she had challenged the notion that free elections would necessarily bring radical Islamists to power:

> I don't know who would win a completely free and fair election. ... it's not at all evident to me that the most extreme factions win. In fact, I think you could make the opposite argument, which is that if people have to go out and campaign, they have to go out and get people's votes, and people can vote not just freely and fairly but secretly, it would be very interesting to see whether people would, in fact, vote for a platform that said our platform is to kill innocent people and take away your rights and send your children off to be suicide bombers or to fly airplanes into buildings. And the good thing about a campaign is that the media should and can ask questions that expose what the true platform and campaign would be. ... Now, it's not a perfect safeguard and to a certain extent you have to trust the people, but we believe in the United States that what the absence of political openness and a press that has the opportunity to examine what political leaders are doing in an open way, that that has produced these dark shadows in which extremists can actually operate.[93]

On the other hand, the results of the Palestinian elections do not repudiate Rice in as stark a manner as some commentators have tried to make the general Western public believe. Hamas's overwhelming victory was, to a large extent, not more than a reflection of the complexities of Palestinian election law and incompetent campaigning on the part of Fatah. One half of the 132 available seats were determined through proportional representation while for the other half a simply first-past-the-post principle was applied. A well-thought out recruitment plan and internal divisions within Fatah that saw many candidates standing against each other thus splitting the secular vote allowed Hamas to gain 74 seats with only 45 percent of the votes. The fact that even under extraordinarily favourable political circumstances Hamas could not manage to gain the majority of the votes against its secular opponents amongst the Palestinian political parties serves as another indicator that Islamist parties might constitute the strongest opposition, yet are unable to generate the support of the majority of the population.

The popular charge of "double standards" in U.S. foreign policy tends to neglect the fact that the U.S. has been rather consistent with its public statements on the possibility of working relationships with Islamist movements. At the beginning of the Bush administration's democratization drive in the Middle East, Richard Haass, then director of the policy-planning staff at the Department of State, had picked up where his Democratic and Republican predecessors had begun laying out the official U.S. stance during the 1990s. According to him U.S. relations with any "fairly elected" government would only depend on how the latter would "treat its own people" and how it would behave on the "international stage" with regard to the questions of "terrorism, trade, the non-proliferation of weapons of mass destruction and counter-narcotics".[94]

The Bush administration's democratization drive suffered yet another setback when in the summer of 2006, Hezbollah's attack on a military patrol guarding Israel's border led to a military response by Israel's army. The White House was suddenly faced with the dilemma that the unilateral, military-based form of counter-terrorism chosen by Israeli Prime Minister Ehud Olmert and his Socialist Minister of Defence Amir Peretz undermined Lebanon's pro-Western government. At this point the short-term interest in the defeat or at least significant weakening of those forces whose goals were "escalation and the widening of the battle field"[95] by threatening Israel and preventing any success in the peace process took precedence over the long-term interest in the democratization of the region. The Bush administration's Jacksonian conviction that regional change can be brought about by military means found reflection in the statement of George W. Bush's long-time confidant and adviser Dan Bartlett, that the President "mourns the loss of every life", but believes that "out of this tragic development" a "moment of clarity" arises which helps to tackle the "roots" of the violence[96] as well as Condoleezza Rice's description of the events as the "birth pangs of a new Middle East".[97]

The Israel-Hezbollah war of summer 2006 therefore highlighted the problems the Bush administration faced when it tried to separate the issue of the Arab-Israeli conflict from its other regional interests or even tried to subordinate it to the pursuit of the latter. Rice's counsellor Philip Zelikow acknowledged as much during remarks at the Washington Institute for Near East Policy which a State Department spokesman later hurried to describe as private opinion:

> For the Arab moderates and for the Europeans, some sense of progress and momentum on the Arab-Israeli dispute is just a sine qua non for their ability to cooperate actively with the United States on a lot of other things that we care about. We can rail against that belief; we can find it completely justifiable, but it's fact. That means an active policy on the Arab-Israeli dispute is an essential ingredient to forging a coalition that deals with the most dangerous problems. I would take that even further. I would say that it is essential for the state of Israel because, in some ways, I do not believe that the Palestinian threat, per se, is the most dangerous threat to the future of the state of Israel. If Israel, for example, is especially worried about Iran and sees it as an existential threat, then it's strongly in the interest of Israel to want the American-led coalition to work on an active policy that begins to normalize that situation. It's an essential glue

that binds a lot of these problems together. And so ironically, even if your primary concern is not the Palestinian danger, you have to give it primary attention while you're looking at other problems as well.[98]

The choice of Robert Gates as the new secretary of defence further strengthened those who adhered to a more consensual approach to U.S. Middle East policy. Donald Rumsfeld's successor had been part of the Iraq Study Group which over strong Israeli objections had described a stronger focus on the Arab-Israeli conflict as a way of generating regional support for the U.S. position in Iraq (United States Institute of Peace 2006).[99]

This task was made easier from the point of view of the Bush administration when Hamas' violent power grab in Gaza effectively ended the power-sharing agreement with Fatah and relieved the United States from having to find an answer on how to deal with Hamas. The ensuing diplomatic frenzy culminated in the Annapolis conference of November 2007 and a new peace process of the same name that was intended to produce a final status agreement between Israel and the Palestinian leadership around President Mahmoud Abbas by the end of President Bush's presidency.

The convening of the Annapolis conference was not only meant to create a new push for serious negotiations between Israel and the moderate Palestinians, but also to engage the Arab world in Iran's containment. It could therefore be interpreted as an implicit acknowledgement on the part of the Bush administration that the plan to subordinate the Arab-Israeli conflict to a wider regional democratization drive had failed. Ironically, this led to a situation where the Middle East policy of George W. Bush's administration began to resemble more and more the traditional approach of George H. W. Bush's White House of regional stability and diplomatic engagement which since the early 1990s had been the subject of much neoconservative ridicule.

6. Conclusion

While the question of a possibly mutually reinforcing relationship between democracy and peace has been receiving ever greater attention, so far U.S. policy-makers have not been able to develop a truly sustainable policy. Even though the end of the Cold War had in many regional contexts put an end to the notion that the U.S. had to choose between the pursuit of either democracy or other "national interests", the Middle East long stood as an example of a region where "exceptional" circumstances prevented a similar change in course.

Under the Clinton administration, peace was to come at the expense of democracy, or at the most, as a precondition for political reform. By framing the issue in this way, U.S. diplomats were able to justify devoting all the energy and resources into the exploitation of what was widely considered to be a diplomatic window of opportunity. At the end, the triple crises of Camp David's failure, the al-Aqsa-Intifada and 9/11 demonstrated the futility of this approach.

The wide-spread acceptance of that fact meant that the incoming Bush administration's attempt to couch its own strategic outlook in the terms of democratization and political reform would resonate positively within the U.S. foreign policy debate. In the context of the Arab-Israeli conflict, the call for the democratization of the Palestinian Authority fell in line with the Israeli and U.S. perception that Israel did not have a true partner for peace on the Palestinian side and should therefore rely on unilateral initiatives.

President Bush's approach to the Middle East differed not only through his stronger focus on democratization in the Arab world, but also the public link of the Arab-Israeli conflict with the situation in the Gulf. In the end, the Bush administration's democratization drive suffered from the fact that it was, in fact, as much subjugated to a more general strategic calculus as was the case during the 1990s. Instead of constituting a mutually re-inforcing relationship, democratization and peace suddenly appeared to hinder each other.

As critics of an over-zealous, ideological application of the "democratic peace thesis" to the Middle Eastern political context have pointed out, the observation of a stable peace between democracies should not lead to the conclusion that peace between non-democracies is not possible.[100] Still, given the historical pattern of Arab regimes blaming domestic failures on "Zionist scheming" or the state of the Arab-Israeli conflict, the question remains valid as to whether it can truly be in the interest of the Arab world's authoritarian regimes to solve the Arab-Israeli conflict. Whether democracy is a result or precondition of peace is more than an academic question, it cuts to the heart of U.S. attempts to forge a sustainable Middle East policy.

Bibliography

Ajami, Fouad. "Iraq and the Arabs' Future". *Foreign Affairs* 82:1 (2003): 1-18.

Beinin, Joel. "The New American McCarthyism: Policing Thought about the Middle East". *Race and Class* 46:1 (2004): 101-115.

Benn, Aluf. "Israel and Arab Democracy". *The National Interest* 80 (2005.): 44-48.

Brumberg, Daniel. "Arab Public Opinion and U.S. Foreign Policy: A Complex Encounter. Testimony before the Committee on Government Reform, Subcommittee on National Security, Veterans Affairs, and International Relations", House of Representatives, Congress of the United States, October 8, 2002, Washington, D.C. http://www.carnegieendowment.org/pdf/files/2002-10-08-BrumbergHilltestimony.pdf (accessed March 17, 2008).

Brynen, Rex. "Cluster-Bombs and Sandcastles: Kramer on the Future of Middle East Studies in America". *Middle East Journal* 56:2 (2002): 323-328.

Clinton, William J. Address to the Nation on the Strike on Iraqi Intelligence Headquarters, June 26, 1993. *Weekly Compilation of Presidential Documents* 29: 1180-1182.

Daalder, Ivo H., and James M. Lindsay. *American Unbound. The Bush Revolution in Foreign Policy*. Washington/D.C.: Brookings Institution Press, 2003.

Djerejian, Edward P. "The United States, Islam, and the Middle East in a Changing World". Speech at the Meridian House International Centre, June2, 1992, in Washington, D.C.

Doran, Michael Scott. "Palestine, Iraq, and American Strategy". *Foreign Affairs* 82:1 (2003): 19-33.

Drake, Laura. "Still Fighting the Last Cold War". *Middle East Insight* 10 (1994): 38-43.

Gates, Robert. "Post Cold War Intelligence". Testimony before the House Foreign Affairs Committee. Congress of the United States, February 25, 1992, Washington, D.C.

Gerges, Fawaz. *America and Political Islam. Clash of Civilizations or Clash of Interests?* Cambridge: Cambridge University Press, 1999.

Haass, Richard N. "Towards Greater Democracy in the Muslim World". Remarks to the Council on Foreign Relations, December 4, 2002, Washington, D.C. www.state.gov/s/p/rem/15686.htm (accessed January 8, 2003).

Indyk, Martin. "Back to the Bazaar". *Foreign Affairs* 82:1 (2002): 75-88.

—. "The Clinton Administration's Approach to the Middle East". Speech at the Soref Symposium. Challenges to U.S. Interests in the Middle East. Obstacles and Opportunities, Washington Institute for Near East Policy, May 18, 1993, Washington, D.C. https://www.washingtoninstitute.org/pdf.php?template=C07&CID=61 (accessed March 17, 2008).

Ish-Shalom, Piki. "Theory as a Hermeneutical Mechanism: The Democratic-Peace Thesis and the Politics of Democratization". *European Journal of International Relations* 12:4 (2006): 565-598.

Kagan, Robert D. *The Arabists. The Romance of an American Elite.* New York: The Free Press, 1995.

Karabell, Zalmay. "Fundamental Misconceptions: Islamic Foreign Policy". *Foreign Policy* 105:3, (1996-97): 77-90.

Kramer, Martin. *Ivory Towers on Sand. The Failure of Middle Eastern Studies in America.* Washington, D.C.: The Washington Institute for Near East Policy, 2001.

Kristol, William, and Robert Kagan. "Toward a Neo-Reaganite Foreign Policy". *Foreign Affairs* 75:4 (1996):18-32.

Lake, Anthony. "Conceptualizing U.S. Strategy in the Middle East". Speech at the Soref Symposium. Washington Institute for Near East Policy, May 17, 1994, Washington, D.C. http://www.washingtoninstitute.org/templateC07.php?CID=63 (accessed March 17, 2008).

Lewis, Bernard. "Did You Say 'American Imperialism'? Power, Weakness, and Choices in the Middle East". In *From Babel to Dragomans: Interpreting the Middle East,* edited by Bernard Lewis, 343-350, New York: Oxford University Press, 2004.

Mann, James. *Rise of the Vulcans. The History of Bush's War Cabinet.* New York: Viking, 2004.

Mead, Walter Russell. "Jerusalem Syndrome". Review of the *The Israel Lobby and U.S. Foreign Policy,* by John J. Mearsheimer and Stephen M. Walt. *Foreign Affairs* 86:6 (2007): 160-168.

—. *Special Providence. American Foreign Policy and How it Changed the World,* New York/N.Y.: Knopf, 2001.

Mearsheimer, John J., and Stephen M. Walt. *The Israel Lobby and U.S. Foreign Policy.* New York: Farrar, Straus and Giroux, 2007.

Moravcsik, Andrew. "Taking Preferences Seriously: A Liberal Theory of International Politics". *International Organization* 51:4 (1997): 513-553.

Nye, Jr., Joseph S. "Can America Regain Its Soft Power After Abu Ghraib?" *YaleGlobal* July 29, 2004, http://yaleglobal.yale.edu/display.article?id=4302 (accessed March 17, 2008).

Pelletreau, Robert. "Islamic Political Activism in Mideast: Muslims are debating the role of Islam in Politics and Culture", Speech at the Council on Foreign Relations. New York, June 6, 1996.

Pickart, George. *The Battle Looms. Islam and Politics in the Middle East.* A Report to the Committee on Foreign Relations United States Senate. Senate Print 103-17. Washington, D.C.: U.S. Government Printing Office, 1993.

Posen, Barry R., and Andrew L. Ross. "Competing Visions for U.S. Grand Strategy". *International Security*: 21:3 (1996-7): 5-53.

Powell, Colin L. "United States Position on Terrorists and Peace in the Middle East". Remarks at the McConnell Centre for Political Leadership, University of Louisville/ KY, U.S. Department of State, November 19, 2001.
http://www.state.gov/secretary/former/powell/remarks/2001/6219.htm (accessed April 7, 2007).

Quandt, William B. "America and the Middle East: A Fifty-Year Overview". In *Diplomacy in the Middle East: The International Relations of Regional and Outside Powers*, edited by L. Carl Brown, 59-74. London: I.B. Tauris, 2006.

Richards, Alan. *Socio-Economic Roots of Radicalism? Towards Explaining the Appeal of Islamic Radicals.* U.S. Army War College: Strategic Studies Institute, 2003
http://www.strategicstudiesinstitute.army.mil/pdffiles/PUB105.pdf (accessed March 17, 2008).

Risse, Thomas. "Public Opinion, Domestic Structure, and Foreign Policy in Liberal Democracies". *World Politics* 43:4 (1991): 479-512.

Rubin, Barry. "The Triumph of the 'Old Middle East'". *Middle East Review of International Affairs* 6:2 (2002): 62-69.

Russett, Bruce. *Grasping the Democratic Peace: Principles for a Post-Cold War World.* Princeton: Princeton University Press, 1994.

Satloff, Robert. *U.S. Policy toward Islamism. A Theoretical and Operational Overview.* New York: Council on Foreign Relations, 2000.

Seliktar. Ofira. *Divided We Stand. American Jews, Israel, and the Peace Process.* Westport: Praeger, 2002.

Sharansky, Nathan. "Peace Will Only Come after Freedom and Democracy". *Middle East Quarterly.* 12 (2005)
http://www.meforum.org/article/666 (accessed on March 17, 2008).

Slater, Jerome. "Ideology vs. The National Interest: Bush, Sharon, and U.S. Policy in the Israeli-Palestinian conflict". *Security Studies* 12:1, (2002): 164-206.

The President. "Prohibiting Transactions with Terrorists who Threaten to Disrupt the Middle East Peace Process", Executive Order 12947, January 23, 1995. *Federal Register* 60: 5079-5081.

The White House. "President Discusses the Future of Iraq, March 26, 2003, in Washington, D.C.", http://www.whitehouse.gov/news/releases/2003/02/print/20030226-11.html (accessed February 13, 2008).

—. "President Bush Discusses Freedom in Iraq and Middle East", Remarks by the President at the 20th Anniversary of the National Endowment for Democracy, November 6, 2003, in Washington, D.C.,http://www.ned.org/events/anniversary/oct1603-Bush.html (accessed March 16, 2008).

—. "President Bush Discusses Iraq Policy at Whitehall Palace", November 19, 2003, in London, http://www.whitehouse.gov/news/releases/2003/11/20031119-1.html (accessed March 15, 2008).

—. "President Bush Calls for New Palestinian Leadership", June 24, 2002, in Washington, D.C., http://www.whitehouse.gov/news/releases/2002/06/20020624-3.html (accessed March 22, 2006).

—. "A National Security Strategy of Engagement and Enlargement", 1996. http://www.fas.org/spp/military/docops/national/1996stra.htm (accessed March 17, 2008).

U.S. Agency for International Development. "U.S. Overseas Loans and Grants (Greenbook)". http://qesdb.cdie.org/gbk/home.html (accessed April 17, 2005).

United States Institute of Peace. *The Iraq Study Group Report*, Washington, DC, 2006. http://www.usip.org/isg/iraq_study_group_report/report/1206/iraq_stu dy_group_report.pdf, (accessed February 17, 2008).

Wirth, Timothy. Testimony at the Hearing of the International Security, International Organizations and Human Rights Subcommittee of the House Foreign Affairs Committee, "US Anti-Terrorism Policy", House of Representatives, Congress of the United States, July 13, 1993, Washington, D.C.

Wolfowitz, Paul. "Clinton's First Year". *Foreign Affairs* 73:1 (1994): 28-43.

Zelikow, Philip. "Strategies for the Multifront War against Radical Islamists", Weinberg Founders Conference 2006, Questions and Answers, September 15, 2006, Washington Institute for Near East Policy, Washington, D.C. http://www.washingtoninstitute.org/html/pdf/Zelikow091506.pdf (accessed on January 23, 2008).

Notes

[1] Barry R. Posen and Andrew L. Ross. "Competing Visions for U.S. Grand Strategy". *International Security*: 21:3 (1996-7): 5-53

[2] *Ibid.*, 14.

[3] Zalmay Karabell. "Fundamental Misconceptions: Islamic Foreign Policy". *Foreign Policy* 105:3 (1996-97): 86.

[4] Walter Russell Mead. *Special Providence. American Foreign Policy and How it Changed the World*, (New York: Knopf, 2001) 184

[5] Paul Pillar, *Terrorism and U.S. Foreign Policy*, (Washington, DC: Brookings Institution Press, 2001) 66-67.

[6] Robert J. Art, *A Grand Strategy for America*, Ithaca/London: Cornell University Press, 2003) 58-64.

[7] Mead, 87

[8] (Quoted in Robert D. Kagan, *The Arabists. The Romance of an American Elite*, (New York: The Free Press, 1995) 7-8.

[9] Jerome Slater, "Ideology vs. The National Interest: Bush, Sharon, and U.S. Policy in the Israeli-Palestinian conflict". *Security Studies* 12:1, (2002): 165, emphasis added)

[10] John J. Mearsheimer, and Stephen M. Walt. *The Israel Lobby and U.S. Foreign Policy*, (New York: Farrar, Straus and Giroux, 2007)

[11] Walter Russell Mead, "Jerusalem Syndrome". Review of the *The Israel Lobby and U.S. Foreign Policy*, by John J. Mearsheimer and Stephen M. Walt. *Foreign Affairs* 86:6 (2007) 161.

[12] Andrew Moravcsik, "Taking Preferences Seriously: A Liberal Theory of International Politics", *International Organization* 51:4 (1997): 513-553; Thomas Risse, Thomas. "Public Opinion, Domestic Structure, and Foreign Policy in Liberal Democracies". *World Politics* 43:4 (1991) 479-512.

[13] Ofira Seliktar, Divided We Stand. American Jews, Israel, and the Peace Process, (Westport: Praeger, 2002).

[14] William B. Quandt, "America and the Middle East: A Fifty-Year Overview" in *Diplomacy in the Middle East: The International Relations of Regional and Outside Powers*, edited by L. Carl Brown, 59-74 (London: I.B. Tauris, 2006) 56

[15] Posen/Ross, 24 and 32.

[16] Bruce Russett, *Grasping the Democratic Peace: Principles for a Post-Cold War World*, (Princeton: Princeton University Press, 1994).

[17] William Kristol and Robert Kagan, "Toward a Neo-Reaganite Foreign Policy", *Foreign Affairs* 75:4 (1996): 20-21

[18] Joseph S. Nye, Jr., "Can America Regain Its Soft Power After Abu Ghraib?" *YaleGlobal* July 29, 2004, http://yaleglobal.yale.edu/display.article?id=4302 (accessed March 17, 2008).

[19] "The 1992 Campaign: Excerpts from Clinton's speech on foreign policy leadership". *The New York Times*, August 14, 1992

[20] Joshua Muravchik, "Conservatives for Clinton". *The New Republic*, November 2, 1992.

[21] Laura Drake, "Still Fighting the Last Cold War". *Middle East Insight* 10 (1994): 42-43

[22] George Pickart, *The Battle Looms. Islam and Politics in the Middle East.* A Report to the Committee on Foreign Relations United States Senate. Senate Print 103-17. Washington, D.C.: U.S. Government Printing Office, 1993, V

[23] The White House. "A National Security Strategy of Engagement and Enlargement", 1996. http://www.fas.org/spp/military/docops/national/1996stra.htm (accessed March 17, 2008

[24] *Ibid.*, 23.

[25] Edward P. Djerejian, "The United States, Islam, and the Middle East in a Changing World", Speech at the Meridian House International Centre, June 2, 1992, in Washington, D.C.

[26] Robert Satloff, *U.S. Policy toward Islamism. A Theoretical and Operational Overview*, (New York: Council on Foreign Relations, 2000) 7.

[27] Fawaz Gerges, *America and Political Islam. Clash of Civilizations or Clash of Interests?* (Cambridge: Cambridge University Press, 1999) 84-85.

[28] Robert Gates, Robert. "Post Cold War Intelligence". Testimony before the House Foreign Affairs Committee. Congress of the United States, February 25, 1992, Washington, D.C.

[29] Anthony Lake, "Conceptualizing U.S. Strategy in the Middle East". Speech at the Soref Symposium. Washington Institute for Near East Policy, May 17, 1994, Washington, D.C. http://www.washingtoninstitute.org/templateC07.php?CID=63 (accessed March 17, 2008.

[30] Timothy Wirth, Testimony at the Hearing of the International Security, International Organizations and Human Rights Subcommittee of the House Foreign Affairs Committee, "US Anti-Terrorism Policy", House of Representatives, Congress of the United States, July 13, 1993, Washington, D.C.

[31] Martin Indyk, "The Clinton Administration's Approach to the Middle East", speech at the Soref Symposium: Challenges to U.S. Interests in the Middle East. Obstacles and Opportunities, Washington Institute for Near East Policy, May 18, 1993, Washington, D.C. https://www.washingtoninstitute.org/pdf.php?template=C07&CID=61 (accessed March 17, 2008)

[32] *Ibid.*

[33] Paul Wolfowitz, "Clinton's First Year". *Foreign Affairs* 73:1 (1994): 40.

[34] *Ibid.*, 40 and 30.

[35] Human Rights Watch 1994

[36] Robert Pelletreau, "Islamic Political Activism in the Mideast: Muslims are debating the role of Islam in Politics and Culture", Speech at the Council on Foreign Relations. New York, June 6, 1996.

[37] Anthony Lake, "The Middle East Moment. At the Heart of Our Policy, Extremism Is the Enemy". *Washington Post*, July 24, 1994.

[38] The President. "Prohibiting Transactions with Terrorists who Threaten to Disrupt the Middle East Peace Process", Executive Order 12947, January 23, 1995. *Federal Register* 60: 5079-5081.

[39] CNN Live this morning. "America under Attack: King Abdullah of Jordan Discusses Fight Against Terrorism". September 12, 2001. http://transcripts.cnn.com/TRANSCRIPTS/0109/12/ltm.03.html (accessed March 17, 2008).

[40] Dennis Ross, "Bin Laden's Terrorism isn't About the Palestinians", *New York Times*, October 12, 2001.

[41] Michael Scott Doran, "Palestine, Iraq, and American Strategy", *Foreign Affairs* 82:1 (2003): 20.

[42] Colin Powell, "United States Position on Terrorists and Peace in the Middle East", Remarks at the McConnell Centre for Political Leadership, University of Louisville/ KY, U.S. Department of State, November 19, 2001. http://www.state.gov/secretary/former/powell/remarks/2001/6219.htm (accessed April 7, 2007).

[43] Martin Kramer, *Ivory Towers on Sand. The Failure of Middle Eastern Studies in America* (Washington, D.C.: The Washington Institute for Near East Policy, 2001); Rex Brynen, "Cluster-Bombs and Sandcastles: Kramer on the Future of Middle East Studies in America", *Middle East Journal* 56:2 (2002): 323-328.

[44] Daniel Pipes, "Getting It Wrong In the Middle East". *New York Post*, November 5, 2001.

[45] Daniel Pipes, "Bin Laden is a Fundamentalist". *National Review*, October 22, 2001.

[46] Joel Beinin, "The New American McCarthyism: Policing Thought about the Middle East", *Race and Class* 46:1 (2004): 101-107.

[47] Alan Richards, *Socio-Economic Roots of Radicalism? Towards Explaining the Appeal of Islamic Radicals*, (U.S. Army War College: Strategic Studies Institute, 2003) 2. http://www.strategicstudiesinstitute.army.mil/pdffiles/PUB105.pdf (accessed March 17, 2008)

[48] Daniel Brumberg, "Arab Public Opinion and U.S. Foreign Policy: A Complex Encounter, Testimony before the Committee on Government Reform, Subcommittee on National Security, Veterans Affairs, and International Relations", House of Representatives, Congress of the United States, October 8, 2002, Washington, D.C. http://www.carnegieendowment.org/pdf/files/2002-10-08-BrumbergHilltestimony.pdf (accessed March 17, 2008).

[49] Martin Indyk, "Back to the Bazaar", *Foreign Affairs* 82:1 (2002): 76.

[50] Richard Haass, "Towards Greater Democracy in the Muslim World", Remarks to the Council on Foreign Relations, December 4, 2002, Washington, D.C. www.state.gov/s/p/rem/15686.htm (accessed January 8, 2003).

[51] Indyk, "Back to the Bazaar", 82.

[52] Barry Rubin, "The Triumph of the 'Old Middle East'", *Middle East Review of International Affairs* 6:2 (2002): 63.

[53] Alan Sipress, "Lawmakers Criticize Palestinians". *Washington Post*, April 6, 2001.

[54] The White House. "President Bush Calls for New Palestinian Leadership", June 24, 2002, in Washington, D.C.,
http://www.whitehouse.gov/news/releases/2002/06/20020624-3.html (accessed March 22, 2006).

[55] Dana Milbank, "An Israeli Hawk Accepts the President's Invitation". *Washington Post*, November 23, 2004.

[56] Nathan Sharansky, "Peace Will Only Come after Freedom and Democracy". *Middle East Quarterly*. 12 (2005)
http://www.meforum.org/article/666 (accessed on March 17, 2008).

[57] Dana Milbank, "A Sound Bite So Good, the President Wishes He Had Said It". *Washington Post*, July 2, 2002.

[58] Charles Krauthammer, "Peace through Democracy". *Washington Post*, June 28, 2002.

[59] Henry Siegman, "Yes, It's Broken. Now Fix It". *Washington Post*, May 19, 2002.

[60] Quoted in Milbank, "An Israeli Hawk".

[61] Quoted in Aluf Benn, "Israel and Arab Democracy", *The National Interest* 80 (2005.): 46.

[62] The White House. "President Discusses the Future of Iraq, March 26, 2003, in Washington, D.C.",
http://www.whitehouse.gov/news/releases/2003/02/print/20030226-11.html (accessed February 13, 2008).

[63] "In Bush's Words 'Advance of Democratic Institutions in Iraq Is Setting an Example'". *New York Times*, September 24, 2003.

[64] James Mann, *Rise of the Vulcans. The History of Bush's War Cabinet*, (New York: Viking, 2004).

[65] Ivo H. Daalder and James M. Lindsay, *American Unbound. The Bush Revolution in Foreign Policy*, (Washington/D.C.: Brookings Institution Press, 2003) 130.

[66] Fouad Ajami, "Iraq and the Arabs' Future", *Foreign Affairs* 82:1 (2003): 18.

[67] Bernard Lewis, "Did You Say 'American Imperialism'? Power, Weakness, and Choices in the Middle East", in *From Babel to Dragomans: Interpreting the Middle East*, edited by Bernard Lewis, 343-350 (New York: Oxford University Press, 2004) 350.

[68] James Woolsey, "At War for Freedom", in: *The Observer*, July 20, 2003.

[69] Greg Miller, "Democracy Domino Theory 'Not Credible'", in: *Los Angeles Times*, March 14, 2003.

[70] Marina Ottaway, Thomas Carothers, Amy Hawthorne, Daniel Brumberg. *Democratic Mirage in the Middle East*, (Washington, DC: Carnegie Endowment for International Peace, 2002) Policy Brief No. 20.

[71] Jon Alterman, "Not in My Backyard: Iraq's Neighbour's Interests", *Washington Quarterly*, 26: 3 (2003) 149-160.

[72] The White House, "President Bush Discusses Freedom in Iraq and Middle East", Remarks by the President at the 20th Anniversary of the National Endowment for Democracy, November 6, 2003, in Washington, D.C., http://www.ned.org/events/anniversary/oct1603-Bush.html (accessed March 16, 2008).

[73] Shafeeq Ghabra, "It's Time to Tear Down the 'Arab Wall'", in *Washington Post*, November 23, 2003.

[74] Quoted in Terence Hunt, "Bush: Mideast Must Move Toward Democracy", in: *Washington Post*, November 7, 2003.

[75] The White House, "President Bush Discusses Freedom in Iraq and Middle East", *op. cit.*

[76] Robin Wright and Glenn Kessler, "Bush Aims for 'Greater Mideast' Plan", in: *Washington Post*, February 9, 2004.

[77] Neil MacFarquhar, "Arab Leaders Seek to Counter U.S. Plan for Mideast Overhaul", in: *New York Times*, March 4, 2004; Steven R. Weisman/Neil MacFarquhar, "U.S. Plan for Mideast Reform Draws Ire of Arab Leaders", in: *New York Times*, February 27, 2004.

[78] "Kingdom Warns US Against Imposing Reforms". *Arab News*, February 20, 2004, http://www.arabnews.com/?artid=39792 (accessed on February 26, 2004).

[79] P.K. Abdul Ghafour, "No Reforms under Foreign Pressure", in: *Arab News*, March 2, 2004, http://www.arabnews.com/?artid=40442.

[80] Zbigniew Brzezinski, "The Wrong Way to Sell Democracy to the Arab World", in: *New York Times*, March 8, 2004.

[81] "The Arab Backlash". *Washington Post*, March 10, 2004.

[82] Bill Clinton, "Closing Address: U.S.-Islamic World Forum, Doha" January, 12, 2004, http://www.brook.edu/fp/research/projects/islam/clinton20040112.pdf (accessed March 22, 2006).

[83] The White House, "State of the Union Address", February 2, 2005, Washington, D.C.,http://www.whitehouse.gov/news/releases/2005/02/20050202-11.html (accessed May 13, 2005)

[84] "Egypt's Brutal Answer". *Washington Post*, February 24, 2005.

[85] Glenn Kessler, "Rice Drops Plans for Visit to Egypt", in: *Washington Post*, February 26, 2005.

[86] Maamoun Youssef, "Egyptian President Orders Election Changes", in: *Washington Post*, February 26, 2005; "Mubarak to nominate himself for Elections, rejects Constitutional Changes", in: *Arabic News*, January 31, 2005, http://www.arabicnews.com.

[87] Condoleezza Rice, "Remarks at the American University in Cairo", June 20, 2005, Washington, DC: U.S. Department of State, http://www.state.gov/secretary/rm/2005/48328.htm (accessed March 22, 2006).

[88] Daniel Williams/Robin Wright, "Controversy Swirls over Egypt Vote", in: *Washington Post*, September 9, 2005.

[89] International Crisis Group Report, (2005) I.

[90] Abeer Allam, "A Political Rival of Mubarak Loses His Seat in Parliament", in: *New York Times*, November 11, 2005.

[91] Michael Slackman, "Egyptian Leader of Muslim Group Calls Holocaust a Zionist 'Myth'", in: *New York Times*, December 23, 2005; Neil MacFarquhar, "Will Politics Tame Egypt's Muslim Brotherhood?", in: *New York Times*, December 8, 2005.

[92] Steven R. Weisman, "Rice Admits U.S. Underestimated Hamas Strength". *New York Times*, January 30, 2006.

[93] Condoleezza Rice, *Roundtable with Saudi Media*, June 21, 2005, Washington, DC: U.S. Department of State, http://www.state.gov/secretary/rm/2005/48401.htm (accessed February 13, 2008).

[94] See Haass.

[95] Assistant Secretary of State David Welch quoted in Robin Wright, "Options for U.S. Limited as Mideast Crises Spread". *Washington Post*, July 13, 2006.

[96] Quoted in Michael Abramowitz, "In Mideast Strife, Bush Sees a Step to Peace". *Washington Post*, July 21, 2006.

[97] Quoted in Robin Wright, "As Mideast Smoke Clears, Political Fates May Shift". *Washington Post*, August 13, 2006.

[98] Philip Zelikow, "Strategies for the Multifront War against Radical Islamists", Weinberg Founders Conference 2006, Questions and Answers, September 15, 2006, Washington Institute for Near East Policy, Washington, D.C. http://www.washingtoninstitute.org/html/pdf/Zelikow091506.pdf   (accessed   on January 23, 2008)

[99] "Israel Rejects Iraq Study Group Proposals". CBS News.com, December 7, 2006,http://www.cbsnews.com/stories/2006/12/07/world/main2237127.shtml (accessed March 17, 2008).

[100] Piki Ish-Shalom, "Theory as a Hermeneutical Mechanism: The Democratic-Peace Thesis and the Politics of Democratization", *European Journal of International Relations* 12:4 (2006): 583.

CHAPTER ELEVEN

LEADERSHIP AND POWER: TONY BLAIR, GEORGE W. BUSH AND THE WAR AGAINST IRAQ

JON ROPER

"How much an obstacle is it to this special relationship you say you want to have on behalf of your two countries that you are ideologically poles apart?"

President Bush: "He can handle his politics in Britain, and I'll handle mine in America. ... I can assure you that when either of us get in a bind, there will be a friend on the other end of the phone".

Prime Minister Blair: "And I think it's important to recognize, as well ... there are very strong alliances that can be formed with people across so-called ideological divides of that type".[1]

In February 2001, on the first occasion that President George W. Bush met with Prime Minister Tony Blair at Camp David, the attendant media were anxious to know what the two men had in common. On the one hand there was a Republican "compassionate conservative" and on the other the architect of New Labour who, together with the former US President Bill Clinton, had advocated the "Third Way" as the articulation of modern progressive politics. It was the first time for thirty three years that a Republican President had met a Labour Prime Minister. Then, Richard Nixon and Harold Wilson had not managed to forge much of a political or personal friendship. Now, at their joint press conference, when asked if they had a shared personal interest, "maybe in religion or sport or music", the President let the journalists share a moment of intimacy. He had observed, to the apparent embarrassment of his guest ("They're going to wonder how you know that, George"), that he and Mr. Blair both used the same brand of toothpaste.

Whether this gave an immediate boost to the sales of Colgate–once marketed in Britain as giving its user a "ring of confidence"–is less important than the fact that even at this first meeting, the two leaders had found themselves in agreement on more than dental abstergents. They identified the foreign policy issue that would come to define their reputations during their respective terms in office: Iraq. At the news conference, Bush outlined his agenda: "to make it clear to Saddam Hussein that he shall not terrorize his neighbors and not develop weapons of mass destruction" and Blair echoed the President's concern: "don't be under any doubt at all of our absolute determination to make sure that the threat of Saddam Hussein is contained and that he is not able to develop these weapons of mass destruction that he wishes to do"[2].

Two years later, Tony Blair supported George W. Bush in a pre-emptive war against Iraq, thereby alienating much of Europe, as well as many members of his own party and public opinion in Britain. To his critics, the British Prime Minister had identified himself as a fellow traveller of the President, offering unhesitating support for American military action in the aftermath of the terrorist attacks in the United States that had taken place a little over six months after their first meeting at Camp David. He had become "no more than George Bush's poodle"[3]. This chapter argues, however, that even prior to George W. Bush taking office, Tony Blair was a leading advocate of humanitarian interventionism to oppose "evil" dictators such as Saddam Hussein. It assesses the "Blair Doctrine", first outlined in a speech to an audience in Chicago in 1999, in terms of its contribution to the contemporary and continuing political debate within the United States over the "Vietnam Syndrome" and its impact on Presidential power. In speaking out against the prospect of American isolationism just prior to the 2000 presidential election campaign, moreover, the Prime Minister revealed that he was never going to be "ideologically poles apart" from its eventual winner, George W. Bush, and the neo-conservatives whom he appointed to his administration.

In an article published in *The Political Quarterly* in 2005, Inderjeet Parmar also points out that Blair and Bush shared "independently arrived at global diagnoses and, in considerable measure, prescriptions"[4]. Furthermore, he suggests, Blair harboured a nostalgic longing for the nation's imperial past and held to a romanticized view of its historical contribution to international stability. Indeed, it was only a last minute intervention by the Labour party's foreign policy commission during the 1997 election campaign that prevented him from proclaiming in a speech in Manchester that he was "proud of the British Empire"[5]. As Prime Minister, his ambition, in Parmar's view, was nothing less than "to preside over the resurrection of a beneficent liberal-imperial world order" that Blair was convinced could be achieved only "by an active Anglo-American alliance"[6].

This chapter traces the outcome of such a vision. It argues that in supporting American action against Iraq, the Prime Minister's ideal of a transatlantic led international community, co-operating with the United States and Britain in the struggle against "evil" and pariah states, ultimately could not be reconciled with the American President's doctrine of unilateral pre-emptive war to preserve national security. Blair's cherished alliance was effectively isolated in the court of world opinion.

In May 1999, less than a month after his Chicago speech, Blair traveled to the capital of Bulgaria. Observing that: "I know that at least one of my predecessors, William Gladstone, would be delighted to see me visiting Sofia", he acknowledged that the nineteenth century Liberal leader, who had unequivocally condemned Turkish atrocities in the country, "was one of my political heroes". Gladstone's "commitment to opposing the persecution of the Bulgarians in the 1870s was unshakeable. He spoke out loudly and clearly of "this civilisation, which has been affronted and shamed"'. For the Prime Minister, with Europe witnessing the contemporary crisis of ethnic cleansing in Kosovo:

> The parallels between then and now are all too tragically clear. Today we face the same questions that confronted Gladstone over 120 years ago. Does one nation or people have the right to impose its will on another? Is there ever a justification for a policy based on the supremacy of one ethnic group? Can the outside world simply stand by when a rogue state brutally abuses the basic rights of those it governs? Gladstone's answer in 1876 was clear. And so is mine today[7].

In the light of the events that were to unfold four years later in Iraq, there is a certain irony in some of Blair's remarks. Subsequently, however, he was often located within the British political tradition that had been shaped by his illustrious role model. For Parmar, therefore, there was "a strong strain of Gladstonian moralism" in Blair's attitude towards international relations. In terms of his foreign policy, Timothy Garton Ash, writing in *The Guardian* on the eve of the Iraq War, defined the Labour leader as "a Gladstonian Christian liberal interventionist". More recently, in a collection of essays exploring the Prime Minster's ten years in office, he characterized the "Blair Doctrine" as "neo-Gladstonian"[8]. In the same volume, Ian McClean commented that as he left office: "the more

perceptive tributes to Tony Blair on his retirement stressed how
Gladstonian he was", but admitted that such comparisons could only be
pursued "up to a point"[9]. Indeed, there may be a different parallel that can
be drawn along a line of transatlantic political latitude.

As Parmar observes, the faith based politics that led him to emphasize
"the utility of Jesus in everyday life" also suggested "something of the
southern US evangelical Protestant" in Blair's character[10]. This chapter
pursues that argument. Blair's blend of moralism and missionary zeal in
taking the nation to war five times during his decade in office is
reminiscent of a Wilsonian perspective on the wider world: not that of the
Labour leader Harold Wilson, another of his predecessors as Prime
Minister, but rather of Woodrow Wilson, the southern protestant and
evangelist for democracy, who as America's President became a principle
architect of its twentieth century perspectives on the wider world.

Blair's approach to leadership, foreign policy and military
interventionism thus can be placed in the historical context of early
twentieth century American progressivism. The chapter concludes by
suggesting how, in a similar way, George W. Bush's commitment to a
muscular foreign policy that emphasized the use of America's military
power in the preservation of its perceived national interest was another
throwback to the early twentieth century, this time to the world of
Theodore Roosevelt. Such historical analogies point to the cultural
continuities that helped to shape contemporary political attitudes on both
sides of the Atlantic at a time of their potential dislocation in the
immediate aftermath of September 11th 2001.

The war against Iraq can be seen as an outcome of the events of that
day, reflecting the grandiose visions, democratic ambitions and imperial
hubris of both the British Prime Minister and the American President. It
would shape their political legacies. For George W. Bush, along with key
members of his administration, however, it was initially also the product
of a desire to reassert the President's power as commander in chief after it
had been eroded as a result of the greatest debâcle of twentieth century
American liberal internationalist and interventionist foreign policy:
Vietnam.

Presidential Power and the Impact of Vietnam

Contemporary neo-conservative views on the role that the United
States should adopt in international relations were forged in the aftermath
of military defeat. America's ill-fated involvement in the Vietnam War
fragmented the Cold War liberal consensus that had until then consistently

sanctioned the President's use of his powers as Commander-in-Chief to commit American forces overseas. The aftershocks of Vietnam were seen most acutely in the widespread reluctance to sanction the President risking American troops becoming embroiled in another such conflict. This shift in attitude was recognised by President Jimmy Carter when he admitted that military power was perhaps not the only solution to foreign policy problems. In a speech outlining a new approach to foreign policy at Notre Dame University on 22 May 1977, Carter put it this way:

> For too many years we've been willing to adopt the flawed and erroneous principles and tactics of our adversaries, sometimes abandoning our own values for theirs. We've fought fire with fire, never thinking that fire is better quenched with water. This approach failed, with Vietnam the best example of its intellectual and moral poverty[11].

Carter tried to move American foreign policy away from the orthodoxies of Cold War nostrums, combining his principled support of human rights with an awareness of the public's desire not to go to war once more. The "Vietnam Syndrome" came to symbolize popular opposition to further military adventurism abroad. Others within Carter's own party, however, were concerned by what they saw as a progressive weakening of American power in the world, dramatized by the Iranian hostage crisis. For disillusioned Democrats, the failed attempt to rescue those held in the American Embassy in Tehran not only helped catapult Carter from the White House, but also left their party in disarray and the United States with a profound sense of ideological dislocation and political malaise.

Ronald Reagan once famously remarked: "I didn't leave the Democrat party. They left me". Towards the end of the 1970s, there was a similar exodus of those neo-conservatives who argued the case that American power, and with it the President's capacity to use military force should he deem it necessary, should be re-vitalized in the aftermath of Vietnam. Their titular leader within the Democrats had been Senator Henry "Scoop" Jackson from Washington State, who had supported Lyndon Johnson's policy in Vietnam to its disastrous end, and who campaigned for the party's presidential nomination in 1972 and 1976.

Most Democrats had rejected Jackson's bids for the White House, opting instead for George McGovern, defeated comprehensively by Richard Nixon in 1972, and then four years later for Jimmy Carter, whose disastrous term in office would help to consign the party to the presidential wilderness for another twelve years. Looking around for a candidate who they felt might inherit Jackson's mantle, in 1980 many of his former supporters opted for the self-proclaimed apostate: Ronald Reagan. These converts to the Republicans, among them Richard Perle and Paul Wolfowitz, who had formerly both worked for Jackson, became neo-conservative advocates of American power symbolized by a strong Executive who could take, if necessary, decisive military action as Commander-in-Chief.

Others made a similar ideological journey. In 1990, for example, in a memorial lecture commemorating the life of the Senator from Washington State, Charles Krauthammer proclaimed that he had "always been proud to call myself a Henry Jackson Democrat"[12]. He had previously written that Jackson was:

> The symbol and the last great leader of a political tradition that began with Woodrow Wilson and reached its apogee with John Kennedy, Lyndon Johnson and Hubert Humphrey. That tradition, liberal internationalism, held that if democratic capitalism was to have a human face, it had to have a big heart and a strong hand[13].

Krauthammer became a leading neo-conservative commentator. Moreover, as these converts to Reagan's Republican party staggered away from the Democrats and the wreckage of Carter's presidency, they concluded that the persistence of the "Vietnam Syndrome" was not only weakening the President's hand but also diminishing America's capacity to pursue its national interests on the world stage.

By the time Bill Clinton recaptured the White House for the Democrats in 1992, the Cold War was over and liberal internationalism seemed less important than more immediate concerns closer to home: "It's the economy, stupid" had been the Democrat's election mantra. Nevertheless, Clinton's foreign policy involved an attempt to reconcile the Carter wing of the Democratic party and those who had not thrown in their lot with the neo-conservatives but who still accepted the "Scoop" Jackson arguments for a robust assertion of Presidential power, if necessary committing military force in the defence of national ideals. Given the controversies surrounding his own conduct during the Vietnam War, Clinton's attitude to military interventionism was ambivalent, but in contrast to Carter, he was prepared to sanction it in pursuit of his foreign policy ambitions. At the end of his first term in the White House, however, Michael Mandelbaum, writing in *Foreign Affairs*, condemned the President's actions in Bosnia, Somalia and Haiti as "three failed military interventions" that had occurred in his first nine months in office and which had set the pattern of "foreign policy as social work". For Mandelbaum, "the Clinton interventions were intended to promote American values" rather than advancing the national interest[14]. In pursuing a humanitarian foreign policy–Carter's human rights agenda backed this time by American military power–Clinton had involved the United States in areas of the world that were disconnected with its strategic interests. As soon as such actions threatened the lives of its military personnel, notably in Somalia, American public opinion reacted. Benevolent intentions proved no match for the continuing influence of the "Vietnam Syndrome".

Clinton's military interventions, up to the moment that American public opinion rebelled, nevertheless became a rallying point for post Cold War liberal progressivism–the "Third Way"–within and beyond the United States. When "New Labour" took office in Britain in 1997, it did so with a commitment to an "ethical foreign policy" that was reminiscent of Jimmy Carter's vision. But it was Tony Blair as Prime Minister who would invest this idealistic skeleton with military muscle: sanctioning the use of British military forces in attempts to find solutions to potential humanitarian disasters. It was a policy which soon resembled Clinton's first term forays into overseas interventionism. As John Kampfner points out, Blair became Prime Minister knowing "precious little about foreign affairs" but within a year he "had defined a new mission for Britain overseas". It involved "a taste for the battlefield"[15].

This propensity to go to war was a new departure for a Labour party, which, when previously in office in the very different circumstances of the 1950s, 1960s and 1970s, had generally eschewed the exercise of military power. Similarly, Labour's enthusiasm for American military action overseas during the Cold War had been typically either tepid or cold. In the Korean War, it is true that Labour's leader and the then Prime Minister, Clement Attlee had accepted that "we'll have to support the Yanks", but on a visit to Washington in December 1950 he tried to persuade President Truman to consider a ceasefire and the withdrawal of UN troops[16]. During the Vietnam War, Harold Wilson, Labour's first Prime Minister after an interval of thirteen years, was asked by Lyndon Johnson to send a "token force" to support the American commitment. The Prime Minister refused the President's request and like Attlee tried to mediate in America's war[17]. James Callaghan was Prime Minister during the period of America's post-Vietnam retreat from military adventurism overseas and while Jimmy Carter was President.

Where Tony Blair differed from his three immediate predecessors as Labour Prime Minister, therefore, was in his determination that "New Labour" should enter the brave new world of post Cold War international relations free from its former shibboleths and able to back its humanitarian aspirations with military force. Indeed, unaffected by the ideological uncertainties that had caused divisions among Democrats in the United

States after the Vietnam War, Blair emerged as the leading and most articulate advocate of "Third Way" interventionism, even to the extent of lecturing Americans on the way forward in the post Cold War world.

The "Blair Doctrine": the idea of International Community

On 24th April 1999, the Prime Minister spoke at the Economic Club of Chicago and outlined his vision of how the international community should co-operate in an age of increasing globalisation to confront threats to peace and security. Tony Blair did so in the context of NATO's military action in Kosovo: the second major combat operation conducted by the alliance, four years after its first intervention in the Balkans in Bosnia and Herzegovina. In a speech which conflated idealism and realism, Blair argued that Kosovo was "a just war, based not on any territorial ambitions but on values". It was a humanitarian mission: "We cannot let the evil of ethnic cleansing stand. We must not rest until it is reversed". The Prime Minister then shifted his argument from abstract justice to pragmatism. Invoking the powerful memory of Munich, he drew the orthodox lesson that, for the previous sixty years, had remained a constant refrain in British–and American–foreign policy: "appeasement does not work. If we let an evil dictator range unchallenged, we will have to spill infinitely more blood and treasure to stop him later".

In the Balkans, the "evil dictator" was Slobodan Milosevic. In extrapolating his argument from the proximate issue of the Kosovo campaign to the application of the principles of an international community to global security, however, Blair drew a direct comparison with another leader who also threatened peace. "Many of our problems have been caused by two dangerous and ruthless men–Saddam Hussein and Slobodan Milosevic". Moreover:

> One of the reasons why it is now so important to win the conflict (in Kosovo) is to ensure that others do not make the same mistake in the future. That in itself will be a major step to ensuring that the next decade and the next century will not be as difficult as the past. If NATO fails in Kosovo, the next dictator to be threatened with military force may well not believe our resolve to carry the threat through.

So the commitment to confront dictators involves a high stakes political and military gamble: success will make other international pariahs think again before risking war, whereas failure will encourage them to ignore threats from the international community with impunity.

Then it was back to idealism. In the post Cold War World, Blair suggested,

> Our actions are guided by a more subtle blend of mutual self interest and moral purpose in defending the values we cherish. In the end values and interests merge. If we can establish and spread the values of liberty, the rule of law, human rights and an open society then that is in our national interests too. The spread of our values makes us safer.

His appeal was to that most fundamental of American sentiments. He quoted an American president in support of his case: "as John Kennedy put it 'Freedom is indivisible and when one man is enslaved who is free?'"

What came to be known as the "Blair Doctrine" thus involved five key tests which would help guide a decision by the international community, working through the a re-vitalised United Nations, to intervene in some of the many cases where "regimes that are undemocratic" were "engaged in barbarous acts". The arguments for intervention had to be irrefutable: "are we sure of our case?" Diplomacy had to be exhausted. Military action should be "sensibly and prudently" undertaken. Furthermore, it should be accepted that interventions might have to be sustained through a long-term commitment of force. Finally, the extent to which national interests were involved should be assessed. Taken together, the mixture of humanitarian sentiments and pragmatic guidelines that the Prime Minister sketched out represented a "Third Way" foreign policy, based on an ideological outlook that was part of "an attempt by centre and centre-left Governments to re-define a political programme that is neither old left nor 1980s right".

In concluding his remarks, Blair admitted that his vision could not be realised without the full commitment of the United States to take a leading role in supporting it. The most powerful nation in the world had to engage with his idea of an international community and had to remain involved with finding solutions to the problems it faced. "I say to you: never again fall for the doctrine of isolationism", because "the world cannot afford it" should America take too narrow a view of its national interest and stand by when international interventions for humanitarian purposes were being discussed[18].

As John Kampfner observes, Blair's speech was based largely on ideas contributed to it by Sir Lawrence Freedman, Professor of War Studies at Kings College London.[19] Subsequently Freedman has maintained that:

> This remains Blair's speech. This is not only because the final draft was not an exact copy of my first draft, but because once the words had been used by the Prime Minister it was the meaning he attached to the words

that was important rather than the meaning I attached to them. The same thoughts could have been expressed in different ways.[20]

The substance of such nuances of interpretation is not made clear, but it might be gleaned from one of Freedman's other publications: his magisterial study *Kennedy's Wars*, in which he argues that it was the successful handling of the Cuban Missile Crisis that led members of JFK's administration to assume that they could control the course of events in other Cold War confrontations. It was this belief that led the United States inexorably down the path to deeper involvement in Southeast Asia and the Vietnam War[21]. Blair was grateful for Freedman's help in framing his speech: unfortunately, *Kennedy's Wars*, which the Prime Minister might also have benefited from reading, was not published until the following year. In developing the idea of "international community" and his criteria for humanitarian interventionism, Blair emerged in American terms as a "Scoop" Jackson Democrat, untroubled by the historical baggage of the Vietnam War.

While Clinton remained equivocal in his commitment to any military action that would involve American troops taking part in a ground war in the Balkans, Blair was convinced that the rightness of the cause justified the risks of confrontation. His gamble worked. Milosevic backed away from war. Indeed, the difference between Blair and Clinton in their respective uses of military power for humanitarian ends was that the Prime Minister's actions–in Kosovo and subsequently in Sierra Leone–were judged to be successful and he derived both domestic and international support for them and from them. They also confirmed Blair's conviction that military solutions could be effective in helping to rid the world of undemocratic regimes and that the United States' involvement in any such campaign was critical to its success.

George W. Bush: "Idealism without Illusions"

In the United States, as Clinton's term in office came to an end, ideological critics of his performance as Commander-in-Chief ensured that the future of foreign policy and the circumstances in which the President's use of American military power could be justified remained a topic of contemporary political debate. The legacy of Vietnam continued to make the issue of military interventionism–whether for humanitarian reasons or not–a contentious one among and between Democrats and Republicans alike.

Seven months after Blair's speech in Chicago, George W. Bush, campaigning for the Republican nomination in the 2000 presidential election, gave his first major foreign policy address at the Ronald Reagan Library in California. Although he focused upon American concerns, Bush's argument, like Blair's, blended values and interests, idealism and realism, concentrating on the core values of freedom and democracy:

> Some have tried to pose a choice between American ideals and American interests–between who we are and how we act. But the choice is false. America, by decision and destiny, promotes political freedom–and gains the most when democracy advances.

There was another quote appropriated from a former American President. It was George Washington who had observed that: "Liberty, when it begins to take root, is a plant of rapid growth."

Bush, like Blair, rejected the isolationist impulse:

> In a world that depends on America to reconcile old rivals and balance ancient ambitions, this is the shortcut to chaos. It is an approach that abandons our allies, and our ideals. The vacuum left by America's retreat would invite challenges to our power.

Instead, he offered a foreign policy based upon: "a distinctly American internationalism. Idealism, without illusions. Confidence, without conceit. Realism, in the service of American ideals"[22]. Leave out the first sentence of that quotation and the word "American" in the last and the rhetoric employed by the then Republican candidate for the Presidency and the British Prime Minister speaking in Chicago is remarkably similar.

That word "American" was, however, crucial. Blair and Bush differed in the relative emphasis they placed on idealism and realism in the context of the idea of an "international community" on the one hand and "a distinctly American internationalism" on the other. Whereas Blair's vision was rooted in a liberal concern that justified military interventionism on humanitarian grounds, the conservative Bush placed more emphasis on defining and defending the national interest of the United States from perceived threats to its security in the post Cold War world. Indeed during the election campaign, Condoleezza Rice, one of his principle foreign policy advisors, in an article in *Foreign Affairs*, criticised the Clinton administration for its failure to adequately define and pursue the national interest, implicitly dismissing the expansive idealism of the "Third Way" and the emphasis that both he and Blair had placed on international co-operation. The Democrats, she argued, were prepared for the United States to exercise its military power only when: "The 'national interest' is replaced with 'humanitarian interests' or the interests of 'the international community.'" Although, for Rice, "'Humanitarian intervention' cannot be ruled out a priori", when weighing the costs and benefits in terms of the national interest a president:

> must ask whether decisive force is possible and is likely to be effective and must know how and when to get out. These are difficult criteria to meet, so U.S. intervention in these "humanitarian" crises should be, at best, exceedingly rare[23].

Neo-conservatives nevertheless agreed with the advocates of the "Third Way" on both sides of the Atlantic that in surveying the contemporary ideological terrain of American politics in the post-Vietnam era, to persuade the public to support the President's use of military power, it was necessary to triangulate between the poles of isolationism and interventionism. Neo-conservative realists maintained a robust and pragmatic view of the efficacy of the use of America's military resources in pursuit of the national interest but still recognised that idealism and realism could coalesce in opposition to the prospect of America's withdrawal from world affairs. In 2000, George W. Bush's disputed election victory brought them back into positions of influence within the new Republican administration.

The Discourse of "Evil"

At what became known as the "Colgate Summit", the reporter's question had thus missed the point. What was remarkable about Bush and Blair, at least in terms of the animating principles of their perspectives on the use of military power, was not that they were "ideologically poles apart" but that they had, from the start, a great deal in common: foreign policy should blend values and interests and America should avoid isolationism from international affairs. Blair's vision of an "international community" and Bush's call for "idealism without illusions" had been attempts to persuade their audiences–in Chicago and in Los Angeles–that when military interventionism to counter "evil" was judged necessary, war could be legitimised by an appeal to the merger between democratic values and national interests. It is significant in this context too that the new President agreed with the Prime Minister that there was "evil" in the world and that on both moral and pragmatic grounds the United States should lead efforts to combat it.

They were both fond of the word. In his Chicago speech, Tony Blair argued for the world to confront "evil" dictators. Similarly George W.

Bush reminded his audience at the Reagan Library that the former President had been: "a hero in the American story. A story in which a single individual can shape history. A story in which evil is real, but courage and decency triumph". At that time, Bush warned, threats to national security remained: "The Empire has passed, but evil remains"[24].

September 11th 2001 proved their point. As Peter Singer observes, when President Bush addressed the nation on the evening of 9/11, he used the word "evil" four times in his brief statement, "setting the tone for the months and years to come"[25]. For both the American President and the British Prime Minister, who, in his statement to the House of Commons following the attacks also characterized their perpetrators as "evil", values and interests now joined to justify military interventionism, first in Afghanistan and then, far more controversially, in Iraq.

In his 2001 State of the Union Address, Bush invested Iraq as a charter member of the "axis of evil". Later that year, ten months after 9/11, speaking to the graduating class at West Point and in setting out the "Bush Doctrine", the President asserted that the United States would be prepared to take pre-emptive military action to counter perceived threats to its national security. He framed his argument with what had by then become familiar rhetorical flourishes:

> Some worry that it is somehow undiplomatic or impolite to speak the language of right and wrong. I disagree. ... Moral truth is the same in every culture, in every time, and in every place. ... There can be no neutrality between justice and cruelty, between the innocent and the guilty. We are in a conflict between good and evil, and America will call evil by its name. ... By confronting evil and lawless regimes, we do not create a problem, we reveal a problem. And we will lead the world in opposing it[26].

The moral certitude that informed the President's rhetoric was the product of his strongly held religious beliefs, which Tony Blair, as a committed Christian, also shared. The common discourse of "evil" thus acted as another bridge across any ideological divide that might have separated the two leaders. They both saw the world in terms of moral absolutes– "good" and "evil", "right" and wrong" –which were derived from the certainties of their faiths. This enabled them to agree on the animating principles of a post 9/11 interventionist foreign policy that aimed to promote the ideal of democracy in the face of the perceived threat from international terrorism.

"Democratic Globalism"

In the 2004 Irving Kristol lecture, given at the American Enterprise

Institute in Washington, Charles Krauthammer recognised that the "Bush doctrine" and the "Blair doctrine" in fact shared a distinctive ideological vision which had been misrepresented by their critics. Indeed, Krauthammer pointed out that what was "often lazily and invidiously called neo-conservatism … is a very odd name for a school whose major proponents in the world today are George W. Bush and Tony Blair". He argued that the American President and the British Prime Minister were making the same case for a particular view of the world: "they are the principal proponents today of what might be called democratic globalism, a foreign policy that defines the national interest not as power but as values, and that identifies one supreme value, what John Kennedy called 'the success of liberty'".

"Democratic globalism" transcended bland ideological definitions: there was "nothing neo about Bush, and there's nothing con about Blair". Instead this new perspective was rooted in established patterns of American thinking about the wider world. It:

> sees as the engine of history not the will to power but the will to freedom. And while it has been attacked as a dreamy, idealistic innovation, its inspiration comes from the Truman Doctrine of 1947, the Kennedy inaugural of 1961, and Reagan's "evil empire" speech of 1983. They all sought to recast a struggle for power between two geopolitical titans into a struggle between freedom and unfreedom, and yes, good and evil.

For Krauthammer, American power, which should be capable of military expression through the President's ability to act as Commander-in-Chief, should be used to realize the ambitions of a foreign policy abandoned by many within the Democratic party after Vietnam. From the 1970s onwards, liberal internationalism, "the foreign policy of the Democratic Party" had been "transmuted into an ideology of passivity, acquiescence and almost reflexive anti-interventionism" except, during the Clinton years in cases that were "morally pristine enough to justify the use of force" but were "devoid of raw national interest"[27]. The events of September 11th 2001 had altered the public mood dramatically. As national security became a political imperative, Krauthammer believed that the President was now able to create the necessary popular consensus for the commitment of American forces overseas in the global "war on terror", using military power untrameled by the "Vietnam Syndrome" and with the support of a like-minded leader across the Atlantic.

In its emphasis on the promotion of American values, the "Bush Doctrine" may thus have staked a claim to the similar moral high-ground as had the "Blair Doctrine". But Krauthammer ignored the fundamental difference between the two visions: Blair's hope that values would coalesce with interests to encourage international co-operation stood in stark contrast to Bush's determination, following 9/11, to take unilateral action where necessary against the "evil" that threatened both American values and interests. This placed him in an impossible political situation. While the Prime Minister agreed with the moral imperatives driving the President in his "war on terror", allying himself with Bush in the build up to military action against Iraq would mean that he was isolated from the very international community whose creation he had encouraged.

The "Blair Doctrine" and the "Bush Doctrine" both made the case for a military campaign to overthrow Saddam Hussein. In his Chicago speech, the British Prime Minister had identified the Iraqi dictator as an international pariah. Blair had already supported American action in 1998, when President Clinton, frustrated at Saddam's lack of co-operation with UN inspectors sent to investigate Iraqi programmes for the production of weapons of mass destruction, authorised a bombing campaign against suspected WMD facilities. In his speech at West Point, Bush, now fully engaged in prosecuting the "war on terror" saw Saddam at the epicentre of a toxic nexus: an "unbalanced" dictator, with weapons of mass destruction, only too willing to supply them to terrorists aiming to destroy the United States. Neo-conservatives in his administration–including Dick Cheney, whose influence as Vice President was then at its height–had advocated an attack on Iraq immediately after 9/11. Following the invasion of Afghanistan and as America turned its attention towards Iraq, it was in arguing the case for war, however, that Blair's dilemma was clearly shown. He supported the Bush administration's intentions but he was unable to finesse the political distinctions that separated his vision of an "international community" from the President's bellicose assertion of America's pre-emptive power to defend its national security.

Nowhere was his task to prove more difficult than within Europe. As John Kampfner observes, Blair's:

> self-styled role as a bridge between Europe and America turned into an attempt to reconcile two seemingly irreconcilable approaches–the need to preserve multilateralism, consensus and the rule of law versus the need to impose a world order dictated by Washington and driven by a simple and ardently held view of right and wrong[28].

While other European leaders–notably in France and Germany–distanced themselves from the "Bush doctrine", it was Tony Blair who, in the end, acquiesced in his support for American military action not least because he agreed with the President's assessment of what was at stake. Faith–both religious and political–played an important role. As the former Labour foreign secretary, David Owen observed, "both Bush and Blair share strong religious beliefs and have an inner certainty that they are men of destiny"[29]. The discourse of "evil" that they had directed against terrorism and dictatorship led to the President and the Prime Minister pursuing military action against Iraq, both convinced of the rightness of their cause.

The convoluted process of weapons inspections, the case for Saddam's possession of weapons of mass destruction, the "slam dunk" intelligence in the US and the "dodgy dossier" produced in the UK thus became the political dramas in a broader context in which Tony Blair, working through the United Nations, struggled to persuade the international community to accept his case for humanitarian intervention in Iraq–his doctrine. Bush supported the effort–up to a point. Yet by asserting his own doctrine of pre-emption, the President inevitably undercut the Prime Minister. America was going to act, if necessarily unilaterally and in defiance of international opinion. In that event, Blair's efforts to build a consensus among the United Nations in favour of the invasion of Iraq would become redundant: a fact that the international community immediately recognised. The British Prime Minister would eventually stand virtually alone and isolated among major world leaders in his continuing support for the President's actions.

Leadership and Hubris

For both Bush and Blair, the final confrontation with Saddam became a test of their leadership. Moreover, for David Owen, their decision to go to war revealed the extent to which both the President and the Prime Minister suffered from hubris: over-confidence in the rectitude of their political and moral convictions and excessive pride in their abilities to act decisively upon the world stage. As Owen observes:

> The Jungian analyst, James Hillman, argues that normally hubris is limited by self-control. "The limiting effect of one's innate image prevents that inflation, that trespassing or hubris that the classical world considered the worst of human errors. In this way character acts as a guiding force."

It was this self-control, he argues, that both Bush and Blair lost in the aftermath of 9/11. In this way: "the centralizing nature of US President George W Bush and the British Prime Minister Tony Blair was such that they were both in search of more power and were therefore particularly susceptible to being swept up with the intoxication of power, following the tragic events of September 2001 in New York and Washington, referred to as 9/11. The war against terrorism was ... the opportunity to strengthen the powers of the President". So:

> Bush and Blair began "trying to create a new legal regime" for avoiding the constraints of international and national law on interrogation and detention after their military intervention in Afghanistan and later Iraq. They planned to build a "new paradigm" to replace the Geneva Conventions that were not allowed to apply to al-Qaeda or Taliban prisoners, and they tried to do all this by themselves, with little or no consultation with friends or allies[30].

Moreover, it became apparent that their personal and political relationship derived much of its strength from their mutual admiration of each other's capacity to take action based upon conviction. In November 2003, after the initial invasion of Iraq had begun to unravel into a continuing fight against an insurgency, David Frost interviewed President Bush and asked of Blair: "what is the key to your working together so well? I mean, it's like you have a special relationship". Bush's reply was simple:

> You know, the key to my relationship with Tony is he tells the truth, and he tells you what he thinks and when he says he's going to do something, he's going to do it. I trust him, therefore. I've seen him under some tough – tough circumstances stand strong. And I appreciate that in a person[31].

Three years later in 2006, during an interview with Michael Parkinson, Blair was asked the question that demonstrated that British commentators still could not understand the relationship between the two leaders. It was similar to that which had been put by the journalist at Camp David: "What do you have in common with George Bush?" But this time Blair's reply had nothing to do with dental hygiene, and was instead reminiscent of Bush's answer to Frost:

> I find him extremely straightforward to deal with and what he says, he does. And I tell you when you are dealing with people at my level ... the people you look out for are the people who say I'm going to do it and they do it. Now you know sometimes that has got its difficulties, its downside as well as its upside but that's what I like about him[32].

What the President and the Prime Minister had identified in one another was a quality of leadership that both admired. Once either of them had determined upon a course of action, the other knew that they could be relied upon to abide by that decision. The problem for Blair, however, lay in the increasing perception in Britain as well as in continental Europe that his desire to play a central role on the world stage and his staunch support for Bush's military interventionism meant that he would sacrifice ideological values to political expediency, ultimately privileging his "special relationship" with Bush over any commitment to European solidarity and the traditional values of British socialism.

Tony Blair's leadership of New Labour brought his party unprecedented electoral success but for many of his critics on the left it came at the cost of old Labour's ideals. Blair–like Bill Clinton– nevertheless appreciated that if adhering to an out-dated and increasingly unpopular ideology comes at the cost of power, it is a luxury that politicians in a democracy can ill afford. In contrast, the leader who transcends ideology, appearing to embody "the spirit of the age" and who can set the political agenda not only domestically but also on the world stage can become a significant electoral asset for a party anxious to stay in power. Blair's leadership style thus differed sharply from that of Clement Attlee, Harold Wilson, or James Callaghan: the three postwar leaders of the Labour party who had also occupied the office of Prime Minister. Just as American neo-conservatives in the 1970s had lost confidence in the Democrats and migrated towards the right, so too did the architects of New Labour see a model of leadership that existed not within the traditions of their own party but one that worked effectively for their Conservative opponents during Margaret Thatcher's long tenure as Prime Minister. It provided an example of what is possible, and was the spur to the transformation of the Labour party under Tony Blair into an electoral force that won three successive general elections. Thatcher, like Blair, changed her party from within, dominating it–and the British political scene–in her case for eleven and a half years and in his for a decade as Prime Minister.

Yet if, as Stephen Graubard points out:

> The retention of office has become the all-consuming ambition in both the White House and at Number 10 Downing Street, with trust and truth the principle casualties of the age of "spin", in societies once renowned for their commitment to civil discourse and debate, leadership becomes a matter of retaining public confidence[33].

For both George W. Bush and Tony Blair, military intervention in Iraq eroded their political credibility. No amount of "spin" could obscure the undermining of the public's faith in their rationale for taking action. The location of Saddam's weapons of mass destruction joined the whereabouts of Osama bin Laden as one of the unsolved mysteries of the "war on terror". While the short-term goal of toppling an "evil" dictator was achieved, the long-term difficulties of combating the insurgency and creating a viable Iraqi state became increasingly apparent.

John Kampfner points out that in the aftermath of the intervention:

> Blair paid the price for a failure of diplomacy. ... Iraq damaged him deeply. ... He had dominated his party for a decade, his authority allowing him to push through foreign and domestic policies even when they were at odds with his MPs and activists–even members of his own Cabinet. For the first time, opinion polls were showing that his personal popularity had dropped below that of his party[34].

Blair stepped down as Prime Minister in June 2007. In his resignation speech to his Sedgefield constituents, he once again rationalized his actions and stood by his convictions.

> Then came the utterly unanticipated and dramatic. September 11th 2001 and the death of 3,000 or more on the streets of New York. I decided we should stand shoulder to shoulder with our oldest ally. I did so out of belief. So Afghanistan and then Iraq, the latter, bitterly controversial. Removing Saddam and his sons from power, as with removing the Taliban, was over with relative ease. But the blowback since, from global terrorism and those elements that support it, has been fierce and unrelenting and costly. For many, it simply isn't and can't be worth it. For me, I think we must see it through. They, the terrorists, who threaten us here and round the world, will never give up if we give up. It is a test of will and of belief, and we can't fail it[35].

Similarly, George W. Bush, was faced with plummeting popularity ratings as the result of the intense domestic criticism of his handling of the war in Iraq. As his presidency entered its final year, he still adhered stubbornly to what Andrew Sullivan describes as the "faith-based rigidity" that had defined his time in office[36]. In an interview with the BBC on February 14th 2007, he was adamant that the "war on terror" had to be fought: "I happen to believe we're in an ideological struggle. And, those who murder the innocent to achieve political objectives are evil people". Moreover, his actions would be vindicated if America stayed the course:

> Liberating 25 million in Afghanistan is part of what I hope people think of when they look at my presidency. ... And I'm happy with Iraq. The... decision to (re)move Saddam Hussein was right. And this democracy is now taking root. And I'm confident that if America does not become isolationist you know, and allow the terrorists to take back over–Iraq will succeed[37].

Conclusion

For both George W. Bush and Tony Blair, foreign policy, in keeping with much else about their leadership styles had more to do with similar perspectives on the expression of power than of differences in their respective ideologies. The vision which they shared was reminiscent of that of the progressives who bridged the ideological divide in America at the turn of the twentieth century and which was exemplified by two Presidents: Theodore Roosevelt for the Republicans and Woodrow Wilson for the Democrats. Their presidencies were the formative influences on twentieth century American attitudes to the wider world. Roosevelt demanded action: the progressive era saw the government and the presidency beginning to expand both in its domestic and notably in its foreign purposes. He also believed that the President should pursue the national interest aggressively in any way not expressly prohibited by the Constitution. As America entered the twentieth century, following the closing of the frontier and the acquisition of overseas territories as a result of the Spanish American War of 1898–during which, in Cuba, Roosevelt himself had led a cavalry charge–the President saw the future role of the United States in projecting its power on the world stage. Moreover, his "corollary" to the Monroe Doctrine, asserted that:

> Chronic wrongdoing, or an impotence which results in a general loosening of the ties of civilized society, may in America, as elsewhere, ultimately require intervention by some civilized nation, and in the Western Hemisphere the adherence of the United States to the Monroe Doctrine may force the United States, however reluctantly, in flagrant cases of such wrongdoing or impotence, to the exercise of an international police power.

Implicit in this assumption was that America had the right to use military force in support of its "civilised" values and its national interests: a consistent theme in the development of its foreign policy as its global influence increased.

Wilson refined Roosevelt's message and his political approach. He endorsed Roosevelt's support for America's growing international pre-eminence, believing in moral guidance and the imperialism of the "idea of America" abroad. It was Wilson, who fundamentally changed America's worldview in the initial years of the twentieth century. Whereas Alexis de Tocqueville had traveled from France to America in the 1830s to see if democracy in America had been made safe as an object for imitation in the rest of the world, some ninety years later Wilson suggested that Americans should now ensure that the world was made safe for American democracy.

Roosevelt's insistence on the exercise of American power–if necessary militarily–overseas, and Wilson's belief that the world might be made over in America's democratic image merged during the progressive era which they defined and became animating principles of American foreign policy in the twentieth century and beyond.

George W. Bush, like Roosevelt, believed in the projection of American military power unilaterally overseas. Moreover, when this was coupled with Woodrow Wilson's democratic idealism, it became a powerful neo-conservative political alchemy. Wilson's ambition to promote the ideals of American democracy worldwide fed into Bush's approach to foreign policy. He proved he was a President prepared to use Roosevelt's means for Wilson's ends: pre-emptively and unilaterally trying to make the world safe for American democracy through the use of military power.

In America, the prospect of failure in Iraq legitimized ideological dissent not only from liberal critics of military interventionism but also amongst conservatives themselves. For the right wing commentator Pat Buchanan, therefore, the "Bush Doctrine" led the President "to embrace Wilsonian interventionism in the internal affairs of every autocratic regime on earth". Neo-conservatives become "anti-conservatives", whose "crusade for democracy will end as did Wilson's, in disillusionment for the president and tragedy for this country"[38]. In Britain, the "doctrine of international community" which Blair hoped would define a new world order, foundered on the rocks of American unilateralism. What John Kampfner refers to as the "combination of naivety and hubris" which characterized Blair's foreign policy, unquestionably tarnished the Prime Minister's political reputation[39].

Woodrow Wilson observed that: "The President is at liberty, both in law and conscience, to be as big a man as he can"[40]. But it is still the case that he is only big as long as he retains the democratic trust of the people. It is the erosion of public confidence that ultimately undermines a democratic leader's political reputation and capacity to use military power. In America, during and after the Vietnam War, what remained at stake was the issue of Presidential credibility in insisting that political problems are tractable to military solutions. If the legacy of "George W. Bush's War" constrains his successor's future capacity to act as Commander in Chief, it implies a recurrence of the neo-conservative nightmare: that the President's capacity to use military power should be conditional rather than absolute in determining the future course of America's relations with the rest of the world.

Similarly in Britain, it was Herbert Asquith, a contemporary of

Roosevelt and Wilson, who considered that "the office of the prime minister is what its holder chooses and is able to make it"[41]. Tony Blair, like Margaret Thatcher before him, wanted to ensure that the Prime Minister's office was the co-equal of that held by other world leaders, including the President of the United States. Remember him talking to Michael Parkinson about his relationship with George Bush: "When you are dealing with people at my level", he said, immediately privileging his position as a leader distanced from those whom in a democracy he has to ask to follow. Yet while Tony Blair may also have a touch of the Roosevelt about him in his attempts to expand the scope of executive power in Britain, it is Woodrow Wilson who is the more intriguing role model for him.

American audiences would recognize immediately the Wilsonian progressive internationalism that imbued the rhetoric of "democratic globalism". Moroever, those who emphasize Blair's Gladstonian heritage should not ignore the philosophical, political and religious connections that can also be made between the nineteenth century British Liberal leader and the American Democrat who became President less than two decades after Gladstone left office. Like Blair, Woodrow Wilson professed his admiration for Gladstone's leadership, oratory and convictions. As President, he demonstrated a similar clarity of moral purpose. His belief in the primacy of democratic ideals, supported by his strong Christian faith, led him to advocate America's involvement in international politics and persuaded him of the necessity to intervene in World War I. In his Chicago speech, Blair argued that the isolationism which Wilson fought to overcome should never be a refuge for a United States that had become disillusioned with the wider world. The Prime Minister's unwavering commitment to the advance of democratic values as a means of achieving peace and collective security would have made him a natural ally of the Wilson who successfully persuaded his European counterparts at Versailles to accept the Covenant of the League of Nations, only to see the United States retreat into what both regarded as its myopic rejection of involvement in world affairs.

Blair's affinity with the American President should be seen not simply in terms of his support for Wilsonian internationalism. While unlikely to suggest, as Wilson did allegedly, that he felt that God had ordained him to become chief executive, Blair was the most overtly religious British Prime Minister since Gladstone himself. Just as Wilson's political convictions— like Gladstone's—were framed in the context of his religious beliefs, so Blair's Christianity must be counted as an important part of his political persona, even if, while in office, he was careful not to over-emphasize his faith in a more secular European age. That religiosity informed his vision of an international community: imbuing his foreign policy with a sense of direction and a desire to preserve civilisation against what he saw as the depredations of terrorist fanatics.

Moreover, although the Prime Minister's former director of communications, Alistair Campbell, remained concerned that: "We don't do God", Blair's religious convictions played well in George W. Bush's White House and may help to explain his readiness to support the President across an ideological divide that was always more apparent than real. As John Rentoul points out, Blair was "the first Prime Minister since Gladstone to read the Bible habitually"[42]. George W. Bush did so too as part of his regular routine. Faith gave further impetus to their shared sense of the importance of giving moral substance to leadership in the international arena. The discourse of "evil" that both leaders adopted led them to believe in the efficacy of applying military power to political problems. Never "ideologically poles apart" Tony Blair and George W. Bush embarked on a policy of "democratic globalism", only to confront the unpredictable consequences of their actions. Iraq became the lens through which their contemporary images, their political legacies and their historical reputations would be reflected. Their agreement to go to war demonstrated that from the beginning of their "special relationship", they indeed had a lot more in common than a shared preference for a particular brand of toothpaste.

Bibliography

Asquith, H.H. *Fifty Years in Parliament, vol. 1*. London: Cassell, 1926

Freedman, Lawrence. *Kennedy's Wars*. Oxford: Oxford University Press, 2000

Graubard, Stephen. *The Presidents*. London: Penguin Books, 2006

Harris, Kenneth. *Attlee*. London: Weidenfeld & Nicolson, 1982

Kampfner, John. *Blair's Wars*. London: The Free Press, 2004

Krauthammer, Charles. "Democratic Realism: An American Foreign Policy for a Unipolar World", *Irving Kristol Lecture* (2004)

Mandelbaum, Michael. "Foreign Policy as Social Work", *Foreign Affairs*, 75:1, (1996):16-32

Owen, David. "Hubris and Nemesis in Heads of Government", *Journal of the Royal Society of Medicine*, 99, (November 2006): 548-61

Parmar, Inderjeet. "'I'm Proud of the British Empire': Why Tony Blair backs George W. Bush", *The Political Quarterly*, 76:2, (April-June 2005), 218-32

Rentoul, John. *Tony Blair: Prime Minister*. London: Time Warner, 2001

Seldon, Anthony, ed. *Blair's Britain, 1997-2007*. Cambridge: Cambridge University Press, 2007

Singer, Peter. *The President of Good and Evil*. London: Granta Books, 2004

Wilson, Harold and Michael Joseph. *The Labour Government 1964-1970*. London: Weidenfeld & Nicolson, 1971.

Wilson, Woodrow. *Constitutional Government in the United States*. New York: Columbia University Press, 1908

Notes

[1] "Remarks by the President and Prime Minister Blair in Joint Press Conference", Camp David, February 23rd 2001
http://www.whitehouse.gov/news/releases/2001/02/20010226-1.html

[2] *Ibid.*

[3] The comment was made in February 2003 by Charles Kennedy, then leader of the Liberal Democrats. See "Blair battles 'poodle' jibes",
http://news.bbc.co.uk/1/hi/uk_politics/2721513.stm

[4] Inderjeet Parmar, "'I'm Proud of the British Empire': Why Tony Blair backs George W. Bush", *The Political Quarterly*, 76:2, 218-32, (April-June 2005): 218

[5] Cited *ibid.*, 226: the incident is recounted in John Kampfner, *Blair's Wars*, (London: The Free Press, 2004) 4.

[6] Parmar, "'I'm Proud of the British Empire'", 218

[7] Tony Blair, "The Kosovo Conflict; A Turning Point for South Eastern Europe", Speech to the Atlantic Club of Bulgaria, Sofia University, May 17, 1999,
www.fco.gov.uk/en/newsroom/latest-news/?view=Speech&id=2149336

[8] Timothy Garton Ash, "In Defence of the Fence", *The Guardian*, February 6, 2003 and "Commentary" in Anthony Seldon, ed. *Blair's Britain, 1997-2007*, (Cambridge: Cambridge University Press, 2007) 633

[9] Ian McClean, 'The National Question' in Seldon, ed., *Blair's Britain*, 487

[10] Parmar, "I'm Proud of the British Empire", 223

[11] A transcript of the speech is available at:
http://millercenter.org/scripps/digitalarchive/speeches/spe_1977_0522_carter

[12] Charles Krauthammer, "America and the Post Cold War World", *The Henry M. Jackson Memorial Lecture* (1990), 7.
http://www.hmjackson.org/downloads/krauthammer.pdf

[13] Quoted by Helen H. Jackson, *ibid.* 5

[14] Michael Mandelbaum, "Foreign Policy as Social Work", *Foreign Affairs*, 75:1, (1996):16-32, 16.

[15] Kampfner, *Blair's Wars*, preface, ix

[16] See Kenneth Harris, *Attlee*, (London: Weidenfeld & Nicolson, 1982) 454, 464.

[17] See Harold Wilson and Michael Joseph, *The Labour Government 1964-1970*,

(London: Weidenfeld & Nicolson, 1971), 264.

[18] Tony Blair, "Doctrine of the International Community", Speech at the Economic Club of Chicago, April 24, 1999
http://www.number10.gov.uk/output/Page1297.asp

[19] Kampfner, *Blair's Wars*, 50-3.

[20] Lawrence Freedman, "Defence", in Seldon, ed., *Blair's Britain,* footnote 624

[21] See Lawrence Freedman, *Kennedy's Wars*, (Oxford: Oxford University Press, 2000)

[22] Governor George W. Bush, "A Distinctly American Internationalism," Ronald Reagan Presidential Library, Simi Valley, California, November 19, 1999
www.mtholyoke.edu/acad/intrel/bush/wspeech.htm

[23] Condoleezza Rice, "Campaign 2000: Promoting the National Interest", *Foreign Affairs,* (January-February 2000)

[24] Bush, "A Distinctly American Internationalism"

[25] Peter Singer, *The President of Good and Evil*, (London: Granta Books, 2004) 143

[26] George W. Bush, "State of the Union Speech", January 29, 2002,
www.whitehouse.gov/news/releases/2002/01/20020129-11.html and
"Graduation Speech at West Point", June 1, 2002,
www.whitehouse.gov/news/releases/2002/06/20020601-3.html3.html

[27] Charles Krauthammer, "Democratic Realism: An American Foreign Policy for a Unipolar World", *Irving Kristol Lecture* (2004)
http://www.aei.org/publications/pubID.19912,filter.all/pub_detail.asp

[28] Kampfner, *Blair's Wars*, 386

[29] David Owen, 'Hubris and Nemesis in Heads of Government', *Journal of the Royal Society of Medicine,* 99, (November 2006), 548-61, 549

[30] *Ibid.*, 549

[31] "Interview of the President by Sir David Frost of BBC TV", November 17, 2003,
www.whitehouse.gov/news/releases/2003/11/20031117-1.html

[32] Interview with Tony Blair, "Parkinson", March 4th 2006,
http://www.itv.com/Entertainment/chatandtalent/parkinson/default.html?guest_id=113

[33] Stephen Graubard, *The Presidents*, (London: Penguin Books, 2006) 693

[34] Kampfner, *Blair's Wars,* 387

[35] Transcript of Tony Blair's Resignation Speech, http://www.uksbd.co.uk/

[36] Andrew Sullivan, "Just be Ready for John McCain and Barack Obama to Swap Sides over Iraq", *The Sunday Times*, February 17, 2008

[37] Transcript of George W. Bush interview with Matt Frei,
http://news.bbc.co.uk/1/hi/world/americas/7246075.stm

[38] Quoted in Michael Foley, *American Credo*, (Oxford: Oxford University Press, 2007) 332

[39] Kampfner, *Blair's Wars*, 387

[40] Woodrow Wilson, *Constitutional Government in the United States,* (New York: Columbia University Press, 1908)

---

[41] H. H. Asquith, *Fifty Years in Parliament*, (London: Cassell, 1926) vol. 1, 185
[42] John Rentoul, *Tony Blair: Prime Minister,* (London: Time Warner, 2001) 351

CHAPTER TWELVE

TALES OF THE TRANSATLANTIC:
"WAR ON TERROR" AS SEMANTICS
AND AS STRATEGY

JAMES BERGERON

The politics of naming is an essential element in the ordering of human relations and affairs.[1] In the philosophy of Walter Benjamin, the power to name is a prime aspect of the Biblical idea of divine creativity: the Word preceded and created the World.[2] In the Beginning, after all, was The Word. By assigning a signifier, Naming establishes relations with both the signified and other social actors. Small wonder, then, that there is a politics of the name as well as a politics of the deed, situations in which the power to Name is contested in a "war of words". This is nowhere more truly so than in the realm of violent conflict. Whether a violent actor is characterized as a soldier, terrorist or patriot; whether the conflict itself is called rebellion, revolution or liberation, shapes and contours war aims, strategies, coalitions, outcomes and consequences. As William Safire has noted, "Every war is entitled to a name".[3]

There is a conceptual difference, of course, between purpose and propaganda, public apologetics and strategic clarity. The European war of 1914-1918 may have been called the "War to End all Wars", the "War to make the World Safe for Democracy" etc., and to some extent these motivators did influence the terms of the struggle and consequences of the peace. But at the level of operations and strategy, the Allies knew that they were fighting a conflict with the armed forces and national resources of Germany and Austria-Hungary; all other considerations flowed from that basic, grounding premise. As the founder of modern strategy Carl von Clausewitz famously stressed,

> First, the supreme, most far-reaching act of judgment that the statesman and the commander have to make is to establish the kind of war on which

they are embarking, neither mistaking it for, nor trying to turn it into, something that is alien to its true nature. This is the first of all strategic questions and the most comprehensive.[4]

The military art is one of strategic and operation planning, as well as of implementation and execution. Such actions use official discourse as raw materials. Further, in a democracy where maintaining public support for major conflicts is a political and practical necessity, government rhetoric is forced into a close relationship with both strategy and action. Rhetoric can thus have a huge impact on reality.

As the Name of the War, the Global War on Terrorism has been highly controversial. Arguments rage over Clausewitz's first of all strategic questions: Does the term conflate disparate strategic objectives, failing to discriminate between them or does it accurately bound a set of related threats? Does it set open-ended and unattainable national policy goals or does it provide strategic clarity?[5] Is the United States at war? With whom (or what)?

Over time, the "GWOT" has become a complex signifier. The label has expanded to encompass not only the response to al-Qaeda and the Taliban in Afghanistan and around the world, but also counter-proliferation efforts against the spread of Weapons of Mass Destruction, the 2003 Iraq War and its aftermath, the remaking of a liberal Middle East, and the effort to contain Iran as a major power in the Gulf region. It bears a heavy burden. And yet, as a Name, the "Global War on Terror" has also a demonstrated remarkable staying power that demands explanation. It has remained a staple of White House discourse since the 11 September 2001 terrorist attacks in New York and Washington and continues to inhabit popular culture. On the fifth anniversary of the invasion of Iraq, President George W. Bush hailed the Iraq campaign as a strategic victory in the "war on terror".[6] The term retains its popularity among the political Right in America.

The GWOT rubric has not been without its competitors. Several attempts have been made to usurp its place or otherwise augment it in governmental discourse, largely without success. Its usage in the media and popular culture has declined–pushed aside by a focus on more concrete conflicts in Iraq and Afghanistan–but no competing totalizing concept has yet displaced it. The next US President faces a challenge in deciding whether to maintain the term with all of its baggage, attempt to replace it with another totalising signifier, or indeed forgo any attempt to employ a single totalizing concept.

The GWOT label has been variously associated with President Bush's personality and strong moral stance, with a Wilsonian strand in neo-conservative thinking, with a desire to bundle dissociated security concerns and with a moralistic approach to politics that tends towards over-simplification and amplification of all threats to a "heroic" existential level. There are parallels here to British political history and culture, as Jonathan Roper has noted in the previous chapter. The British government of Tony Blair was a close ally of the Bush Administration in the "war on terror". The Prime Minister often spoke in similar terms when discussing terrorism, Afghanistan or Iraq. But there were differences as well, both then and especially under the Premiership of Gordon Brown. A comparative exploration of the GWOT label, as rhetoric and as strategy, offers insight into how governments and leaders in the US and UK conceptualize threats and craft responses–rhetorical and real–in full knowledge of intense scrutiny by the world's media and each other.

The first section focuses on the emergence of the GWOT concept–and its implications–in the first weeks after the attacks of 11 September 2001. Section two explores some aspects of modern government policy making and institutional culture that might go towards explaining the enduring nature of the GWOT label. The third section considers the rivals to GWOT and explores the reliance on founding stories as essential raw material in current American international security discourse. Section four explores the national security discourse of the Labour Government under Gordon Brown. The concluding section considers the conceptual and strategic effects of GWOT and offers some thoughts on both semantics and strategy for a new US Administration.

The Name of the War

The idea of a "war on terror" has a long history. It was used in the late nineteenth century to describe police actions against radicals and anarchists, who sometimes called themselves "terrorists".[7] The British proclaimed a "war on terrorism" against Jewish and Arab extremist attacks in Palestine during the late 1940s. Ronald Reagan used the term frequently during his presidency. But Reagan's usage was consistent with the habit of US Administrations to "declare war" on social problems during the Post-World War II era. Examples include the War on Drugs, War on Poverty, Nixon's "War on Cancer" and the War on Crime.

Declaring a war on terror is lingistically and legally ambiguous. In international law, war was traditionally a condition that only states could enter into. After 11 September, there is a growing precedent in international law for a state to be in a condition of war with an NGO that employs violent means. This finds support in United Nations Security

Council resolutions recognizing the United States's right of self defence against the perpetrators of the 11 September attacks, as well as the NATO invocation of Article 5 of the Washington Treaty, triggering collective self defence under Article 51 of the United Nations Charter in response to an armed attack on a member state.

It is now generally accepted that the United States is in a state of belligerency with the al-Qaeda organisation and perhaps its direct affiliates and allies such as the Taliban. The Afghan War of 2002 fell within pre-existing international law as collective self-defence against a state who had directly supported the 11 September attacks against the United States, thus assuming responsibility for those attacks. Further, few would reject the proposition that states and governments need to improve their resilience against terrorist attack, their intelligence sharing, their surveillance of air and sea traffic, port security and other aspects of homeland defence. Even considered within the paradigm of countering criminality, all of these measures are necessary and prudent. Beyond those traditional benchmarks, however, controversy continues to reign. "War" is normally understood in terms of a concrete opponent, not a method of violence. If the pursuit of a "war on terror" is to be more than the "war on drugs", then concrete actors and interests need to be identified. Without such granularity, the risk of vagueness is high.

On the evening of 11 September, in his first press release after the attacks on the World Trade Center and the Pentagon, President Bush referred to winning the "war on terror".[8] But the rest of the statement was couched more in terms of a crime or catastrophe. There was more than a passing parallel to rhetoric of the "war on drugs" kind or other such bureaucratic devices. The lines of policy and of language that would define the GWOT did not yet appear to be formed.

Those policy lines would be established with remarkable rapidity. On the morning of 12 September, during a meeting with his National Security Team, Bush emphasized that the attacks "were more than acts of terror. They were acts of war"–an odd juxtaposition of two terms that the President would subsequently attempt to merge.[9] This would be "a new kind of war",[10] a war that would be different from those which had come before with an enemy that attacks and "runs for cover. But it won't be able to run for cover forever". It was to be "a monumental struggle of good verses evil". But Bush also emphasized that the American way of life would not change, nor essential freedoms be restricted.

British Prime Minister Tony Blair also issued a statement on 12 September.[11] For Blair the "tragedy" in America was the result of an attack on the whole democratic world, and the "very notion of democracy". The terrorists are devoid of humanity, mercy and justice. And the response would be wide ranging:

> People of all faiths and all democratic political persuasions have a common cause: to identify this machinery of terror and to dismantle it as swiftly as possible. With our American friends, and other allies around the world, this is the task to which we now turn.

Blair appears be the first to depict the attack as one on democracy, rather than the United States alone. Further, the language Blair employed on 12 September, and later, spoke more to a "Global Policy against Terrorism", than to a war as such:

> The USA will be considering the action it considers appropriate against those found to be responsible. But beyond that, there are issues connected with such terrorism that the international community as a whole must consider: where these groups are, how they operate, how they are financed, and how they are supported, and how they are stopped.[12]

Blair emphasized that this would not be retaliation against Muslims or against Islam as such.

The next major statement was again Blair's, to the House of Commons on 14 Sept.[13] Once again, emphasis was placed on an attack on "basic democratic values" and on the civilized world, "an attack on the free and democratic world as a whole". A separate strand of obligation was derived from the loss of hundreds of UK citizens in the attacks, "In the most direct sense, therefore, we have not just an interest but an obligation to bring those responsible for account". That statement is interesting in its juxtaposition of Britain's *interest* in responding to an attack on the civilized world, and its *obligation* to respond to attacks on its citizens. Blair delivered perhaps the first "with us or against us" message:

> The objective will be to bring those who have organised, abetted and incited this act of infamy; and those that harbour or help them have a choice: either to cease their protection of our enemies; or be treated as an enemy themselves.[14]

The Prime Minister also made the first major post-9/11 linkage of terrorism to weapons of mass destruction:

> We know that they [the terrorists] would, if they could, go further and use chemical or biological or even nuclear weapons of mass destruction. We know, also, that there are groups or people, occasionally states, who trade

the technology and capability for such weapons. It is time this trade was
exposed, disrupted and stamped out.[15]

His policy vision would include a review of extradition law, finance and
money laundering, and the links between terror and crime. It also began
the conflation of terrorism, the threat of WMD terrorism and counter-
proliferation.

The next day, President Bush made his first post-9/11 weekly radio
address to the nation.[16] A message primarily for internal consumption, the
international *leitmotif* of Blair's speech to Parliament is absent. What are
stressed are the "different and long war" concept, American unity and
American exceptionalism. In what would be a recurrent theme, the
President noted that "A terrorist attack designed to tear us apart has instead
brought us together as a nation." Crisis showed America at its best: in
terms of the courage of the fire fighters and police officers, of citizens
coming together "to pray, to give blood, to fly our country's flag".

> Great tragedy has come to us, and we are meeting it with the best that is in
> our country, with courage and concern for others. Because this is America.
> This is who we are. This is what our enemies hate and have attacked. And
> this is why we will prevail.[17]

The notion that an attack on the United States is an attack on national unity
has a long pedigree, triggering integrationist rhetoric that finds its roots in
the Civil War. To the appeal to unity, President Bush added the argument
for national exceptionalism: the actions of Americans in response to attack
uniquely qualify the American character as a whole as superior. It is this
nobility of character that is under attack, not some paltry foreign policy
position.

Tony Blair rounded out the first week of public pronouncements with
his CNN interview of 16 Sept.[18] Responding to the question of whether
war had been declared on the United States, Blair accepted that "Yes,
whatever the legal or technical issues about the declaration of war, the fact
is that we are at war with terrorism." Once the attackers of 11 September
had been dealt with,

> …there has then to be an agenda that we construct at an international level
> that involves the whole of the international community in dismantling the
> machinery of international terrorism, how it is financed, how these people
> move around the world, the countries that harbour them and give them
> help. At every single level, we have to pursue and dismantle this
> machinery of terror.[19]

Again, care was taken to reassure the Muslim community.

With the benefit of hindsight, it is striking how quickly the themes that would dominate political discourse over the coming six years were crafted. By 12 September, the President's main themes of good verses evil, an unconventional and long war on terrorism, an attack on American identity and way of life, an image of an enemy in hiding and a counter-intuitive appeal for life to go on as normal were all in place. Over the course of the week, Prime Minister Blair added greater emphasis on an attack on democracy and the civilised world, the need for an international policy against terrorism and the linkage between the terrorist threat and WMD proliferation. Both eschewed focusing on concrete opponents such as al-Qaeda for an abstract conflict with "terror" itself. This had the effect of making the conflict abstractly existential, rather than political or geo-strategic, and thus also potentially unlimited in scope. Of course, no one had as yet named the guilty parties (although all suspected al-Qaeda in Afghanistan by this time), and waiting for proof before crafting the Name of the War was apparently not an option in the first days after the attack. Both Bush and Blair emphasised that this conflict was not with Muslims, or Islam. Blair differed from Bush, at this stage, by raising the Middle East Peace Process in connection with his recipe for a solution.

These building blocks of transatlantic rhetoric came together in President Bush's Address to a Joint Session of Congress on 20 September.[20] Once again the exceptionalist and integrationist themes loomed large, but so did the international dimension of the conflict, the gratitude for the support of peoples and governments worldwide, and particular thanks to Tony Blair who was in the audience. "Once again, we are joined together in a great cause". The perpetrators of the act of war against the US were named as al-Qaeda, led by Osama bin Laden, with the assistance of the Taliban regime in Afghanistan. His demands to the Taliban were delivered.

The President could have stopped there, allowing his "war on terror" to narrow its focus into a war on al-Qaeda and the Taliban regime in Afghanistan. In a major decision on both rhetoric and strategy that would have large consequences, he did not: "Our war on terror begins with al-Qaeda, but it does not end there. It will not end until every terrorist group of global reach has been found, stopped and defeated." The US would direct all means of national power "to the disruption and defeat of the global terror network". The enemy in hiding analogy was employed: The US would "drive them from place to place, until there is no rest."[21] And the world was put on notice:

We will pursue nations that provide aid or safe haven to terrorism. Every nation, in every region, now has a decision to make. Either you are with us, or you are with the terrorists. From this day forward, any nation that continues to harbour or support terrorism will be regarded by the United States as a hostile regime.[22]

On 20 December 2001, the White House's Coalition Information Centre released a scorecard for the first one hundred days of the "Global War on Terror".[23] It was one of the first, if not the first, use of the GWOT term as a proper title. From that point on, the GWOT entered political and popular discourse. In February 2003 the White House issued the *National Strategy for Combating Terrorism* which formally defined the terms of the struggle as against "premeditated, politically motivated violence perpetrated against non-combatant targets by sub-national groups or clandestine agents.[24] A US Global War on Terrorism service medal was created the following month.[25]

The Institutional Dimension of GWOT

Choosing GWOT as the Name of the War had a number of significant effects. GWOT undeniably captured the global public imagination, reflecting the widespread anger and revulsion against the attacks of 11 September by means that were clearly "terrorist" in orientation and perpetration whatever the outer boundaries of the concept might be. There was much truth in President Bush's emphasis on a "new kind of war" (new to the United States at least) and awareness of American vulnerability. The country and the world woke up on 12 September to a greater realization that terrorist groups or fringe organizations could manipulate modern technologies and complex networks such as air transport to inflict incredible damage. As a result, the GWOT name had a strong unifying effect in the first weeks after the 11 September attacks when the fear of further attacks loomed large.

The hard question that soon emerged was whether this new threat was better characterised as an aspect of globalization and technology in the hands of radical or criminal elements and thus essentially a policing, intelligence and infrastructure resilience problem, or whether the situation was that of "war" with terrorist NGOs and their state supporters. Were "spectacle" terrorist attacks here to stay, as a new fact of life that could be managed but not eliminated in a free society or could that threat be addressed within the American Way of War predicated on a totalizing struggle, existential stakes and the prospect of true victory over one's adversaries? Could one juxtapose a new kind of war with an old kind of war talk?

The "Global War on Terrorism" label made clear that the situation was indeed one of war, not only of policing. It was also a war that aimed at victory. That war would include as adversaries the perpetrators of 11 September, all terrorist groups and (before long) rogue states and WMD proliferators. As Samantha Power has noted, the "war" label become a defining framework for the national response.[26] This approach had the effect of maximizing the prerogatives of the Federal Government over those of the States, of the President as Commander in Chief over Congress and of the Department of Defense over other branches of the Executive. Declaring the war to be "on terror" also helped the Administration to keep its options open as to how broadly or narrowly it would act in the first instance.

But Presidents alone cannot Name wars. That requires the support of the media, expert commentators and think-tanks, the civil service, the military and ultimately the public in establishing a new rhetorical and normative label of such importance. As a Name, GWOT found both support and resistance within these institutional cultures.

At the level of substance, GWOT was a hard pill for some parts of the military to swallow. It appeared to be a battle waged primarily by special forces, intelligence and the CIA. There was a much reduced function (beyond the subjugation of Afghanistan and later Iraq) for the traditional armed forces. Secretary of Defence Donald Rumsfeld fought a long battle to transform a heavy US military into a lighter, more agile security actor that was better posed to tackle the Global War on Terrorism. In October 2003 an apparently leaked memo from Secretary Rumsfeld appeared in the press.[27] In it, he wondered whether the Department of Defence–large and used to fighting conventional wars–was changing fast enough to deal with the new security environment. Were news ways to organise, train, equip and focus required? How can we measure success? A key concern was the educational dimension, countering the influence of radical Islamic schools and clerics, as a key factor in the struggle.

Rumsfeld's memo was in line with his broader goals of a streamlined and "transformed" military, but it also set out very clearly the dual nature of the problem. On the one hand, the US was engaged in the occupation (as it then was) of an Iraq that had been invaded because of the threat of weapons of mass destruction. On the other, the underlying threat of radical Islamic terrorism was ideological and educational. Perceptions were key weapons in such a struggle. The "global war on terrorism" had tended to conflate al-Qaeda, rogue states and WMD proliferators into a monolithic threat. But how to deal with them, when actions against one side of the doctrinal monolith seemed detrimental to other fronts?

At the level of Pentagon policy process, however, GWOT was more attractive. After all, "GWOT" is an acronym and that was not unrelated to its usefulness. Most briefing *and thinking* in the Pentagon is done through the medium of Power Point. A slide medium requires that concepts and strategies be presented in bullet format within the limits of the slide and the constraints of elegant presentation. It is not an extended narrative form of discourse, with exceptions, dependent or conditional clauses, etc. Rather, statements are short, clear, sharp but often conceptually incomplete or misleadingly simplistic. In such an environment, acronyms are essential. Several can be linked to policy objectives on a single slide, allowing for the grand illustration of coherent government action. On a single slide. In doing so, they take on symbolic and semiological meaning, as a kind of covering myth that stands for a complex signified. Even better than the "global war on terrorism" label, the GWOT signifier conveys a complex, problematic and contestable idea as though it is a statement of material fact. It takes on the qualities of a noun rather than of an argument.[28]

A second consideration in the policy process is "branding", reminiscent of Madison Avenue approaches to advertising in the 1950's. It is not enough to understand and communicate "the right thing to do". Rather, "the right thing to do" must be given a policy title that makes it distinct, and which allows a service, or a given senior commander, to link that concept to their own status and fortunes. There are close associations here to hierarchy. New leaders often invoke a new discourse to infuse their new headquarters with their vision and authority, as well as a test of alertness and loyalty. It should be kept in mind that senior commanders rotate approximately every two to three years in the US and British military; Defence Ministers last perhaps a year longer than that on average. Speaking in the right tongues–and knowing when to change voices–is an increasingly essential attribute of the successful staff officer.

A third phenomenon of military policy making is the need to link a great number of long term spending programmes and procurement policies to current strategic objectives of interest to the Executive and to Congress. The Global War on Terror became a first-order organising principle for this purpose from 2002 to approximately 2005. Various high-ticket spending projects and most of the security cooperation programme with friends and allies were publicly justified primarily and at times almost solely, on their utility to the GWOT.

New War and Old Stories[29]

The Global War on Terrorism label brought forth challengers and supporting visions from several points of the political spectrum. One of the first came from President Bush himself: The coinage of GWOT in the image of the Old West. His comments of the first week after 11 September made reassuring links to the past, with references to posses, "smoking them out and getting them on the run", etc. More akin to policing than war, the Old West analogies demonstrated an early variant of a recurring strand in GWOT discourse–of linkage to founding memories and myths in the American story–as Eliade put it, an "eternal return" to the time of beginnings that endows current practice with sacred meaning.[30]

Almost from the time of its coinage, GWOT vied with another competitor appealing to the "eternal return" of an America chasing its own Tale. This was the neo-conservative suggestion of "World War IV" as a signifier for the current state of affairs. In November 2001, Eliot Cohen characterised the conflict with al-Qaeda and the Taliban as an opening salvo in a fourth world war (the Cold War serving as World War III) that necessarily included regime change in Iran and Iraq as well as the destruction of al-Qaeda.[31] Founding neo-conservative Norman Podhoretz adopted and promoted the concept, stressing the rightness of US actions, particularly in Iraq, and the monolithic nature of a threat that included Iran as a clear and present danger.[32] A third proponent of World War IV, ex-CIA director James Woolsey, took the concept to its next logical step with a forceful stance on tyranny and authoritarianism throughout the Middle East, including current US partner regimes. In April 2003 Woolsey singled out Egyptian President Hosni Mubarak and the Saudi Royal Family by name as proper targets for a US push for democracy in the Middle East.[33]

"World War IV" outdoes GWOT in terms of framing a monolithic and totalizing threat. It also strives for a greater linkage to founding conflicts in the American story of itself and to the call for national mobilization for a protracted struggle that the story recalls and legitimates. It makes explicit the hard issue of current relations with authoritarian regimes in the Middle East and the need to confront religious extremism in its Pakistani, Saudi, and Egyptian heartlands. Yet it did not achieve popularity or widespread usage beyond a neo-conservative hard core. For one thing, President Bush did not adopt the term, the critical variable in establishing a new grammar for the conflict. Further, as Peter Beinart has pointed out, accepting World War IV implies a counter-intuitive acceptance that the Cold War was World War III, a notion which runs counter to popular understanding that the US avoided World War III–a nuclear conflict-by exercising restraint and not engaging in a rollback attempt against the Soviet Union.[34]

The second contender came out of the Pentagon in July 2005 in speeches by Secretary Rumsfeld and the Chairman of the Joint Chiefs of Staff. This was a rebranding of the conflict as a struggle against Islamic extremism. General Richard Myers explained that the GWOT label over-emphasized the military role in the conflict. He foresaw a greater diplomatic, economic and political dimension to US efforts in the future.[35] National Security Advisor Steve Hadley joined the chorus: "It's more than just a military war on terror. It's broader than that. It's a global struggle against extremism. We need to dispute both the gloomy vision and offer a positive alternative".[36] But the new initiative was short lived, possibly due to the over-eagerness of the global media to depict the change as a climb down or policy defeat, rather than a pragmatic readjustment of discourse. In a speech in Texas on 3 August, President Bush cited the "war on terror" several times, making it clear that the President Was Not For Turning.[37] "Make no mistake about it, we are at war". Similar addresses followed on 24 August and 28 September 2005. The new term did get some usage in Pentagon planning and briefings that summer, but could not stand up against the simplicity and plasticity of GWOT or its power of reference. As a final footnote, the Pentagon's penchant for political acronym and catchphrase could be seen at work. Global Struggle Against Violent Extremism–GSAVE–results in a positive-sounding signifier that could not have been accidental.[38]

The next contender, yet another return to Old Stories, linked radical Islam to twentieth century European fascism. The idea had random use for a few decades until picked up by Christopher Hitchens after 11 September as "fascism with an Islamic face" and now promoted as the neologism Islamofascism by Norman Podhoretz and others.[39] For Hitchins, the parallels between al-Qaeda, the Taliban and other adherents to radical Islam with fascism are many, including a glorification of heroic death, obsession with past empires and current humiliations, anti-Semitism, a cult of the leader and of one great book, and an emphasis on sexual conformity. Admitting that the state-centric aspects of European Fascism are missing, Hitchens points out that the dream of the Caliphate is not too distant from that of a revived Roman Empire or of Greater Germany.[40]

President Bush employed the term in a speech on 7 August 2006, stressing that Islamo-fascism was an ideology both real and profound and again on 10 August referring to "Islamic Fascists" after the arrest of two dozen Britons suspected of plotting a massive hijacking of transatlantic flights.[41] But the response from the media and Muslim society was swift in coming, with several calls to reign in the term as a dangerous conflation of Islam with both terrorism and fascism.[42] Islamofascism quickly faded from White House discourse.

There are some parallels between al-Qaeda, the Taliban and aspects of European fascism. It is not the purpose of this chapter to engage in that debate. But the interesting point here is that the use of the Islamofascist term by leading neo-conservatives (although not by the President) seems to be precisely motivated by that part of the neologism where linkage to European fascism is weakest–the totalitarian integration of radical Islam in a nationalist and secular corporate state, closely allied with capitalism, industry and the military–in an effort to integrate Iran (but probably not Saudi Arabia) more explicitly into the Global War on Terror. Islamofascism harkens back yet again to founding stories, this time the defining struggle of the Allies in World War II against Nazi Germany and Fascist Italy. As Niall Ferguson pointed out, it tends to link current efforts to those of the "Greatest Generation" in a struggle that defined American power and identity in the twentieth century.[43] What might replace it?

Enter the "Long War". The term had been around for some time. In September 2003 James Carafano argued that that the United States was engaged in a "long war against terrorism" that had a parallel in the Cold War, with Iraq as the opening campaign and occasional flashpoint, as Korea was for the Cold War.[44] About his book of that title published in April 2005, Carafano significantly noted that the name captures the only element of the war with which everyone agrees. "We can't agree it's global, we can't agree it's terrorism, but we all agree generally it's a war...[and] it's going to be long".[45] The term was picked up by Central Command Commander General John Abazaid in 2004 and began to get official legs in Washington late in that year. President Bush made reference to the "long war" in his 2006 State of the Union Address.[46] The Pentagon gave its imprimatur in the form of its 2006 Quadrennial Defense Review which included a chapter on "Fighting the Long War".[47] The new term was explained as representing new thinking about how the current conflicts would be prosecuted. Greater investment would be made in special forces, surveillance technologies such as unmanned aerial vehicles, language skills and cultural knowledge.[48] A new emphasis on partnership with friendly states in unstable parts of the world was required. In fact, it depicted less a "global war" than a global counter-insurgency campaign linked to a counter-proliferation policy and two conflicts in Iraq and Afghanistan.

Perhaps the most important word retained was "war". The Long War echoed the Cold War in its depiction of longevity, its ideological nature, and its development of new military instruments fit for purpose. It may also, depending on one's view of the Cold War, frame the current conflict as one capable of being won by wearing down the enemy in a struggle of cold attrition. But there was an unavoidable sense of loss of clarity in the "Long War" concept.

By the end of 2006, discourse fatigue was setting in for the GWOT and its semantic friends. In December, departing Secretary Rumsfeld stated that he regretted the use of the term "War on Terror" by the Administration, as it had raised unrealistic expectations.[49] There was no "war on terror"–terror was a weapon in the hands of extremists.

> The word "war" conjures up World War II more than it does the Cold War, and it creates a level of expectation of victory and an ending within the 30 or 60 minutes of a soap opera. And it isn't going to happen that way. Furthermore, it's not a war on terror. Terror is a weapon of choice for extremists who are trying to destabilize regimes and impose their–in the hands of a small group of clerics–their dark vision on all the people that they can control. So "war on terror" has a problem for me, and I've worked to try to reduce the extent to which that's used, and increase the extent to which we understand it more as a long war or a struggle or a conflict, not against terrorism but against a relatively small number, but terribly dangerous and lethal, violent extremists.[50]

On 27 March 2007, the Democratic staff director of the House Armed Services Committee sent a memo advising the staff to avoid colloquialisms such as the "war on terrorism" or the "long war", and cease to use the term "global war on terrorism" in their drafting of the annual Defense Authorization Bill. Staffers were to be more specific, and refer to concrete operations such as Afghanistan or Iraq.[51] There was political purpose, of course: excising GWOT from discussions over Iraq also removes the al-Qaeda link and tilts the understanding of Iraq towards a "civil war" perspective with less justification for US involvement.

In April 2007, the new commander of the US Central Command, Admiral William Fallon, quietly retired use of the "Long War" term.[52] The change was apparently in response to fears by Gulf allies that it implied a long US military presence in the region. Also out at CENTCOM were references to Jihadists and Islamofascism. Although the President continued to make reference to the long term nature of the current struggle, primacy in the Name of the War once again quickly reverted to War on Terrorism, now often employed without the "Global".

A similar trend could be observed in Britain: Prime Minister Blair had rarely used the "war on terror" term since 2005.[53] In December 2006, the Foreign Office advised the government to cease use of "War on Terror" terminology. A spokesperson for the department said the government wanted to "avoid reinforcing and giving succour to the terrorists' narrative by using language that, taken out of context, could be counter-productive."[54] In the following month the UK Director of Public Prosecutions refuted the GWOT concept in no uncertain terms. Speaking about the London terror attacks of 2005, he stressed that:

> London is not a battlefield. Those innocents who were murdered...were not victims of war. And the men who killed them were not, as in their vanity they claimed on their ludicrous videos, "soldiers". They were deluded, narcissistic inadequates. They were criminals. They were fantasists. We need to be very clear about this. On the streets of London there is no such thing as a war on terror, just as there can be no such thing as a war on drugs. The fight against terrorism on the streets of Britain is not a war. It is the prevention of crime, the enforcement of our laws, and the winning of justice for those damaged by their infringement.[55]

Such a statement is powerful. But it should be noted that it is also consistent with the institutional position and needs of the police, and Crown Prosecution Service. Once again, where one sits appears not unrelated to where one stands.

In April 2007, Hilary Benn, International Development Secretary in the Blair government told a group in New York that the "war on terror" has been a misleading and counter-productive term, and confirmed that the UK government would cease using that term.[56] Benn saw "war on terror" as misleading because it over-emphasized the military dimension of the conflict and implied a greater unity among terrorist phenomenon that actually exists; counter-productive in that it gave small terrorists everywhere a great sense of identity, a sense of being a part of something bigger.

War on Terrorism retains its primacy in White House usage as of the time of writing in March 2008. Beginning in 2006, however, some new planks of support where added to the rhetorical armour of the GWOT in Presidential addresses. Once again, these drew on founding stories. Thus, the statements of Osama bin Laden should be heeded, the President has stressed, with reference made to the mistakes of those who ignored Lenin and Hitler.[57] Japan and Korea are put forward as examples of America's civilizing mission, a counter to those who believe that the US should "cut and run" in Iraq.[58] The spectre of Vietnam has been raised to foreshadow the fate of those who would be left behind by an American withdrawal from Iraq.[59]

Perhaps the most interesting of current reference points is the depiction of the global war on terror as the opening chapter in the "defining ideological struggle of the 21st century" for liberty and democracy against the "dark vision" of hopelessness and despair peddled by Islamic terrorists and authoritarian states. In an important speech in September 2006, President Bush set out in great detail the nature of this threat as the two sides of Islamic radicalism–Sunni al-Qaeda and Shia Iran–"just as dangerous, and just as hostile to America, and just as determined to establish its brand of hegemony across the broader Middle East".[60]

> The Shia and Sunni extremists represent different faces of the same threat. They draw inspiration from different sources, but both seek to impose a dark vision of violent Islamic radicalism across the Middle East. They oppose the advance of freedom, and they want to gain control of weapons of mass destruction. If they succeed in undermining fragile democracies, like Iraq, and drive the forces of freedom out of the region, they will have an open field to pursue their dangerous goals. Each strain of violent Islamic radicalism would be emboldened in their efforts to topple moderate governments and establish terrorist safe havens.[61]

And thus,

> This is the great ideological struggle of the 21st century–and it is the calling of our generation. All civilized nations are bound together in this struggle between moderation and extremism. By coming together, we will roll back this grave threat to our way of life. We will help the people of the Middle East claim their freedom, and we will leave a safer and more hopeful world for our children and grandchildren.[62]

The emphasis on an existential ideological struggle with Islamic radicalism in both its Sunni and Shia forms achieves again the conflation of al-Qaeda-informed terrorism, the regional challenge of Iran and the more general problem of counter-proliferation. It also throws into high relief the global struggles for liberty and democracy across the world as necessary elements of US national security. There are faint echoes of founding stories in the evocation of the generational calling, a recalling of the "Greatest Generation" theme. But the irony of this perhaps final attempt to craft a totalizing label for the Administration is that the invocation of a "great ideological struggle" draws on a language not liberal but Soviet.[63] Coined primarily by Lenin, used extensively during the Brezhnev era and still a favourite term of the unreconstructed Left, "ideological struggle" has deep roots in the discourse of European communism.[64] It brings neo-conservatism full circle to its left-liberal origins.

A Scottish Enlightenment: GWOT under Gordon Brown

The Labour government of Gordon Brown has taken a decidedly different path in its political rhetoric, notwithstanding a close alliance with the United States in matters of operations and policy regarding anti-terror operations, missions in Afghanistan and Iraq, and counter-proliferation. One month after the June 2007 terrorist actions in London and Glasgow, Prime Minister Brown made a statement on security to Parliament.[65] In it, he set out Britain's "three lines of defence" against terrorism, being (1) heightened checks at overseas airports and seaports, (2) through a robust and unified border force using the latest biometric identification techniques and (3) through a national biometric ID card system to be implemented in 2009. He went on to address proposed anti-terror legislation and the need to provide commensurate safeguards in a free society:

> Mr. Speaker, liberty is the first and founding value of our country and security is the first duty of government. The British way is that every measure we take to enhance security is complimented by additional protections against any arbitrary treatment and in defence of the liberties of the individual.[66]

Terrorism and violent extremism, Brown noted, must be tackled at its foundations

> Through debate, discussion, dialogue and education as we tackle at root the evils that risk driving people, particularly vulnerable young people, into the hands of violent extremists.[67]

Brown's statement was notable for its inclusions and exclusions. Included was a defence of British liberty, assurances that necessary actions to battle the terrorist threat would not infringe civil liberties, a promise that enhanced police powers would be accompanied by special procedures of judicial oversight and parliamentary accountability and the need to socialize and educate those in British communities who might be vulnerable to the extremists. Excluded was any link to a global war (or even battle–the preferred British term) against terrorism, to the security missions in Iraq and Afghanistan, the threat of WMD proliferation by rogue regimes or the need to remake the Middle East. In short, while the threat of domestic terrorism and extremism is the centrepiece of the statement, the issue is not conflated with wider agendas or objectives.

Five days later, Prime Minister Brown and President Bush spoke on the lawn at Camp David, at the wrap up of Gordon Brown's first visit to the US in his new role. In his opening remarks, President Bush spoke to the new White House *leitmotif*:

> ...we're writing the initial chapters of what I believe is a great ideological struggle between those of us who do believe in freedom and justice and human rights and human dignity, and cold-blooded killers who will kill innocent people to achieve their objectives...We also recognize that if you're involved with an ideological struggle, then you need to defeat that one ideology with a more hopeful ideology, and that's why it's very important for us to defend and stand with these young democracies in Afghanistan and Iraq...success in Afghanistan and Iraq will be an integral part of defeating an enemy and helping people realize the great blessings of liberty as the alternative to an ideology of darkness that spreads its murder to achieve its objectives.[68]

Brown's response was polite, supportive, yet different. He too spoke of the shared values of Britain and the United States, which he defined as: "the joint inheritance of liberty, a belief in opportunity for all, a belief in the dignity of every human being". On terrorism, Brown asserted that "terrorism is not a cause, it is a crime, and it is a crime against humanity." Pressed during questions and answers by the press as to whether that meant something different from "war on terrorism" and hearing again the President's vision of a long ideological struggle against evil, cold-blooded killers, Brown responded that he absolutely agreed that

> ...we're in a generation-long battle against terrorism, against al-Qaeda-inspired terrorism, and this is a battle for which we can give no quarter; it's a battle that's got to be fought in military, diplomatic, intelligence, security, policing and ideological terms...So we are at one in fighting the battle against terrorism, and that struggle is one that we will fight with determination and with resilience, and right across the world...And in a sense, the battle we are facing with international terrorism is a battle between our values, which stress the dignity of every individual, and those who would maim and murder, irrespective of faith, indifferent to human life, often simply for propaganda effect, and of course with devastating effects, both on the communities they claim to represent and the whole world.[69]

So, not much difference, then? Battle verses war, generations-long and fought across the world with those who would maim and murder. They are close visions, as should be expected from two leaders whose armed forces and police are cooperating very closely together in the field and who appear to share many fundamental values. But the characterization of the opponent as "evil" does not appear to easily roll off this Prime Minister's tongue, nor does the phrase "ideological struggle" given the continued existence of a traditional Left wing of his own Party. The "not a cause but a crime" remark was a subtle but flat challenge to the notion this is a grand conflict of ideologies, as the press realised at Camp David. Brown seems more comfortable with the need for cultural education to keep the vulnerable from falling into the clutches of criminal extremists. That seems to be as close to "ideological struggle" as Brown gets. There is also no linkage of the al-Qaeda threat to missions in Iraq and Afghanistan. Given the growing involvement of al-Qaeda in Iraq by that time, the linkage would have been easy to make. But Brown did not seem to be interested in merging separate structural challenges.

Most of President Bush's speeches on GWOT were delivered before a military audience, very much "on home ground". In October 2007 Prime Minister Brown visited British troops in Basra.[70] His remarks focused on the troops professional service, their bravery and courage and the good work they were doing in helping to rebuild Iraq. The sense was of reconstruction and nation building. The opportunity to push the boundaries of linkage to wider agendas was not taken up.

On 25 October PM Brown gave a speech on liberty that further developed the themes of his statement on security in July.

> A passion for liberty has determined the decisive political debates of our history, inspired many of our defining political moments, and those debates, conducted in the crucible of great events, have, in my view, forged over time a distinctly British interpretation of liberty–one that asserts the importance of freedom from prejudice, of rights to privacy, and of limits to the scope of arbitrary state power, but one that also rejects the selfishness of extreme libertarianism and demands that the realm of individual freedom encompasses not just some but all of us....So instead of invoking the unique nature of the threats we face today as reason for relinquishing our historical attachment to British liberty we meet these tests not by abandoning principles of liberty but by giving them new life.[71]

Brown recites the long list of British abuses of liberty but argues for the gradual emergence of a concept of liberty rooted in tolerance, based fundamentally on dignity for all and due process against the exercise of arbitrary power. In striking the balance between liberty and security,

In my view, the key to making these hard choices in a way that is
compatible with our traditions of liberty is to, at all times, apply the liberty
test, respecting fundamental rights and freedoms, and wherever action is
needed by government, it never subjects the citizen to arbitrary treatment,
is transparent and proportionate in its measures and at all times also
requires proper scrutiny by, and accountability to, Parliament and the
people.[72]

And further,

By insisting that liberty is and remains at the centre of our constitution, we
rightly raise the bar we have to meet when it comes to measures to protect
the security of individuals and communities against the terrorist threat. For
me, this means that any necessary steps we take to enforce security must
always be accompanied by the strongest of safeguards to ensure there is
scrutiny, accountability and transparency in the decisions that are made
and that at all times we preserve the primacy of independent courts and
strengthen accountability to Parliament.[73]

Brown's statements reflect the traditional liberal concern with the threat
posed by the state to the individual, even in circumstances of terrorist
threat. The invocation of greater transparency, enhanced individual
protections, judicial review and Parliamentary accountability supported his
requests for greater police and surveillance powers. The argument invokes
one of the deepest of British founding stories, that of the liberal
inheritance, to argue that necessary executive interference in private life is
justifiable if balanced by greater supervision by other parts of the state
system such as the Courts and Parliament. And that is the point: Brown is
arguing for greater police powers and heightened public surveillance. But
he does so within the liberal constitutional paradigm and discourse
tradition, with much less emphasis on the threat of an "evil other" which
inhabited his predecessor's political rhetoric.

At the heart of Brown's discourse on liberty and security is the notion
of a human dignity based on tolerance which runs throughout many of his
public addresses. "A belief in the dignity of every human being" (30 July
07), "By history and conviction, we–in Britain–are bearers of the
indispensable idea of individual dignity and mutual respect" (12
November 2007), and indirectly through a steady stream of arguments for
cultural education and awareness, better community relations, improved
living conditions and support for development in Africa. There is a strong
parallel to the political addresses of Barack Obama who made dignity a
centrepiece of his campaign for the Democratic Party presidential
nomination.[74]

Considerations for a "Post-GWOT" Administration

The US Administration that takes office in January 2009 will be faced with the question of how much of the Bush Administration's foreign policy discourse to keep and what to replace. Because of the very close association of the Global War on Terror with President Bush, it is not likely that Obama, seeking to establish his foreign policy, will continue to emphasize the term. That leaves open the question whether a new totalizing concept should be employed or whether the effort to encapsulate terrorism, rogue states and WMD proliferation in a sole signifier should be abandoned.

This chapter began with an invocation of Clausewitz and of the strategic danger of misunderstanding the nature of a war one was setting out on. As Record and others have argued, GWOT tended to conflate structurally disparate foreign policy objectives, leading to a blurring of strategic clarity and possibly effective decision-making.[75] In this sense, GWOT was strategically overbroad. After 11 September, the United States was not in a condition of belligerency with global terrorist organisations, but with al-Qaeda and its affiliates. Hardening US defences against terrorist attack did not need GWOT rhetoric–the ruins of the World Trade Centre were motivation enough. By casting so wide a rhetorical net, the United States risked alienation of states that feared interference in domestic matters and worried European allies who strongly supported a global policy against terrorism, but were cautious about a "war". Further, Iraq and Iran, being states–even if rogue ones–are subject to a different calculus of deterrence than a "near-virtual organisation" such as al-Qaeda has become since losing its base in Afghanistan.

But does it matter if the Administration employs a populist rhetoric so long as the decision-makers share strategic clarity amongst themselves as to the true nature of their foreign and security policy? That depends on how narrow the club of decision-makers are. In a modern state, military and security operations are planned by hundreds and executed by thousands of staff officers. Professionals, they will act in good faith on the discourse that has been promulgated by the Administration in speeches and in policy documents, and will act and try to think accordingly. That will pull strategy in the direction of the rhetoric. The only alternative is for the small circle of decision-makers to rather explicitly bypass the staff process and attempt to direct operations on the ground from the top, often referred to as the "long screwdriver" effect. This is damaging both to morale and to effective military planning. It should be avoided.

Then there is the international dimension. The United States has a wide range of partners in its efforts to combat global terrorism, to dissuade Iran from pursuing atomic weapons and limit its negative influence in the Middle East, and to prevent the proliferation of weapons of mass destruction and ballistic missile technology. But few see these challenges as monolithic. Conflating them under a totalizing concept appears to have been counter-productive. The prudent, strategic move would be to abandon the attempt.

What then of the use of historic metaphor or founding story? As has been illustrated, none of the attempts to do so have met with particular success, with the exception of GWOT itself. In every other case, the historical differences are too great to allow comparison with a current political agenda. A national myth or founding story–precisely because it has been placed on a cultural pedestal–cannot be joined with the "post-Golden Age" of the Present without the Present seeming to fall short. Better to stick to founding principles, or better yet good ones.

If there is a public discourse best able to engage with domestic audiences on security as well as to reach out to Muslim communities, the Iraqi people, Iranians and others caught up in the current situation, the experience of the GWOT signifier would favour the discourse and policy of the "liberal inheritance", a regard for the rule of law, due process, human rights and most fundamentally, a regard for individual dignity. In her recent book *Chasing the Flame* (2008), Samantha Power has called for dignity as a foreign policy objective, infusing the "how" of intervention with a greater respect for the subjects of intervention.[76] It involves asking people what they want rather than telling them what they need. That insight resonates with the tangled fortunes of GWOT and of the need for a better American and international public diplomacy and strategic vision.

Bibliography

Barthes, Roland. *Mythologies*, trans. A. Lavers. London: Jonathan Cape, 1972.

Carafano, James and Paul Rozensweig, *Winning the Long War: Lessons From the Cold War for Defeating Terrorism and Preserving Freedom.* Westminster, Md: Heritage Books, 2005.

Clausewitz, Carl von. *On War*. Edited and translated by Michael Howard and Peter Paret. Princeton: Princeton University Press, 1976.

Eliade, M, *The Myth of the Eternal Return or, Cosmos and History.* Princeton: Princeton University Press, 1965.

Fitzpatrick, Peter and James Henry Bergeron, eds. *Europe's Other: European Law between Modernity and Postmodernity*. Aldershot: Ashgate Press, 1998.

Jacobs, Carol. *In the Language of Walter Benjamin*. Baltimore: Johns Hopkins University Press, 1999.

Lenin, V. I. *Collected Works*. Moscow: Progress Publishers, 4th English Edition, 1964.

Podhoretz, Norman. *World War IV–The Long Struggle against Islamofascism*. New York: Doubleday, 2007.

Power, Samantha. *Chasing the Flame, Sergio Vieira de Mello and the Fight to Save the World*. New York: Penguin Press, 2008.

Record, Jeffrey. *Bounding the Global War on Terrorism*. US Army War College Carlisle Paper, 2003.

United States, White House, *National Strategy for Combating Terrorism* (2003), www.whitehouse.gov/news/releases/2003/02/counter_terrorism/counter_terrorism/strategy.pdf.

Notes

[1] The views expressed are in a private capacity and do not necessarily reflect the official policy or position of the United States Government or the North Atlantic Treaty Organization

[2] Walter Benjamin, "On Language as Such and on the Language of Man". See generally Carol Jacobs, *In the Language of Walter Benjamin*, (Baltimore: Johns Hopkins University Press, 1999).

[3] William Safire, "Islamofascism", *New York Times*, Oct 1, 2006. www.nytimes.com/2006/10/01/magazine/01wwln_safire.html.

[4] Carl von Clausewitz, *On War*, ed. and trans. by Michael Howard and Peter Paret, (Princeton: Princeton University Press, 1976) 88.

[5] Jeffrey Record, "Bounding the Global War on Terrorism", *US Army War College Carlisle Paper* (2003) www.carlisle.army.mil/ssi/pubs/display.cfm?pubID=207

[6] White House, Press Release, "President Bush discusses Global War on Terror, 19 March 2008, www.whitehouse.gov/news/releases/2008/03/20080319-2.html.

[7] *New York Times*, April 2, 1881.

[8] White House, Press Release "Statement by the President in his Address to the Nation", September 11, 2001, www.whitehouse.gov/news/releases/2001/09/20010911-16.html.

[9] White House, Press Release, President Bush Meets with National Security Team, September 12, 2001, www.whitehouse.gov/news/releases/2001/09/20010912-4.html.

[10] The first use of the term "a new kind of war" came in a televised phone call with Major Rudy Giuliani and Governor George Pataki on September13, 2001. See *CNN.com*, "Bush, Pataki, Giuliani: We Will Rebuild", September 13, 2001, http://archives.cnn.com/2001/ US/09/13/bush.transcript/index.html.

[11] 10 Downing Street, "11 September Attacks: Prime Minister's Statement" September 12, 2001, www.number10.gov.uk/output/Page1597.asp.

[12] *Ibid.*

[13] 10 Downing Street, "Prime Minister's statement to Parliament in response to terrorist attacks in the United States", September 14, 2001, www.number10.gov.uk/ output/ Page1598.asp.

[14] *Ibid.*

[15] *Ibid.*

[16] White House, Press Release, "President Addresses Nation in Radio Address" September 15, 2001, www.whitehouse.gov/news/releases/2001/09/20010915.html.

[17] *Ibid.*

[18] 10 Downing Street, "Prime Minister's Interview with CNN: We Are at War with Terrorism" September 16, 2001, www.number10.gov.uk/output/Page1599.asp.

[19] *Ibid.*

[20] White House, "Address to a Joint Session of Congress and to the American People", September 20, 2001, www.whitehouse.gov/news/releases/2001/09/20010920-8.html.

[21] Soon to be more strikingly described in Old West terms as "smoking them out, getting them on the run, and bringing them to justice".

[22] *Ibid.*

[23] "Raw Data: War on Terror, First 100 Days", *Fox News*, December 20, 2001, www.foxnews.com/story/0,2933,41275,00.html.

[24] United States, White House, *National Strategy for Combating Terrorism* (2003), www.whitehouse.gov/news/releases/2003/02/counter_terrorism/counter_terrorism/strategy.pdf.

[25] United States, White House, Press Release, "President of the United States establishes Global War on Terrorism Service Medal", March 12, 2003. www.whitehouse.gov/news/ releases/2003/03/20030312-6.html.

[26] Samantha Power, "Our War on Terror", *New York Times*, July 29, 2007, www.nytimes.com/2007/07/29/books/review/Powert.html?_r=2&ref=books&oref=slogin&oref=slogin

[27] "Rumsfeld's war-on-terror memo", *USA Today*, October 22, 2003, www.usatoday.com/news/washington/executive/rumsfeld-memo.htm?loc=interstitialskip. *See also* "After grim Rumsfeld memo, White House supports him", *USA Today* 22 October 2003, www.usatoday.com/news/washington/2003-10-22-defense-memo-usat_x.htm?csp=1, "Rumsfeld: Mainly a Style Thing", *Christian Science Monitor*, October 24, 2003, www.csmonitor.com/2003/1024/ p01s01-usmi.html.

[28] Roland Barthes, *Mythologies*, trans. A. Lavers (London: Jonathan Cape 1972). For my previous development of the semiology of the policy process, see "Europe's Emprise: Symbolic Economy and the Postmodern Condition" in

Europe's Other: European Law between Modernity and Postmodernity edited by James Henry Bergeron and Peter Fitzpatrick, (Aldershot: Ashgate Press, 1998).

[29] This section title is a modification of "New Europe and Old Stories" by Peter Fitzpatrick. See Fitzpatrick and Bergeron (1998), *supra.* n.25.

[30] M. Eliade, *The Myth of the Eternal Return or, Cosmos and History* (Princeton: Princeton University Press, 1965) 10-11.

[31] Eliot Cohen, "World War IV: Let's call this conflict what it is" *Wall Street Journal*, 20 Nov 2004, http://opinionjournal.com/editorial/feature.html?id=95001493.

[32] Norman Podhoretz, "World War IV: How it Started, What it Means, and Why we have to Win" *Commentary*, Sept 2004. *See also* Norman Podhoretz, *World War IV–The Long Struggle against Islamofascis,* (New York: Doubleday, 2007).

[33] Charles Feldman and Stan Wilson, "Ex-CIA Director: US Faces World War IV, *CNN.com*, April 3, 2003, www.cnn.com/2003/US/04/03/sprj.irq.woolsey.world.war/.

[34] Peter Beinart, "Is this really World War IV?" *Los Angeles Times*, December 9,2007.

[35] Eric Schmitt and Tom Shanker, "Washington recasts terror war as 'struggle', *International Herald Tribune*, July 27, 2005, www.iht.com/articles/2005/07/26/news/ terror.php.

[36] *Ibid.*

[37] Richard W. Stevenson, "President Makes it Clear: Phrase is 'War on Terror', *New York Times*, August 4, 2005, www.nytimes.com/2005/08/04/politics/04bush.html.

[38] Fred Kaplan, "The Global War on Bad Slogans", *Slate*, July 26, 2005, www.slate.com/ id/2123412/.

[39] Christopher Hitchins, "Defending Islamofascism: It's a valid term. Here's Why" *Slate*, 22 October 2007, www.slate.com/id/2176389/, Podhoretz, *supra* n. 29.

[40] *Ibid.*

[41] Richard Allen Greene, "Bush's language angers US Muslims", *BBC News*, August 12, 2006, http://news.bbc.co.uk/2/hi/americas/4785065.stm. *See also* Katha Pollitt, "Wrong War, Wrong Word" *The Nation*, August 24, 2006, www.thenation.com/doc/ 20060911/pollitt.

[42] *Ibid.*

[43] "War of the World: Conversation with Niall Ferguson", October 19, 2006, Institute of International Studies, University of California at Berkeley, http://globetrotter.berkeley.edu/people6/Ferguson/ferguson06-con5.html.

[44] James Carafano, The Long War against Terrorism" Heritage Foundation, Press Commentary, September 8, 2003, www.heritage.org/Press/Commentary/ ed090803a.cfm.

[45] Quoted in Bradley Graham and Josh White, "Abizaid credited with popularizing the term 'Long War', *Washington Post*, February 3, 2006, www.washingtonpost.com/wpdyn/content/article/2006/02/02/AR2006020202242. html. *See* James Carafano and Paul Rozensweig, *Winning the Long War: Lessons*

From the Cold War for Defeating Terrorism and Preserving Freedom (Westminster, Md: Heritage Books, 2005).

[46] White House, Press Release, "President Bush delivers State of the Union Address", January 31, 2006,
www.whitehouse.gov/news/releases/2006/01/20060131-10.html.

[47] Anne Scott Tyson, "Ability to Wage 'Long War' is Key to Pentagon Plan", *Washington Post*, February 4, 2006, http://www.washingtonpost.com/wp-dyn/content/article/2006/ 02/03/AR2006020301853.html.

[48] Simon Tisdal and Ewen MacAskill, "America's Long War", *The Guardian*, 15 February 2006, www.guardian.co.uk/world/2006/feb/15/politics.usa1.

[49] Eric Rosenberg, Rumsfeld says he regrets the phrase 'War on Terror', *San Francisco Chronicle*, December 13, 2006, www.sfgate.com/cgi-bin/article.cgi?f=/c/a/2006/12/13/ mngecmumq71.dtl.

[50] *Ibid.*

[51] "Republicans, Democrats spar over use of term "Global War on Terror" to include Iraq Action", *International Herald Tribune*, April 4, 2007, www.iht.com/articles/ ap/2007/04/04/ america/NA-GEN-US-Congress-Terrorism.php.

[52] Michael R. Gordon, "US Command Shortens Life of 'Long War' as a Reference", *New York Times*, April 24, 2007,
www.nytimes.com/2007/04/24/washington/ 24policy.html.

[53] Sam Knight, "British minister dumps 'War on Terror' in New York speech" *Times Online*, April 16, 2007,
www.timesonline.co.uk/tol/news/uk/article1660976.ece.

[54] Jason Burke, "Britain stops talk of 'war on terror'", *Guardian*, December 10, 2006, www.guardian.co.uk/politics/2006/dec/10/uk.terrorism.

[55] Clare Dyer, "There is no war on terror", *Guardian*, January 24, 2007, www.guardian.co.uk/politics/2007/jan/24/uk.terrorism.

[56] "Benn to Criticise 'War on Terror'", *BBC New,* April 16, 2007,
http://news.bbc.co.uk/ 2/hi/uk_news/politics/6558569.stm.

[57] White House, Press Release, "President Discusses Global War on Terror", September 5, 2006, www.whitehouse.gov/news/releases/2006/09/print/20060905-4.html

[58] White House, Press Release, "President Bush Attends Veterans of Foreign Wars National Convention, Discusses War on Terror", August 22, 2007, www.whitehouse.gov/news/releases/2007/08/print/20070822-3.html, *see also* "President Bush Discusses Importance of Freedom in the Middle East", January 13, 2008, www.whitehouse.gov/news/releases/2008/01/print/20080113-1.html.

[59] *Ibid.*

[60] *Supra,* n. 55.

[61] *Ibid.*

[62] *Ibid.*

[63] See Andrus Pork, "The Concept of Ideological Struggle: Some Soviet Interpretations" 24 *Government and Opposition* 3, (July 1989) 283-93.

[64] V. I. Lenin, *The Ideological Struggle in the Working Class Movement, Put Pravdy* No. 77, 4 May 1914, from V.I. Lenin, *Collected Works*, 4th English Edition (Moscow: Progress Publishers, 1964), Vol 20, 277-80.

[65] Downing Street, Gordon Brown, Statement on Security, July 25, 2007. www.number10.gov.uk/output/Page12675.asp.

[66] *Ibid.*

[67] *Ibid.*

[68] White House, "President Bush Participates in Joint Press Availability with Prime Minister Gordon Brown of the United Kingdom" July 30, 2007. www.whitehouse.gov/news/ releases/2007/07/print/20070730.html.

[69] *Ibid.*

[70] 10 Downing Street, "PM's address to troops in Basra", October 2, 2007, www.number10.gov.uk/output/Page13381.asp. See also similar remarks in December 2007, "Address to troops in Basra, December 9, 2007, www.number10.gov.uk/output/ Page14037.asp.

[71] 10 Downing Street, "Speech on Liberty", October 25, 2007, www.number10.gov.uk/ output/Page13630.asp.

[72] *Ibid.*

[73] *Ibid.*

[74] Spencer Ackerman, "The Obama Doctrine", *The American Prospect*, March 24, 2008, www.prospect.org/cs/articles?article=the_obama_doctrine.

[75] *See* Record, *supra*, n.4.

[76] Samantha Power, *Chasing the Flame, Sergio Vieira de Mello and the Fight to Save the World* (New York: Penguin Press, 2008) See Carne Ross, "Hero of our time", *New Statesman*, March 13, 2008, www.newstatesman.com/200803130045.

CONTRIBUTORS

Martine Azuelos is Professor of Anglo-American studies at the Sorbonne Nouvelle-Paris III University, where she directs the Research Centre on Anglo-Saxon Economies (CERVEPAS). Her research deals with contemporary economic issues in Britain and the United States, with specific emphasis on labour market issues, entrepreneurship and innovation performance, and the United States' role in driving globalisation and regional integration in the Americas. More particularly, she has written on trade policy and NAFTA, and co-edited *Intégration dans les Amériques: dix ans d'ALENA* (Paris: Presses de la Sorbonne nouvelle, 2004).

Carine Berbéri is Lecturer in British Studies at the University of Tours. She has published several articles about British attitudes towards the European Union. She is also the author of *Le Parti travailliste et les syndicats face aux questions monétaires européennes* (Changing Attitudes to European Monetary Questions: the Labour Party and British trade unions), Paris: L'Harmattan, 2005. Her research interests are principally in the field of British politics, with a particular emphasis on the relationship between Britain and Europe.

Lars Berger is Lecturer in Politics and Contemporary History of the Middle East at Salford University/Greater Manchester, UK. He received his M.A. in Political Science, Islamic Studies and Sociology as well as his Ph.D. in Political Science from the Friedrich-Schiller University Jena/Germany. In 2006-07 he was a British Academy Fellow at the Department of Politics at Newcastle University. Dr Berger has studied and travelled widely in the Middle East focussing in particular on Egypt, Saudi Arabia and Israel. In 2002-03, he was one of two Germans to participate in the American Political Science Association's Congressional Fellowship Program. In 2007, the German Middle East Studies Association (DAVO) recognized his research with an award for the best Ph.D. dissertation of that year.

Jim Bergeron (BA Regent's College, JD/MA Syracuse, LLM London) is Political Advisor at Striking Force NATO in Naples, Italy. He was previously lecturer in European Law at University College Dublin, visiting lecturer at the University of London and City University and visiting research fellow at Cambridge. He has published several articles in the fields of legal history, postmodern approaches to law, antitrust and international security. His contribution to this volume is made in a purely private capacity.

Juliette Bourdin is Lecturer in American Studies at the University of Paris VIII-Saint-Denis. Her field of research deals with American foreign policy, and more particularly with US-China relations.

Ann Lane is Reader in International Politics at Kings College London and has taught at the Joint Services Command and Staff College, Defence Academy UK since 1999. She was formerly Lecturer in Politics at The Queen's University of Belfast. She is author of several books and numerous articles dealing with UK involvement with the former Yugoslavia. Her contribution to this volume is made in a purely private capacity.

Lori Maguire is Professor of British and American Studies at the University of Paris VIII. She received her doctorate in Modern History at St. Antony's College, Oxford. Her research interests include both British and American foreign policy. She is the author of *Anglo-American Relations with the Free French* (Macmillan, 1996) and *Conservative Women: A History of Women and the Conservative Party* (Macmillan, 1998) and co-author of *La démocratie au XXe siècle* (Atlande, 2000) as well as numerous articles.

Fatma Ramdani teaches English at the University of Lille III and is currently a doctoral student in the American Studies department at the University of Paris 3. Her thesis topic is "The American stance at the four United Nations conferences on women (1975-1995)". Her research focuses on the framing of US foreign policy at the United Nations conferences. She attended a six-week Fulbright seminar entitled "The reconciliation of American diversity with national unity" at New York University's Multinational Institute of American Studies in summer 2005.

Jon Roper is Professor of American Studies at Swansea University. His research interests encompass American political ideas, the American Presidency and the impact of war on American politics, culture and society. He is the author of *Democracy and Its Critics* (1989), *The*

American Presidents: Heroic Leadership from Kennedy to Clinton (2000), and *The Contours of American Politics* (2002). Other edited books include (with John Baylis) *The United States and Europe: Beyond the Neoconservative Divide* (2006) and *The United States and the Legacy of the Vietnam War* (2007).

Pauline Schnapper is Professor of contemporary British studies at the University of Paris Sorbonne Nouvelle (Paris III), with a special interest on European and foreign policy. She is the author of a number of articles and *Le Grand Malentendu: la Grande-Bretagne et l'Europe*,Presses de Sciences Po, 2000, and *Le Royaume-Uni et la Sécurité européenne, 1989-2000*.

INDEX